The Faculty in College Counseling

THE FACULTY
IN COLLEGE COUNSELING

Melvene Draheim Hardee

COORDINATOR OF COUNSELING
FLORIDA STATE UNIVERSITY

with two chapters by Orrin B. Powell

ASSISTANT COORDINATOR OF COUNSELING

McGRAW-HILL BOOK COMPANY, INC.

New York   Toronto   London   1959

THE FACULTY IN COLLEGE COUNSELING

To B. Lamar Johnson, who as teacher,
administrator, and spokesman for
higher education has inspired the
recording of these ideas.

IN FOCUS

Before we can tackle the problem of advising and directing our students satisfactorily, we must develop a philosophy on which to base our actions. . . . It does not seem reasonable to allow a student to pick and choose his studies from the curriculum without asking any questions as to what the courses are, what relationship they have to other courses, and where they may eventually lead. Yet that is exactly what we have done, assuming that by some mysterious process the desired results will be achieved. The folly of this practice has been brought sharply to our attention during recent years. The losses resulting from such haphazard procedure have been shocking. These losses can in part be attributed to failure in academic planning; in part they must be charged to lack of planning and guidance with regard to the host of problems which cluster about a student's academic work. . . . The direct effect that financial, personal, social or health difficulties have upon academic performance should be easy to detect. If we see this connection and are convinced of its importance, our philosophy of guidance will certainly take cognizance of it.

Archibald MacIntosh
Behind the Academic Curtain

Preface

In his book *The Spirit of St. Louis,* Charles Lindbergh makes this statement:

> Ideas are like seeds, apparently insignificant when first held in the hand. If a wind or a new current of thought drifts them away, nothing is lost. But once firmly planted, they can grow and flower into almost anything at all, a cornstalk or a giant redwood—or a flight across the ocean.[1]

What Airman Lindbergh states can be applied to the central thesis of this book, *The Faculty in College Counseling.* As an idea, faculty counseling is not altogether new, but the *coordination* of the work of faculty members who counsel with other aspects of counseling *is* relatively new. This idea has been planted in a number of colleges and universities throughout the country. Where such planting has been effected, the growth process is under way; the idea, cornstalk or redwood in size or guise, is observable.

Reflecting these transplantations, this book has been written for the use of at least five different groups. (1) The volume is thought to be useful as a source book for general and academic administrators in colleges and universities who make decisions concerning the placement of students in programs of study and the progression of these students toward an academic goal. (2) Similarly, this book is designed for the use of administrators (directors and coordinators) of programs of counseling who are responsible for implementing institutional philosophy through this particular aspect of individualized instruction. (3) With the focus of the writing placed upon the faculty member himself, it is reasonable to assume that teachers in institutions of higher education will use the book for reference and discussion. (4) Over-all, if the book has value for the professional worker in the field, it is assumed that advanced students preparing for positions in institutions of higher education as administrators and teachers will profit from a study of the presentations. (5) Finally, the book should attract readers from among professional personnel in the secondary schools—superintendents, principals, guidance directors, and

[1] Charles A. Lindbergh, *The Spirit of St. Louis,* Charles Scribner's Sons, New York, 1953, p. 288.

vii

counselors—who are attempting to effect better articulation between secondary school and higher education.

The materials illustrating the "transplantations" have been contributed by representatives of all five groups in written or oral poll and through more informal exchanges of ideas. Much of the material has been "kitchen-tested" by the author in her visitations to various campuses where, as program consultant, she has engaged in spirited discussions on the premises of the book with representatives of the five groups named above. The author has, in addition, presented the basic ideas inherent in the book for the scrutiny and criticism of colleagues in professional meetings (round-table and panel discussions).

The basic ideas or premises are several. Among them are these: (1) The faculty member is indispensable in the counseling process; (2) there are specific methods, philosophically sound and decidedly practical, which can be utilized in the in-service training of faculty members in their assignment to counseling; (3) the *diversity* of kinds of counseling to be found on college and university campuses is good as long as some *unity* can be effected for the benefit of both the student and the institution; (4) this unity of purpose and practice on the campus can be facilitated through the merger of efforts of administrators, faculty members, and students, planning and working together; (5) the program of counseling in higher education builds upon the program of counseling in the secondary school; and (6) the expectation of parents concerning the counseling of son or daughter is a factor to be reckoned with in present-day programs of higher education.

The author has done her best to survey institutional practices through three national polls and one regional review in the past eight years. It is, however, quite possible that some very good work in the area of coordination of counseling has escaped attention for one or another reason, and this is regrettable.

If the reader believes that "ideas are like seeds," he will recognize the possibility of the transplantation of some very healthy notions about faculty counseling (and its coordination) to the good soil of neighboring institutions. The attempt of this book is to portray for the five groups mentioned the cornstalks and redwoods of faculty counseling—coordinated!

Since no man is an island, as John Donne contended, and since certainly no *writing* man—or woman—is an isolate, this book reflects a compounding of ideas—a chain of thoughts—a merger of things seen and read. The author herewith acknowledges these compounds.

First, to the hundreds of representatives of colleges and universities who answered not only one—but several—questionnaires sent by the author, she expresses deep appreciation. In this day when the arrival of one questionnaire evokes a shudder from the busy administrator, special credit is due to those who completed the questionnaires and, in addition, wrote lengthy supplementary reports and included other descriptive materials. May this book, in a measure, reflect their contribution.

Second, to the members of the division of student personnel of Florida State University and to the teaching staff who contributed special sections, the author expresses her thanks. Appreciation is extended to each member of the staff of the office of coordinator of counseling. Particular credit goes to Bert Powell, assistant coordinator, for his chapters on orientation and student participation, as well as for his aid in tabulating the data from the several surveys. Finally, the author is greatly appreciative of the unflagging interest of Mrs. Jean Blasberg in this project and of her constant encouragement and support in its final stages.

Melvene Draheim Hardee

Contents

CHAPTER 1 *The Coordination of Counseling Services in Colleges and Universities*

The present-day observer of activities in higher education may well feel that he is witnessing the construction of thousands of arks by innumerable Noahs, working feverishly by day and by night to prepare for the flood of students prophesied to sweep over the academic lands by 1970. College and university business wizards and architectural experts are working together to acquire *Lebensraum* and to make the wildernesses habitable. Twelve-story skyscraper dormitories, ground-hugging residence cottages, circular and spiraling edifices in brick, block, and wood are rising up. The race is against time and for the purpose of institutional survival, for the worried Noahs know the consequence of being caught with their dormitories half done and their classrooms only blueprinted.

But housing the swelling numbers by day and by night is only a part of the problem—the most dramatic and visible part, perhaps. There are other worries which beset institutional planners—worries about obtaining teachers with high qualifications (or even without) to "keep school" in the edifices once they are delivered by the contractor. There are worries, too, about the kinds of education which shall be "installed" in the spanking new classrooms—general, special, technical, etc. There are concerns—quiet murmurings at first but rising in volume—about the personalization of education, the individualization of instruction. And at this juncture, those individuals classified as student personnel workers begin to reach for blueprints, to study budgets, and to join in the search for additional qualified staff members.

If the twin concerns of the highly activated Noahs are (1) getting buildings and teaching staff and (2) giving the best instruction to each student, where does the planning for student personnel programs come in—or go out? If the student horde can be housed and fed, certain "personnel" anxieties surely will be allayed. If the collegiate populace of 1970 can be disciplined and entertained outside class time, certain other

1

personnel concerns will diminish. If the multitude can be viewed as single individuals in the growing crowd, then the millennium in collegiate learning will have been attained.

THE QUEST OF THE STUDENT

The needs of students have been written about in countless articles and books, attention being called to such specific needs as civic, family, personal, recreational-aesthetic, social, and vocational. It has been urged that college and university administrators give attention to the general needs of all students as well as to particular needs of individual students. This emphasis upon the over-all learning and specific well-being of students—intellectual, social, emotional, spiritual, and physical—is expressed by Brumbaugh and Berdie: [1]

. . . . The student's learning processes and his actual potential for learning must be considered in planning his education. His attitudes and emotions, prejudices and biases, rigidity and flexibility, also must be considered. . . . Paramount in this point of view is the recognition of individual differences existing between students. Individualized and personalized education can be provided only if teachers and educators are fully aware of differences in the abilities and backgrounds of students. Differences in interests, personality characteristics, socioeconomic backgrounds, cultural activities, and information status must all be considered by educators.

The understanding needed by educators to enable them to discern the individual differences in students deserves study. The manner in which the understanding of individual faculty members can best be broadened and deepened has not yet been fully determined. That the role of the faculty member as confidant, adviser, and friend is becoming increasingly important is attested by comments such as these: [2]

Already and without special stimulus students make their way to us for advice, or "just to talk things over," in efforts to integrate all their activities, including studies and their participation in the life of the college community, their personal problems, employment, the choice of vocation, the significance of the events of the day, into some more meaningful life. They are, in fact, apprentices, and they seek guiding craftsmen and some more experienced comradeship. Experimentation with systems of counseling, advisorships, and tutorial programs has been marked in the period we are considering. It is sometimes weak on the side of the supply of information that is based upon first-hand experience or acquaintance with the rapidly changing developments.

[1] A. J. Brumbaugh and Ralph F. Berdie, *Student Personnel Programs in Transition,* American Council on Education Studies, Washington, October, 1952, pp. 7–8.
[2] John M. Gaus, "A First View: The University-wide Approach," in Joseph E. McLean, *The Public Service and University Education,* Princeton University Press, Princeton, N.J., 1949, pp. 197–198.

Seeking to meet his individual needs relating to family, educational, vocational, and other concerns, the student approaches this craftsman and more experienced comrade. As Havemann and West [3] point out, the literary stereotype of the college or university professor has been that of a younger, somewhat more vigorous, but equally kindly Mr. Chips. His delight lies in books, long walks, quiet conversations, flowers, birds, and students. He is brilliant in discourse and gifted in wit despite being absent-minded about meals, appointments, and general grooming. The professor of the novels is a kind of pedagogical Scattergood Baines, straightening out the lives of students without claiming credit. (The female counterpart of this educator-craftsman and comrade is not noted. It is likely that the description fits her in many respects.)

That faculty members have assumed the responsibility for assisting students is affirmed in institutional records. [4] It is noted that faculty and administration "in the early days" offered students educational guidance, financial help, and health supervision and that they even did some basic work in keeping personnel records, dispatching reports to parents and preparing summaries of procedures involving students. While no systematic program of educational guidance is observable, there is considerable evidence pointing to the fact that such guidance existed informally and was accepted as a responsibility of each teacher.

That faculty members of the present day will continue to serve the individual student in the rising tide in so informal a fashion is doubtful. [5] The technological age has touched the educator. He has become less of an ambling, shaggy-dog "do-gooder" and more of "an organization man." Jostled in the crowd of students, this present-day educator has seen former low student-teacher ratios abandoned. He has been forced to consider the use of television and other mass media to supplement classroom presentations. He (or she) is participating in new methods for appraising student progress, for classifying and grouping students, for changing the traditional time pattern of higher education. These changes in *modus operandi* in the classroom portend change in the pattern of student advisement—in a reconsideration of the role of the teacher as a comrade and craftsman. It is becoming increasingly evident that the faculty member will dispatch this role more adequately as he works *in combination with* those persons who are trained specifically in the field of student personnel and counseling.

[3] Ernest Havemann and Patricia Salter West, *They Went to College,* Harcourt, Brace and Company, Inc., New York, 1952, p. 252.
[4] Eugenie Andruss Leonard, *Origins of Personnel Services in American Higher Education,* University of Minnesota Press, Minneapolis, 1956, pp. 65–66.
[5] Ray Briggs, "Professor 1957—A Profile," *Saturday Review,* Sept. 14, 1957, p. 19.

WORK IN COMBINATION

As Brumbaugh and Berdie [6] point out, a knowledge of students, relating to their interests, personality characteristics, socioeconomic backgrounds, cultural activities, and information status, must be gained by educators. It is not enough for the professionally trained personnel worker to have and to hold this understanding. The sharing of information, with adherence to ethical practices, between the professionally trained student personnel worker and the faculty member; the devising of ways for their working together in the interests of students; the refinement of methods for increasing this effectiveness of working relationship—these are of vital concern to college and university personnel.

A recent report covering the status of education beyond the high school [7] affirms clearly that all teachers must complement and assist the professional counselor as part of a team. While the latter can do much by way of specific testing and supplying specialized information to teachers and students in groups, in most instances, the individual counseling of students will fall to teachers who must be adequately informed and competent in performance.

Significantly, a group of college and university educators has referred to a pressing "future need" and, in so doing, has provided a statement of over-all objective for this book: [8]

To achieve a higher degree of integration between the student personnel services and instructional programs. In their effects upon the student, these two aspects become parts of one and the same educational program. Among the methods recommended are (a) the use of policy committees with strong representation from the teaching faculty; (b) the making available of facts about students and student needs to academic administrators and faculty curriculum committees; (c) in-service training programs for selected members of the faculty interested in improving their interviewing and counseling techniques; (d) case conferences involving instructors, faculty advisers, and personnel workers; (e) study groups of teachers and personnel workers, dealing with areas of common ground, such as group dynamics, general education, extra-class aspects of the learning process, and the like.

In succeeding pages, consideration is given to the several means suggested above as well as to other methods of providing opportunity for integration. However, as Williamson [9] points out, some articulate understanding of the philosophies of education current in the educational scene

[6] *Op. cit.*

[7] The President's Committee on Education Beyond the High School, *Second Report to the President,* Washington, July, 1957, p. 42.

[8] *Future Needs in Student Personnel Work,* American Council on Education, Washington, 1950, p. 6.

[9] E. G. Williamson, "Professional Preparation of Student Personnel Workers," *School and Society,* 86:3–5, Jan. 4, 1958.

in America is needed, in addition to technical competence and some abilities for working in combination. He contends that, since the college or university is a community of scholars dedicated to furthering the intellectual and personal development of students and faculty, it follows that all services should be so administered that they contribute to the realization of these objectives. This sophisticated understanding of the nature of the educational enterprise must obtain if "the high art of helping individuals to develop their lives to the fullest" is to endure.

PREVAILING PHILOSOPHIES OF EDUCATION

One might, with profit, conjecture about the reason for this "future need" to integrate student personnel services and instructional programs in institutions of learning. To a considerable extent, the philosophical concept inherited or adopted by an institution has accounted for its prevailing practices. Taylor,[10] in discussing the philosophical principles that underlie programs of education, designates three: the rationalist, the neohumanist, and the instrumentalist.

Briefly stated, the *rationalist* programs seek to develop the intellectual virtues, conforming, in the process, to fairly rigid principles for the cultivation of man's reason. Commenting on programs of this type, Lloyd-Jones says: [11]

In spite of the high-sounding pretensions of personnel workers, if they work in a situation largely rationalistic in nature, and especially if they themselves have not critically explored the educational outcomes of the various philosophies of education, they will probably find themselves consigned to certain roles that support the rationalistic character of the educational program and also provide a narrow and inadequate scope for their efforts as personnel workers who are interested in "the whole man."

The second category—that of the *neohumanist* philosophy—can be described as having its unity in the cultural heritage of western civilization, its curriculum being based upon the natural sciences, social sciences, and humanities. Neohumanism is a philosophy of dualism, with recognition of the importance of both mind and body. Lloyd-Jones comments: [12]

This is the philosophy that prevails most widely in education at the present time. It provides a situation that has given personnel work a wide open field.

[10] Harold Taylor, "The Philosophical Foundations of General Education," in *General Education,* Fifty-first Yearbook of the National Society for the Study of Education, University of Chicago Press, Chicago, 1952, part I, pp. 22–23.

[11] Esther Lloyd-Jones, "Changing Concepts of Student Personnel Work," in Esther Lloyd-Jones and Margaret Ruth Smith (eds.), *Student Personnel Work as Deeper Teaching,* Harper & Brothers, New York, 1954, p. 9.

[12] *Ibid.,* p. 11.

The personnel worker who holds a neohumanistic philosophy believes that student needs can be met by analyzing each special need, supplying a specialist to meet that need, and then relating these specialists in some kind of firm pattern of relationship that appears administratively logical. The assumption seems to be that if the connections and relationships exist externally between and among the pieces and parts, these can then be transferred inward by the student to reinforce the unity and harmony of his experiences and contribute to his growth.

The third concept—that of *instrumentalism*—achieves unity in centering upon the individual student. In a program designated as instrumentalist, one may find a curriculum broadly elective, experimental in type, and pragmatic in aspects of its operation. Taylor describes instrumentalism as a philosophy of individualism concerned with the full development of the individual in the development of his society.[13] It is the instrumentalist philosophy, rather than that of rationalism or neohumanism, comments Lloyd-Jones, which presents the principles to which student personnel workers contend they adhere.[14]

All in all, it is unlikely that any one of the philosophical concepts appears in pure form on any single campus. An educational institution numbers many individuals, teachers and students, with such a variety of aims and goals that a single "pure and unadulterated" philosophy of education is difficult, if not impossible, to implement. However, one can, with reasonable assurance, categorize an institution as "having tendencies toward" one or another philosophy of education or of being in the process of moving from one concept to another. This characterization of a college or university is likely the reflection of rationalist, neohumanist, or instrumentalist influences at work and in evidence in the institution's history.

Disunity on a college campus may result from the fact that the institutional philosophy is not understood or recognized by student personnel workers and the various departmental staffs. Misunderstandings are likely to occur when educational philosophies held by one or another group are in conflict. Similarly, lack of integration between student personnel services and instructional programs may result from philosophies "in transition" and from procedures newly initiated in any transitional era. Opportunities need to be made available on college campuses for a frank discussion of these matters of institutional philosophy. Pressures of daily routine should not preclude cooperative study which hopefully results in specific suggestions devised for reconciling the personal and professional aims of individuals with the over-all philosophy of the institution.

[13] Taylor, *op. cit.*, pp. 42–43.
[14] Lloyd-Jones, *op. cit.*, p. 12.

In recent years, the evidence of a growing number of institutional surveys denotes a recognition on the part of governing boards and administrators of a need to determine and define the underlying philosophical concepts of the institution and to review the activities which result. Educational practices in conflict with or in contradiction to the underlying philosophy may be discerned, discussed, defended, or abolished. In this process of self-survey (see Chapter 17 of this book), a searching study of the student personnel program is in order.

CLEAVAGES ON CAMPUS

Relative to the matter of reconciling personal and professional goals of administrators with the philosophy of the total institution, much may be said. It can be seen that desire on the part of certain individuals for more favored status has resulted in cleavage between the student personnel staff and instructional personnel. Student personnel workers have sometimes given the impression that they are a group apart, a group annointed and enthroned close to top-level administrators. A study of administrative charts in the various colleges and universities would confirm this "near-topness" in the positions occupied by personnel workers. As a result, salaries for workers in student personnel programs have oftentimes been more desirable than those of teaching faculty. Increasing numbers of student personnel positions have been created. This, together with the favor accorded student personnel workers by administrators, has created suspicion in other encampments. When the head of the department of chemistry asks for, but is denied, a new teacher in his department, and the dean of students asks for, and gets, a new counselor for student activities, the schism widens appreciably. The head of the chemistry department desires to receive the same additions to his staff and the same budgetary consideration for himself and his people as he sees bestowed upon the dean of students. The competition in the market place for space, staff, salary increments, and special consideration has been more than lively; it has, in fact, been deadly.

Such statements as the following, taken from institutional surveys, attest the homicidal tendencies of some "academic men" who view the expansion of student personnel services and the subsequent contraction of areas of instruction:

The division of instruction is responsible for making curricular activities truly educational. The division of student personnel is responsible for the learning that goes on in extracurricular activities—student government, student publications, athletics, music, dramatics, club activities, and social affairs.

In its recommendations, the university study committee has attempted to suggest a clear-cut differentiation between the duties of the division of instruction and the division of student personnel. At the same time, it has recognized their interrelatedness and the vital importance of the services performed by the division of student personnel. To this end, the study committee recommends:

> That a special committee consisting of the dean of students, the dean of men, the dean of women, and two persons outside the division of student personnel (preferably one or both from outside the university) review the policies of the division of student personnel, particularly those governing student activities, services, and costs, with a view of reducing personnel and costs.
>
> *Comment:* There is substantial feeling in the university that the division of student personnel has overexpanded. A significant number of the faculty feel that proportionately it costs too much to operate this division. The university study committee believes therefore that the division itself should review carefully its program, its policies, and its services to determine whether it is in a defensible position.

With feeling such as this evidenced, it is little wonder that administrators in higher education insist upon welding together student personnel services with instructional programs. One may legitimately ask: Is the student personnel service a kind of "Campus Colossus"? Is the growth in student personnel programs dwarfing development of the various academic areas? Within a given institution, is the presence of organized student personnel services in conflict with institutional philosophy? Are student personnel services out of balance with respect to other program emphases? If so, how can balance be restored? If not, how can the impression of imbalance be corrected? These and other questions relating to the peaceful coexistence and the productive partnership of all areas of educational activity demand attention.

It is the thesis of this book that the integration of student personnel and instructional programs may be brought about—not by accident—but by vigorous, persistent action.[15] This fusion of the elements of the institutional program results from study, recommendation, legislation, trial-error, and trial-success activities in a continuous process. The Great Facilitator in the fusion is the *faculty member himself*. In the process of integration, as cited earlier in this chapter, all teachers must complement and assist the staff of professional student personnel workers as part of a team. In this book, close-ups of team operation are provided and descriptions of prevailing practice enunciated. The fusion of student personnel and instructional programs *with the faculty as facilitators* is a subject for considerable discussion—not merely one to be encompassed in a single volume.

[15] Melvene Draheim Hardee, "The Coordinator of Counseling: His Role in Administration of Student Personnel Services," *Occupations*, 30:396–399, March, 1952.

ACCENT ON COUNSELING

Any attempt on the part of institutional planners to provide for the individualized and personalized education of students will eventuate, at some point, in provision for *counseling*. The counseling of students is one important aspect of the offerings in the student personnel program. Commenting on this, two consultants cited earlier remark: [16]

Counseling services must be provided for students. These services, coming from many sources in the college, must help students make educational and vocational plans, maintain good mental hygiene conditions and achieve a satisfactory religious and ethical philosophy. Increasingly, counseling is regarded as personal counseling. Students are approached as individuals who cannot be divided into various problem areas, and counselors must be skilled in many areas rather than being specialists merely in one and disregarding other aspects of adjustment.

Supplementing this judgment is an observation of Morse,[17] who notes that a small proportion of students will need a great deal of counseling help; many will benefit from some; a large proportion will solve their immediate problems in their own way.

A perusal of a number of college handbooks, bulletins, and catalogues will reveal the extent to which provision for counseling is made and, in all likelihood, will reflect something of the philosophical concepts of education held by a particular institution. Four institutions describe as follows their counseling services or their position with reference to such services:

SOUTHERN LIBERAL ARTS COLLEGE: College freshmen need varying amounts of assistance in making adequate and satisfying adjustments to their new college world and its responsibilities and opportunities. W_____ College provides this assistance through a counseling service. This service is an integral part of the educational program of the college and accompanies the student throughout his college career.

MIDWESTERN TEACHERS COLLEGE: Every student at M_____ College has several kinds of counselors. Each of your teachers will counsel you, if you request it. In addition, you will have a specially assigned personnel counselor and a curriculum counselor. The six personnel counselors welcome you to their offices whenever you want to talk with them. Perhaps you are not sure what vocation you wish to follow, or if you have chosen a vocation, you do not know which curriculum will best prepare you for that vocation. Your personnel counselor will be glad to help you analyze and interpret your interests, apti-

[16] Brumbaugh and Berdie, *op. cit.*, p. 9.
[17] Horace T. Morse, "General Education and Individual Guidance," in Melvene Draheim Hardee (ed.), *Counseling and Guidance in General Education*, World Book Company, Yonkers, N.Y., 1955, p. 6.

tudes, and abilities in terms of present-day needs and opportunities. Your curriculum counselor is assigned to you as soon as you and your personnel counselor have chosen the curriculum you are to follow.

MIDWESTERN COLLEGE: The number of advisers and counselors available to students in A_____ College rivals the number of specialists available to a Hollywood actress or a retired race horse. These advisers and counselors include hall advisers, faculty counselors, and the counseling service. Two upperclass students will live in the freshman hall with you your first year. These hall advisers are conglomerates of walking catalogues, helping hands with freshman week, registration, social problems, "homesickness" emergencies. Your faculty counselor will help you through your entire career, especially with your courses, requirements, etc., but he will also be a counselor in all areas of community living.

SOUTHERN STATE COLLEGE: The primary purpose of the residence-hall counselor is to provide an atmosphere and promote a means whereby the student may develop self-guidance. The counselor is especially concerned in these fields: (1) problems of personal adjustment, (2) social growth of students, (3) the development of leadership qualities, and (4) academic growth. The activities and duties of the counselor are directed toward these goals.

Something of the diversity and variety of counseling services can be seen in the four examples given. These, in turn, give rise to the question concerning a working definition of counseling in educational institutions —a common understanding of *what it is* and *is not*.

Hahn and MacLean,[18] commenting on the nature of counseling psychology, affirm that it is a process which takes place in a one-to-one relationship between an individual troubled by problems with which he cannot cope alone and a professional worker whose training and experience have qualified him to help others reach solutions to personal problems. The authors emphasize these characteristics of counseling: It is a professional clinical service, centered upon the problems and needs of the client, based upon the accuracy of counselor prediction, and resulting in client-made decisions.

As is evident, the emphasis in the foregoing definition is upon the professionally trained counselor, termed the clinical or counseling psychologist. Contributing a definition with somewhat wider application, Wrenn [19] states:

Counseling in a broad sense includes all of those personal contacts with students by individuals who are consciously attempting to understand and assist them by the specific procedures utilized in personal interviewing. The interview may be extensive or brief. It may involve a great deal of participation on the part of the counselor, or it may involve situations in which almost all

[18] Milton E. Hahn and Malcolm S. MacLean, *Counseling Psychology*, McGraw-Hill Book Company, Inc., New York, 1955, pp. 6–10.
[19] C. Gilbert Wrenn, *Student Personnel Work in College*, The Ronald Press Company, New York, 1951, p. 57.

of the initiative rests with the student. Counseling in this sense may or may not be preceded or accompanied by measurement or other attempts to understand the student's background and characteristics. Counseling even in the broad sense, however, must be more specific than mere conversations. There must be some felt need on the part of the student, whether expressed or not, and some intent to help on the part of the counselor.

In both definitions, there is (1) emphasis upon the one-to-one relationship, (2) a focus upon problems and needs of the client, (3) willingness on the part of the counselor to aid and assist, and (4) a recognition of some general structuring for the interview.

Likenesses and differences between teaching and counseling have been much debated, with objectives and methods of teachers and counselors undergoing scrutiny. The appraisal of process and product emerging from classroom and counseling cubicle has ensued. Dressel [20] contends that counseling—whether academic, vocational, or personal—can facilitate work in the classroom and the student's personal adjustment if counselors attempt to develop on the part of counselees a rational method for solving problems which is likewise stressed in academic courses.

Wrenn [21] acknowledges the fact that there is similarity between counseling and teaching in that both (1) deal with information to be considered or transmitted, (2) require validation of data, (3) exact a method of presentation which is varied to meet individual needs, and (4) reach conclusions or generalizations. He believes that the vital difference is that information dealt with in counseling is information *about* one of the participants and that the content of the learning experience in counseling *is* the student himself.

McConnell,[22] giving the point of view of an educational administrator, resolves some issues in the great debate in his analysis:

We might assume . . . that most faculty members should serve as adviser-counselors; that some teachers, with more time and some training, should carry greater responsibility in a total counseling program; and that the work of the latter is merely an extension of the services of the former. We might also assume that the modern college or university should provide specialized counseling services conducted by professionally trained staff, and that these services, too, are actually extensions of the services of their faculty colleagues.

In this point of view, there is assurance given that one phase of the work of a teacher is his counseling and that the work of specialized

---

[20] Paul Dressel, *General Education: Exploration in Evaluation,* American Council on Education, Washington, 1954, p. 275.

[21] C. Gilbert Wrenn, "Some Emotional Factors in Counseling," in *Guidance in the Age of Automation,* Syracuse University Press, Syracuse, N.Y., 1957, pp. 34–43.

[22] T. R. McConnell, "A University President Looks at Student Personnel Work," an address to the American College Personnel Association, Buffalo, N.Y., 1954.

counselors supplements and extends the service provided by faculty members. Thus it can be seen that "the high art of helping individuals to develop their lives to the fullest" is an obligation to be shared by all educators within an institution. The dispatching of the advisement and counseling function with vigor and creativity by faculty members *in combination* with professional personnel is the continuing emphasis of this book.

SPECIAL AREAS IN COUNSELING

Earlier in the chapter it was stated that the real facilitator in the fusion of student personnel services with instructional programs is likely to be the faculty member himself. The service of the faculty member in the counseling program of institutions is the concern of this book. To ascertain the level of operation of the faculty member and to assess the function he performs, one must review the needs of college-age students which are met through counseling. These are, in part, reflected in the provision made by the institution for individualized and specialized help.

In a poll of eighty-nine institutions of higher learning (see App. A), inquiry was made about opportunities extended to students for counseling. The author is mindful of the fact that students are not divisible into discrete parts; nonetheless a listing by types of offering, such as is shown in the questionnaire, was necessary for the consideration of respondents. It would appear from the tabulation that the majority of institutions provide placement, health, vocational, educational, psychological, and residence counseling as well as counseling for veterans. A sizable number of institutions provide for religious counseling; specialized help in reading, speech, and hearing; psychiatric services; and marriage and family counseling. Few institutions, it would seem, provide special advisement for the foreign student.

Kinds of service	*Number of institutions reporting*
Placement counseling	80
Health counseling	79
Vocational counseling	78
Educational counseling	76
Psychological services	75
Veterans' counseling	72
Residence counseling	71
Religious counseling	69
Remedial reading	69
Speech and hearing	69
Marriage and family-adjustment counseling	49
Psychiatric services	35
Foreign-student advisement	10

Some special counseling services mentioned in addition to the above were as follows:

Admissions counseling
Rehabilitation of the handicapped
State sanatorium dismissals (special counseling)
Finance and budgeting advisement
Student-activities counseling or group organization counseling
Testing (individual and group) and follow-up counseling
Scholarship advisement
Human relations laboratory (group therapy)
Remedial aid in mathematics
Discipline and conduct aid
Selective service or military advisement
Higher-level study skills counseling

There is considerable variation existing among institutions with respect to the amount and kind of special counseling, as is evidenced by the following comments:

Educational counseling

SMALL MIDWESTERN LIBERAL ARTS COLLEGE: We have a special program of freshman orientation.

LARGE EASTERN METROPOLITAN UNIVERSITY: Some of our colleges and divisions carry on educational counseling with some students.

MIDWESTERN TEACHERS COLLEGE: Our freshman counseling is systematic, but our upperclass counseling is haphazard.

SOUTHERN LIBERAL ARTS COLLEGE: Educational counseling is available for freshmen through orientation-class teachers; for upperclassmen, the help is available through heads of the departments.

Residence counseling

LARGE MIDWESTERN UNIVERSITY: Residence counseling is available in all housing for girls and in men's halls and fraternities.

SOUTHERN UNIVERSITY: We do not have it yet in all dormitories.

WESTERN STATE COLLEGE: Residence counseling is provided for girls in our organized program, but for boys, only to a limited extent.

SOUTHWESTERN TEACHERS COLLEGE: We are only now beginning our program of residence counseling.

Psychiatric counseling

MIDWESTERN TEACHERS COLLEGE: Psychiatric counseling is not available on campus but may be obtained through referral to the county mental health agency.

SOUTHERN UNIVERSITY: This type of counseling is available to our students one-half day a week.

WESTERN STATE COLLEGE: We refer students to the psychiatrist in the local community.

EASTERN UNIVERSITY: We refer cases to the proper state authorities.

These comments serve to illustrate the fact that considerable difference in kind and degree of counseling exists with respect to educational, residence, and psychiatric services. These same differences are likewise to be observed with respect to vocational, health, financial, and placement counseling.

ORGANIZATIONAL PATTERNS IN COUNSELING

In so far as the staffing of the various counseling services is concerned, the persons named in the questionnaire (App. A) as having definite responsibilities relating to the counseling of students include the following: [23]

The dean or director of student affairs and assistants
The chief admissions officer and his staff
The head physician and staff of nurses and technologists
The dean of men and women and their staffs of residence counselors
The director of the bureau of vocational guidance and counselors
The director of placement and placement counselors
The director of academic counseling and the faculty advisers
The director of the testing bureau and psychometrists
The counselor for student organizations
The foreign-student adviser
The director and counselors in clinics such as psychology, speech, reading, writing, marriage counseling
The head of the veterans' counseling bureau and assistants
The chaplain and other religious counselors
Etc.

In sixty-four institutions, the centralization of counseling activities resided with the dean of students, director of student personnel, or director of student affairs. In nineteen institutions, responsibility for counseling was centered in the offices of director of student counseling, director of student advising, coordinator of counseling, director of guidance, dean of women, dean of men, or director of admissions. In six institutions, responsibility was not centered in a single office or with a single individual.

Some descriptive comments concerning organizational patterns were given as follows:

[23] See also App. D for findings of Fred J. Vogel, "Study of Concepts and Practices Relating to the Allocation of Certain Student Personnel Responsibilities in Selected Institutions of Higher Learning in the United States," a thesis submitted in partial fulfillment of the requirements for the Ed.D. degree, Florida State University, 1958.

SOUTHERN LIBERAL ARTS COLLEGE: The director of guidance works with the dean of women in coordinating counseling services.

MIDWESTERN LIBERAL ARTS COLLEGE: We have no coordinator of these services. The director of student advising attempts to guarantee that cooperation exists.

EASTERN LIBERAL ARTS COLLEGE: The director of placement, director of admissions, and assistant to the dean have specific coordinative responsibilities shared with those of the dean of the college.

WESTERN STATE COLLEGE: We have a decentralized program with coordination made possible through the office of personnel coordinator.

Among the various methods used by institutions to effect internal or departmental coordination were meetings of the staff of student personnel workers in councils and committees on a weekly, semimonthly, or monthly basis; individual conferences between members of the staff; and publications circulated among the staff. One institution mentioned the fact that eleven different area committees in student personnel and counseling met regularly for coordinative planning. In contrast, another commented that all planning is done on a very informal basis, person to person, over a cup of coffee. Such statements as these reflect progress:

Our decentralized program of counseling services gives a segment of responsibility to each student dean and some responsibility to academic deans and department heads.

With centralization of effort coming about through coordination, we find a more meaningful approach to problems and less chance for overlapping of function. Teachers and counselors are helped to deal with the student as an entity, all having more complete information about him.

In our program of coordinated planning, more persons are made to feel responsible. We are able to use a greater percentage of faculty leadership in the total program.

In other instances, the lack of unified effort existing among faculty members and student personnel staff can be seen as follows:

We have an inadequate administrative tie-in with faculty advising which could be overcome by proper coordination.

We need a greater integration of effort with the teaching faculty.

Our program tends to compartmentalize the faculty and the counseling group which would not be the case if coordination were good.

Perhaps our weakest points are in relation to (*a*) coordination of student counseling services with academic advising and (*b*) coordination of general student services with similar services offered in the separate colleges and schools within our university.

Thus a summary of statements received from the eighty-nine respondents points to (1) the lack of unity in goals among personnel workers, including counselors, (2) the breakdown of communications (internally) between student personnel administrators and counselors in the various specialty areas, (3) the dissimilarity of goals between instructional areas and student personnel and counseling areas, and (4) the breakdown of communications (externally) between the members of the teaching faculty and the student personnel and counseling groups.

THE INTEGRATION OF COUNSELING AND INSTRUCTIONAL PROGRAMS

The function of the contemporary student in higher education is to learn. In the event of inability to learn, the student does not fulfill his function. The institutional resource which he will seek for help in overcoming the disability is, in most instances, the counseling resource. Its purpose is to aid the student in achieving his educational goals and in making maximum use of his abilities. *This function weds counseling—an important aspect of student personnel—with instruction and justifies its existence.* The failure of instructional personnel to claim professional counselors as partners (and vice versa) in the educational enterprise results in devastating crosscurrents which tend to throw a student off his educational course. The urgent need is for understandings to be effected between and among teaching faculty and professionally trained counselors.

To achieve these understandings among factions, administrative planners must provide opportunities for teachers (as educators) and counselors (as educators) to learn together. And what shall be the focus of their learning? This answer is suggested: The content of the daily lesson shall be *the student*—who is he? How shall he be educated?

Is there a particular counselor or adviser to whom a student must go when his problem is academic in nature? Personal? Vocational? Religious? Marital?

How are students informed of the counseling services?

May a student consult more than one person in the process of solving a problem? If so, how does he make the transition easily and naturally from one counselor or adviser to the other?

How shall a second counselor, working on the student's problem, be informed of the work of the first?

Shall there be a report of the progress of the student as he works toward a solution of his problem? If so, to whom shall this report be available?

With whom shall confidential information about the student reside? Where shall results from tests and placement examinations be kept?

Shall there be a periodic check made on the student to determine the progress he is making on his problem? How shall such a check be made? What persons are involved?

If the progress of a student in working out a problem is slowed down, who shall recommend action to facilitate its solution?

What assistance shall be given to the student in summarizing and evaluating his counseling experiences?

With reference to the foregoing, it is hoped that the teaching faculty may become as effective in "educating" as are the best counselors, that the professional counselor will achieve as great distinction as the best teachers, and, further, that teacher-educator and counselor-educator, working in combination, can weld together the segments of a campus wherein the whole student learns.

If this is the goal, then the program of student personnel, including counseling, and the program of instruction deserve to be organized in such a way as to ensure the coordination of effort of individuals in both groups. This working of administrators, teachers, counselors, advisers, and students *in combination* is underscored further by the following statement: [24]

It is in the spirit of the pilgrim that many instructors and their students seek that guidance by which they may affirm "the new creation." . . . As pilgrims they are able to realize the fundamental possibilities of counseling—in the classroom, in student activities, and with individual students. They may not have the perfect skills, they may be lacking in professional knowledge, they may feel more inadequate than their students, they may distrust the manners and contributions of professional counselors, yet, despite all, they have begun the long and sincere trek of the pilgrim. If this spirit increases in college faculties, the observer will concomitantly see the further development of counseling as a well-acknowledged element in the role of the college teacher.

SUMMARY

This initial chapter has served to emphasize the need in institutions of higher education for achieving a greater degree of integration between the student personnel program and that of instruction. The utilization of the faculty member at appropriate levels in the student personnel program, particularly in *counseling,* can do much to facilitate the desired integration.

In ensuing chapters, the concept of the whole student is discussed with reference to institutional wholeness. The work of the faculty adviser—his role, his training, and his successes and persisting problems—is viewed. Similarly, the role of the noncounseling faculty member and of the staff employee is discussed. The elements essential to the coordination of programs of counseling are enumerated, with emphasis placed

[24] Herbert Stroup, "The College Teacher as Counselor," *School and Society,* 85:121–122, Apr. 13, 1957.

in a succeeding section upon student records and reports. Suggestions for the articulation of high school counseling with that of college are posed. Illustrating the achievement of successful integration of student personnel and instructional units is a chapter covering practices for orienting new students. Consideration is given to the role of the parent with reference to the adjustment of the new student. Following this, counseling functions performed by students are enumerated. The coordination of counseling services by means of the case conference and the case study is illustrated. Finally, the ongoing studies relating to the integration of student personnel services and instruction and to utilizing the faculty member are cited.

The "new creation" referred to earlier may well be that accomplishment of *an integration of effort of all who work and learn together on a campus*—the teaching faculty, advisers, general and academic administrators, directors of counseling, and nonacademic personnel in cooperation with parents, high school guidance staff, and the community at large.

CHAPTER 2   *The Whole Institution and the Whole Student*

The phrase "university as a whole" is used often in oratory and print. As conceived, the educational institution *has* a wholeness or unity. Its purpose and objectives reflect a singularity of aim which is to provide the learner with experiences which will change him as an individual. At the outset, all who subscribe to the purposes and goals of a particular college or university will agree that some harmony of beliefs and similarity of idea about the education of youth must exist. Assuredly, these same persons would affirm that college and university personnel must work within the framework of the whole institution in achieving personal and professional goals. As was indicated in Chapter 1, a primary goal is that of achieving a higher degree of integration between student personnel services and the instructional program. These two aspects become parts of one and the same educational program in their effects upon students.

At what point is it that conflicting departmental and individual interests threaten this oneness? Why must faculty loyalties be divided and institutional purposes split? Under what circumstances are the objectives of one group of faculty members misunderstood or misinterpreted by another? Why must attention be increasingly given to the integration of all institutional effort? Why, specifically, is there such a pressing need to consider ways and means of integrating the program of counseling with the program of instruction?

WHO THINKS WHAT OF WHOM

Teachers on the Campus

In the results from the poll of eighty-nine institutions cited in Chapter 1, such comments as these were observed:

LARGE WESTERN STATE UNIVERSITY: The relationship between our faculty and specialized counselors is poor.

19

MIDWESTERN STATE UNIVERSITY: In our program we do not give attention to enlisting the interest of the teaching faculty.

SOUTHERN LIBERAL ARTS COLLEGE: There is too little faculty participation in the total counseling program of our campus.

SOUTHWESTERN STATE TEACHERS COLLEGE: Faculty overloads prevent their participation in student guidance as fully as would be desirable.

As one university administrator affirms, the faculty is the most important group on the campus, and "everything that makes an institution of higher learning springs from the faculty."[1] The lack of cooperation between the counseling group and the instructional personnel is serious. There is evidence of the fact that the segmented college or university is attempting to deal with the fragmented student, which attempt is, of course, fantastic.

The failure on campuses of faculty to be enthusiastic about the counseling program, with its specialties—academic, vocational, personal, psychological—arises in part from concepts of *self* and *job* held by teachers as well as from concepts which the teacher group holds of professionally trained counselors. On most campuses there are teachers who hold particular points of view about counseling. As stereotypes there are the following:

1. There are those who feel that the relationship between teacher and student is a near-sacred one. These educators believe that the learning situation in which teacher and student participate is something of a private affair. There is a possessiveness voiced by teachers who comment "my students," "my classes," "my subject-matter field," their students seeming virtually to be "academic wards." These teachers will tolerate no "interference" of the special counselor in the educational process; the classroom "oracle" feels that he, better than anyone else, can minister to *all* the needs of *all* the students under *all* conditions.

2. A goodly number of teachers not included in the former group advance the opinion that *anybody can counsel*. They regard vocational counseling as "much ado about nothing" and psychological counseling as strictly faddish. These faculty members are advocates of the brand of guidance which begins and ends, "Son, I know that if you will work hard, everything will turn out fine." An occasional pat on the back and thick layers of reassurance at periodic intervals constitute the necessary personal follow-up.

3. There is a small but nonetheless vocal group who believe that students who are old enough to come to college are mature enough to have solved all their problems. Each member of this group of "rugged realists" affirms that he or she made a vocational choice at age twelve

---

[1] Monroe E. Deutsch, *The College from Within*, University of California Press, Berkeley, Calif., 1952, p. 56.

and stuck to it thereafter. Furthermore, each member claims to have circumvented most of life's problems by employing scientifically accurate methods to reach conclusions. This group, whose ranks fortunately are thinning, would instruct the officers of admissions in their institution, "Send us no problems. We want only happy, well-adjusted, and mature seventeen-year-olds in our classes."

4. A wary group of teachers, feeling that counseling is on trial, look with the skeptic's eye at the professional counselor, seeking to limit his function and his realm of influence. These faculty members are sure that the counselor will find only a *few* students in the institution who need his help. They assume, furthermore, that these few students will be used as objects of clinical experiment, with the results being so theoretical, detached, and scientifically stratified that they will not change in the least the behavior of the greater group of students on campus.

5. A more voluble set of pedagogues, recognizing that counseling is here to stay and in a mood to provide counselors with plenty of business, take the view that, with a counseling program under way, the "traditional responsibility of teachers" (concern for students) is inoperative. This select group of teachers expects the "clairvoyant counselor in the ivy control tower" to anticipate most problems of student life on the campus before they occur. They adopt the view that no longer does a faculty member need to be concerned with anything except lectures, examinations, and scholarly papers. With this transference of responsibility for the "whole student" to the counselor, the renaissance of "the professor" is effected. He can thus begin to think about students as quiescent recipients of knowledge, as "disembodied intellects"—all of which will be much simpler for him.

6. Then there is the group of ascetics among faculty who state early a positive allergy to doing faculty advisement. At the moment they perceive the possibility of being named to the program of educational advisement, they break out in a rash of resistance. They argue a primary dedication to teaching in the college but not advising for the college, pleading an overload of teaching, extension courses, research, field and committee work, and family pressures. They reject in-service training, record keeping, report writing, and details generally. They beg for a palliative for their suffering. They will be happier if they just *teach!*

Fortunately, there is a sizable number of college teachers who demonstrate an attitude of "suspended judgment" and of acceptiveness. These teachers seek to learn how the purposes of the total institution can be facilitated by work of professional counselors and how, as teachers, they can fit into the counseling program as "faculty facilitators" of student adjustment. If they are approached about taking on faculty advising duties, they agree, pledging their cooperation to learn how to carry on their jobs.

Counselors on the Campus

What are some common stereotypes of thinking which handicap counselors in their working relationships with the teaching faculty? (The misunderstanding certainly cannot be all on the side of the teacher group.)

1. There are some counselors who give the impression that they were first to discover "the total individual." The *gestalt* approach, they believe, has never quite been accepted by teachers with limited training in the field of psychology. Nor do these counselors have much hope that the great mass of educators will ever perceive the individual in his totality. They are quite sure that the teaching professor, immersed in the intricacies of economics, history, engineering, has no real knowledge of the student and has no wish to acquire such knowledge.

2. There are some counselor "prima donnas" who regard themselves as omniscient in their work. They feel that they can communicate *only* with *other counselors*, that the magic ring of specialdom includes only persons with a given number of credit hours in interviewing, testing, and personnel research. Outside the charmed circle are the great masses of "just people" who teach, manage dormitories, and administer offices on a university campus. "Operation nil" would seem to describe the communication between this self-styled brain trust of counselors and the larger group of "generalists."

3. Some zealous counselors, having gone off the deep end in graduate school, come to the surface convinced that *all* students need counseling. These same counselors put forth a herculean effort to see that the wayward, confused, and questioning—together with all their friends, classmates, and roommates—are "brought in" for help. Posing as campus Samaritans, these counselors adopt the motto "We will help you with your problem, even to finding one for you."

4. There are a few "big brother" counselors who feel that they must protect large numbers of students from the well-intentioned but misguided efforts of a fumbling, bumbling faculty group. This attitude ranges all the way from an expression of annoyance on the part of the counselor when some faculty member's name is mentioned, to an actual statement, "Professor Able doesn't know how to handle this at all." In these instances, the remark usually circulates back to Professor Able, the latter retaliating with the statement that Counselor Cain is poorly adjusted himself and under no conditions should be counseling others.

5. A small, select group of counselors seem to be of the opinion that they must work with only a small, select group of students. These

"specialty seekers" search out the really good "cases" which can, they feel, be fruitfully used for research, publication, and presentation before learned societies. The "run-of-the-mill stuff," they affirm, is not for them. They gravitate to and grapple with only the very best student problems, thus fulfilling, they feel, their destiny as deities.

6. One group of loud-voiced skeptics among the counselors has viewed with alarm the inclusion of faculty in the program of academic advisement for students. This clique of counselors resents the fact that the name "counselor" is oftentimes given to the faculty adviser. These persons feel that the profession is surely "on the skids" now that "just anybody" is accorded a counselor halo. The world—and their prestige—is, alas, too much with them.

Fortunately, as in the case of the teacher group, there are more than a few counselors who, with growing insight, have adopted the "suspended-judgment" viewpoint and an acceptive attitude toward the faculty. They believe that, if one teacher can be found who views with a reasonable degree of understanding the processes of human adjustment, there will be found another ninety-nine teachers who can be "educated." This group of counselors plan their strategy wisely and win esteem by sensible service contributions, aimed at aiding the teacher who serves as a faculty adviser as well as the faculty member who is not undertaking a student-advisement function.

COUNSELING AND THE TOP–LEVEL ADMINISTRATORS

A wedding of instruction and counseling can scarcely take place if the top-level administration is not in favor of such merger. The attitude of the administrators is reflected in public pronouncements but is better shown in professional activities sponsored by them. Among the activities encouraged by wise administrators to wed uneasy factions in the larger institutional setting are the following:

1. The faculty conference or workshop staged at the opening of school or at intervals during the year (see App. F–2)

2. The appointment of standing committees within the institution to deal with all-college or university problems which recur, such as the curriculum committee, the committee on faculty professional relations, the committee on tests and measurements, the committee on student affairs, etc., including persons from the student personnel area and counseling together with instructors and academic division heads and deans.

3. The appointment of committees whose assignment is for a shorter time period to consider problems of all-school concern—a committee to study and advise with respect to the use of the library, enforcement of

campus traffic rules, planning for parents' day, homecoming, orientation for new students, etc.

4. The designation of faculty as a whole to engage in institutional self-study with an eye to discovering areas of weakness and of strength with respect to the total educational structure, covering instruction, business management, and student affairs

5. The consolidation by means of legislative action of areas of instruction and of student personnel (see Chapter 9)

There is ample evidence of the fact that there are pressing problems on campuses of most institutions and that these can be effectively resolved by chemists, psychologists, social scientists, mathematicians, business administrators, counselors, and others, working together in inspired study.

The aforementioned five activities afford opportunity for faculty members in the large institution to appreciate the viewpoint of one another. In institutions of smaller enrollment, this mutual viewing may be effected by means other than those of faculty conference, standing committees, ad hoc committees, and evaluation and study groups. However, this high-quality working relationship does not necessarily come about just because the institution is small, although it is true that in the small institutions a very considerable number of the staff operate in duality or in a three-in-one role, dispatching functions of the teacher and counselor or of teacher, administrator, and counselor.

If the top-level administration of a college or university provides the opportunity for reciprocal working relations among faculty members, the following is made easier: (1) cooperation of academic deans, department heads, and the director of counseling and (2) cooperation of the teaching faculty and the counseling staff. Interdisciplinary "combine" is oftentimes facilitated by moves emanating from the top level in administration. Lacking the top-level "union," mergers at grass-roots level do come about, but often more slowly. The hope is that personnel in instruction and counseling will find opportunity to work together and, once brought together, will find means for communicating ideas. Commenting on the manner in which members of the Quaker faith have promoted group relations, Stuart Chase cites the fact that these principles can be factored out of their meetings: participation and involvement of members in problems and solutions; careful listening; periods of silence to delay emotional responses; permissive leaders; equality of status for all members; priority of facts over opinions; a moratorium on questions which stir emotions and cause sides to form.[2]

[2] Reported by W. W. Blaesser, "Elements of a Well-rounded College Student Personnel Program," in J. P. Culpepper and others (eds.), *Report of the Southern College Personnel Association Work Conference*, August, 1952, p. 11.

Blaesser, in reviewing these activities, suggests that it might be appropriate for student personnel workers to formulate a set of human-relations principles covering person-to-person, intragroup, and inter-group relationships with students, college presidents, academic deans, business managers, faculty, personnel specialists and generalists, maintenance staff, townspeople, etc.[3]

RELATIONSHIPS BETWEEN THE DIRECTOR OF COUNSELING AND DEANS AND DEPARTMENT HEADS IN INSTRUCTION

What are the possibilities for effecting a good working relationship between the director of the counseling service and the academic dean or the department head—a two-person, one-to-one relationship? In view of some comments from the poll cited earlier, the possibilities would appear to be bright:

MIDWESTERN LIBERAL ARTS COLLEGE: We have a good—but informal—relationship.

WESTERN STATE COLLEGE: There is excellent cooperation on mutual problems; we have periodic attendance of deans and department heads at meetings of the personnel council.

SOUTHERN TEACHERS COLLEGE: There is a very fine working relationship which has been established by means of a coordinating committee which is composed of heads of all campus departments.

EASTERN CITY UNIVERSITY: The relationship is "spotty"—excellent in certain instances but poor in a majority of cases.

These generally encouraging reports may be accounted for in several ways; for one thing, counseling as an institutional service has undoubtedly been sold first to the top-level administrators. This group have participated in the planning which has resulted in the addition or extension of counseling services; they feel themselves to be a part of the plan and are not suspicious of it. Furthermore, administrators are expected to take the broad view of the institution and its welfare and to lift their sights above the confines of a single segment of the educational offering.

The director of the counseling service needs this support from administrators in instructional areas and needs to take into account anything which would tend to weaken the relationship. Perhaps the greatest deterrent to good cooperation is that of insufficient time for deliberation and communication. Executives are often pressed to make decisions quickly. In haste, some matters involving the welfare of students come to be viewed from only one angle—the academic.

[3] *Ibid.*

One administrator in a program of counseling services explains her recent endeavor:

This year I have been holding conferences with each of the academic deans, going over what types of assistance we are ready to offer students and discussing with them the techniques to follow when we become *involved* in academic counseling, as we are bound to do at times. This has been a time-consuming project but the cooperation has been splendid. Every dean has promised to discuss student personnel services in early faculty meetings or to talk with special units of their administration on academic advisement.

With what shall these face-to-face contacts between administrative personnel be concerned? A multitude of things, doubtless, some of which are these:

1. The similarity of goals among special counselors, teachers, and administrators for the assistance of students

2. The specific ways in which counselors *can* facilitate the work of teachers and administrators

3. The points at which cooperation between counselors, teachers, and administrators may break down

4. The evaluation of results regarding cases of students wherein there was optimum, minimum, or an absence of cooperation of counselors, teachers, and administrators

5. A long-range plan to ensure that aid and assistance will be given particular groups of students as well as each individual within the group

Deans and heads of instructional departments need to take time to acquaint themselves fully with the student's problem before making decisions which will affect the student, his parents, and the college or university. When an academic dean writes a letter to parents without consulting the director of counseling in order to gain a picture of the "whole student"—his life in the residence hall, his participation in student activities, his performance in part-time work, etc.—there is evidence of a lack of integration between instruction and counseling. Similarly, when deans of instruction or department heads give advice to a student concerning his achievement *without* reference to accumulated data about the student (see Chapter 10) or without benefit of conferences with counselors who have observed the student, there is evidence of poor working relationships. The participation of deans and department heads in the case-conference activity or in the case study of a student (see Chapters 15 and 16) has great potential for the education of the academician concerning the needs of the whole student.

Nor is the lack of cooperation between administrators in academic areas and the director of counseling solely the fault of the former. The director of counseling—together with members of the counseling staff—has been content in some instances to see administrative decisions made hastily. The comment has been, "It's their prerogative; top brass operates that way." Members of the counseling staff may accept without protest an administrative action of doubtful value. It is all too easy for them to toss off an executive's handling of a student's case with the comment, "That's the way it has to be as long as Dean Rough is in the driver's seat."

It is the responsibility of the director of counseling to assist Dean Rough or Dr. Tumble of the administration in keeping apprised of problems of both individual and group concern which occur among students. This comes about through participation of these educators in committees, study experiences, informal conferences, the case conference or case study, and by means of written aids such as are described throughout this book. Deans and department heads need to know what the counseling program is accomplishing and what their particular contribution to the program should be. One administrator in counseling recounts this experience: [4]

A few years ago we decided that our relationships with university administrators and department heads were not as close as we would like them to be, so the staff of the Student Counseling Bureau organized an open house and coffee hour in the Counseling Bureau and invited departmental chairmen, deans, associate deans and assistant deans, the president of the university and his vice presidents, and other administrative officials. We were very pleasantly surprised when almost everybody who was invited came to the open house. Every staff member had a specific assignment and was responsible for a certain number of guests—introducing them to other bureau staff members, answering their questions, providing them with as clear a picture of bureau aims and activities as possible. Afterward, we noticed a much more receptive attitude on the part of many people when we had to approach them for one reason or another.

COOPERATION EFFECTED BETWEEN MEMBERS OF THE INSTRUCTIONAL AND COUNSELING STAFFS

What of the relationship between teachers and professional counselors? Are the stereotypes outlined in the early pages of this chapter so enduring that a working relationship cannot be effected in the academic lifetime of teacher or counselor? Decidedly not, is the answer. Some of the possibilities for merger of efforts are described below.

[4] Ralph F. Berdie, "Some Relationship Problems in Counseling," in Ralph F. Berdie (ed.), *Roles and Relationships in Counseling*, Minnesota Studies in Student Personnel Work, no. 3, University of Minnesota Press, Minneapolis, 1953, pp. 26–27.

Opportunities to Know Each Other

The first requisite is for teachers and counselors to become acquainted with one another. Such a meeting does much to dispel doubt about who does what and how. A respect for the individual and his or her specialty is paramount in the building of good working relationships. Meetings of faculty members and the counseling staff similar to that cited earlier for administrators and the counseling staff are certainly desirable. In order that the gesture not always be one of "Come up to our house," one director of a program of counseling has recommended that members of the counseling staff spend time in interdisciplinary educative experiences —visiting the campus art museum, attending a chemistry lecture open to the public, taking part in a series of coffees sponsored by the English department, and other activities designed to introduce the counselor to a number of areas of instruction.

Opportunities to Work Together

Teaching faculty and counselors should make the most of opportunities provided by the administration to work together. Teachers are included on administratively appointed committees and study groups for the reason that they figure in an important part of the student's educational experience on campus. Instructors should, therefore, share these experiences gained from the classroom with those who work with students in a counseling or extraclass capacity. Counselors are chosen for membership on these committees on the basis of their close association with students. They, too, have experiences to share with instructional personnel. In these sessions, it is important for both groups to operate as freely as possible from bias—for the instructor to approach the topic *not* as a champion of departmental rights, and the counselor, *not* as a champion of individual student rights—but for both to view the problem at hand with "warm objectivity," evidencing a primary interest in the "whole student in the whole institution."

Commenting on relationships of this nature, one administrator of a counseling bureau declares: [5]

More real cooperation can be obtained if we consider cooperation realistically instead of idealistically. Ideally, cooperation demands that the cooperating parties be similarly motivated toward the same goals and in substantial agreement about the best ways of attaining those goals. When these conditions exist, cooperation is an almost automatic and natural outcome. However, I frankly doubt whether we have yet reached that acme of educational theory and

[5] William Gilbert, "Relationships Between Counseling Organizations and Other Divisions," in Ralph F. Berdie (ed.), *Concepts and Programs of Counseling*, University of Minnesota Press, Minneapolis, 1951, p. 43.

practice where we are always motivated toward the same goals. The main educational goals of a great many elementary physics instructors, for example, still consist simply in producing students who have learned a respectable number of physical laws and principles. And the main educational goals of a great many clinical counselors still consist simply in freeing a respectable number of students from handicapping emotional blockages to positive growth.

He concludes with the observation: [6]

> As a prerequisite for the development of effective and efficient working relationships, each organization within a college or university needs to work out a fairly clear set of fundamental principles for operations and policies. Concerning these there should be no yielding unless a broader decision is made to alter the functions of the agency. In order to ensure future development, each agency should also work out a set of long-range goals which it will work toward as opportunity presents itself. . . . Many compromises may have to be made at this long-range level and much patience may be required before these secondary goals can be reached.

Cooperation on Joint Problems

Perhaps the greatest gain in the building of a working relationship among educators comes through the mutual deliberation of counselor and teacher on the problems of a particular student. When Jerry Genesis, the freshman, gives evidence of failing in two of his subjects at mid-semester and when he shows a decided indifference about or fear of his status, the counselor to whom he is referred will, in all likelihood, seek the help of the instructors in the courses in an effort to understand Jerry's state. Some counselors will find that a number of teachers have considerable knowledge about Jerry and have taken time to evaluate his progress and to give him help. Generally speaking, the role of the trained counselor is one of collecting these observations and reports of action and of discussing the implications of Jerry's behavior with resident advisers and other specialized personnel. As a result of this coordinative activity, the counselor may formulate a hypothesis concerning the "why" of Jerry's failure. This aids in the later construction, in collaboration with Jerry, of suggestions for his future action.

Commenting on this method of effecting good working relations through consideration of actual cases, one expert states: [7]

> I would stress . . . the in-service training and upgrading of the personnel staff itself by the encouraging of individual study and the stimulation of regular group meetings, including discussions of actual case situations.

---

[6] *Ibid.*, pp. 44–45.
[7] Ordway Tead, "Integrating Personnel and Teaching Functions in College," *The Educational Forum*, 17:408, May, 1953.

The extension of such study beyond the circle of personnel and counseling staff is, of course, recommended. (See review of a case in Chapter 15.)

Having obtained information from the faculty member about the behavior of Jerry, the counselor has a responsibility for a systematic follow-up with the faculty member. This aspect of "case handling" is all too often omitted in the press of time. What happened to Jerry in the process of counseling? Did he withdraw from school? Did he drop certain courses? Did he obtain tutorial help? Did he forgo some part-time work which was cutting into his study time? Did he, through counseling, gain a more objective attitude about a family situation which was bothering him? Did he begin intensive psychotherapy? Information as to what happened, collected by the counselor and shared with members of the teaching faculty who participated in the case study, is important in effecting good working relationships between members of the instructional and counseling staffs.

The Case Conference

While the counselor-teacher (one-to-one) relationship is practically unbeatable, considerable importance may be placed upon the case-conference activity. The "multisided" student can be viewed in a relatively short time when those persons who have worked with him are given opportunity to consider his total educational adjustment. In the opinion of one group, the case conference is characterized by the following: [8]

a. The conference proceeds through three recognizable stages: the accumulation of data and experience; interpretation of this material; the planning of action and the assignment of specific responsibilities.

b. In the course of the conference, the participant comes to understand that it is not a tribunal; he understands, unless the case is exceptional, that it is not a simple matter of low ability or lack of effort which has given rise to the performance that made the conference necessary.

c. The participant comes to feel that he has information and insight of some value to the whole group working on the problem—and that he can make a real contribution.

d. He develops new insights and attitudes toward this student and/or all students, and toward his colleagues.

e. Having his methods, achievements, and purposes in a specific matter under very direct attention, he reviews his estimate of these.

The case conference seeks to determine the facts about a college student through a polling of those who know him. His life in the

[8] *In-service Training at Stephens College,* a mimeographed report prepared by the Committee on In-service Training for the Board of Curators, 1947, p. 5.

residence hall, his behavior in class, his part-time work experiences, his counseling experiences, his social activities—a review of these assists in the construction of the whole picture of the student. In some instances, off-campus personnel, including community or religious youth workers or representatives from social agencies, veterans' administration, and rehabilitation groups, may be included with profit in the case conference. Having participated in one such conference, a religious youth worker commented that he felt it had been his finest educational experience of the year. He had gained (1) new ideas as to how the philosophy of aiding the whole student was implemented by cooperative faculty action, (2) new information about the counseling services and methods of referral, and (3) a particular admiration for members of the teaching faculty who attempt to provide individualized instruction.

Counseling by Teaching Staff

Reference made earlier in this chapter to faculty advising serves to call to the attention of the reader the trend toward extending certain counseling responsibilities to members of the teaching faculty. A more detailed consideration of this activity appears in Chapters 3 to 7. The extension of this responsibility should be accompanied by (1) assistance given to these faculty advisers for carrying out the assignment, (2) opportunity for faculty advisers to participate in some aspects of policy making relating to advising, and (3) adequate recognition accorded to teachers for their work as advisers.

Written Aids

The use of written aids constitutes another method for promoting understandings which are necessary if teachers and members of the counseling staff are to work together. Commenting on the publication of a *Newsletter* directed toward bettering relationships between the student counseling bureau and the faculty, one administrator states: [9]

The *Newsletter* . . . contains reports of bureau activities, summaries of personnel research studies, particularly those coming out of the bureau, occupational information obtained from United States and state publications and professional journals, summaries of relevant articles appearing in journals, descriptions of books and materials available in the Occupational Library of the Student Counseling Bureau and other matters of professional interest. The fall issue each year contains a directory of Student Counseling Bureau staff members, along with a brief description of their professional qualifications and the areas of student counseling in which each is particularly interested.

Georgia Institute of Technology and Indiana University make use of a folder-type leaflet which is easily enclosed in an envelope and which

[9] Berdie, *op. cit.*, p. 26.

can be mailed to all faculty members. The University of Minnesota, the University of Colorado, Tennessee Agricultural and Industrial University, University of Kansas City, and University of Florida issue a larger directory of similar coverage. At Texas Agricultural and Mechanical University a specially prepared "At-a-Glance Guide to Student Personnel Services" (large sheet 9½ by 14½ inches) contains information relative to the various student personnel services, roles of different members of the educational community, and information relative to making referrals. The Guide may be posted on a bulletin board for handy reference or placed under the glass top of a teacher's desk. (See App. G.)

THE WHOLE STUDENT

How does the college student figure in the working relationships being built between and among (1) administrators in the area of instruction, (2) directors of programs of counseling, and (3) teaching faculty and counselors? This question necessitates a look at the admission of Jerry Genesis to college. By what means was he—and the other new students —recruited?

Public relations experts and catalogue-handbook writers have rivaled the makers of seed and shrub order books in their publications. Promises of early flowering, of fullest bloom, of hardy growth and maturation have been evident in both. The nurture and care of the sapling—be it the weeping willow in the yard or a Woeful Willie in the classroom— would seem to be similar if the statements cited from college publications in Chapter 1 are to be believed. The studied sowing by educational ad writers of such terms as "personalized education," "individualized instruction," "guidance in decision making," and "counseling toward personal adjustment" is obvious. Missing only in the educational blurbs is the covering sentence, "This sapling guaranteed to grow to a height of five feet in a single season or your money cheerfully refunded." [10]

And thus the question: Are these students fulfilling *their* anticipated growth? What is happening to the *rosa floribunda* on our campuses as they experience transplantation from high school to college? Is the student's hope for the transplant being fulfilled?

The student new to the campus is seeking a variety of things, a mixture of the academically and socially acceptable: an extension or intensification of general education, an exploration of a vocational area or areas, the refinement of certain social skills, a search for a mate, a fulfillment of parental expectations, a wish to move upward socially or

[10] From an address by Melvene Draheim Hardee, "Counseling in General Education," American Psychological Association, Division 17, New York City, September, 1954.

culturally, and so on. Whatever the goal or combination of goals, the student needs (1) to acquire ideas and attitudes which will give direction to his life and (2) to observe patterns of conduct which make sense.

Writing of the need for the new student to find adults who will aid him in achieving a feeling of personal worth and serve as models for the building of his life, one writer declares: [11]

... identification with faculty is a powerful preventive of problems and is at the same time a very great incentive to a student to "stretch himself" to equal the stature of his new faculty acquaintance.

It makes no real difference to the student whether this faculty member be a full professor, an associate, or an instructor, as far as rank is concerned, nor is it important that he or she bear the label of dean or department head or counselor. The important thing is that the person be *real*, that his or her influence be salutary. In speaking about the obligation of those who would guide young people, one psychologist declares: [12]

... if he who offers guidance is a whole person with real roots in human culture, he cannot help conveying directly or indirectly to every client what he himself sees and feels and the perspective in which his own life is lived.

The "he" who offers guidance is as often a teacher or administrator as he is a counselor. Of stated importance is the *quality* of the faculty member—his sound, rich, generous, and wise personality, as Murphy affirms.[13] The new student has anticipated, in most instances, this kind of mentor.

Furthermore, the student new to the campus expects no such fragmentation of campus life—and his education—as he all too often finds. He is disconcerted when he observes the competition among departments and between persons, the indifference of educators or their insensitivity toward one another. All too often the student is himself caught in these "academic circumstances" which hamper rather than facilitate his growth in the academic soil of his selection.

THE STUDENT AS THE FOCUS

In the foregoing section, the statement was made that administrators should provide opportunities for teachers and counselors to learn together. The following are excerpts from a group discussion of faculty

[11] Sister Annette, "Psychological Principles," in Paul J. Brouwer (ed.), *Student Personnel Services in General Education,* American Council on Education, Washington, 1949, p. 249.

[12] Gardner Murphy, "The Cultural Content of Guidance," keynote address, American College Personnel Association, Chicago, 1955.

[13] *Ibid.*

personnel in a woman's college. The meeting is one of a regular discussion series and, as publicized in advance, is concerned with *the attitudes which contribute to good counseling and teaching*. The interdisciplinary nature of the group can be seen in the designation of the professional field of the panel member and the audience participant.

The members of the panel include a department head in home and family life, a teacher of mathematics, a clinical psychologist, a teacher of religious education, a teacher of social science, and a teacher of humanities. The moderator is a counselor in the occupational guidance unit.

MODERATOR: In viewing our topic for discussion (What are the attitudes which contribute to good counseling and teaching?), could we ask first, what do we mean by an "attitude"?

HEAD OF FAMILY LIFE: The way a person behaves.

CLINICAL PSYCHOLOGIST: There is probably real difficulty in separating attitude from action; there are muscular activities involved in an attitude. We might say that it is a predisposition toward doing something.

HEAD OF FAMILY LIFE: Is there any way other than viewing one's actions that people can discern one's inner attitude?

MODERATOR: A teacher once confided in me, "There is a girl in my class whom I just cannot like—but I always treat her with respect." One day the roommate of the girl came to the teacher and asked, "Why is it you don't like Jean?" Despite the "respect" with which the teacher felt she was treating Jean, this "respectful" attitude could not mask her true feelings.

TEACHER OF SOCIAL SCIENCE: I think we are prone to suppose that actions are identical when one is "playing" and when one isn't. My belief is that there is no other way people can pass judgment on us *except* by taking into account our action.

MODERATOR: What is one attitude which characterizes the good teacher?

TEACHER OF MATHEMATICS: Respect for the individual.

TEACHER OF PHYSICAL EDUCATION [audience]: Also, a sincere desire to be of service to the individual, understanding, sympathetic.

HEAD OF ART: What is involved in respect for the individual?

TEACHER OF MATHEMATICS: For one thing, it is the desire to help the student develop to his fullest capacity.

CLINICAL PSYCHOLOGIST: Back to your illustration of the faculty member who did not like the student—this person made a judgment. In this instance, the faculty member was not *acceptive* of the student, likely for reason of some behavior that this student exhibited which was different from that of others.

HEAD OF FAMILY LIFE: Respect doesn't necessarily mean approval. In acceptance, you pass no judgment on the opinion of another. You recognize that he holds the right of entertaining such an opinion.

TEACHER OF HUMANITIES: I had a student in class who after three class meetings came in and told me she was not getting anything out of art. I asked her what she expected to get. She answered that she wanted to *judge* art and that she wasn't being given this chance. Further, she said she had been out of school two years, wanted good grades but wasn't a good student. I felt that she was in a state of anxiety about taking a test scheduled for the next day. I adopted a kind of attitude of tolerance, I guess. My first impulse might have been to suggest that she drop the course, but instead of doing this, I took about half an hour before my next class to try to find out why she felt competent to judge art.

TEACHER OF RELIGIOUS EDUCATION: I am interested in the comment "I adopted an attitude." Is this possible?

TEACHER OF HUMANITIES: You mean this sounds artificial—like a mask which I pulled on?

[The audience engages in discussion, several speaking on the point of the teacher's responsibility for clarifying the objectives of the student who is entering a course or proceeding with it.]

TEACHER OF HUMANITIES: I am confused about your frequent use of the word "responsibility." Who is responsible for the student's learning other than the student herself? I am referring to learning in the advising situation as well as in the classroom. I don't feel that I am "responsible" for the student either as a teacher or an adviser.

TEACHER OF SOCIAL SCIENCE: Perhaps you are responsible for putting the student in the hands of those who have such responsibility—a dean or other administrator.

CLINICAL PSYCHOLOGIST: Aren't you responsible for creating a permissive atmosphere in both classroom and conference session so that students may express themselves—reveal their attitudes?

TEACHER OF RELIGIOUS EDUCATION: This is not only a psychological attitude to be developed by teachers and counselors; it is actually a religious one.

TEACHER OF HUMANITIES: Would you say then that my primary objective as a teacher of humanities is to provide an atmosphere in my classroom which could be termed "free" or "permissive"?

[Discussion in the audience on the primary objectives in the several fields follows.]

HEAD OF BUSINESS EDUCATION: A primary objective in my field might be to develop good business citizenship.

TEACHER OF MUSIC: In mine, it would be to develop all-round music understanding.

TEACHER OF MATHEMATICS: I think that the good teacher of mathematics is thinking of the individual and fullest attainment of her possibilities *regardless* of achievement in mathematics. The development of the total person comes first.

MODERATOR: Would you say that you have a specific objective for each student in your class?

[Some audience participation which leads to the next illustration.]

TEACHER OF RELIGIOUS EDUCATION: I had a conference with a student on her schedule, and after a bit she confessed that all she wanted to do was to transfer the following year to the University of M_____ and have as much time for dating as possible. At this point, I got Dean C_____ on the telephone and asked, "What is the subject in which you can major that would require the least work?" Now, what was my objective?

TEACHER OF BIOLOGY: Possibly your aim was to gain the favor of the student?

TEACHER OF FRENCH: On the contrary, wasn't your main objective to make the girl extremely uncomfortable?

CLINICAL PSYCHOLOGIST: You appeared to accept the girl's ideas. I hope you didn't have any mental reservations about what you did.

TEACHER OF RELIGIOUS EDUCATION: No, I didn't. When I finished talking with Dean C_____ on the telephone, the student said, "It sounded pretty bad when I heard you put the question that way to the dean." Right then, we started our conference in a manner in which I don't think we could have otherwise.

HEAD OF BUSINESS EDUCATION: Weren't you really saying to yourself, "Now this is just an elementary attitude that this student is taking. During this two-year period, I am going to work with her to help her prepare for M_____?" I think that you were assuming a responsibility for guiding her toward some better goals.

TEACHER OF HUMANITIES: I guess we could say that you accepted her expressed point of view all right. The point is, would the student have learned by any other method or attitude that you might have used? Would your study beforehand of materials in the counseling folder—test scores, high school grades, family background—have given you a lead on a different attitude to take?

CLINICAL PSYCHOLOGIST: I don't think so. His acceptance of this student and her ideas at face value didn't particularly derive from things he could have read about her in advance. There are several points we might consider here. It deals with our limitations as faculty advisers. We know there is only a certain amount of time that any one adviser can devote to a student. The faculty member may need to set limits in order that one student not usurp so much time that he has too little left for other advisees and other students in his class. Then certainly there is a limit to what we can actually *do* for a student. We cannot manipulate the individual or her environment. We cannot decide for an advisee what her life goal will be. In short, we cannot make decisions *for* the student. We can assist students in their growth toward better decision making within the limitations of our time.

TEACHER OF FOOD AND NUTRITION: This is not easy. Frequently, students have been used to working to please somebody else—high school teacher or principal or parents. Often in class, they will ask, "What do you want on this paper?" They will flounder, and badly at first, when a *mandate* or *prescription* of what to do is withheld.

TEACHER OF RELIGIOUS EDUCATION: I remember that in a class of seniors some years ago I asked, "What do you want out of this course? Why did you enter the course? How would you like to be treated?" I got the notion from their responses that they wanted to be treated as adults. So, the course was conducted accordingly. The group decided that grades would not be faced until the end of the course. The students agreed to do any reading that they needed to and I was to post the reading assignments. Well, seven girls flunked, and the dean called me in. His point was that there hadn't been any indication of this impending failure on the mid-semester reports. But, this was once in my life that I taught a whole semester with no worries about grades!

CLINICAL PSYCHOLOGIST: Had you made it clear to the students that some of them might fail?

TEACHER OF RELIGIOUS EDUCATION: Oh, yes, and they understood that I would not "watchdog" over them. At the end when grades were assessed, one girl said, "Because of the wonderful relationship of teacher and students—and student to student—I assumed that I was doing better than I actually was."

TEACHER OF HUMANITIES: Was there any chance for them to come in to find out about their grades?

TEACHER OF RELIGIOUS EDUCATION: Oh, yes, they were free to come in at any time to ask about their grades. During the semester, only three girls out of twenty-five came in to discuss their work. None of those three were in the group of seven who failed.

[Audience participation on the topic of teacher responsibility for student achievement.]

MODERATOR: We have been talking about attitudes characteristic of the good teacher and adviser, the first being *respect for the individual*. In our consideration, we faced up to some of the primary objectives of our particular area of specialty; we viewed several examples of our *modus operandi* and raised questions about the use of particular methods indicative of particular attitudes held by the teacher; and we faced the question, "Who is responsible for the student's achievement?" We have by no means exhausted ourselves on the first attitude, respect for the individual student, but we must turn to other attitudes which you have named as important for the good teacher and adviser.

The foregoing discussion illustrates to some extent the kind of cooperative learning which may proceed when faculty members meet together to discuss *the student, the faculty,* and the *working relationships of both.* Some readers will dismiss the example as "impossible in our institution." Others will concede, "We could be doing some of this—on a limited scale, of course." Others will have had similar experiences in small group discussion of this nature in faculty conference, in-service training sessions, department meetings, etc. It is recognized that, in large institutions particularly, much of the discussion in faculty meetings is directed to the expansion of curriculum, course changes, and "institutional business," with the regrettable result that the matter of teacher-student relations is rarely placed on the agenda for discussion. Outlined below are questions which appear to have merit for discussion, institution-wide.[14]

1. Do we recognize how little we know about the student population that we are serving and will serve?

2. How much real examination have we done of our own curricula? How segmented is the hierarchy in which we work? How much do we know of the role which society is asking us to perform?

3. If the total faculty does not analyze the curriculum in higher educa-

[14] From "Contemporary Youth in Higher Education," a keynote address by Ray Birdwhistell, anthropologist, University of Louisville, Third Annual Work Conference, Southern College Personnel Association, Mars Hill, N.C., 1954.

tion, how can the workers in student personnel interpret it to students?

4. Can we ask a few counselors or psychiatrists to handle the emotional problems of the entire collegiate group?

5. Must counselors and psychiatrists be condemned to failure and/or to gadgetry because we fail to ask society to pay for the services which its members are receiving? Should the colleges handle the emotional problems of its students, or should an institution operate a referral service to off-campus agencies?

6. If we decide to train students for membership in the community, is our present college-activities program really equipping our student body for the job? Is the time spent with students by our deans of students and staff justified in light of the performances of college graduates in their respective communities?

7. In a culture which will give fewer and fewer jobs to students with A.B. and B.S. degrees, do we have a right to deceive the student with a job-oriented undergraduate curriculum, particularly when the graduates of every professional school are crying for a broader background?

8. Do we as a faculty group recognize that we live in a society which now has a forty-hour week and will probably within fifteen years have one of twenty-five or thirty? Do we recognize that we must train for a useful leisure rather than the job? Do we recognize that an increasing role of education will be to keep students off an overcrowded labor market, extending schooling for more and more American youth?

9. Do we recognize that, in the present day, more and more people will be postponing the rearing of families? Will we provide dormitories and apartments for young married couples who can have children and participate in the parenthood training program?

Viewing the range of questions, one moves next to ask: How can the resources of an entire college or university community be energized to give direct and dedicated consideration to these problems which cut across all areas—the humanities, the social sciences, the biological and physical sciences—and which involve the professional fields, the academic program planners, and the financial experts?

Some important considerations are undoubtedly these:

1. What is a college student? What are his hopes, dreams, aims, and aspirations?

2. After whom (among the adults in contemporary society) has the collegian chosen to pattern? For what reason?

3. What are the values of the college man? On what can he be compromised? Regarding what does his integrity never waver?

4. How does the college man or woman make decisions? What are the intellectual processes of which he is capable? What part have his

emotions played in his learnings up to now? To what extent will his emotions continue to educate him?

5. What are the limits to which the young adult can stretch himself? How shall he be helped to approach these limits?

6. To sum it up, what of the contemporary student in higher education? What is he, intellectually, physically, psychologically, spiritually?

That consideration of matters such as these is possible in a large university is evidenced by the following statement of an administrator: [15]

From time to time the student counseling bureau invites all the faculty and staff to a series of lectures or lecture discussions on topics which we feel are pertinent to their roles as advisers or counselors. We have in the past had meetings on problems of predicting academic success, personality measurement, etc. The program for the current year is as follows:

THE PSYCHOLOGY OF THE UNIVERSITY-AGE ADOLESCENT

November 7   Developmental Aspects of the College-age Adolescent: Dale P. Harris, Professor and Director, Institute of Child Welfare

November 14   Social Needs of the University-age Adolescent: Ben Willerman, Associate Professor of Psychology and Senior Student Personnel Worker

November 21   Abilities and Aptitudes of the University Adolescent: Wilbur L. Layton, Associate Professor of Psychology and Assistant Director, Student Counseling Bureau

December 5   Mental Health and Illness in College-age Adolescents: Myron G. Messenheimer, Mental Hygienist and Assistant Professor

December 12   Vocational Interests of the University Adolescent: Theda Hagenah, Associate Professor of Educational Psychology and Assistant Director, Student Counseling Bureau

THE STUDENT AS AN INGREDIENT

Perhaps it will be the students in their naïveté—but also in their trust of faculty members—who will bring unity to the campus where disunity threatens. When student problems are studied by the faculty and administration, who better than *students* should join in the study to interpret "to the elders" some of the intellectual, physical, psychological, and spiritual drives of their youthful contemporaries? That students can serve with teachers, administrators, and counselors in conferences and on policy-making committees has been proven by such institutions as Syracuse University, Mills College, Chico State College, Stephens Col-

[15] From a letter directed to the author by Theda Hagenah, Associate Professor of Educational Psychology and Assistant Director, Student Counseling Bureau, December, 1957.

lege, and by others. (Some noteworthy cautions are cited by Stroup.[16])

When students, teaching faculty, administrators, and counselors sit down together to talk about the whole student in the whole institution, some consideration will need to be given to questions such as these:

1. Is there an over-all policy concerning the counseling of students? Is it understood by students, teaching faculty, administration, counselors, and clinicians?

2. Are there definite procedures which have been established for carrying out the policies? How did the procedures originate? Are these practices known to all—students, teaching faculty, administration, counselors, and specialists—on campus?

3. What are the responsibilities and duties of each faculty member who works with students? Are these responsibilities known and understood by him? By others who cooperate with him?

4. What authority is vested in persons who have been given counseling or advisement functions? Are the limits of this authority clear?

5. Are the talents of the various teachers, counselors, clinicians, and specialists in the program being used to good advantage? What are the possibilities for better utilization of special abilities?

6. Are there established channels of communication between and among counselors, teachers, administrators, and students, parents, high school personnel, and off-campus agencies? Are the channels used effectively?

7. Is the program of student counseling effective? How well are the immediate and ultimate objectives of counseling being attained?

8. Are the policies and the procedures of counseling reviewed frequently in light of changes in the institution and in society generally?

9. Is there opportunity for some faculty and students to participate in revision of counseling policy and procedure?

10. What are the means by which the various activities of the institution can be better integrated to aid the student who is seeking to integrate his educational experiences? What cooperative action can be initiated?

The goal in such deliberations directed toward the counseling of students is to effect understandings among all college and university groups, with individuals working *in combination* and without fear, distrust, contempt, and indifference. The counseling cloth must be cut to the educational pattern. The dedication is, and will continue to be, the whole institution for the whole student. No substitute of the "segmented university" existing to aid the "fragmented student" is acceptable.

[16] Herbert Stroup, "Values and *Disvalues* of Faculty-Student Committees," *Personnel and Guidance Journal*, 35:289–292, January, 1957.

SUMMARY

The aim of this chapter has been to recount something of the nature of good working relationships between (1) administrative officers in the academic and counseling areas and (2) members of the instructional and counseling staffs. The focus has been the student who seeks help from individuals in the several groups. Specific questions were raised to test some aspects of institutional wholeness, these in particular concerning the assigned responsibilities for advisement and counseling, the channeling and collection of information, and the review and evaluation of policies and practices in the program of counseling.

In the chapter to follow, attention is drawn to the special role of the faculty member as an adviser. The intention of specific faculty service as well as the extent to which it is proving effective is given detailed consideration.

CHAPTER 3 *The Role of the Faculty Member in the Program of Counseling*

Who, in 1925, in predicting things to come in higher education would have said that in the brief span of twenty-five years a movement would be under way designed to educate faculty members after they had presumably been educated? In earlier times, the professor with a learned degree in the A, B, C's—astronomy, botany, classics—or with a penchant for philosophy or flute could set up schoolkeeping on his own pedagogical premises. The teacher of flute kept to his studio except when he taught an occasional class in music theory. He was known to give five to eight lessons a day in flute, and in between times he composed or arranged for flute.

Those were the days of splendid isolationism not only for flutists but also for laboratory technicians with withdrawal tendencies, assorted linguists dedicated to their translations, and artists in water color, oils, and silk screen who, like Garbo, wanted only to be alone. That they were called out of their crannied existence to counsel little bands of new and forlorn freshmen, as well as surprising numbers of mature-looking upperclassmen, is the theme of this discussion.[1]

What is the purpose of this trend which seeks to "retool" the accomplished faculty flutist who has wanted, chiefly, to pipe his tunes like Pan "down by the river"? Conceivably the aims are as follows:

1. To extend or delegate to him, as a third-level counselor, certain of the responsibilities of professionally trained counselors

2. To return the faculty member to his rightful role as friend and confidant of the student

To effect both of these objectives, administrators are directing their efforts toward sensitizing the faculty member to the plaints of students,

[1] Based on a panel discussion "Studies of Behavior in Human Relations Education," by Melvene Draheim Hardee, American College Personnel Association, Chicago, March, 1955.

many of whom need only a sympathetic ear. This sensitization of the faculty member may hopefully result from experience in the counseling program together with the in-service training provided.

Throughout this book, the designations *faculty counselor* and *faculty adviser* are used somewhat interchangeably. (In the opinion of the author, the designation *adviser* is more apt in view of the functions performed by the faculty member. The use of the term *counselor* tends to imply a formal training or special experience in helping individuals to make wise choices or solve personal problems. While a few faculty members serving in a program of institution-wide counseling may have this combination of specialized training and experience, this is by no means the prevailing pattern.) To merit the designation of faculty counselor or faculty adviser, the faculty member will perform functions more far-reaching than those of an enrollment officer and registration clerk. (See chapters to follow.) One authority believes the role of the faculty counselor or adviser to be that of *coordinator* of all behavioral data pertaining to the counselee and his progress.[2]

FACULTY ADVISEMENT—ITS INTENT, EXTENT, AND SUCCESS

In a recent survey of practice in 218 colleges and institutions, some questions posed by the author were these (see App. B):

1. What are the types of counseling in which faculty serve? How successful is their service? What are the means by which faculty receive their training? How successful are these methods?

2. Of what importance is the service of faculty members in counseling?

3. What types of counseling do faculty members not do?

4. What improvements in your institution would you suggest for the use of faculty personnel in counseling?

While a more detailed treatment of the results is given in the tables at the end of this book, it is essential for the reader to note some of the over-all trends in participation of faculty members in programs of counseling. For example, in all 218 institutions, with student enrollments varying from less than 750 to more than 5,000, faculty members are used in the area of academic counseling (see Table 1). In 171 of these institutions, faculty members do personal-social counseling. Somewhat fewer— 153 institutions—report the use of faculty members in vocational counseling. In ninety-eight colleges and universities, faculty members participate in religious counseling, and in eighty-four institutions they perform health counseling. Respondents to the questionnaire give varying reasons

[2] Eugene L. Shepard, "The Role of the Faculty Counselor in General Education" in Melvene Draheim Hardee (ed.), *Counseling and Guidance in General Education*, World Book Company, Yonkers, N.Y., 1955, pp. 161–178.

for the use of faculty members in the counseling of students. Approximately sixty-six respondents agree in the following (see Table 5):

The faculty member is in a position to be of great help to students. He is their first and nearest point of contact. He is most familiar with academic needs of students as well as with the content of the academic areas.

Thirty-six replies tend to confirm the statement:

Counseling is a part of the educational program. Faculty counseling is a natural result of the teaching-learning situation.

Some thirty-one replies contend:

Counseling provides the means for faculty to know and understand students better, as well as the stimulus for their continued professional growth and development.

Among other reasons cited by twenty or more respondents are the following:

Faculty counseling aids in the integration of the various factors of education, relating counseling, teaching, and the student's total life experience.

The success of a counseling program is dependent on the participation of everyone. The faculty is the heart of the educational program.

Faculty counseling accentuates the service-to-students aspect. It makes possible the assistance of someone who is interested in students personally, who is accessible to them, and who is in a position to reach many students.

As for the quality of performance in counseling, a brief review of the data contributed would show that, on a scale ranging from poor to excellent, the faculty member's performance is most often rated as good (see Table 2). Twelve institutions having student enrollments of less than 750 report that faculty members assigned to academic counseling are doing an excellent job. Twenty-five institutions in this category term the performance of faculty members as good. Six schools of this size report that their faculty personnel do a fair job of student advisement, whereas no institution in this category indicates that a poor job is being done by the faculty. (See Table 2 also for results in institutions with larger enrollments.)

In all institutions surveyed, it would appear that the most commendable work is being done by the faculty in the area of academic counseling, with performance in personal-social counseling in second place, and performance in vocational counseling in third place.

THE ADMINISTRATION AND COORDINATION
OF FACULTY ADVISEMENT

While Chapter 9 deals somewhat more in detail with the problems of coordination of counseling in colleges and universities, an indication of the variety of practice in programs is presented here with use of specific examples. Responsibility for organizing, executing, and coordinating the work of faculty members who counsel may be assigned to (1) a single individual in either the student personnel area or an academic area; (2) several individuals within an area or from different areas, working in conjunction; (3) a board, committee, or council; (4) a counseling center; or (5) an individual aided by a committee. The administrative arrangement adopted by the institution is probably the one that best fits the local situation in view of institutional philosophy and purpose, the personnel available to do the job, and the available budgetary support.

Administration by an individual in the student personnel area or in an academic area

UNIVERSITY OF THE SOUTH: The dean of students, who is also dean of men, acts, in the first capacity, to coordinate the entire advisory system—freshman through senior year. Students are assigned by him to advisers.

COLGATE UNIVERSITY: A staff of sixteen graduate students and sixteen members of the faculty, termed preceptors, are responsible for the advisement of the entering class. Their work is organized under the director for the preceptorial program.

Administration by several individuals working in conjunction

UNIVERSITY OF UTAH: The director of general education and the dean of students serve as co-chairmen of the board of general-education counselors. This pattern of organization has kept the lines of communication open and has made it possible for general-education counselors, clinical counselors, and curriculum committee members to work together.

HARPUR COLLEGE: Academic advising is provided by the faculty and coordinated by the dean of students. Freshman students are assigned to an adviser by the dean of students with the help of the counselor of students and the admissions counselor.

UNIVERSITY OF OREGON: The dean of the College of Liberal Arts has an assistant, a faculty member, designated as director of lower-division student advising. Aiding him on problems which arise is the director of student affairs, who is a member of the committee on advising.

Administration by a board, committee, or council

HARVARD UNIVERSITY: Faculty members who counsel constitute a board of freshmen advisers, with the freshman dean serving as chairman.

KENT STATE UNIVERSITY: The president appoints a guidance committee which is composed of faculty, administrators, and personnel people and which has considerable continuity in its membership. Recently the committee recommended a coordinating council composed of representatives of all the special services, academic areas, and faculty advisers. The chairman of the guidance committee is also chairman of the council.

Administration by a counseling center

VIRGINIA STATE COLLEGE: The college counseling service is the over-all agency of the college for stimulating and coordinating the program of counseling. The service is directly responsible to the president, its policies being subject to approval by the president and the executive council.

Administration by an individual working in conjunction with a committee

SAN FRANCISCO STATE COLLEGE: The advisory system operates under the general direction of the associate dean of students. He is assisted by the committee on advising made up of one faculty member from each division of the college.

STANFORD UNIVERSITY: The lower-division office, which is charged with the servicing of advisers as well as lower-division students, is located in the registrar's office, and the registrar assumes the executive responsibility for maintaining the advisory program. In this function, the registrar is responsible to the faculty committee on lower division.

OREGON STATE COLLEGE: The personnel coordinator gives leadership to the academic counseling program. He is the executive officer of the personnel council and is assisted in his function by a coordinating committee which studies student personnel services in each school as well as for the institution as a whole.

Within a large institution, each of the several schools or divisions may have its own program of faculty advisement, the programs being coordinated for the institution as a whole by one individual or a committee. An example exists at Ohio State University where the Colleges of Arts-Sciences, Education, Engineering, Agriculture, and Commerce each sponsor a counseling program fitting its own needs. Provision is made through the junior council of the university for a review of matters common to the several colleges and pertaining to the precollege counseling, scheduling, and instructional and educational advisement of undergraduate students.

The foregoing brief descriptions show to some extent the variety in organization and administration of faculty counseling within selected institutions. The organization of the program will affect to a considerable extent the selection of faculty personnel for counseling, the plan for assigning counselees to them, the method of in-service training, and the over-all coordination of faculty advisement with other guidance services of the institution. (See Chapter 5.)

LIMITATIONS SET FOR FACULTY ADVISERS

Reference was made in an earlier chapter to the fear of some professionally trained counselors that a member of the teaching faculty assuming the role of "counselor" would produce results dangerous to the business. Can we expect the faculty member who is trained professionally in flute to be a bull-in-the-china-closet counselor? Will he who learned the intricacies of his musical instrument with ease at five be able to learn the techniques for advising students easily at thirty-five? How much more damaging is the occasionally inept counseling of the professional flutist than is the occasionally bungled flute playing done by a professional counselor? These are questions which perplex the program director or the committee in charge of faculty advisement.

One educator reminds his readers that counseling is an activity which by its very nature demands philosophical warranty. He affirms that, when an individual engages in an enterprise which deliberately and intimately affects the lives of other people, he should have convincing reasons for his action.[3]

In the preceding pages of this chapter, college and university administrators express some of the convincing reasons for the use of faculty members as counselors. At this point it would be well to state the limits to which faculty members may be permitted to go in this enterprise which deliberately and intimately affects the lives of others.

In the survey cited earlier in this chapter, 104 institutions declare that members of the teaching faculty do not attempt to handle cases of emotional or deviant behavior which fall outside the behavioral pattern of students adjudged reasonably normal (see Table 6). Furthermore, respondents from thirty-eight institutions declare that testing—both administration and interpretation—is out of bounds for faculty members. Approximately twenty-four institutions look with disfavor upon the intrusion of faculty members into areas of administrative or coordinative planning which involve policy making, evaluation, and in-service training. A sizable number of institutions ensure that health counseling, personal-social counseling, and vocational counseling are done by professional personnel and not by the faculty counselor. Finally, a scattering of schools will not allow their faculty counselors to engage in financial counseling, remedial speech and reading activities, and marital counseling (see Table 6).

Experience has shown that there are some faculty members who are by nature unafraid to tackle any problem of any student. On the other hand, there are faculty members who would bolt the program of counseling if the counselee broached a personal problem. How can the all-knowing problem solver among the faculty advisers be curbed? How can the faculty member who wants to see and hear no evil be encouraged to listen to the student's problem in order that he may make sensible referral of it to the specialist?

[3] D. Luther Evans, "The Professor and the Counselor," *Educational Research Bulletin,* 33:57, Ohio State University, Mar. 10, 1954.

Part of the answer to these questions comes in the careful selection of faculty members for their advising and counseling responsibilities. There is a continuing need for the "right" people to be recruited to the program of counseling. Once they are recruited, the need exists for in-service training (cooperative learning activities) through which the silk-screen artist, the hurricane-hunting meteorologist, and the afore-mentioned flutist may learn the techniques for performing their jobs as counselors or advisers.

SELECTION OF FACULTY ADVISERS

In the poll of institutions previously cited, some thirty-one respondents pointed to these problems relating to faculty advisement:

SMALL SOUTHERN STATE UNIVERSITY: There is a feeling on our campus that counseling is an extra duty imposed in addition to teaching.

WESTERN STATE AGRICULTURAL COLLEGE: The faculty are too busy to do a good counseling job, probably because they are disinterested in their work.

SOUTHWESTERN LIBERAL ARTS COLLEGE: Since everyone is expected to assist in the academic counseling program, we get some who are neither strongly interested or motivated.

WESTERN STATE UNIVERSITY: It is not only a matter of selecting qualified faculty members to do student advisement, but it is also a matter of dis-couraging from our program faculty members who are not qualified to advise students.

A study of policies and practices in various institutions indicates that these factors are important in matters of selection.

1. The view which the administration takes of the service of the faculty member assuming the role of counselor

2. The participation by academic deans and department heads in the selection of faculty personnel for counseling

3. The criteria of selection applied to faculty

No program of all-college counseling will prosper if the administra-tion minimizes the venture or is indifferent to it. Faculty members gen-erally will rally to a counseling "cause" if the administration rallies. To some critics, this is to say that faculty members are politely acquiescent—that they will "snap to" when the commanding officer gives the order. If this is true, then one would certainly expect to find some hypocrites in the counseling ranks: those who genuinely do not want to counsel students but who make a show of doing it in order to keep face with the administration. That there are some faculty members who evidence this veneer of willingness to counsel when they are basically unwilling to do so is probably true. Perhaps a somewhat larger number of faculty members catch their enthusiasm for counseling from top-level administrators who reflect a sincere interest in the work of the faculty counselor, encourage his efforts, give him reward or recognition of one kind or another, and work to facilitate the counseling job he is doing. This influence of administrators on the program of counseling is a most salutary one. One university administrator speaks forthrightly in addressing faculty counselors in their initial meeting:

> It is most fortunate on this campus that not all of the counseling is done by those who are specialists in counseling. I think that would be a grave error, even if we had the money to do otherwise. It is most fortunate that a majority of those who take part in student counseling are regular teachers of the various subject fields on this campus. That is as it should be. If we do our job well, then we will be less misunderstood and less vulnerable to criticism than we would be otherwise.
>
> I hope, therefore, that you will not accept your duties in a perfunctory manner—just as a chore to be done—but rather that you will look upon this as perhaps one of the most difficult of all things to do but something which, if a college professor cannot do it, is a sad commentary on the professor!

There are other statements of administrators which mirror the institution's philosophy as well as the personal convictions of the officers in charge. These statements, aside from public pronouncement, may be noted in introductions to faculty handbooks, manuals for faculty advisers, and other printed materials depicting the counseling program.

With the support of top-level administrators given to the program of counseling, it naturally follows that these officers should figure in the process of selecting faculty advisers. The need for the services in counseling of the teacher of historical geology or of the associate professor in Greek must be understood by the department head and dean, and approval for such service made in joint conference. This ensures that the faculty member, department head, academic dean, and director of counseling clearly understand the kind of service which the faculty member will provide, the amount of time it will require, and the conditions under which the activity will proceed. An agreement made in combination forestalls the later criticism that "the dean makes poor selections" or that "the department head lets some staff members talk him out of appointment to counseling" or that "the director of the counseling program is too little informed about academic matters to make good teacher-counselor selections."

It goes without saying that the faculty member who is appointed to do counseling deserves to be *invited* to serve in the program rather than to be drafted or to be told that he must volunteer his services! Once the decision concerning the service of the faculty member is made, a formal acknowledgment of the appointment is in order. (See App. F-1 for

letter sent by a coordinator of counseling to faculty counseling personnel.)

With reference to specific criteria used in the selection of faculty
members for counseling, this can be said. The least useful criterion is
the one occasionally voiced by an academic dean or department head,
"Well, Professor Drydock might as well counsel. We can't seem to fill
his classes and he ought to have something to take up his time." The
allocation of Drydock to either a newly established or an old-line program of counseling bodes no good. Students get the word about the
caliber of ineffective counselors much as they get the word about ineffective teachers, with the result that Drydock sits in splendid isolation
as a counselor just as he did as a teacher.

The only respectable criteria for use in selecting faculty for the counseling role are those concerned with (1) the interest of the faculty member in counseling, (2) the ability of the faculty member to deal effectively with students in a one-to-one relationship, and (3) the willingness
of the faculty member to learn the fundamentals of his counseling responsibility.

A thought-provoking set of counselor criteria has been set forth by
the committee of advising chairmen at Stephens College. Faculty advisers in this institution assist in schedule making, counsel on academic
progress, consider the personal-social problems of students, and make
proper referral to specialists, thus serving as a coordinator of counseling
for each of their advisees. The criteria for selection of faculty for the
advising responsibility at Stephens College are these: [4]

1. Sensitivity to human relationships: interest in working with students;
ability to sense another's emotion; patience and the ability to learn; genuine
receptive and interested attitude
2. Objectivity: capacity for controlled sympathy; open-mindedness; recognition of one's own fallibility; sense of honor
3. Flexibility in ways of working with others: ability to make essential com-
promises as the occasion demands; maturity of emotional patterns
4. Respect for another's individuality: ability to accept the student as he
is, on his own level of adjustment; willingness to give the student freedom to
work out his own solutions to problems; confidence in the student's integrity or
ability for growth
5. Concern for the operation in everyday living of the moral and spiritual
values
6. Readiness to make the most of opportunities for growth as a counselor-
teacher
7. Possession of an alert, clear, and creative mind which is stimulating to
others

[4] *Handbook for Advisers*, Stephens College, Columbia, Mo.

In an effort to develop a measure of interest for selecting faculty counselors, Koile administered a professional activity inventory for college teachers to 500 college teachers, 290 of whom were counseling teachers and 210 noncounseling teachers, and who represented forty-six colleges and universities in twenty-five states. He then selected 105 counseling teachers and 105 noncounseling teachers for his analysis, using matching techniques. Each counseling teacher chosen for the experimental group was matched with a noncounseling teacher on the basis of sex, broad teaching field, type of college, academic rank, and the highest degree held. The two groups were matched according to their means and standard deviations on each of the following: age, years of college teaching, and years of other teaching. They also were matched on a group basis according to geographic area. Thus, counseling and noncounseling teachers chosen for the development of a scoring system were matched case by case on five variables and by groups on four variables.

For the subjects in the study conducted by Koile,[5] the following appear to be true:

1. Women tend to be more interested than men in faculty advising activities.

2. Instructors and assistant professors combined as one group obtained higher mean scores than did associate and full professors combined as another group.

3. Teachers who do not hold the earned doctorate appear to be somewhat more interested in faculty counseling activities than those who hold it.

4. College teachers in the two age groups in the middle are more interested in faculty advising activities than teachers in the youngest and the oldest groups.

5. The college teacher's field of preparation appears to be associated with interest in faculty counseling activities. (High means were obtained by applied arts and sciences and the social sciences groups, and low means by the humanities and natural sciences groups.)

6. Interest in faculty advising activities tends to increase with increases in the number of years of noncollege teaching experience.

7. Teachers in state teachers colleges and state regional colleges apparently have greater interest in faculty counseling activities than do teachers in liberal arts colleges.

8. There is not sufficient evidence available from the research to suggest that the length of college teaching experience is related to interest in faculty counseling activities.

9. The geographic area from which the subjects were drawn seems to have no significant relationship to interest in faculty advising activities.

It is evident that, as student enrollments mount and as deans and department heads become more involved in the complexities of hiring

---

[5] Earl A. Koile, "Characteristics of College Teachers Interested in Faculty Counseling Activities," *Journal of Counseling Psychology*, 2:32–34, spring, 1955.

faculty, finding classroom space, outfitting laboratories and other instructional units, their considered meditation on who shall counsel may wane. Certainly the experimental projects which attempt, like that of Koile, to point out some factors for sound adviser-counselor selection may go untried. Administrative heads need to review various programs of faculty advisement in current use in institutions of higher education (see examples in succeeding chapters). These descriptions of program indicate that the effectiveness of the program of faculty advisement rests in large measure upon careful preplanning and upon sound working relations to be effected among faculty members, administrators in academic areas, and the director or committee in charge of counseling.

THE FUNCTION OF THE FACULTY MEMBER WHO COUNSELS

Two faculty members of a state university, when asked to define their function as counselors for freshmen and transfer students, replied as follows:

FACULTY MEMBER IN THE DEPARTMENT OF CLASSICS: Educational advisement is supervised training in curricular selections. The curriculum is a storehouse of resources which a student must learn to draw on wisely. A wise selection both of courses and of schedule hours enables the student to attain his educational goals with the greatest efficiency and economy of time. Educational counseling or advisement should aim both to eliminate the wasted energy which characterizes so much of the student's program and also to open up time for elective work which broadens the content of an individual's education.

FACULTY MEMBER IN THE DEPARTMENT OF ENGLISH: The faculty counselor undertakes the responsibility of helping individual students plan the program of study which will meet university requirements and at the same time fit the needs of the individual students. If the student is undecided as to major or professional choice, it is the responsibility of the counselor to urge him to give thought to the matter, to direct him to sources of information which will help him make a decision, and to aid him in any way in thinking through the problem.

While it is likely that the functions of the faculty members serving as counselors may vary among institutions, their duties may be similar to these: [6]

1. The faculty adviser explains to the student the program of general or basic education as it relates to the first two years of college, to the major of the student (if he has expressed interest in a major), and to preparation for life pursuits generally.

2. The faculty adviser plans with the student a schedule of courses with a consideration of the over-all year's work. This may be accomplished through a

[6] Melvene Draheim Hardee, "General Education and General-educational Counseling," *School and Society*, 74:4, July 7, 1951.

consideration of the offerings set forth in the various publications of the institution, by considering the student's strengths and needs as revealed by a study of high school tests and grades and of college entrance tests, by personal interview, and by judgments as to his ability contributed by high school principals and teachers.

3. The faculty adviser assists the student in exploring his major field. To accomplish this, he will interpret the various departmental publications of the university; in addition, he may refer the student to a special consultant in the field or to the counselors in the vocational guidance office. Finally, he may recommend particular extraclass or part-time work activities for the consideration of the student.

4. Likewise, the faculty adviser assists the "undecided" student in exploring a major field. This is accomplished by referring him to experts in several fields of specialty, to counselors in the vocational guidance office, to the bureau of testing for supplementary testing, and to various extraclass activities wherein interests may be explored and experiences gained.

5. The faculty adviser serves as a "faculty friend" to the student by demonstrating a personal interest in him and in his adjustment to college; by serving as a central contact person in obtaining suggestions, which can be used to help the student, from residence counselor, teacher, or department head; in giving suggestions concerning the student to the residence counselor, teacher, or department head; and by allowing the student freedom to make his own choices after the limitations, alternatives, and consequences involved in a decision are pointed out.

6. The faculty adviser serves as a link between the student and the administration by counseling the student on matters of failure, on the procedures for dropping or adding courses, on eligibility for the various exemption examinations in general education, and on admittance to special remedial classes or clinics.

Speaking of the limitations placed upon faculty advisers, program planners of Wheaton College sound these cautions: [7]

1. A counselor cannot make decisions for a counselee, but he can be a sympathetic listener and even offer various possible solutions to the student's problem.

2. A counselor cannot increase the native ability of his counselee, but he can encourage the maximum use of the ability he knows he has.

3. A counselor should not attempt to solve serious maladjustments involving physical or mental disorders but should refer such cases to proper professional agencies.

4. A counselor cannot reduce the academic or employment load of a floundering counselee, but he can make recommendations that such adjustments be made.

5. A counselor should not criticize a fellow teacher to a student, but he can make a friendly approach to any teacher if that teacher is involved in the student's problem.

[7] *Counselor's Manual*, Wheaton College, Wheaton, Ill., 1949, p. 3.

6. A counselor should not tell a student his I.Q. and psychological scores, but he can indicate areas in which he seems weak or strong.

7. A counselor cannot be a good counselor and betray a student's confidence on matters of a confidential nature.

These outlined functions and accompanying cautions give some indication of the nature of the task assumed by the faculty adviser. With such a wide range of responsibilities evident, it is generally agreed that the faculty member schooled in the liberal arts or trained in a specialty field must be prepared for dispatching these duties. The flutist "playing at counseling" with no real understanding of his role strikes a note a bit more ominous than that of the trained counselor engaging in a musical hobby with little show of competence.

If faculty counseling is intended to produce counseling but not coddling, orientation but not domination, self-direction but not dependency,[8] some thoughtfully presented how-to-do's are in order.

SUMMARY

In this chapter attention has been called to the trend for using faculty members as advisers for students. In the discussion, some administrative patterns have been cited. In addition, there has been coverage of the limitations placed upon faculty advisers, the procedures for selecting faculty members for advising duties, and their assignment to specific functions. Recognizing the fact that the "bits and pieces" of programs are helpful in a limited degree only, the author has included in the chapter to follow some "whole cloth" of institutional practice in advising. The aim is to give the reader a more detailed view of advising procedures in a number of selected institutions, both public and private, in various geographical areas.

[8] Lonzo Jones, *Bulletin for Lower Division Counselors*, Indiana State Teachers College, p. 8. (Mimeographed.)

CHAPTER 4 *Promising Programs in Faculty Advisement*

In the preceding chapter, emphasis was placed upon the role of the faculty adviser, with attention centered on some general functions of advisers in programs with differing organizational patterns. Throughout this book, the author cites instances of working and workable practice in counseling. The single citation, however, fails to give the whole picture of the work of the faculty adviser. It is, therefore, the purpose of this chapter to report somewhat more complete views of twenty selected programs of faculty advisement. To so report, the author has relied upon supplementary information—letters, handbooks, and other materials—which has accompanied the return of various questionnaires.

The programs reported in this chapter are (1) those tried and tested over a period of time and (2) those operating in various parts of the country, in institutions with varying philosophies and objectives and differing student enrollments. It will be obvious to the reader that a sizable number of the programs are found in institutions designated as state-supported and having relatively large student enrollment. In the instance of the small institutions, the informality of the advising process may defy precise description.

The programs chosen for review appear to have some or all of the following characteristics:

1. A statement of philosophy and/or program objectives is evident.

2. A program structure can be seen: method for assigning advisers, system for conducting student interviews, periods designated for interviewing and report making, etc.

3. Criteria exist for the selection of faculty advisers.

4. Functions of faculty advisers are enumerated.

5. Selected information about students is available for the use of advisers.

6. Faculty advisers contribute to student records.

7. In-service training for advisers is provided.

8. Persons trained in student personnel procedures and/or counseling direct or assume a major role in the program.

9. The program has continuity for students from first to fourth years in college.

10. Consideration is given to the needs of the whole student.

11. The areas of operation for professionally trained counselors are stated.

12. There are evidences of good integration of effort among administrators, teachers, and professionally trained counselors.

13. Channels of communication between and among students, advisers, teachers, administrators, and counselors are provided.

14. A system of program evaluation is evident.

In addition, some unique aspects of programming may be seen:

1. The manner in which *a college within a university* provides for the academic needs of its students—University of Chicago, State University of Iowa, Cornell University, etc.

2. The manner in which students undecided about a major are aided—Michigan State University

3. The specialty designations in function assumed by some faculty advisers—San Francisco State College

4. The reimbursement of faculty advisers—University of Illinois

5. The inclusion of spiritual emphases in program objectives—Wheaton College

6. The ways in which faculty advisers may work with students who carry counseling responsibilities—Teachers College of Connecticut

7. The evolution or development of program—Brigham Young University and University of Denver, etc.

Obviously, some very good programs did not come to the attention of the author or could not be included here for reasons of chapter length. With an apology for failure to include all that is known about all that exists, the author moves ahead to present selected programs of faculty advisement in which the reader may discern "something old, something new, something borrowed. . . ."

THE FACULTY ADVISER PROGRAM AT ARIZONA STATE COLLEGE [1]

A good deal of attention has been given by the members of the coordinating committee for curriculum development and advisement to the improvement of a program of educational advisement together with related phases of vocational advisement and planning that would reach all students enrolled at the Arizona State College at Tempe. In their efforts to develop and improve a program of

[1] *A Manual for Faculty Advisers*, 1955–1956, pp. 1–9. (Mimeographed.)

educational and vocational counseling that would reach all students, the members of the coordinating committee proceeded with several simple but basic assumptions. These assumptions are:

1. All college students need some help in making educational and vocational plans. Stated in another way, it is assumed that all college students differ greatly in their needs for educational and vocational guidance and counseling.

2. Educational and vocational guidance and counseling is but one phase of a total guidance and counseling program. Each student must be looked upon as a whole person. The educational and vocational phases of his adjustment must be dealt with in light of the total knowledge of him as a whole individual.

3. If all students are to receive help in making educational and vocational plans, a rather large staff of advisers or counselors will be required.

4. Many faculty members are prepared through training and experience to do educational and vocational counseling of the normal type required by most individuals.

5. The total service load of each faculty member includes some service activities in addition to teaching. Educational and vocational advisement and counseling is one type of service activity.

6. A program of educational and vocational advisement and counseling by faculty advisers to be successful must be coordinated with all other phases of the counseling program of the college.

For a time, faculty advisers were referred to as *curriculum advisers.* The term *faculty adviser* or *faculty counselor* is to be preferred since their responsibilities involve a good deal more than simply advising on curriculum matters. Selection of faculty advisers is made in terms of each of the majors or fields of specialization offered under the major curricula of the college. Thus, each faculty adviser is expected to know and understand the requirements of the curriculum and field of specialization in which he is advising. To facilitate this, a plan is under way whereby faculty advisers also serve as members of the curriculum development committees. Those who share directly in the development of curriculum regulations and requirements should not only understand them but also be able to interpret them to students. Likewise, actual work in curriculum development is closely related to vocational needs and training requirements. Those participating in this work should have a rather good working knowledge of vocational information and requirements in the several career fields for which a given curriculum provides training. In addition, those who have been selected to serve as faculty advisers will give attention to developing the art and skill of counseling.

After experimentation with a number of methods and devices for carrying on educational and vocational advisement through faculty advisers, the procedure now is to give special emphasis to freshmen during their first year and to transfer students during their first semester or year. The program for freshmen involves a scheduled meeting during freshman week. Details of this meeting are worked out by the respective academic deans or adviser chairman. In this meeting, the faculty adviser will have opportunity to become acquainted with each of his advisees. Every new freshman will have an approved program of studies signed by his adviser. During the first semester each adviser will encourage his advisees to make an appointment with him for the purpose of planning a second-semester program of studies. The same procedure holds for planning the program for the sophomore year.

From the freshman year on, advisement is not mandatory nor are students required to have programs of studies approved by their advisers. Every effort is made to continue adviser-advisee relationships throughout the four years or during the time that a student remains in college. The *ideal* would be an adviser to whom students could turn with their serious problems, not that the adviser would be able to solve them all, but, rather, that he could offer friendly and helpful advice including the referral of complicated problems beyond his own knowledge to competent agencies.

The profiles of the freshman placement test results from the College Testing Service are available for each advisee. One or more briefing sessions on the interpretation of test results is held, with advisers expected to attend these meetings before the profiles are made available. In interviews with freshman advisees, the following factors are thought to have a bearing upon progress and achievement: (*a*) aptitudes, interests, and personal characteristics; (*b*) health; (*c*) work load, both in school and out; (*d*) educational and vocational objectives and plans; (*e*) harmony of educational and vocational objectives; (*f*) financial problems; (*g*) parental attitude toward college; (*h*) personal problems and conflicts; (*i*) home situation; (*j*) study conditions; (*k*) commuting problems; (*l*) acceptance by peers; and (*m*) participation in extracurricular activities.

In counseling with advisees, the adviser is asked to keep in mind the following factors: (*a*) satisfaction with the curriculum under which the advisee is registered; (*b*) the general progress including semester and accumulative scholarship indices; (*c*) over-all curriculum requirements; (*d*) general-education requirements; (*e*) requirements in the major or field of specialization; (*f*) desired sequence of courses; (*g*) course prerequisites and restrictions, etc.

It is the hope of the program planners that a close personal relationship between the faculty adviser and his advisees will develop and that this working relationship will do much to overcome the student's discouragement in his course work, this being responsible for the high mortality rate between the lower and upper divisions of the college.

FACULTY ADVISEMENT AT BRIGHAM YOUNG UNIVERSITY [2]

At Brigham Young University support is given to the educational premise that every member of the faculty has a responsibility for advising and working with students outside the classroom. When the counseling service was first established in 1945, about thirty-five carefully selected members of the faculty were given reduced academic loads in order to engage in scheduled counseling. They were assigned to serve in the counseling service where they were also given in-service training in the interpretation of tests and in counseling procedures. This technique was followed to acquaint a large number of the faculty

[2] From a letter directed to the author by Wesley P. Lloyd, Dean of Students, Sept. 29, 1955.

with the educational gains to be derived from a well-organized student counseling program.

It soon became evident that professors whose training and interest were primarily in the subject-matter fields, although being helpful to the counseling service [3] and the student, were not devoted to spending time in counseling that might detract from the academic field for which they had been trained. In an adjusted arrangement, counseling has been established on a professional basis with a counseling staff trained specifically for the work and supplemented by the contribution that can be made by faculty members from the subject-matter areas.

These professionally trained counselors meet on occasion with faculty members of the academic departments, discuss with them fundamental problems that affect both the academic and nonacademic life of the student, and assist faculty members in an understanding of student capacity and achievement. It is understood by all deans and department chairmen that staff members of the counseling service are available to meet with them on request and to be of any desired assistance in this technical field.

A further service which coordinates and integrates the teaching and counseling program occurs when the department head and the academic dean receive from the counseling service certain psychological test scores and ratings made by students within their department. Certain individual scores are, of course, confidential in nature and are not distributed. Future plans provide for greater attention to in-service training of faculty counselors who are given special counseling responsibility by the deans of the colleges or the heads of departments.

The case-study technique and the case conference are procedures used commonly through the office of dean of students and the counseling service. The case *study* is used not alone for a solution of the case at hand, but also to point out ways in which various campus services should be coordinated and integrated for the good of the student. The case *conference,* on the other hand, is a type of clinic in which an urgent student problem is met by representatives of the counseling service, the health service, the discipline office, the dean's office, or another campus agency that can add needed information about the student.

The group methods for studying students operate largely within the counseling service. These methods are established through objective and systematic study. The group methods in counseling are supplementary to and do not substitute for individual counseling. They are pointed ordinarily at problems that are general to the group and do not need individual attention.

A major attempt at integrating the efforts of faculty administrators and counselors for in-service training has come about through the initiation of faculty workshops. Under the direction of the administration, all members of the faculty meet during the week preceding registration and work realistically on problems of educational method and the objectives of the university. In these conferences, faculty members engage in two specific phases of training:

[3] See Antone K. Romney, "The Developments of a University Counseling Service," *School and Society,* 70:330–331, Nov. 19, 1949.

1. They discuss problems that are not limited to any one academic department but are university-wide in nature. Some of these matters are administrative and require understanding on the part of faculty members.

2. They consider problems that are specific to their own department with special reference to teaching method and results.

The faculty workshop is not a lecture series. It is organized both for and by the faculty and challenges the initiative and thought of the entire university staff.

FACULTY ADVISING OF FRESHMEN AT CARNEGIE INSTITUTE OF TECHNOLOGY [4]

The freshman mentor system in the College of Engineering and Science, the Department of Industrial Management, and the School of Printing Management has for its main function the individual guidance of freshmen. Each freshman is assigned a mentor from among his own teachers or the faculty of the department in which he is enrolled. These mentors are carefully selected by the chairman of the committee on freshmen of the College of Engineering and Science with the help of the department heads and deans whose staff members are involved.

The number of freshmen assigned to a mentor varies from year to year, depending upon the number of full-time faculty members available. Six or seven students constitutes an average load. Some mentors meet with their groups as a whole but the more effective contact is by definitely arranged appointments with individuals. The more able as well as the scholastically deficient student should have equal opportunity to confer with his mentor.

The adjustment to college life presents many problems to the average freshman, and for many of them the new situations with which they are confronted lead to confusion and discouragement. The mentor can do much to help the student through this difficult period.

The mentor is the person to whom a freshman can go for assistance in delineating his problems and deciding on steps toward their solution. In general, the mentor is the liaison between the student and the various agencies offering special services. If the problem is delineated as one based only on lack of information or faculty orientations, the mentor may be able to supply this directly and in many problems can assist the student in working out the steps to be taken. In many instances, however, the mentor will feel that the student should consult the dean of the college or division, the freshman course advisers, the bureau of measurement and guidance, the department of student health, or the dean of men, as seems most appropriate. The mentors meet at convenient times to discuss mutual problems and receive some instructions from the psychologists in the bureau of measurement and guidance. Referrals of students to the bureau occur in problems of testing, correction of reading deficiencies, and counseling on personal problems.

[4] From an explanation, "Functions of a Mentor" (mimeographed), accompanying a letter from Douglas F. Miner, former Director, Division of Student Personnel and Welfare, July 1, 1953.

FACULTY ADVISING AT CHICO STATE COLLEGE [5]

Every faculty member, whether he has a formal list of advisees or not, has the opportunity to be of help to students in many ways outside the classroom. Counseling of students is considered to be an integral part of every staff member's responsibility and work load. Much counseling of students has to be done by the teaching staff. While the counselors in the college spend most of their time working with students individually and in groups, they obviously cannot see every student when he happens to need help. Part of the responsibility of the associate dean of students is to coordinate an advising program, with all teaching-staff members participating, with the student personnel office, which is a source of help and service to all faculty and students.

The faculty-student advisory system at Chico State is organized as follows:

1. Advisers are selected on the basis of interest areas or objectives of students.

2. Plans for faculty advising are made in cooperation with the division chairmen.

3. In general, faculty members in a division advise students whose educational objectives fall in their area of instruction.

4. Most faculty members have some advisory responsibilities.

It is recognized that there are variations among faculty members with regard to (a) nonteaching responsibilities and activities, such as serving as chairman of master's candidates' committees, field work, other committees, etc., (b) interest in and preparation for student advising, and (c) teaching load. Faculty members who would like to be advisers are encouraged to make this known. Conversely, any who prefer to be relieved of responsibility in this area are asked to express their desire. Some faculty members, regardless of the division in which they teach, are selected as "special advisers" for certain groups of students. These groups are primarily (a) provisional students—those admitted with less than five recommended units from high school or who score below 20 per cent on a college aptitude test, (b) students undecided concerning their educational objective, and (c) foreign students.

Information provided the adviser includes an adviser's information sheet to be filled out by the entering student which will serve as a basis for his initial and subsequent conferences, a copy of his high school transcript, achievement and college aptitude scores of tests taken when the student enters college, program-planning work sheets, an evaluation sheet from the registrar, notes and record of any previous interviews with the advisee, and the student's class schedule.

Staff members in the student personnel office assist advisers in numerous ways, the most frequent of these being conferences with advisers on problems with individual students and the counseling of students referred to the student personnel office for personal, vocational, or academic counseling. As for in-service training, the following is stated: [6]

[5] *Faculty Adviser's Manual,* Student Personnel Office, Chico State College, 1954, pp. 1–4.
[6] In a letter directed to the author by Hugh M. Bell, former Dean of Students, Apr. 20, 1954.

A few years ago we conducted a series of in-service training programs for faculty advisers, at which time various aspects of the personnel program were presented and discussed by the faculty advisers. We conducted interviews with students, presented test scores, discussed the use of personnel records. These in-service training sessions were conducted on a voluntary basis but were attended by most of the advisers.

EAST LOS ANGELES JUNIOR COLLEGE [7]

Guidance in this institution is understood to be all those experiences associated with the appraisal, induction, instruction, and adjustment of the student in the educational program which lead him to maximum self-realization as an individual living and working in our democracy.

Counseling is one aspect of the personnel program. The college offers the services of a trained staff to students who wish assistance in solving problems which are personal, social, academic, or occupational in nature. The first meeting of a student with a counselor may occur when the student comes to East Los Angeles Junior College to take the entrance examinations. If the student is entering during the fall semester, he may receive assistance in program planning from a counselor during the summer months. If the student is entering in the spring, faculty advisers are available to assist him during the regular registration period.

In order to implement the philosophy of guidance for all students, an orientation course, Psychology 9, is offered to first-semester students. The purposes of the course are to give certain necessary information to all students and to furnish them an orientation to the various measuring devices used in college. The course may prepare students for counseling, illuminating their need for special help and informing them as to what counseling resources are available. Each student has a folder in the counseling office in which are placed results of his performance on the entrance tests and the basic battery given in Psychology 9, records of vocational and academic planning, and any other guidance information.

The majority of instructors have advisory responsibilities. Each adviser has the responsibility for familiarizing himself with lower-division academic requirements in a given field of training and the general graduation requirements of the junior college. Because of his experience in his field, he is able to suggest valuable elective courses to students.

As a part of his orientation to the college organized through the Psychology 9 class, each student plans a semester-by-semester program of required courses to meet his academic objective. These plans are checked by a counselor for required courses, and the student presents the plans to his assigned adviser for review and suggestions of electives. The adviser is usually well acquainted with the student's work and, consequently, able to give valuable advice concerning curriculum, choice of upper-division institution, or reevaluation of choice.

The counseling staff acts as consultants to the advising staff who may have

[7] From a description of the East Los Angeles Junior College guidance services accompanying a statement to the author by Mary H. Kirby, counselor.

questions pertaining to course requirements or the transferring of students to four-year colleges and universities.

FACULTY ADVISING AT EAST TEXAS STATE TEACHERS COLLEGE [8]

The office of student personnel and guidance is an administrative department and also an instructional department. As an administrative and service department with three full-time staff members, the unit operates directly under the president. The office is responsible for all counseling, including specialized counseling and faculty counseling; all testing; the orientation program for new students; personnel record system (other than the academic record which is kept by the registrar); job placement, part-time student employment, and other forms of financial aid. As an instructional department, the office operates under the dean of the college. An elective course in applied psychology for freshmen, a one-hour orientation course for all new freshmen, and a counselor training program at the graduate level are offered.

Faculty counselors are designated as general-education counselors. Their assignment is to work with freshmen and sophomores for academic program planning and for other assistance, occupational and personal-social. Earlier, a faculty counseling planning committee initiated the activities of the group of faculty counselors, raising such questions as who would select faculty counselors and what criteria would be used? It was agreed that each individual of the twelve-member planning group would identify those faculty members who, in his opinion, possessed desirable personal qualities—emotional maturity and stability, a genuine interest in working with individual students in a counseling relationship, and a willingness to work to acquire some skill in counseling. It was decided, in addition, to ask a committee of department heads to compile similar lists. From these lists, the college president, the dean, and the director of student personnel would designate faculty counselors for the next academic year.

The designated faculty counselors have taken part in a series of discussions to formulate details for the fall orientation and counseling activities. In addition, they have studied the process of counseling and instruments used in counseling. In the course of their study, the group constructed a bibliography, did voluntary reading, and held discussions on interviewing, testing, behavior dynamics, and problems common to college students.

During the two and one-half days which are spent with the faculty counselor in orientation activities, the student is encouraged to consult his counselor on problems which arise. The student is required to see his counselor if a change in course schedule is desired. (These latter contacts are referred to as *casual* in contrast to those initiated by the department and designated as *scheduled.*) Three weeks after classes have begun, the faculty counselor meets his counselees in a group and later individually to discuss each student's attitude toward his academic load; the final arrangement of his class; study and

[8] From a letter directed to the author by Earl A. Koile, former Director, Office of Student Personnel and Guidance, Mar. 17, 1953. Also, Earl A. Koile, "Faculty Counseling Faculty Style," *Personnel and Guidance Journal*, September, 1954, pp. 22–25.

part-time work schedule, if employed; the student's living arrangements; his participation in out-of-class activities; and his general impressions of college life. At the group meeting, the faculty counselor usually provides each student with an outline of effective study habits and a time-planning sheet.

Instructors prepare mid-semester reports on all undergraduates who are doing unsatisfactory work in their courses. Faculty counselors interpret these reports to their counselees and assist in planning remedial steps.

EASTERN OKLAHOMA AGRICULTURAL AND MECHANICAL COLLEGE [9]

It is the belief of this institution that there is a definite relationship between guidance functions and classroom teaching. This is thought to be particularly true when guidance is defined as a process of assisting individuals in their adjustment to personal, social, educational, and vocational situations.

In accordance with this philosophy, all faculty members serve as advisers to students. While it is recognized that not all persons are equal in training and personality for the task of advising, it is assumed that all faculty members are interested in students and have a sympathetic understanding of their problems. This trait together with a knowledge of sources in the college to which students with special problems can be referred for help enables a faculty adviser to do an efficient job.

Advisees are assigned by the dean of students or his representative. Factors considered in assignment are vocational interest, personality, friendship, and desires of student and faculty member. Assignments may be changed at the request of either the faculty member or student. In so far as possible, there is equality in the number of advisees assigned to advisers.

The adviser is the staff member with the greatest responsibility for the degree of development a student achieves in his experiences with the college curriculum. The adviser assists the student as follows:

1. Helps him to become acquainted with the college, the faculty, and other students until he feels a sense of belonging
2. Helps him to select a vocation if he is undecided
3. Aids him in planning his educational program
4. Assists him in following a work-study schedule
5. Guides him in his personal maturity and in acquiring social skills
6. Assists him in solving his personal problems

No adviser is expected to be qualified to help all his advisees with all their problems. Principles which govern the referral of students to staff with specialized training are as follows:

1. Referral should be made to a person by name.
2. The adviser should usually talk with the person to whom a student is referred before the student sees him.
3. In certain cases, it is psychologically better for the adviser to accompany the student to the person to whom he is referred.

[9] From the *Advisor's Handbook* and a statement directed to the author by Gerald F. Williams, Dean of Students, November, 1957.

4. Referral should be made only after the student sees and accepts the reason for it.

5. The student should be encouraged to return to the adviser after the referral to discuss the results.

6. The adviser should follow up the referral.

The adviser has two major responsibilties concerning student personnel files: (1) to use them and (2) to transmit to them any significant information secured concerning the student, the knowledge of which would help other faculty members understand him better.

Advising days are scheduled three times during the school year. Classes and laboratories are suspended for one half of the day and the time is devoted to advisers' conferences with advisees. These periods occur at the end of the first nine weeks, at the end of the first semester, and at the end of the second nine weeks. Students secure their nine-weeks and first-semester grades from their adviser during these conferences. The adviser writes a letter to the parents of his advisees three times during the year. These letters are prepared in duplicate and delivered to the dean's office where envelopes are addressed and the copy filed in the student's personnel file.

FACULTY ADVISING AT KENT STATE UNIVERSITY [10]

Four-fifths of the total faculty are engaged in advising, with their advising loads varying in size. There are a number of specialized services which supplement the work of the faculty adviser. A university guidance committee is the policy-forming group. A recommendation of this committee resulted in the formation of a coordinating committee composed of representatives from all offices on the campus which do personnel work. This committee selects from its membership an executive committee of three. The foregoing represents an attempt at coordination within the framework of decentralized control. Decentralization of personnel functions is considered desirable, with the major responsibility for advisement resting with the teacher-adviser.

A deliberate attempt is made to involve all faculty members in advisory responsibilities, with assignments being made in these ways:

1. Several departments designate members who are to advise with new students. The office of student advising assigns students to these advisers.

2. Some department heads assign students, who are majors, to advisers in their departments after an initial screening interview. These assignments are then reported to the office of student advising so that records will be properly distributed.

3. The majority of assignments are made through the office of student advising. A faculty member is consulted before he receives a list of advisees, and he knows that these students have requested him as an adviser. When a student is changing major fields—and has a subsequent change of adviser—he will request the faculty member of his choice.

[10] From letters directed to the author by L. S. Hadley, Director, New Student Week, June 29, 1953, and Apr. 30, 1954. In addition, information from the *Guide for Faculty Advisers*. (Mimeographed.)

The major responsibility of the faculty adviser is educational advising, assuring smooth and effective progress toward graduation. However, the adviser is urged not to avoid counseling with the student about vocational goals, study and reading difficulties, personal problems, and so on.

The size of the advisory load is intended not to exceed twenty-five students. The adviser is to confine himself to that group of advisees except in instances where the members of a department are sharing the same office space and wish to pool their advisory responsibilities. Where records are available, this has been found to be workable. Caution is requested, however, on the matter of signing student requests (adding or dropping class) on the basis of doing the student a kindness *unless* the regular adviser is fully aware of the circumstances surrounding the request.

The director of student advising conducts individual conferences with faculty advisers, usually at their request. In addition, the director attends departmental meetings on invitation, with more than half the meeting time being spent in discussion of problems of advising. Large group meetings have also been used, and the issuing of bulletins is a part of the coordination of activities.

ADVISING AT MICHIGAN STATE UNIVERSITY WITH SPECIAL REFERENCE TO ADVISEMENT OF STUDENTS WITH NO DECLARED MAJOR [11]

Each of the nine colleges at Michigan State University has a chief enrollment officer whose duty it is to direct and coordinate enrollment among the enrollment officers (advisers) who actually work with the students in planning their programs toward graduation. The chief enrollment officer assigns students to individual enrollment officers, maintains records on enrollment-officer loads, keeps close liaison with other chief enrollment officers and the registrar's office, and works closely with the chief enrollment officer of the basic college. Each chief enrollment officer is concerned with the planning of the programs for the students for their first two years, and each is concerned with those students who will work in a field offered by his college.

The basic college chief enrollment officer is responsible for the no-preference students. When a student applies for admission to Michigan State University, he is asked to list his major field of study or to declare no preference. Those declaring no preference are assigned to an enrollment officer who is a teacher in the basic college. Enrollment officers for no-preference students have been very carefully selected to ensure that they are very much interested in the personal problems of the students as well as in their academic progress. These enrollment officers not only work with the students in planning programs, but they also help them in sampling various curricula. The enrollment officer encourages the students to go to the counseling center for tests of aptitude, interest, and the like, and finally encourages students to declare a major at the proper time.

The student, however, does not have to declare a major until he reaches

[11] From a letter written by John N. Winburne, Assistant Dean of the basic college, to W. Hugh Stickler, Florida State University, June 27, 1955.

junior standing: the achievement of 92 credits with a C average. However, students begin to declare majors the first term they are enrolled as no-preference. Some delay the decision and make it only under the threat of not being allowed to register.

This percentage of no-preference students ranges from 15 to 18 per cent from term to term. Students change majors constantly; in a recent term there were over 450 changes of preference made by all students. Many of these were no-preference students changing into a major field. There are large numbers in no-preference each fall term, but this number decreases steadily each term through summer term.

The no-preference student, once he selects a major, is much more stable in his choice than the person who comes with a major definitely in mind. The no-preference student tends to change his major once from no-preference, while the person who comes with a major tends to change twice. The grade-point average for no-preference students is somewhat lower than the average student: 2.30 as against 2.41. This 2.41, however, includes graduate students, so that the grade-point average may not be significantly lower for this group.

In discussing enrollment with various people throughout the institution, one could safely say that there is no movement or interest on the part of anyone to do away with this particular classification.

COUNSELING IN THE NEW YORK STATE COLLEGE OF HOME ECONOMICS, CORNELL UNIVERSITY [12]

Appointment of Specially Trained Counselors

About 1930 the college administration decided that the counseling of students, which had been the divided responsibility of all staff members, could be improved by the addition of personnel trained in the profession of counseling. It had sensed the soundness of the belief that was growing in the educational world that the counseling of human beings was a specialized piece of work and that the employment of persons whose training had had as a primary aim the development of a high degree of competence in this profession would add strength to the educational program of the college.

The administration recognized the invaluable contribution that each staff member must always make to the growth and development of the individual student and that a counseling program can be carried on adequately in an educational institution only when it includes cooperation with members of the teaching staff who are also closely associated with the students.

At the present time, the objectives and the total organization of the college, including the functions of the counseling staff, are explained to all new staff members in a formal orientation program each fall. The dean and the class counselors make up the committee on admissions. In view of their responsibilities with students, they are aware of the abilities, personal qualities, and interests which make for success in the college. From time to time an admis-

[12] An exposition, "Relationship between the Teaching Faculty and the Counseling Service in the New York State College of Home Economics at Cornell University," January, 1958, contributed by Jean Failing, Chairman, Counseling Service.

sions forum is held in which the admissions policies and procedures are explained to members of the faculty who wish to attend. Annual reports on the work of the admissions committee are made to the faculty.

The counseling staff, composed of four class counselors and the placement and associate placement director, has three guidance functions—educational, vocational, and personal. To be effective, the counselor must know the subject-matter areas of the college, the course content and objectives, as well as vocational opportunities for home economics. The counselor to whom the student is assigned on entrance continues as the student's counselor until she is graduated. In general, the entering class is assigned as a group to a counselor.

The members of the counseling staff teach a two-credit course in orientation to college life. This course offers freshmen an opportunity to discuss common problems and to obtain information which will enable them to make the best possible use of the college environment. The discussions include such topics as study habits, vocational planning, effective educational planning, and relationships with others.

The counselors' records of individual students include information secured through the formal application and admissions interview material; educational and vocational plans developed in the orientation course; vocational interests as they develop and change; a list of extracurricular activities; the academic records; test scores; part-time and summer employment. The counseling service on occasion sponsors a testing program, often in cooperation with the university testing service. The purpose of this additional testing is to provide counselors and staff with information on students' general ability and special strengths and weakness in academic areas.

The one person responsible for coordinating the counsel given in the College of Home Economics is the class counselor. Relationships between the counselor and the college faculty may consist of a direct exchange of information between faculty member and counselor, or the exchange of information through a student referred by the counselor or placement secretary to a faculty member or by a faculty member to the counselor or placement secretary. There is exchange of information between the class counselors and the office of dean of men and dean of women, the university placement office, the medical office, and university residential halls—all with the purpose of coordinating the activities which relate to the welfare of the student.

FACULTY ADVISING AT SAN FRANCISCO STATE COLLEGE [13]

The advising system at the college is headed by the coordinator of advising, who has faculty status and who spends three-fourths of his time in this capacity. Under the general direction of the associate dean of students (counseling), the coordinator works directly with the committee on advising, composed of so-called coordinating advisers (one faculty member from each of the major divisions of the college) and four permanent members from various areas of the student personnel program. Designations of groups of faculty advisers in-

[13] From the *Adviser's Handbook* and a letter directed to the author by John T. Palmer, Coordinator of Advising, Jan. 15, 1958.

clude (*a*) general-education advisers who advise lower-division students completing the general-education requirements; (*b*) major advisers who advise students in major fields of curricula; (*c*) minor advisers who advise students electing minor programs; (*d*) transfer advisers who work with students transferring into the institution and who have not yet elected their major fields of work; and (*e*) credential advisers who advise those students planning to qualify for one of the state teaching credentials.

The coordinating advisers take responsibility for working with the faculty advisers in their respective college divisions in the operation of the advising system and assist the coordinator of advising in its improvement. In addition, these coordinating advisers secure information from the advisers in the divisions concerning procedural difficulties, and then work with the coordinator in arriving at workable solutions. The coordinating advisers assist in planning programs of in-service training designed to increase the effectiveness of advising with students. An important responsibility occurs in their assisting the coordinator of advising in selection of advising personnel and the appraisal of their performances.

A faculty adviser is commissioned to do an interpretive, preventive, and sometimes a corrective job. The adviser interprets to the student the needs of society as expressed in terms of curriculum requirements. In addition, the adviser in a sense interprets the student to himself. Finally, when the student has made an error in judgment, the adviser helps him to view the error and its effects and to explore with him the corrective measures that may be taken.

Information provided the adviser includes (1) data provided by the admissions office indicating previous academic work taken in high school or at another college; (2) forms indicating the proficiency of the student in speech, reading, and writing on the basis of examinations given during the admissions process or during orientation; (3) form given to the student by the student health service after physical examination; (4) a list of general-education requirements of the college; and (5) the approximate total score on the entrance exam.

Packets containing the above information are prepared prior to the start of each semester by the student personnel office. These packets are retained by the general-education advisers, usually until the latter part of the sophomore year, at which time the student transfers to a major adviser who then receives the advising packet from the general-education adviser.

FACULTY ADVISING AT SARAH LAWRENCE COLLEGE [14]

Upon entrance to Sarah Lawrence College, the student is assigned to a registration adviser who has some knowledge of her gained from the application form and from replies to detailed questions concerning her intellectual and personal interests, her relations with others, her attitude toward her own education, and other aspects relating to her life goals. This adviser (or counselor) discusses the possibilities for study with the student, arranging for interviews

[14] From an exposition, "Education and Guidance," by Esther Raushenbush, former Dean of the College. (Mimeographed.)

with particular teachers. This adviser remains as "don" for several weeks until
the student is well embarked on her course of study. Through weekly contacts,
the student apprises the don of her progress. It is possible for the registration
adviser to remain the permanent don, or, if it is appropriate, he transfers her at
the end of three or four weeks to a permanent don, perhaps one of the faculty
with whom she is studying.

In his role, the don helps the student plan her working time; if the work is
going badly, he discusses the difficulties with the student, having some knowledge as to whether these represent a general problem in the student's college
life or whether the difficulty relates only to work in a particular course at a
particular time. Three times a year the don writes a report on his view of the
progress of the student. This report is available to her teachers.

Not all college teachers care to or are competent to serve in the role of don.
Some teachers believe that the college professor's function is to impart to students as much knowledge of the subject as they can assimilate and that his
responsibility for the student ends there. In any institution there will be instructors whose range of interest in students is limited to what they can learn
about the subject. These people are not asked to act as dons.

Often in the last year or two a student will have a don from her field of
major interest; this is particularly true if she is considering graduate work.
Each year, each student indicates which faculty member she would like to
have for a don, and if he is willing to serve in that capacity—and has the
time to do so—he agrees. The principal basis on which this relation is established and maintained is one of friendly understanding. Since most members
of the college faculty believe that the psychological attitudes, the emotional
patterns—in fact, the general life experience of students—affect greatly what
they learn and what significance their learning has for them, their interest in
students goes beyond the students' interest in the particular subject. For this
reason most of the teachers look on the function of the don as part of the
teaching process, which, in this instance, it is.

A program of individual guidance such as this is time-consuming. The time
requirement is balanced in part by the fact that there are fewer courses in
the Sarah Lawrence curriculum in proportion to the student body than most
colleges have; students take fewer courses; each teacher teaches fewer. The
student takes three courses a year with the expectation that she will spend
about a third of her full working time each week on each course. Each student, therefore, works with three teachers instead of four or five. Each teacher
is thus able to work with fewer students, teach fewer courses, and give more
time both to individual conference work with his students and to counseling.

FACULTY ADVISING IN THE COLLEGE OF LIBERAL ARTS,[15] STATE UNIVERSITY OF IOWA

The liberal arts advisory office is charged with the responsibility of implementing and supervising the advisory program of the college. Each student
upon enrollment is assigned to an adviser by the advisory office. Students with

[15] From a statement describing the liberal arts advisory program and accompanying
a letter from Dewey B. Stuit, Dean, July 29, 1953.

well-defined academic interests are assigned immediately to the departments of their choices; the departments in turn are expected to assign the students to specific staff members. Nonmajors and preprofessional students are assigned to special advisers who have indicated an interest in student advisement. Faculty members assigned to the special liberal arts advisory program serve as counselors only for students having no departmental affiliation and for special preprofessional training groups, such as medicine, engineering, dentistry.

The advisory program for nonmajors exists (1) to help the student become better oriented to the college; (2) to assist the student in planning a program of studies that will afford the best educational experience for him; (3) to discuss occupational fields and ways and means through which the college experience can be of maximum value; (4) to follow the progress of the student; and (5) to refer him, when necessary, to other agencies for assistance.

To accomplish this, the adviser or counselor needs to have (1) an understanding of the counseling process; (2) a familiarity with all resources, curricular and extracurricular, which will aid in the development of the student; (3) a familiarity with the rules and regulations of the college and university; (4) an understanding of the psychological test scores used routinely in counseling; (5) knowledge of the agencies to which students can be referred for help; and (6) the authority to promote the best interests of students.

In-service training sessions and staff conferences are held periodically throughout the academic year. Topics under discussion in these sessions include the nature of counseling, the use of psychological test scores in counseling, sources of occupational information, and individual cases.

The purposes of the preprofessional student counseling programs are designed (1) to help the student formulate his program of studies so that he will be able to meet entrance requirements of the college of his choice; (2) to inform the student of new developments pertaining to his preprofessional training; (3) to discuss with the student his abilities, interests, and motivations with respect to his chosen field; (4) to encourage the development of latent talents to increase the student's academic resourcefulness; and (5) to refer the student to other agencies for special assistance.

The purpose of the departmental advisory program is to help the student select those courses within and outside the department which will enable him to meet graduation requirements. In an effort to ensure that departmental advisory work is dispatched with a minimum of confusion and expenditure of time, the following policies are observed:

1. Assignment of majors to specific staff members who are interested in and have an aptitude for this sort of work

2. Scheduling of departmental meetings for majors early in each semester for discussion of academic requirements, vocational opportunities, and other matters of special interest

3. The working out with the student of a program of studies for the entire undergraduate career

4. The scheduling of at least one individual interview with each student each semester

5. The keeping of adequate records of the progress of all majors

It is recognized by the administrators of the program of advisory services that, while students assigned to a department have theoretically decided upon their field of academic interest, there are many whose choices have been made on superficial or inadequate bases. Thus, the departmental adviser is requested to prepare himself to (1) handle some of the same problems as are handled by advisers for nonmajors or (2) refer the students to an agency which is prepared to discuss such problems with them.

A folder containing essential information needed for effective counseling and advisory work is prepared for each new student. This folder accompanies the student throughout his college career and contains a record of all official actions taken concerning the student and a statement of his academic background, together with such other information as individual advisers may wish to include. If the student changes from nonmajor to major status or from one department to another, the record is sent from the former adviser to the new adviser by way of the liberal arts advisory office.

FACULTY ADVISING AT STEPHENS COLLEGE [16]

The advising program is directed by the dean of students who delegates the direct supervision of the program to the director of counseling services. This latter officer is responsible for the selection each year of the faculty members who will serve as members of the board of advising chairmen. These persons are not professional counselors as a rule but are selected from those faculty members who are reasonably experienced in counseling and who have shown a willingness to give extraordinary attention to the Stephens advising program.

The members of the board of advising chairmen are each assigned a selected group of faculty advisers numbering approximately eighteen. All faculty members are enrolled in one of these groups which meet at stated times for discussion. Thus each adviser-teacher is connected to the administration in two ways:

1. As a teacher, his functions head up in the office of the dean of instruction.
2. As adviser, in the office of the dean of students.

While administratively these two are distinguishable, in actual practice and in educational aim there is the closest kind of cooperation and mutual assistance.

The student's counseling folder contains information and appraisals which portray (1) the student as an individual, (2) her potentialities, (3) her strengths and weaknesses, and (4) the breadth of her interests and activities. Among the items are the student's cumulative record, the admissions counselor's confidential report, the course plan sheet, personal information from parents, transcript of credits, and general correspondence.

The counseling service relates itself to the faculty adviser and the college advising program in various ways and at several levels of functioning:

1. Counselors receive referrals from advisers and work directly with the student referred.

---

[16] From *Manual for Advisers*, 1957, and Stephens College *News Reporter*, March, 1956. Also, Eugene L. Shepard, "A Three-level In-service Training Program for Advisers," *Personnel and Guidance Journal*, 36:48–50, September, 1957.

2. Counselors serve in a consulting or advisory capacity to an adviser regarding appropriate techniques or procedures to be used in the adviser's counseling with a particular advisee.

3. All advisers receive test data summaries on all advisees.

4. Since the college advising program heads up in the director of counseling services, the members of the counseling service staff take an active part in the training and improvement program for advisers, either by serving as members of the advising chairmen group, as participants in the seminar programs, or as consultants to advising groups.

The chief functions of the counseling service are to supply general counseling and testing services to students, to consult with and assist faculty members who are working with students, and to contribute to the in-service training of faculty for their particular counseling or personnel functions.

ADVISING AT TEACHERS COLLEGE OF CONNECTICUT [17]

Each spring certain faculty members are chosen by representatives from the student personnel division and appointed by the president of the institution to serve as advisers to a number of students in the incoming freshman class. They, with student counselors chosen from the junior class, guide new students through preorientation. At the beginning of the academic year, the advisees are reassigned so that the junior counselors and members of the senior class each counsel with one freshman. The particular duties of the faculty advisers and the student counselors consist of aiding in the orientation of advisees to the college, advising them during their first registration, and checking their academic and social-personal progress during the year.

Faculty advisers are selected on the basis of their student-personnel point of view. A series of in-service training meetings are held in the spring of each year. There is discussion of general duties and responsibilities, specific information concerning college policies, departmental requirements, and the general aspects of counseling.

During the summer, advisers receive the names and addresses of advisees, a résumé of the spring discussions, and a reminder of events to occur during freshman week. Upon arrival on campus in September, advisers receive the counseling kit containing the orientation program and other information pertinent to meetings. Advisers attend the preorientation-week activities with their advisees and student counselors. During one of their conferences with advisees, there is discussion of the traditions and history of the college and what the college experience should mean.

Follow-up conferences of adviser and advisee are held during the year. Anecdotal reports concerning the emotional, social, and academic adjustments of students are submitted periodically to the director of student personnel.

The student counselors attend a series of in-service training meetings similar to those described above for the faculty advisers. In their training the emphasis is placed on the importance of their responsibility and the fact that they may

[17] From the *Faculty Handbook* and a letter directed to the author by Philip I. Clark, Jr., former Director of Student Personnel.

serve the student as a peer. The freshman advisees are assigned to student counselors as far as is possible on the combined basis of their area of major academic interest, commuter-resident status, and hometown area.

During the summer each student counselor writes to his counselees, and, if possible, contacts them in person. The student counselors inform future new students where they will meet them on their first day on campus. They attend, with their counselees, all the meetings and events indicated in the orientation program. Throughout the first year student-counselor–advisee meetings are held. After the mid-point of each term, each upperclass counselor reports on the academic, personal, and social adjustment and progress of his advisees.

ADVISING IN THE COLLEGE OF THE UNIVERSITY OF CHICAGO [18]

In this institution, students in the college are assisted by faculty advisers in planning their academic work. These advisers constitute the staff of the dean of students in the college, it being the responsibility of this officer to coordinate the relations of each student in the college with the university. The advising of students is one of the noncurricular services administered by the dean of students in the university.

The advisers in the college are members of the faculty, who are freed from approximately a third of their instructional duties. It is felt that this plan improves upon that in many colleges wherein advising is considered to be an activity carried on by all or by some members of the faculty in addition to their full-time work as teachers. With each adviser carrying on two-thirds the normal quota of instruction, research, or examining in the college, he can give from six to eight hours a week to conferences with students at times convenient to him. Under this plan, advising becomes a part of the total service rendered by some members of the college faculty.

Members of the faculty are asked to serve as advisers only if they are interested in this type of service and have demonstrated their ability to work with students individually. Professional training in counseling is not expected. The appointment of faculty members to counseling is not made until there has been time for the individual to become familiar with the structure of the university. An advising assignment usually specifies at least three years of service.

The various aspects of an adviser's work are discussed frequently, and regular meetings are held for considering particular phases of their business. With no fixed manual on advising in use, the advisers follow general bulletins and special instructions prepared by the dean of students in the college. Perhaps the most effective training comes through the association of the new appointee with an experienced adviser, this being facilitated by their sharing of offices. The approximate load of an adviser is 120. Both men and women serve as advisers, each one counseling men and women students. Whenever possible, a student is given an adviser whose instructional work is in the field of his principal interest. Liaison between advising in the college and the academic

[18] John R. Davey, "Advising," in *The Idea and Practice of General Education*, University of Chicago Press, Chicago, 1950, pp. 325–333.

counseling of all divisions is made easier by the fact that the offices of the advisers, the dean of students in the college, and the divisional deans of students are all located in one area. Many referrals of students are made to the departmental counselors in the student's final year of residence in the college, since over 80 per cent of the college students expect to enter a division or a professional school.

The first meeting of a new student and his adviser occurs in a group meeting wherein there is discussion of the regulations of the university, registration procedures, and other matters of immediate, practical interest. A second meeting occurs when student and adviser get together for a registration conference. At this time results of the placement tests are known, and with this knowledge of the student's interests, educational expectations, and vocational preferences, the adviser draws up the first registration plan. The planning of a student's program is not a mechanical, routine matter. While results from placement tests do indicate conditions to be filled, it is likewise true that the academic means of fulfillment must fit each particular case. For instance, students deficient in reading or writing or the fundamental mathematical skills are required to plan programs which make it possible to remove the deficiencies.

The next contact of adviser and student occurs about six weeks after classes have begun at which time there is a review of the student's progress in his studies. There is an attempt made to evaluate the extent to which balance has been achieved between academic work and other activities. Students are urged to come in whenever they encounter a difficulty of any kind. The student is summoned for a special conference whenever there is a report of unsatisfactory progress. In the course of an academic year, an adviser would likely have six interviews with each member of his group and possibly double this number with some.

As can be expected, parents of students often consult advisers; advisers often request that parents confer with them. In conferences such as these, the adviser attempts to interpret the objectives of the student to the parent and likewise to interpret the educational program of the college.

Close cooperation of the heads of college houses and the academic advisers is necessary. Reports of academic progress go regularly to these heads of houses, and they, in turn, submit to the dean of students in the college their observations regarding the study habits and general behavior of students. Informal consultations between both staffs occur whenever the academic work of a student or his conduct in the residence house calls for joint action. Although the adviser is not responsible for counseling students on all kinds of problems, he is expected to locate the nature of the student's trouble and to know to which source an appeal must be made. In this regard, the adviser serves *to coordinate* the advice given by several of the agencies and/or to bring together persons who can plan in combination for the welfare of the student. It is to be pointed out likewise that the adviser does not act as a disciplinary officer nor is the adviser responsible for determining the academic status of any student.

FACULTY ADVISING AT UNIVERSITY OF DENVER [19]

In 1946 a group of twenty carefully selected faculty members were given intensive training in counseling techniques and basic philosophy by various members of the student personnel services and the psychology department. They met every Saturday for two quarters. After this training period, they were assigned counselees and worked under rather close supervision of the groups named. Some of these faculty counselors worked on an overload basis, counseling ten hours per week in addition to their fifteen-hour teaching load. Others counseled one-third teaching time, which was set at fifteen hours per week on the basis of five hours in the classroom and two hours of preparation per class session. Three years later the faculty-counselor program was discontinued for various reasons, and a staff of professionally trained people was appointed. However, the original group of twenty is, in the majority, still on campus, and the members continue to counsel with students, refer cases to the counseling services, and participate in the faculty advisers' program. They constitute an excellent interpretive medium for counseling and serve as a liaison between faculty in general and counseling.

The counseling office is responsible for the faculty advising program. The current practice at the University of Denver is to assign students for curriculum advising to the department of their stated major or field of specialization. The departments are then responsible for assigning students to staff members, usually on the basis of lower-division students (freshmen and sophomores) and upper-division students. There is little continuity in these assignments. There is a special group of advisers for preprofessional trainees, medical technology students, students from abroad, etc. Students who are not ready to declare a major are advised by the counseling staff with the help of three or four specially appointed faculty members. The counseling office furnishes all departments with folders on their advisees. It also prepares and distributes to every faculty member a faculty adviser's manual for orientation purposes. This manual is revised every year and is alluded to by the faculty as the "Advisers' Bible."

For training purposes, *all* departments appoint a representative and an alternate to meet with the director of student counseling to consider questions contributing to more efficient advising and better understanding of the student as an individual. The group, as a whole, decides on the frequency of meetings; some years they meet once a month, others twice a quarter, for a period of two hours each time. The program is set up on the basis of topics requested by the members of the group. Usually, the requests cover such topics as the adequate use of resources, the role of the adviser, the relationship between counseling and advising, the significance of tests, vocational goals, adequate preparation and training, health and emotional problems of students, etc. Consultants for these meetings are carefully selected from the university personnel or from outside sources. Prior to meetings, reminder notices are sent out which bring to

[19] From a letter directed to the author by Esther M. Dimchevsky, Director, Student Counseling, University of Denver, Aug. 1, 1957.

the attention of the members various problems affecting the welfare of students. The faculty advisers are also furnished with *"U" at DU,* one of the freshman manuals originally edited by the counseling office. The participants in this group are expected to report back to their departmental meetings the significant points and problems brought to their attention at the advisers' meeting. They also make curricular and other recommendations to the administration.

In addition, panel presentations on counseling and student problems are presented at general faculty meetings. Counselors serve as consultants on various faculty committees. The dean of students and director of student counseling are members of the student life committee of the faculty senate.

Last year the counseling staff met with each department to discuss vocational and training problems connected with that particular department as seen in counseling. At these meetings the head of the department usually presented the philosophy of the department, the type of student who should undertake a major in it, the opportunities in the field, etc.

Student cases are reviewed, at which time the faculty concerned are invited to participate. The mental hygiene department is always on this mailing list to receive information sent out by the counseling office. Personal contacts with individual faculty members are effected, with discussions leading from specific considerations to the general fitness of curricula and services. Copies of special studies and reports are sent to the various departments or to individual faculty members on request.

FACULTY ADVISING AT UNIVERSITY OF ILLINOIS [20]

This counseling service includes an equivalent of thirteen or fourteen full-time central staff members who are clinical or counseling psychologists and about seven part-time faculty counselors. Most of the faculty counselors spend one-fourth of their time or about eight actual hours per week in the counseling service. This proportion of their salary is carried in the budget of the service, the teaching department carrying the rest. Faculty members are chosen jointly by the counseling service and by the deans of the colleges—and in some instances by the department heads. There is no system of assigning a certain number of students to these counselors, but instead their hours are available for counseling appointments just as is the case of the full-time members of the counseling staff. The faculty counselors' work is with freshmen and other students; they do not only educational and vocational counseling but also personal counseling to the limit of their abilities.

Before beginning their counseling work, these faculty members get a pre-service and in-service practicum course which is about the same as the one given to advanced graduate students in clinical counseling except that there is less emphasis on theory. The faculty counselors make referrals to the central staff when they feel that a student's problem is beyond their depth. These counselors are not housed in the same building but it would be to the advantage of all if they were located centrally. Joint staff meetings are held once a

[20] From a letter directed to the author by William M. Gilbert, Director, Student Counseling Service, Mar. 11, 1957.

month. Individual testing is done in the service; in addition, administration and scoring of freshman guidance tests are done for all incoming freshmen. The service has the right to make recommendations regarding regular increases in rank and salary for faculty counselors. These may be made directly to the provost. In practice, the director of the service gets in touch with the department heads commenting:

> Mr. So-and-so, who, as you know, is a faculty counselor with us, has been doing an unusually good job of counseling. How would you react to an increase in salary (or rank) for this next year?

This practice is further outlined in a statement of policy made by the provost in March, 1949:

> A positive program of counseling services to students, based on the best clinical and guidance practices, has become and should remain an integral part of the educational experiences we offer to students. The persons who do this type of work well should be rewarded for it and advanced in rank and salary in proportion to their excellence. Recommendations for changes in rank and salary of personnel listed in the budget of the student counseling service, in so far as counseling services are concerned, will originate with the director of the service and the college offices to the general administration.

Before the institution of this policy, faculty advisers were released from a portion of their teaching time and in addition received what amounted to a bonus for their counseling services. This resulted in the awkward situation that counselors were in effect being paid for more than 100 per cent of their university time. It also resulted in a feeling on the part of counselors, and in some cases on the part of the department head, that counseling functions were actually serving to prevent the permanent increases in salary and rank which the counselor would otherwise obtain. The new program of giving formal recognition by means of recommendations for increases in rank and salary seems to be working out very well.

ACADEMIC ADVISING AT VASSAR COLLEGE [21]

The college advisory system aims to help the student to discover her own capacities, to find the program of college work that will develop her powers, and to learn where she can best use her trained abilities in society. The plan is based upon the belief that, since the central activity of the college consists in making contact between the student and the curriculum, the teacher is the best college adviser and, furthermore, that the good teacher always concerns himself with the student as a whole person.

The dean, as executive officer of the faculty and chief academic adviser, is ready to consult with students upon any question pertaining to their plan of study, standards of scholarship, or other academic interests. The associate dean serves as general academic adviser of all advanced-standing students. The assistant dean is especially concerned with the interests of freshmen and serves

---

[21] From the Vassar College *Catalog,* the *Handbook for Academic Advisers,* and a letter directed to the author by Marion Tait, Dean, July 21, 1953.

as chairman of the group of general academic advisers to whom freshmen are assigned for guidance upon their arrival at college.

The dean, the associate dean, and the assistant dean are members of the coordinating committee on academic advising. This committee, which includes nine members elected by the faculty, is responsible for the formulation of advising policies, for the appointment of academic advisers, and for the review of interdepartmental programs of related studies.

As the student proceeds through her course of study, she is assigned to a succession of advisers, each of whom in turn assists her in the planning and carrying out of her work. The faculty adviser is guided by his own competence and interest in defining the limits of advising. On the one hand, no adviser should feel that he must undertake psychotherapy; on the other hand, no adviser limits himself purely to the advising on departmental courses. The adviser should make his own decision as to his competence to deal with a situation. If he feels unable or unwilling to cope with a problem, he should use other available resources—the study counselor, the dean's office, the psychiatrist.

The advising of students prior to their arrival at college and through the period necessary to adjust first-year programs is assigned to the committee on admission and to the general academic advisers. The assistant dean, assisting the chairman of the committee on admission, serves as a link between the advising of the student during the summer before her entry and the advising of the student during her first year. Freshmen may call on her for help at any time.

The general academic advisers, teaching members of the faculty selected from all departments, are assigned by the assistant dean to advise the student from the time of her arrival at college until she has selected her program of related studies. In many cases the general academic adviser will also be the house fellow in the student's house.*

Once the related-studies program is selected, the advising of students in planning either an interdepartmental program or a departmental program is assigned to a new adviser. Interdepartmental-program advisers are chosen by the coordinating committee for their special knowledge in fields of interdepartmental study. Departmental advisers are designated and assigned by the departments.

In her senior year, the advising of a student may pass to the instructor of the central advanced course in her program of related studies or to the director of her independent work, if that work is the culmination of her senior program. In this guidance for the work of the final year the instructor of any of her other courses may be asked to collaborate. This arrangement is usual in interdepartmental programs.

* Under this plan two teaching members of the faculty live in each residence hall, assuming responsibility for general advising and participating in regular seminars to discuss the policies and problems of the residential college. They are included in the group of general academic advisers and constitute a committee of the faculty under the chairmanship of the dean. They are given a reduction in their teaching load; independent apartment units are provided, and meals in the house dining room. The positions are open to married as well as single members of the faculty.

FACULTY ADVISING AT WHEATON COLLEGE [22]

The specific reasons for a counseling program at Wheaton College are detailed as follows:

1. To recognize individual differences and attempt to discover each student's special interests, abilities, and needs, to the end that a college program may be outlined which will make the maximum use of these interests and abilities and, in so far as possible, meet his needs

2. To make possible a personal touch between faculty and students, a relationship which has become more and more difficult to maintain because of large classes, busy schedules, and the resulting more or less formalized instruction found in higher education today

3. To make a certain faculty member responsible for the personnel materials relating to a particular student in order that maladjustments may be prevented or corrected

4. To make known to each student through the interpretation of vocational and aptitude test results the broad areas in which he could reasonably be expected to succeed

5. To encourage students to study the needs of society to discover where their particular abilities are most needed and can count most for Christ and His Kingdom

6. To assist students in spiritual problems and encourage them to be regular in their daily devotions and open minded in their search for divine guidance through searching the Scriptures and other factual data

Students are assigned to counselors on the basis of their expressed interest and with assurance that a department counselor would direct a student away from his department if another department could better minister to the student's needs.

Counselors are notified of their assignments and given some personal information about their counselees late in the summer in order that they may have sufficient information to make an initial approach by letter before the students arrive on campus. The day before new-student registration, counselors are supplied with information relative to the student's previous schooling and the percentile ranks on tests recently administered. By the end of the first month, counselors have interviewed each counselee and shortly thereafter submit their initial reports on a two-page questionnaire. Later reports are submitted on a half-page mimeographed report blank. The frequency of reports depends upon the needs of the particular counselee. There is no hard and fast rule as to the form of the report, but the following six questions are covered frequently:

1. What are his objectives and goals (academic, personal, spiritual, and vocational)? To what extent has he progressed toward these goals?

2. What are his strengths and deficiencies as a student?

3. Has he been working up to capacity?

[22] From *Counselor's Manual,* 1949.

4. Has he developed socially (adjustment to college community, poise, normal participation in student committees and organizations)?

5. *a.* What are his special problems, if any, and what progress has been made in solving his problems?

b. Can you summarize what advice has been given and what progress has been made in solving problems?

6. What recommendations do you have for his further development?

After counseling reports have been checked by the coordinator of the new-student program, they are forwarded to the deans and others responsible for student adjustment. After serving this function, they are filed in the student's cumulative record where they are made available to counselors reporting, administrative officers, and departmental advisers.

SUMMARY

As indicated in the introductory remarks of this chapter, the twenty programs chosen for brief review were those operating in various sections of the country and illustrating several institutional types—those with differing objectives, student enrollment, and program emphases. In addition, some or all of the fourteen characteristics stated earlier apply to the programs described. As mentioned, the author could not possibly include descriptions of all the noteworthy programs which have come to her attention in the several polls. For this, apology is offered.

Some readers will speculate upon the presence of paper plans as compared with true operational systems. Sometimes the plan which exists in the very small college seems to defy description, the working relationships among students, teaching faculty, and administrators seeming to evolve naturally and "planlessly." In other instances, the elaborate structure in print at a flourishing institution bears little resemblance to the feeble system actually in force. The author was amused to read a description of faculty advising submitted by the dean of a well-known university which rang with his convictions of its adequacy and excellence. In contrast, a statement from a faculty adviser in the same institution gave a decidedly different view:

Our faculty advisement program is practically nil. For the past two years five freshmen have been assigned to each member of the college faculty who has volunteered for the program. A get-acquainted meeting was held on two nights in our campus soda shop where each faculty member sat in a group arrangement with his five advisees. Beyond that, nothing happened. Perhaps two or three faculty members invited the students into the home, and perhaps a dozen or so students visited their adviser in his office during the first semester (usually after mid-terms) but that has been the extent of our program. The adviser really has little to be to his advisees except an initial rather than sustained friend. The adviser does not register the student nor have any other responsibility for him. This system has not caught on but we will go along with it passively for another year. We feel mighty uneasy about what we are not doing.

That the *spirit* for doing adequate faculty advising is willing but the *flesh* is weak is an acknowledged fact on many campuses. Overburdened with more than a full load of teaching, committee work, field service— and possibly research—the faculty member may be gliding along rather than marching resolutely toward a goal set for him. It is the lag between *what is* and *what should be* that occasions such comments as this: [23]

... the university provided me with a freshman adviser to whom I was to go when my first month's grades were turned in and regularly thereafter once a month. My particular adviser was an ascetic-looking assistant professor in English, very scholarly and by no means interested in callow freshmen. He had a half dozen other freshmen besides me to advise, and his technique was to get rid of us as quickly as possible.

Every month he gave me my grades and said, "That's fine; you're doing very well." I said, "Thank you," and walked out. In later years when I became interested in the institution of freshmen advisers, I questioned numerous students on the campus and found not one who had received more advice from his than I had from mine.

Such comment gives rise to the suggestion by Aaronson [24] that there is a need for full-time counseling systems, with professionally trained, readily available counselors, in place of the present part-time faculty counseling. Thorpe,[25] however, maximizes the good that faculty members can do in making themselves available to students who wish to confer periodically with them on academic or other matters. He remarks that some of these students suffer from maladjustments of personality, transitory and fairly minor in nature, which some serious attention on the part of the instructor could alleviate.

From the foregoing descriptions of counseling programs, there will be seen ways in which the work of faculty advisers is combined with that of professionally trained counselors. The importance of the task in improving reciprocal working relations between the two is emphasized by Wrenn: [26]

[23] Ernest Havemann and Patricia Salter West, *They Went to College,* Harcourt, Brace and Company, Inc., New York, 1952, p. 260.

[24] B. S. Aaronson, "The Influence of Three Areas of Scholastic Maladjustment in Forcing Veterans to Leave School," *School Review,* 57:52, January, 1949.

[25] Louis P. Thorpe, "Mental Health Practices at the College Level," *Mental Health in Modern Education,* Fifty-fourth Yearbook of the National Society for the Study of Education, University of Chicago Press, Chicago, 1955, part II, p. 249.

[26] C. Gilbert Wrenn, "The Role of Faculty Advisers in a Personnel Program," *Occupations,* 19:3, April, 1941.

Faculty advisers and trained counselors must cease being either afraid or contemptuous of each other. The trained man is there to help the untrained one or to relieve him of a burden of responsibility, not to prove that the latter is incompetent or unworthy. The professional counselor or personnel worker would do well, likewise, to trim his sheets and sail a little nearer to an adequate recognition of how powerful an ally the faculty adviser can be, if care and judgment are used. There need be no fear that the trained counselor will "work himself out of a job" by giving recognition and dignity to the role of a faculty adviser. The more the average professor and adviser know of student human nature and symptoms of poor adjustment, the more demand there will be for trained specialists.

A supportive stand is taken by MacIntosh in a book directed to parents of college-going students. Surveying conditions and practices in 276 American colleges, the author summarizes as follows: [27]

The part which the faculty can play in guidance depends upon a number of conditions. For many faculty members, the amount of teaching they have to do may preclude their participation or may limit it to guidance which they give in connection with teaching itself. Others will have neither interest in this kind of extra nor a desire to learn about it. Some, with the opposite point of view, will welcome the chance to take an active part in guidance. If together with their interest they show an aptitude, such teachers after some training may prove to be valuable additions to the guidance staff.

It is with an underscoring of approval for these last two statements that the author turns next to a consideration of the aspects of in-service training of faculty advisers. The "trimming of sheets" and the "sailing ... nearer to an adequate recognition of one's allies," as stressed by Wrenn, may hopefully result from the education or reeducation of faculty members in cooperative programs of study and training.

[27] Archibald MacIntosh, *Behind the Academic Curtain,* Harper & Brothers, New York, 1948, pp. 139–140.

CHAPTER 5 *The In-service Training of*
Faculty Members

Quick and painless learning about counseling for the faculty member new to the program of counseling cannot be ensured. No sure-fire correspondence course or ten easy lessons intended to transmit the knowledge and skills desired seem to have been perfected. Without doubt, the best possible assistance to faculty members selected to counsel students should be given. In support of this contention one expert writes: [1]

Advising students regarding their choice of courses and the relationship of this choice to their goals, abilities, and interests is a complex operation. At its best, it provides an instructor with insights and understandings which broaden his outlook, increase his understanding of students, and improve his teaching. Academic advising by instructors does not of itself automatically bring about these changes and improvements. This implies that in-service training in student personnel work should be made continually available to all staff at all levels of the service.

A poll taken in 1948 of ten experts in the field of student personnel work revealed that approximately 250 to 300 colleges and universities over the country were sponsoring some type of in-service training program for their faculty members who served as advisers or counselors to students. In 1950, one investigator studying returns from ninety colleges and universities reported that fifty-three schools made provision for the in-service education of their faculty counselors.[2] In 1953, a complete issue of the official publication of the National Association of Deans of Women was devoted to the matter of in-service education for faculty.[3] A growing number of handbooks and guidebooks for faculty members

[1] B. Lamar Johnson, *General Education in Action,* American Council on Education, Washington, 1952, pp. 60–61.
[2] Carroll L. Miller, "Counseling by Faculty Advisers," *Educational and Psychological Measurement,* 10:451–454, autumn, 1950.
[3] *Journal of the National Association of Deans of Women,* vol. 16, no. 2, January, 1953.

doing advisement gives evidence of the fact that, in the development of counseling programs in higher education, faculty members not professionally trained as counselors are carrying important responsibilities.

In the survey of 218 institutions cited, respondents indicated the means by which faculty were trained, commenting on the success of these methods (see Table 3). Forty-four respondents indicated that in-service training for faculty counselors was given, but there was no designation as to the type of training. A summary of particular activities appears as follows:

Group meetings were held in thirty-seven institutions; conferences for faculty counselors were sponsored in thirty-four colleges and universities; courses were available for counselors in twenty-five institutions; printed materials constituted the chief means of in-service training in twenty-three instances; services of lecturers and specialists were used in twenty. In nine institutions faculty workshops were sponsored. An additional nine respondents mentioned "experience" as a means of in-service training. One may pause to conjecture about this last, wondering just what experience, offered in what form, at what intervals would best supply this training.

Concluding the review, twenty institutions admit that little or no in-service assistance is given to faculty counselors. The author speculates as to whether or not all faculty members in the program are sufficiently well trained before taking over the assignment. Possibly the counselors have, over the years, "learned on the student" (viz., "experience" as indicated by nine previously cited schools). It may be that, in some institutions, in-service training is conducted in so informal a fashion that respondents adjudge the experience to be not truly worthy of designation.

INFORMAL TRAINING PROGRAMS

The informal programs are, in general, characterized by two factors:

1. They proceed to orient teachers to their counseling duties through activities that are not separated from the total faculty orientation.

2. They proceed with an instructional tempo which allows the faculty to absorb ideas gradually rather than meet them head on.

In training programs of the informal type, faculty members learn of the institution, its curricula, its student body, its faculty and staff through a year-long, somewhat more leisurely set of activities, social and professional. Ideas are shared and information exchanged at lunch tables, in departmental meetings, on the golf links, and in various other faculty gatherings. Without doubt, these informal activities can go a long way in meeting the objectives set up for training faculty counselors.

FORMAL PROGRAMS OF TRAINING

In the more formal programs of training for faculty counselors, consideration is given to such items as these:

1. The aims and objectives of the faculty advisory system
2. The philosophy of general or basic education
3. The departmental curricula
4. The means devised for the communication of faculty counselors with chairmen of general education, department heads, academic deans
5. The ways of working with students who demonstrate varying strengths in their interests, abilities, and aptitudes [4]

In addition, in-service training attempts to impart to faculty members some specific information about (1) the content of courses in both general and professional areas; (2) the methods used by teachers of particular courses; (3) the relationship of earlier learnings of the student to the new situation in college; (4) the importance of high school tests and grades in predicting a student's success in college; (5) the relationship of general-education courses to the major which the student declares; and (6) the relationship of scores made on college entrance examinations to the selection of course work.

Finally, the more formal training program for counselors is directed toward assisting the faculty member in (1) recognizing all aspects of a student's problem; (2) conducting effective interviews with students; (3) using test data, grades, and evaluative summaries in the counseling process; (4) assisting the student to analyze himself objectively; and (5) facilitating the referral of the student to a specialist capable of working with him on a particular problem.

In viewing the success of training methods designed to help faculty members to perform effectively as counselors, representatives of the 218 institutions comment as follows: Twelve respondents label the program of in-service training for academic advisement duties as excellent; forty-five consider this training to be good; thirty-two institutions describe the training as fair.

In addition, the training given to faculty members for their duties as vocational counselors was adjudged in three institutions as being excellent, in twenty-four as being good, and in twenty-two as being fair. (See Table 4 for other evaluative ratings for in-service training of faculty members doing personal-social, religious, and health counseling.)

Heading the list of suggestions made by respondents in answer to the question, "What improvements or changes would you make in the

[4] Paul C. Kelso and Melvene Draheim Hardee, "Cooperative Learning Experiences of the Faculty," in Melvene D. Hardee (ed.), *Counseling and Guidance in General Education*, World Book Company, Yonkers, N.Y., pp. 287–305.

program of faculty counseling?" was the declaration: "More and better in-service training is needed for counselors" (see Table 7). Accordingly, this chapter devotes itself to a consideration of some promising practices in the in-service training of faculty counselors and to suggestions for improving these programs generally.

ALL–INSTITUTION FACULTY MEETINGS

A number of colleges and universities customarily sponsor a faculty conference or institute which, in most instances, precedes the opening of school in the fall. The aim of such a program is to orient new faculty members to the institution, to reorient veteran members of the faculty to institutional aims, and, in general, to begin the school year on a note of captured collective enthusiasm. It is interesting to observe that topics under study by the faculty are often student-related, covering broadly or in some detail the range of problems of the "whole student."

At Stephens College, the fall faculty conference extends over a period of three days, during which time there is consideration (in general convocation and in small groups) of the student and her general and specific education.

At Central State College (Wilberforce, Ohio), faculty members met in 1952–1953 to discuss "Inter-personal Relations on the Campus." A very considerable portion of the opening remarks of the president was directed to the need for treating the individual student as a total personality rather than contributing to his segmentation through course specialization.

At Southern University, the preschool conference of 1955 was organized about the theme "Improving the Self-directive Power of Students through Adjustment Services." At Tuskegee Institute an all-faculty conference in 1946 focused upon "An Effective Guidance Program for the Institute."

Chico State College has held a series of faculty conferences concerned with general education, the student personnel program, and student activities in the college program. Attendance at the conference has been voluntary for faculty members. In addition, a limited number of students have been participants.

At Florida Southern College, discussion groups of the faculty conference centered their attention on these questions:

1. What should be the purposes of our college guidance program?
2. What are good guidance practices and how can they be best used in our classrooms?
3. How can students, teachers, and administrators of this college arrive at a common educational purpose?

At Florida State University, the entire faculty has met for a day and a half to consider such topics as "Report of the All-university Study Committee" (1954); "The Students We Teach" (1955); and "Grading Practices We Follow" (1956). (See App. F-2 for the 1955 program.)

With an all-institution emphasis being placed early in the year on needs of students and institutional resources for meeting these needs, the stage is set for the in-service training sessions of faculty counselors. These sessions may, with profit, center upon some of the technical aspects of counseling if sufficient orientation to the matter of individualizing education is given in the all-institute sessions. Lacking such institution-wide emphasis in a conference, the responsibility for orienting faculty advisers along these lines falls upon the director or committee in charge of the faculty advisory system. As one investigator remarks: [5]

> Too often the philosophy of the college, its goals, its traditions never become known to the faculty members; frequently, the significance of a broad academic program is not clearly perceived and the academic regulations not understood. Accordingly, the adviser, because of his dearth of information and his inadequate appreciation of his role, is unable to do more than approve courses and this in a very perfunctory manner.

SEMINARS, CONFERENCES, AND WORKSHOPS FOR ADVISERS

Colleges and universities which sponsor seminars, conferences, and workshops for faculty advisers report the treatment of a variety of themes and topics. In an effort to give the reader an idea of the scope of coverage as well as the specialty of program in which some institutions excel, the author has designated several program emphases, introducing them with a descriptive topical heading.

Assisting the Counselor in Determining His Role

At the University of Rhode Island, the office of advisement and counseling sponsored a series of seminars of counseling with some fifty-five members of the faculty participating. The discussions were based upon the following questions:

1. What is the student-adviser relationship?
2. What do we know and what should we know about our advisees?
3. What are the problems in faculty advising?
4. What is the place of faculty advising in higher education? (See summary of Seminar Four in App. E.)

At Stephens College, the first meeting of a recent fall session had as its topic "What the Admissions Counselor Says about Stephens College in the Field." A motion picture, "The Lonely Night," served in a second

[5] Miller, *op. cit.*

meeting to depict a problem of some students. A third meeting re-
volved around a discussion of "What Kind of an Adviser Are You?" The
final meeting of the year was labeled "Coping with the Problem Parent."

Assisting the Counselor in Understanding the Student

Florida Agricultural and Mechanical University has conducted a
series of meetings in the fall semester, the first being concerned with
the role of the faculty adviser in the university program. Subsequent
meetings have covered the use of test data in counseling, the use of
occupational information, and assisting the marginal student.

At Southern State College, an initial meeting has dealt with a general
orientation of the faculty adviser to the student personnel point of view.
Following this, three meetings have been concerned with (1) concepts
of intelligence, (2) the counseling record, and (3) tests and their interpretation.

At State Teachers College, Lockhaven, Pennsylvania, meetings of
general faculty are held on the first Monday night in each month. Following this session there is an advisers' hour. Content of the advisers'
meeting has been extended to cover such things as (1) bibliography of
available books dealing with interviewing; (2) assistance which can
be given to students on study problems; and (3) the construction of
graphs of ability and achievement for each advisee, noting those who
are working beyond capacity, those not working up to capacity, and
those who by reasons of ability and achievement need to be counseled
concerning their vocational goals.

Providing the Counselor with Information about Course Work

At Florida State University, the program of general education is reviewed in each fall seminar for the 150 educational counselors. One
presentation took the form of a panel discussion in which eight teachers
in the humanities course work spoke on "The Contributions of the Areas
in Humanities to the Needs of Particular Students." The speakers presented five-minute talks to the counselors, allowing a half hour for
questions and answers. The large assembly broke up into small groups
for a further consideration of courses in humanities.

In a seminar held for faculty counselors of students undecided about
a major, members of the departments of chemistry, physics, meteorology,
and geology presented a review of opportunities for students enrolling
in the physical sciences. A subsequent meeting was held in the spring
on the topic "General Education Offerings in the Biological Sciences,"
with the departments of botany, bacteriology, physiology, and zoology
participating.

Assisting the Counselor in Effecting Working Relations with Institutional Personnel

As stated in Chapter 2 of this volume, the concept of wholeness of the institution is furthered when members of the faculty and administrative staff are given information about the work of specialists within the institution and when they proceed to use this information wisely. In a hallmark publication relating to the work of the teacher as a counselor, there are cited some eighteen institutional resources, ranging from the academic deans and department heads to the community and its various resources.[6]

The faculty counselor needs to know of similar resources on his campus and in the community. The supplying of counselors with directories of guidance services which include the name of the officer in charge, the location of the office, and the telephone number is helpful. In addition, the instituting of a training program for advisers to cover the work of specialty areas is commendable. The College of Letters and Science of the University of Wisconsin has sponsored these sessions with participants as shown:

1. Student counseling center and student health: director of student counseling center, director of student health department, and director of the neuropsychiatric section of the student health department

2. Financial aids and student housing: director of admissions who is the chairman of the committees on undergraduate scholarships and loans, director of the housing bureau, and director of residence halls

3. Student activities and advising students with low six-weeks grades: dean of men, dean of women, and associate dean of the college

4. Faculty advising, especially the academic advising of superior students: chairman of the standing committee on advising in the college and the dean of the college

One area of particular interest for faculty advisers is that of testing and individual appraisal. In a program of decentralized services wherein the testing unit is apart from the counseling center, there is need for experts in measurement to discuss with faculty advisers the use of test profiles, application of results from a specific test, and other technical aspects of a testing program. These presentations should be made with some flexibility, recognition being given to the most elementary as well as the more complex factors in a testing program.

A chief problem in in-service training through seminars, conferences, and workshops is that of finding a time when all persons involved will be free to attend. Florida Agricultural and Mechanical University sched-

[6] Donald J. Shank and others, *The Teacher as Counselor*, American Council on Education Studies, ser. 6, no. 10, Washington, 12:32–35, October, 1948.

ules meetings at 7 o'clock in the evening during the fall session. At Howard University, a workshop for mentors, tutors, and advisers is held prior to the opening of school, with the deans of men and women planning the four-day experience. Skidmore College reports a three-day workshop on advising, also held before classes begin. In their 1953 session, attendance was voluntary, with more than 90 per cent of the faculty members returning early from their vacation to take part.

In addition, the setting or locale for learning is important, as is affirmed by respondents at Sacramento State College who suggest the following:

Some greater amount of in-service training with new faculty members and a continuing channel to the "veteran" members would be of help. This would preferably be in the nature of a faculty retreat where a leisurely reexamination of all objectives, and our contribution to these, would be possible.

Lacking time and good location for full meetings of the advisory group during the year, some colleges and universities resort to the circularization of printed materials in order that faculty counselors be informed of current or changing procedures, of scheduled dates for counseling, reporting, or registration.

PRINTED MATERIALS

Chief among materials of a printed nature are handbooks (see App. H), which are sponsored by a number of institutions. Mimeographed or printed, these contain a variety of aids for the faculty member. One investigator, having studied faculty advising in nineteen liberal arts colleges, reports: [7]

Slightly fewer than half of the schools have manuals for advisers. The principal aim of most of these manuals seems to be to provide accurate information regarding prerequisites and requirements. The only exception is a manual that encompasses a complete training program, covering basic personnel techniques and philosophies as well as course data.

An examination of the handbooks cited in App. H shows a wide range of materials, including such subjects as (1) the philosophy of faculty advisement, (2) functions of advisers, (3) descriptions of curricula in the general studies and professional schools, (4) rules and regulations pertaining to choice of subjects and registration, (5) regulations affecting students in their campus living, (6) suggestions for interviewing, (7) test interpretation, (8) referral process and referral agencies, (9)

[7] Mary Ann Tinsley, "The Faculty Adviser in the Liberal Arts College," *Personnel and Guidance Journal*, 34:220, December, 1955.

consideration of problems of students undecided about a major, and (10) case studies of particular students.

Editing the publications are chairmen of advising committees, deans of general studies, the director or coordinator of counseling, the dean of students, or dean of men or women. This responsibility for compiling and editing materials, in most instances, appears to be placed with the person who is responsible for supervising the program of faculty advisement.

In addition to manuals and handbooks, some institutions sponsor the publication and distribution of news-type leaflets. One such publication is the *Coordinative Notes* series of the office of coordinator of counseling at Florida State University. This publication, issued once a month for the first six months of the year, is organized in two parts: Part I for all counselors (residence-hall, vocational, upper-class academic, etc.) in the program of decentralized services of the university and Part II directed to faculty advisers for freshmen and transfers specifically. Included in Part I are explanations of (1) mid-semester progress check, (2) case-conference method, (3) examples of program coordination, (4) counseling and registration for spring semester, and (5) college and career days. The second part includes (1) reminders to faculty advisers for turning in materials to the office of personnel records, (2) the scheduling of conferences with students early in semester, (3) suggestions for working with students on their unsatisfactory status, and (4) a "testimonial" of a student regarding the assistance given by the faculty adviser.

A third type of publication distributed in some institutions as an in-service training aid is the directory of guidance and counseling services. If working relations are to be maintained or improved in the total institution, faculty advisers need to know the names, locations, and particular functions of persons performing personnel and counseling duties. In the small college or university, this information may be common knowledge. In the large institution, however, where change in personnel and office location is frequent, a listing of personnel in the form of a directory is needed.

Among institutions sponsoring a directory for use of students and faculty are Bucknell University which publishes a *Directory of Services Available to Students;* Indiana University, *Directory of Student Counseling and Personal Services;* Georgia Tech, *Got a Question?;* University of Texas, *Problems? Here's Help;* and Florida State University, *Directory of Guidance Services.* A novel device, available to students and faculty at Tennessee Agricultural and Industrial State University, is a cardboard guidance wheel which rotates to indicate, with a pointed arrow, the particular service which a student may consult for a specific problem.

FORMAL–COURSE PROVISIONS

In the poll of institutions cited in this book, some twenty-five respondents indicated that in-service training through formal course offerings was provided for faculty members who served as counselors. In a number of instances, this category included those colleges or universities whose faculty counselors leave the campus to obtain formal training in guidance and counseling as graduate students in another institution. For this investment of a teacher's time in night classes, Saturday classes, or summer sessions, a stipend or additional remuneration is sometimes given.

A distinctly different arrangement was worked out at Mississippi State College. In the summer of 1948 there was offered on campus a six-weeks course, graduate level, meeting one and one-half hours per day, five days per week. All fees were waived for college employees, and approximately 50 per cent of the forty-six persons enrolled in the course registered for credit, regardless of the fact that many held advanced degrees. The group was composed of freshman counselors, department heads, major advisers, and members of the counseling and testing committee. Two sections per day were organized in order that conflicts with teaching schedules might be prevented. If an instructor did not have a full teaching schedule, the enrollment in the counseling course was considered to be 25 per cent of a full load. Thus, an instructor who was assigned only 75 per cent of teaching time could draw full salary for the summer through participation in the counselor course. For those who had a full teaching load or were employed on a twelve-months basis, a small stipend was given for enrollment in the course.[8]

THE INDIVIDUAL CONFERENCE

In reporting procedures of training being used among 243 institutions including (1) public land-grant institutions, (2) state colleges and universities and separate professional and technical schools, (3) state teachers colleges and normal schools, and (4) state junior colleges, one investigator discerned that the case conference, use of small groups, individual conferences, and lectures were activities most widely used. Singled out, the individual conferences were reported as being used in sixty-one training programs or by 49 per cent of the total group. Most schools, however, reported using more than one method or procedure in conducting their training programs.[9]

[8] D. W. Aiken, "Securing Faculty Cooperation in the Student Personnel Program," *Educational and Psychological Measurement,* 9:470–476, pt. II, autumn, 1949.

[9] Carl O. Eycke, "A Survey of In-service Training Programs for Faculty Counselors in State Supported Colleges and Universities in the United States," a thesis presented

The individual conference of the faculty counselor with the program director or a resource person can, of course, be focused upon a variety of items. In the study cited, Eycke [10] found that well over half of the institutions give assistance to the faculty counselor in test interpretation and the use of student personnel folders. Interviewing methods and referral procedures are reviewed in most of the institutions. Test interpretation, interviewing, and referral procedures in combination made up the content of in-service training generally and of the individual conference in particular.

Some of the most productive of the individual conferences of faculty adviser and director of the counseling program have been centered upon the specific problems of a student. The faculty adviser's opening statement is often this: "Jerry Genesis seems to be having considerable trouble with biology (or history, English, humanities). I wonder how he can be helped."

A consideration of Jerry's high school background, his college entrance tests, his schedule of classes, study habits, extra class and work activities, his general health, and his motivation for college then ensues, with the faculty adviser and the program director viewing these together. Questions are posed by both counselor and director, appropriate lines of action are discussed, and some tentative solutions reached. In no instance should the program director do all the talking or assume the "taking over" of the student's problem. Rather, the activity is one of faculty adviser and counseling director working in combination.

An advisory program which does not make provision at some point for individual conferences between director (or coordinator) of the program and the individual faculty adviser cannot long endure. The occasionally perplexed or harassed faculty artist, physicist, agronomist, or linguist needs the security of knowing that there is someone to whom he can turn who conceivably knows more than he knows about a student's problem or knows where the answers can be found. As one administrator points out, "You must not become so heavily involved in the well-being of the individual student that you override and neglect the personality needs and intellectual demands of the faculty members with whom you are dealing." [11]

The program administrator will listen to many woes and grievances from faculty advisers, not all concerning him, but many directed toward "the counseling system," "the perniciousness of administrators," "the thanklessness of students," "the high cost of living," etc. The practiced ear

in partial fulfillment of the requirements for a M.A. degree, Ohio University, June, 1956, p. 101.

[10] *Ibid.*

[11] John G. Darley, "The Faculty Is Human, Too," an address presented to the Southern College Personnel Association, Atlanta, Ga., December, 1955.

extended to students should also be extended to these now-and-then-frustrated faculty members. Oftentimes after some serious outpouring, the unburdened faculty adviser will come up with a good idea for improving the counseling program, and the time in "therapy" will have been well spent!

THE CASE CONFERENCE

As has been cited, the case conference is a frequently used type of in-service procedure. Opportunity is afforded the faculty counselor for learning more about his counseling responsibility when he participates in the review of a student's problem which may include the several areas—academic, vocational, personal-social, and health. This activity, as described by Shepard,[12] proceeds as follows:

> The case-conference method is an administrative device for the collection of up-to-date information and the securing of the combined judgment of staff members concerning a student's progress and problems. These conferences are under the supervision of the director of counseling services. They may be initiated by any member of the faculty who feels that such a staff review would be helpful. Those invited to participate in such a conference will include all those members who are working directly with the student, such as her teachers, adviser, residence counselor, dean, and college physician. The case conference is probably one of the most effective procedures for helping teachers and others to understand a particular student and her behavior through the sharing of information and insights, plus a means for getting cooperative action initiated by those most able to assist the student.

Conducted as a learning session, the case conference aids the faculty adviser in recognizing the work of specialized personnel on campus who share the responsibility for assisting the student in solving problems. In addition, the faculty counselor may observe the resources of the institution as a whole and the possibilities of action undertaken in combination with others. Some faculty advisers who have come to their first case conference with trepidation or actual skepticism have stayed to talk at length with a residence-hall counselor, instructor, or physician. Chapter 15 of this volume portrays a recording of a case conference which reviews some problems of adjustment of a student from abroad.

The coordination of follow-up information resulting from the case conference is important. A residence-hall counselor commented to the chairman of the case-conference group, "The possibilities for assisting students through the case-conference method are unlimited when each of us is kept informed of the steps in the resulting action." This dis-

[12] Eugene L. Shepard and staff, "Meeting Student Needs Through Counseling," *Stephens College News Reporter,* vol. 15, no. 3, March, 1956.

semination of information about the student's progress is made in memoranda, in a telephone conversation, or in conference with those who need to know of the action.

AREAS OF IN–SERVICE TRAINING NEEDING NEW OR RENEWED EMPHASIS

In the continuing effort to make the good better and the better best, a number of practices in the in-service training of faculty members merit study. Among these areas to be reviewed critically are (1) the improvement of working relations in the total institution between and among faculty counselors and others charged with guidance and counseling responsibilities; (2) the improvement of the workshop or group method; (3) the consideration of problems of emotional adjustment of students; (4) the inclusion of students in aspects of in-service training; and (5) the initiation or maintenance of a systematic evaluation of in-service training.

Improvement of Working Relations in the Institution

Commenting on working relations, one administrator in counseling in a Midwestern college states: "We would like to chart more clearly and carry out more completely the communication between the groups charged with personnel work and the instructors who serve as counselors for our students." A similar goal is cited by another director of counseling, who states: "One of the most important things is to increase general knowledge of what people in different offices are doing and of the ways in which students can be led to make the maximum use of the facilities we have available."

The availability of directories and other listings does not, of course, ensure harmonious working relationships. Faculty members who work with students must make personal contact with their colleagues who also work with students. Commenting on this, one respondent affirms:

It is the belief of program planners at our institution that coordination is developed through personal acquaintanceship. In this institution, the director of the student counseling center, who is a clinical psychologist, invites faculty advisers to informal coffee hours in the counseling center. As a consequence, the attitude of the faculty adviser who refers a student to the center suggests to the student that the procedure is a friendly one carried out in terms of the persons involved and not through dispassionate machinery.

One investigator [13] recommends the use of the demonstration case work-up as a technique for more formal group study. In the experiment

[13] Barbara A. Kirk, "Techniques of In-service Counselor Training," *Personnel and Guidance Journal*, 34:206, December, 1955.

reported, cases were selected on the basis of the student's need for assistance beyond the facilities of the school, these requiring, for the most part, clinical counseling or diagnostic work. In this more formal procedure, the faculty counselor obtains training through conferences with experienced, professional personnel to whom the student was earlier referred. The skills to be developed by the faculty counselor are those relating to the identification of students for referral, the making of the referral, and the follow-up counseling of the student after referral.

The possibilities for initiating, maintaining, and improving good working relations between the faculty adviser and the professional counselors, the health staff, and the residence-hall staff—to single out only three groups—are illustrated by the following:

The professional counseling staff and the faculty adviser

A desirable relationship between faculty advisers and the professional counseling staff is described by a respondent of the University of Delaware:

If counselors do their jobs adequately they will be able to offer to the faculty adviser such data as test scores and their possible significance for curricular and vocational planning, information as to a student's relative intellectual strengths and weaknesses, inadequacies in basic skills, etc. The counselor will go beyond these descriptive data, however, and attempt to explain the pattern of individual differences in terms of its positive as well as its negative aspects. He may try to help the adviser to understand the student as an individual in the light of family background, personal history, and individual idiosyncrasies in order that the student be aided in avoiding situations which could produce confusion, frustration, and dissatisfaction.

The health staff and the faculty adviser

Commenting on the improvement of working relations among groups, an administrator cites the program of New Haven State Teachers College:

The health staff has been eager to develop a channel for referring selected students to the various counselors in the school. To date, informal conferences regarding particular students have been held, and there has been collaboration in referring a few students for diagnosis and study. More exchange of information with faculty advisers is occurring.

The residence-hall staff and the faculty adviser

A respondent from Texas Technological College calls attention to this important aspect:

In the dormitory supervisory program there has been much evidence of bringing into a single focus the educational experiences of students. The increasing requests on the part of academic personnel for information about the general pattern of day-to-day activities of the student—particularly if his academic achievement is poor—mark growth in cooperation between these areas.

These and other relationships need to be reviewed by the director or the committee in charge of the program of institution-wide counseling. Provision for the initiation of cooperative endeavor as well as for the continuance of such activity is frequently made through workshop or small-group sessions at which representatives of all units and agencies meet to discuss their common problems.

Improvement of the Workshop or Group Method

Much of the in-service training of faculty members is carried on through group procedures; therefore, an analysis of methods for teaching teachers to counsel and for demonstrations of actual practice in effecting good working relations between and among faculty advisers, administrators, special clinicians, and counselors is desirable.

Gordon [14] writes of the experiment carried on at Kansas State College for training college faculty in counseling. He calls attention to the following requisites of good group procedure:

1. Clarification by the leader of his role
2. The structuring of the group situation
3. The use of flexible patterns of action
4. The carrying through of a policy of "permissiveness" in group procedure
5. Learning by doing and by feeling
6. The introduction of "extra content"
7. Good preplanning done by the director
8. Use of live case narratives
9. Role playing by participants
10. Use of a reference file in a central location available to participants
11. Dissemination of actual tests and other materials used
12. The utilization of resource personnel

An analysis of the goals of workshop training are said by Gibb and Gibb [15] to be concerned with (1) initiating or keeping the group action moving; (2) regulating or influencing the direction and pace of the group; (3) informing or bringing information or opinion to the group; (4) supporting or encouraging the ideas of other group members attempting to hold the group together in order to accomplish its task; and (5) evaluating or attempting to get the group to evaluate its decisions, goals, or procedures.

---

[14] Ira J. Gordon, "Guidance Training for College Faculty," *Journal of the National Association of Deans of Women*, 16:69–76, January, 1953.

[15] Jack R. Gibb and Lorraine Miller Gibb, *Applied Group Dynamics*, University Bookstore, University of Colorado, Boulder, Colo.

The adoption of suitable procedures for group work comes slowly. It is evident that "doing what comes natcherly" is often the *modus operandi* in colleges and universities. Administrators and other leaders overlook or postpone a searching analysis of the group method for reasons of lack of time or of access to training methods. On this score, one respondent in the survey of 218 institutions cites his procedure:

As a matter of fact, I simply do what experience and common sense seem to indicate should be done and do not bother about group dynamics, anthropological excursions, or sociological interludes. It is not that I do not realize that research and experience in new fields involving group dynamics and applications of new techniques are accomplishing value; it is rather that I am untrained in the new techniques and feel skeptical about playing around on the edges of fields with which I have little knowledge.

As programs of in-service training continue, a sizable number of participants will recognize that the smoothing of sharp edges of conflict or the resolution of tangles resulting from misunderstandings and misinformation is entirely possible if effective techniques for group work are employed.

The Consideration of Problems of Emotional Adjustment of the Student

In Chapter 3 some consideration is given to the extent to which the faculty counselor is called upon to deal with the problems of emotional adjustment and deviant behavior of counselees. If it is agreed that students cannot very well separate their emotional selves from their academic selves, it stands to reason that faculty counselors will sense or be apprised of the emotional involvements of some of their students. Two investigators suggest that in-service training be broadened to include a study of the dynamics of human adjustment: [16]

The consultants frequently recommended that more faculty counselors be oriented to the nature of emotional problems and given some training to help them identify such problems. By identifying such problems early, college advisers and counselors can help students with those problems before they become so severe as to require more specialized attention.

The Inclusion of Students in Aspects of In-service Training

With the focus of training for counseling being placed upon the student and how he can be aided in achieving self-direction, there is strong argument for including students in the program of in-service training for counselors. Use of students in demonstration interviews, on panels and symposia, in reporting results of program evaluation—these

[16] A. J. Brumbaugh and Ralph F. Berdie, *Student Personnel Programs in Transition*, American Council on Education Studies, Washington, October, 1952, p. 25.

are but a few of the ways in which students may serve in the program of training. Most students are quick to accept responsibilities which they are equipped to handle and to refrain from accepting tasks which put them in unwarranted positions of leadership.

Continuing and Systematic Evaluation of the Program of In-service Training

If study and evaluation of instructional areas for better teaching of *students* are desirable, then study and evaluation of the instructional process for *teaching teachers to counsel* are deserved. Questions such as these are recurrent: How effective, over-all, is the program of in-service training? How effective is a single technique used in training? How effective is the contribution of one person or a group of persons to the training program?

It is probably true that most judgments about the effectiveness of a program of in-service training are made "off the cuff" and frequently without benefit of a systematized evaluation. While the "feel of the program" as adjudged by those in it is important, the feeling of one or two persons is not likely to be representative of the total group. A systematic polling or a collection of judgments of counselors in terms of representative samples is doubtless more reliable.

Some institutions which have experimented with methods for evaluating the in-service training of faculty counselors have procedures to suggest. At Southern State College, the faculty counselor is asked to evaluate each seminar session through use of a check list prepared as a grid with (1) the topic ranged on the left-hand side of the sheet and (2) the degree of understanding obtained marked at the top in gradations of response as (*a*) I still don't understand this topic; (*b*) I have a vague idea about the topic; (*c*) I think I understand the topic very well. Topics covered included judgments on the personnel point of view, the concept of intelligence, and testing and test interpretation.

At Florida State University, a seminar for faculty advisers was evaluated with respect to the following: [17]

1. Content, or what the program included

2. Organization and presentation, or the arrangement of content, sequence of events, devices for presentation, timing of events, arrangement of scheduling of activities, and so on

3. Participation, or the work of individuals who shared in the program and contributed to it

4. Materials, or the production of mimeographed and printed items, the charts and displays, the test profiles, etc.

[17] Melvene Draheim Hardee, "A Program of In-service Training for Teacher Counselors," *Junior College Journal*, 22:456–458, April, 1950.

5. Setting, or environment, including the place and time of meeting
The specific breakdown of items under each heading included the following:

Content

1. Explanation of ways of conducting a group meeting with twenty counselees for purposes of giving information to them on routine matters
2. Information on conducting an individual interview
3. Information about registration procedures
4. Explanation of the make-up of the *Manual for Counselors* and its coverage
5. Explanation of the placement and exemption examinations and of the psychological test
6. Interpretation of the students' high school test scores and high school grades
7. Explanation of the records to be kept by counselors for their personal files and for the office of personnel records
8. Review of the kinds of problems the typical student might face in a first year
9. Explanation of the responsibilities of educational counselors in dealing with student problems

Organization and presentation

The content was presented by a variety of means including the following:
1. Five individual speeches
2. Three demonstrations or skits of two or more people
3. Two panel discussions
4. Two question-answer sessions with ten resource persons answering questions
5. One wire recording
6. Three dialogues

Participation

The total number of participants was twenty-six persons, including the coordinator of counseling, dean of students, chairman of the council of deans, guidance committee of six members, deans of men and women, director of the test service bureau, director of vocational guidance, director of the psychological clinic, assistant director of the School of Library Training and Service, principal of the demonstration school, chairmen of freshmen mathematics and English, supervisor of personnel records, chairman of general education and his area chairmen, and four educational counselors.

Materials

The materials were limited to *The Manual for Educational Counselors,* the *University Catalog,* the *Freshman Bulletin,* the *Schedule of Courses* for fall, the *Suggested Program of Study for Freshmen,* and the personal data summary of Tommy Case, a hypothetical student.

Setting

The setting chosen was a large parlor in one of the women's residence halls, centrally located and convenient to the dining room, bus stops, and administrative offices. One reason for the choice of a residence-hall parlor in preference to an auditorium setting was the fact that both men's and women's residence-hall counselors were invited to participate in the seminar sessions. The meeting of educational counselors and residence counselors on the latter's "home ground" seemed to afford opportunities for mutual cooperation and the beginning of working relationships. The actual amount of time spent in seminar was five and one-half hours each day. There were two twenty-minute recess periods, morning and afternoon.

At the conclusion of the fall seminar for educational counselors, the coordinator issued to all persons in attendance a questionnaire to be checked and returned before the scheduling of counseling interviews. It was the wish of the coordinator and the advisory committee to obtain *immediate* reactions to the in-service experience. The tabulation of results revealed the following:

1. The seminar was of more-than-average value (81 per cent).

2. No counselor considered the seminar to be of no value, and only two deemed it of little value.

3. The organization and presentation of materials were deemed excellent by the majority of respondents.

4. The content was adjudged useful and helpful by a high percentage of counselors.

5. A large percentage of respondents would have preferred fewer participants.

6. Materials and setting were adequate for the majority.

7. The consensus among counselors was that a following year's program might include more factual information on the general-education program together with more intensive coverage of techniques of interviewing.

8. New ideas for a subsequent year covered greater use of visual aids, a more detailed consideration of test scores and testing, actual use of a student in the demonstration of interviews between counselor and

counselee, and a separation of "experienced" counselors from "new" counselors.

It is agreed that the proof of the counseling pudding lies in its taste to the student consumers. If the program of in-service training has been effective, the result may likely show in the improved counseling done by the faculty members. The collection of comments from counselees is therefore important. Wheaton College asks students to rate the faculty counselors' performance in a check of twenty-nine items and to contribute narrative comments in addition. Some of the statements to be adjudged by students are these:

I believe that my faculty counselor is interested in me as a person and wants to help me succeed in life as well as in college.

My faculty counselor took time to discuss my interests, abilities, etc., with me before advising me as to my proper course of study.

My faculty counselor referred me to others when I needed special help, etc.

A recent comprehensive evaluation of the freshman advisory program at Miami University (Oxford, Ohio) included a polling of freshmen, upperclassmen, students who had withdrawn in the freshman year, parents, faculty advisers formerly serving in the program, and those currently serving. From the results obtained, the committee of freshmen advisers prepared sixteen recommendations covering new practices for the program as well as revisions of continuing practice.

Program strengths and weaknesses emerge when a scientific study of the training process is instituted. Thus the program of in-service training for faculty members who counsel calls for continuous evaluation. (See also Chapter 17.)

SUMMARY

A considerable number of faculty members affirm that attitudes engendered in students are "caught" and not "taught." Perhaps the "feeling for" counseling which faculty members will hopefully acquire comes through a *catching* rather than a *teaching* process.

However, some critics and observers of the educational process contend that there are many things which cannot be acquired through learning; instead, these are granted as a birthright. One conjectures about the venture under study wherein faculty members are educated or re-educated in ways of dealing with counselees and advisees. If the flute-playing faculty member does not possess the gift of competency in counseling, can he acquire it? The answer is, "Hopefully he may acquire it *with assistance.*"

From the content of this chapter, the reader may assume with some justification that faculty counseling and advisement are here to stay and that they will likely increase in scope and intensity. Accordingly, the chapter has stressed the need for in-service training, types of formal programming, content and method used in the program of in-service training, and some areas needing special emphasis.

In the chapter to follow, consideration is given to the persisting problems that plague the director of the program of faculty counseling and advisement, the faculty member who participates in the program, and the student, on the receiving end. As these persisting problems in their universality are faced and solutions found, the institution's wholeness is immeasurably enhanced.

CHAPTER 6 *Persisting Problems in Programs of Faculty Advisement*

It is possible that the reader might assume from the foregoing chapter that the success of the program of faculty counseling is assured with the careful selection of faculty members and with their gentle nurture and care thereafter. Such is not always the case. Occasional reedy dissonances which emanate from the studio of the faculty flutist sound the warning that all is not well. When these disharmonies merge with the faulty or faltering notes from other studios and cloistered offices, then the "happy days" cadence of the program is ended. What are these irritants which denote, in a cacophony of sound, counseling out of control?

Basing his ideas on a study of twenty-one colleges and universities, James H. Robertson [1] has enunciated several principles which he believes should govern a program of advising in higher education. He arrives at these principles after a rather full analysis of the policies and procedures in effect in the schools he visited. His principles are as follows:

1. The advising program should be so organized that the faculty are responsibly involved and are not merely co-opted clerks. The program should be so arranged that each faculty adviser is expected to explore with his students significant questions about the rationale of graduation requirements, the intelligent choice of vocational and professional objectives, the need for a strategic plan in achieving maximum benefit from the college.

2. Since not all faculty members are willing or able to be useful advisers to undergraduates, there must be provision for selection and rotation.

3. The pressing problem of the proper relationship between the various professional agencies and the academic advisory staff must be explored and clarified. Mutual understanding, respect, and confidence can come in part through the accumulated experiences of day-to-day contacts through personal knowledge of each other. So important is this direct, personal awareness, however,

[1] James H. Robertson, "Academic Advising in Colleges and Universities—Its Present State and Present Problems," *North Central Association Quarterly*, vol. 32, no. 3, January, 1958, pp. 228–239.

that it should not be left to casual, accidental telephone conversations or cor-ridor conferences. Specific activities must be provided for.

4. The accumulated information and insights derived from academic ad-vising should be made available in some effective set of records to the college as a whole. Further, these data should be available to appraise the outcomes of the college program.

5. If the academic advisory program is to have full acceptance and vigorous growth, there must be continued publicity for the program both within and without the college. The purposes of the program need to be conveyed to students, parents, alumni, secondary school teachers, and counselors as well as to the faculty and administration of the institution itself.

That all is not as well as it might be in the faculty adviser's province is cited by Iffert.[2] Reporting student reactions to college facilities and services, he cites ten items receiving the lowest ratings, six of these in order of importance being as follows: (1) assistance from counselors on how-to-study techniques, (2) assistance from teachers on how-to-study techniques, (3) services of the faculty adviser in helping the student select first-term courses, (7) quality of counseling assistance given on problems of educational and vocational choice, (8) opportunity for in-formal social contacts with faculty members, and (9) assistance from academic deans on problems related to course work.

In an article devoted to the more efficient use of faculty members in programs of counseling, one educator calls attention to the need for im-proved selection of faculty members, improved working conditions, and more intensive and extensive in-service training.[3] These aspects are among those treated in this chapter. However, the administration of the faculty counseling activity is suggested as a first important considera-tion (see Table 14).

ADMINISTRATIVE PROBLEMS

A continuing question on a number of campuses is, "How shall the program of faculty advising be organized?" As a number of polls and surveys tend to indicate, the program is most often administered through the office of the dean of students of the institution or by the personnel dean within a given school or college. The integration of faculty advising with the total program of institutional counseling seems to be ensured fairly well in this administrative design.

Divisions of student personnel or areas similarly named should be sensitive to the scathing criticism leveled by their colleagues in the

[2] Robert E. Iffert, *Retention and Withdrawal of College Students*, Bulletin no. 1, Government Printing Office, 1958.

[3] A. Gordon Nelson, "The College Teacher as Counselor," *Educational Forum*, 18:349–357, March, 1954.

academic areas—that of "empire building." If the assignment of the program of faculty counseling to the area of the dean of students is construed to be the undeserved building of a bigger domain, then the administrative planners should take heed. Interesting program organizations are seen as follows:

Some institutions have found it the better part of wisdom to meet the personal and academic needs of students through the designation of more than one counselor for each student. At San Francisco State College, for instance, there are these special designations for faculty advisers: (1) those who advise students in major fields of curricula, (2) minor advisers to advise students electing minor programs, (3) transfer advisers to work with students transferring into the institution who have not yet elected their major fields of work, and (4) general-education advisers who work with students in the lower-division general-education program.

At Central State College (Wilberforce, Ohio), each student has an assembly unit counselor who is concerned with the total development of the student. He has, in addition, an academic adviser who specializes in educational counseling.

At Central Michigan College, the student personnel division maintains an extensive program of counseling which includes (1) group advisers in the division of student personnel whose responsibility it is to help students to think through problems of emotional, social, and vocational nature, (2) curriculum counselors who are members of the faculty giving assistance to students in selecting their program of study, (3) departmental counselors—the department head or persons named by him—who guide students in selecting courses needed for a major or minor, and (4) interdepartmental counselors who aid students who are earning majors or minors in courses selected from two or more departments.

While it is admittedly difficult to classify the problems of students rigidly—academic, vocational, personal-social, emotional—and to allocate the responsibility for counseling in each to a special set of faculty advisers or professional counselors, some institutions have found this the solution for ensuring the best service to the whole student by the whole institution. Country-wide, some great debates have been waged over how much of the responsibility for the welfare of the whole student shall be given to the major area (school, college, or department) in contrast to that given to the area of student personnel. These debates which seek to clarify the issues are profitable. In the last analysis, however, the tailor-made program devised for the particular campus with its particular aims, budgets, facilities, and personalities is an inevitable choice.

THE LAMENT ABOUT LOAD

A primary irritant of the faculty counselor is that concerned with the academic load. The advising job is done without released time and in addition to the regular classroom teaching, committee assignments, research and special study, extension service—all this and heaven, too! Some faculty members contend that they are devoting fifty hours per week to the service of the institution and that the assignment of counseling responsibilities adds another ten or twenty hours. Others, a bit more realistic, will affirm that the counseling of students cannot be assessed on a weekly time basis but rather that there are peak periods and pressure times which unfortunately often occur when faculty advisers are constructing, administering, and correcting examinations or are preparing for a recital, dramatic presentation, or a program off campus.

Directors of counseling and academic deans have attempted in some institutions to assay the work load of the faculty counselor. The results have been generally helpful. The process usually requires that the faculty member look searchingly at his daily or weekly investment of time as it is distributed among activities concerned with preparation for teaching, the classroom presentation, the paper correction, the committee service, and other assigned duties. Faculty committees at work on such a survey recognize that there is a differential of time investment in such departments as art, music, drama, and athletics, as contrasted with such other departments as English, history, chemistry, and business administration. Frequently, as a result of studies of this type, faculty investigators of teaching load have noted that the competent teacher will successfully accomplish many things, including student advisement, whereas the less competent teacher will lag behind in over-all output, the difference being the way in which Teacher Able utilizes time available to him and how he organizes for his several responsibilities and dispatches them.

The matter of releasing time for counseling by reducing the adviser's teaching load or curtailing extension or field activities poses some problems for administrators. If each of twenty faculty members is to be released from three hours of instruction in order to counsel, then four or five other faculty members must "take up the slack." Administrators declare that this is virtually impossible in times when budgets are strained and faculty members hard to find.

Several institutions have tried to make allowances for the counseling assignment and to release time for it. At Bradley University, sixteen freshman advisers assigned fifty counselees each are freed of two periods of instruction a week. At New Jersey State Teachers College, a counseling hour is a scheduled weekly event, and during that hour no classes are conducted. At Stephens College, advising days are designated at several times during the academic year, with classes suspended in order that (1) advisers and students meet in conference and (2) advisers have adequate time to write the letters to parents which are required.

In the last-named institution, prospective faculty members are told at the time of hiring that student advisement will be a part of their service to the college. Likewise, at DePauw University, new faculty members understand when they are employed that some student advisory service will be expected of them. This anticipation of the counseling responsibility does much to stabilize the faculty member who is later handed the counseling folders of twenty-five new students or is summoned to a counseling seminar or an in-service training session.

Another aspect of load has to do with the number of advisees assigned to the faculty adviser. The figure of twelve to fifteen counselees is often cited as the optimum in load, but, in more instances than not, the actual number of counselees assigned to an adviser exceeds twenty-five. When the numbers mount, the faculty member, caught in the pressures of time, may limit his function to that of "telling the student what to take each semester." If, for this reason, the process of advisement reduces itself to assembly-line treatment of students, then a lower limit on numbers per counselor is certainly to be desired.

Again, the number of advisees which can be capably handled may be an individual matter, for some faculty advisers seem to do as well with twenty-five students as with fifteen. It is difficult to assay the working relationship between a counselor and a counselee, but it is reasonable to believe that better rapport is effected when adequate time is available for doing the job.

With the problems of students varying in kind and degree, administrators find it difficult to effect the best assignment in number of students for each adviser. Anticipation of student problems is not always possible, for background information consisting of principal's comment, high school grades, and autobiographical sketches does not always delineate the magnitude of a new student's problem. The plight of one homesick, poorly adjusted, under-achieving freshman may consume the same amount of time as that taken by five reasonably well-adjusted and adequately achieving students.

The system of assigning students to faculty advisers deserves consideration, for a wide range of practice exists on this score. At Stephens College, for instance, some ten items are taken into account:

1. The faculty adviser's characteristics as a person, his field interest, teaching load, extraclass load, experience in counseling, and sometimes his own expressed wishes and preferences

2. The number of advisees and advisers in the total program

3. The preferences of students with respect to advisers

4. The specialty area of the student

5. The adjustment problem of the student

6. The assignment of students from abroad to advisers having some knowledge of that culture

7. The variation in assignment of "types" of students to one adviser

8. The preference of the admissions counselor

9. The general congeniality of adviser-advisee: their home towns, acquaintanceship of members of their families, age and sex of the adviser

10. The comprehensiveness of the student's needs rather than the vocational interest alone

Grinnell College reports having tried assigning students to faculty counselors on the basis of ability—superior students in one group, students with academic problems in another, students with similar academic interests in still another. This system was discontinued, however, in favor of a more recent plan which consists of assigning students to an adviser in such a manner as to ensure heterogeneity of groups.

In the College of Letters and Science of the University of Wisconsin, the method used is that of assigning the freshman to an adviser who is one of his teachers during the first semester. The assumption is that the relationship thus established will continue for the remainder of the freshman-sophomore years. This arrangement imposes the necessity of switching advisers after classes begin, since there is no way of knowing in advance of the opening of school which teachers will have which freshmen. The program planners feel that this difficulty could be remedied if the students could indicate at the time of admission (1) the subjects they are likely to take and (2) the subject field in which the adviser is preferred. It would then be possible to assign a large number of students to advisers during registration week. Finally, there is the continuing problem of the limited number of full-time faculty members who teach first-semester freshmen classes and to whom a growing number of incoming freshmen are assigned.

Another aspect of grouping can be seen in the plan of Mount Holyoke College wherein each adviser is given a group of freshmen all of whom are in the same residence hall. The academic adviser is thus enabled to maintain close contact with the head of the residence hall and the student government officers in the hall, keeping informed about the non-academic life of advisees.

The privilege of selecting his own adviser is extended to the student in several institutions. At both Carleton College and Walla Walla College, at the beginning of each year the student is given a list of faculty members who serve as counselors. The student is requested to choose three persons in first-, second-, and third-order preference. At Carleton College it is specified that at least two of the three be his present instructors. In both instances, Carleton and Walla Walla, it is noted that the student will be given his first choice unless that adviser has a full quota of advisees by the time the preference sheet is submitted.

At East Texas State Teachers College, assignment of students to a faculty counselor on the basis of departmental and curricular interests was ruled out since student curricular interests could not be accurately determined in advance in time for assignment. Departmental assignment, it was felt, put an undeserved premium on the immediate choice of major for some students. The system adopted was that of *arbitrary assignment* of students to faculty counselors, which facilitated the cutting across of departmental lines and aided in the assignment of students with no definite educational and occupational choices.

A "best" method for all institutions to use in matching counselor and counselee probably defies description. The "best" would need to fulfill local requirements—preferences of certain academic areas, availability of certain faculty members for counseling, time available for conferences prior to registration, and information available for the use of counselors at the time of initial conferences. It would be advisable for institutions to study the frequency of change of major on the part of students in the freshman and sophomore years if assignment by major preference is followed. Certainly, it would be advisable for the program of counseling to be so organized that "recruitment" of majors by certain academic areas would be minimized.

THE AVALANCHE OF PAPER WORK

The feeling about student advising as an added burden of responsibility arises, too, from what the adviser must do in addition to conferring with the student. Frequently, the requirements of the job in terms of record keeping and reporting are not anticipated. The faculty member is deep in the heart of the counseling activity when he feels the press of clerical duties. As can be expected, the paper-work requirements vary among institutions, depending upon the degree of formalization of the program.

In some institutions, no item other than the student's schedule of classes is required, and this is frequently dispatched in the student's own handwriting with the adviser merely affixing his signature. In other institutions, narrative reports are required for the permanent files or for the uses of academic or personnel deans, the registrar, and the central counseling office.

At the University of Bridgeport, the faculty adviser submits to the office of student personnel a comprehensive report at the end of the semester. Included in the report are a description of the advisee; comments about the adviser-advisee relationship; notes about the student's scholastic, personal, and social adjustment; and general remarks and recommendations. (See App. N for the interview report form used in the Grinnell College program of faculty advising.)

At Lindenwood College, reports of all counseling conferences are made in triplicate, one copy being sent to the guidance office, another to the dean, and the third being retained by the faculty counselor. These reports constitute a running record of the efficacy of the program and provide for continuity in the guidance of the student. Eight reportings are made during the year, at times of schedule making and registration as well as at intervals when grades are released.

At Wheaton College, four reports are submitted by faculty counselors, the first at the end of the first four weeks of school, and the second at the conclusion of the seventh week. A third report is submitted at the end of the semester, and the fourth is effected after an interview with the student in the thirteenth week. The reports cover the student's attitudes; life purpose; grades and ability; time schedule; problems of family, social, spiritual, and emotional nature; financial needs; academic load; and selection of major.

Some institutions, "feeling the feelings" of faculty advisers concerning the paper-work expectations, have contributed ways and means of assistance. At San Francisco State College, stenographic service and dictating machines are provided by the student personnel office for faculty advisers in order that they may dictate notes concerning their advisees.

The office of student personnel and guidance of East Texas State Teachers College addresses all envelopes sent by faculty advisers asking students to report. In addition, this office prepares the notice, leaving sufficient space for counselors to fill in the salutation, hour and day of scheduled appointment, and other comments.

At Southern Methodist University, a central secretarial service is provided for the assistance of advisers in communicating with students and in preparing records and reports. Instances of the kind cited are few, however, with the more usual practice being that of the faculty advisers writing the reports somewhat laboriously in longhand when part-time help from a departmental secretary or student assistant is not forthcoming.

If assistance for dispatching the adviser's paper work is lacking, it may be compensated for to some degree by materials provided for doing better counseling. At the University of Connecticut, the academic counselor is furnished with an IBM student test record which assists him in determining the quality of work done by the student in high school and his expected performance in college as evidenced by reading scores, scores in English usage, and other areas.

At Allegheny College the following things are furnished to the faculty adviser:

1. Background information sent by the freshman to the college during the summer, together with a letter to his adviser which discusses tentative goals

2. Profile of inventory test scores

3. Reading profile

4. Aids for interpretation of the freshmen inventory tests

5. Digest of test results

6. Application for major field and adviser-change slip

7. Departmental load chart

8. Cover sheet explaining the system followed by the deans' committee for collecting advisers' and teachers' reports on students in academic difficulty

9. Individual report sheets for students in academic difficulty

10. Student self-appraisal in the objectives of general education

(See App. E-3 for data sheet used at University of Rhode Island.)

Perhaps no institution has achieved the millennium in providing faculty advisers with all the information which is needed by them for doing the job of advisement. More could probably be done in every institution, but the question would be, "Who would do it?" And those who are designated to provide the materials frequently ask the attendant question, "How well are these materials being used?" The answer to this lies in the systematized evaluation of the work of individual faculty advisers, and more, much more, needs to be done in this area, as a later section of this chapter affirms. On the matter of more help for advisers, this can be said: With academic administrative offices generally overtaxed, with secretarial pools nonexistent in most institutions, and with limited budgetary allotments for printing and mimeographing, the prospect of more help for advising personnel is dim.

ADVISING STUDENTS IN GROUPS OR INDIVIDUALLY

With the number of advisees assigned to an adviser remaining large and with the prospect of increased assistance to advisers not too bright, some institutions approve the group method for advisement of students. Not only does the group method allow for a saving of time in coverage of certain required information but it also makes possible desirable types of interaction between and among advisees and adviser.

At Colgate University, for instance, groups of students frequently meet with the preceptors for the evening meal and then adjourn to one of the lounges in the Student Union for a discussion period. In East Texas State Teachers College, faculty counselors meet new students in group arrangement five times in the first two days of the orientation period. These group meetings precede the individual conferences which are devoted to program planning.

At the College for Teachers in Buffalo, group sessions are held each semester for purposes of discussing current college issues and encouraging group thinking and exploration. Although the agenda for these sessions is suggested by the office of the dean of students, the junior counselor and the faculty adviser may develop their own program in terms of group interests and needs.

Inaugurated at the University of Bridgeport is a plan for weekly meetings which are held with freshmen advisees at the beginning of each semester and which follow the principles of group guidance as distinguished from classroom instruction. In this university, advisees assume considerable responsibility for organizing and conducting the meetings by preparing questions, making reports to the group, and inviting guest speakers, both faculty and upperclassmen.

Franklin and Marshall College sponsors a plan whereby students are divided alphabetically into thirteen groups, each under the supervision of a faculty group leader who is adviser for the freshmen in his group. The groups meet twice a week for one hour at a time when no regular classes are scheduled, attendance being compulsory. Discussions have centered around fraternities, study habits, student activities, college regulations, guidance, history of the college, placement and part-time jobs, athletics, selective service information, and boy-girl relations. Invited to serve as group observers and assistants to the faculty group leaders are upperclass students preparing for the ministry or for teaching, social work, and psychology.

The foregoing review covers a representative sample of advisement through group arrangement which colleges and universities have found useful. It is conceivable that a great deal more will be attempted by program directors to effect group advisement of students within a given major area. A dean of a school of business administration, for instance, has proposed that the initial conference for the purpose of working out a schedule of course work be a group activity, with "counseling" to follow during the year as individual problems arise. That the nature of the schedule-making conference is more "group" than "individual" is a belief held by more than one academician. The proof of the individual's particular need in such an initial contact with the faculty adviser must then be demonstrated. Other group activities of an orientation nature offered as courses, credit or noncredit, and designed to orient the student to his new environment are discussed in Chapter 12.

A slightly different accent on group activities is seen in the socialization of student and adviser. At Wisconsin State College at Oshkosh, a group meeting of students with faculty counselors is held on the first day of freshmen orientation. It is scheduled for mid-afternoon, and the counselor may serve light refreshments for the group. At the College of Wooster, a counselor's tea is sponsored at the opening of school, the informal event being held in the evening at the counselor's home or at a place selected by him or her. At Randolph-Macon College, advisers are encouraged to entertain their advisees in their homes during the year.

During the first week of the fall session, East Texas State Teachers College underwrites a freshman supper with the counselor group, which is held in the college cafeteria. Freshmen who are married may bring their husbands or wives. An evening program of games follows the supper, with the counselor free to participate or not, as he chooses, in the game period.

At Florida State University, the faculty adviser and new students are scheduled to meet as a group in a two-and-a-half-hour period, one portion of which includes a noon box lunch. The student pays fifty cents for the box lunch which is prepared by a catering service and is distributed from two central campus locations.

While it is recognized that the group handling of advisees cannot take the place of the individual interview, it is possible to fulfill some aims and objectives of the program of advisement through the group method. Wider experimentation with these plans deserves to be done in most colleges and universities.

Notwithstanding the well-intentioned efforts of the faculty adviser, there are those students who choose to remain out of contact with their adviser, thus complicating the work he is required to perform. On campuses where the enrollment is large, the contact of adviser and advisee infrequent, the distance between the adviser's office and the student's residence hall great, there is need for attention to be given to "bringing in the students." Some advisers prefer having advisees enrolled in their classes, this making it possible for adviser and student to get in touch somewhat more easily.

In the introductory pages of the *Manual for Counselors* of Carleton College appear these remarks: [4]

Our idealist's bias is evident in even so small a matter as that of sending notes to our advisees suggesting that they come for a conference; we rebel against sending the notes because we feel that they *ought* not to be necessary. But necessary they are, nonetheless. Students ought not to be lazy and indifferent, but some are. They ought not to be shy, but some are so hesitant that not even a charm school graduate cum laude could persuade them, in one try, that they should accept willingly the hand that is extended to them. When

[4] *Manual for Counselors*, prepared by the North Central Study Committee on Liberal Arts Education of Carleton College, 1950, p. 2.

such a student does not come of his own accord, the perfectionist counselor can come to two conclusions—both wrong: (1) He can conclude that the student who is not intelligent enough to come for help of his own accord does not deserve help; that he probably would not profit by it if he received it; or (2) he can conclude that he himself has failed as a counselor because he was unable to impress the student on first meeting with his friendliness and with his desire to be of assistance. Yet for the counselor to have to send a note renewing his offer of assistance is not a confession of failure—no more than the second invitation to a guest to remain a little longer is a confession that one has failed as a host.

At East Texas State Teachers College, the counselor is asked to write a note informing the counselee that the unkept appointment should be rescheduled. If the student does not appear for the second appointment, the counselor informs the office of student personnel and guidance, setting the time and place for a third meeting. The office of student personnel sends the letter which designates this meeting. After the appointment hour for this meeting has passed, the faculty counselor notifies the student personnel office regarding its outcome.

Few advisers would contend that the failure on the part of the student to answer the summons for a conference is an evidence of growing self-reliance. More would affirm that the breaking of appointments or the failure to make them when they are really needed is an evidence of the student's continuing immaturity. More often than not, the student who neglects answering the request of his counselor for a conference at a crucial time is the same "johnny-come-lately" who will stand in line weeks later expecting more than his due share of attention. Somehow and in some way, say the irritated faculty advisers, this student needs to learn the lesson that those who come too late may receive too little.

SPACE FOR ADVISING ACTIVITIES

Although only a small amount of space is devoted herein to this irritant, it deserves much more consideration. In all too many institutions, the program of counseling has been installed without benefit of adequate housing. A common sight in some institutions is that of six or more faculty members counseling with all stops open in a room of surprisingly small proportions, with no privacy of interview being possible.

A sizable number of offices are secreted away in remote parts of the campus which defy location by word or by diagram. "Obstacle courses," seemingly devised to keep students from finding their faculty adviser, handicap the program. While a faculty counseling service may begin with humble housing, it is obvious that the morale of faculty members is seriously affected when no improvement is made after a year or two.

A convenient location for faculty counselors, with space provided for files, and a telephone to facilitate the coordination of each student's problems are minimum essentials.

FOR HOW LONG SHOULD ADVISING CONTINUE?

Much of the literature concerning the advisement of students deals chiefly with the freshman. Some institutions are hopeful that, once the freshman has survived the onslaught of the first-year "plagues," his second, third, and fourth years will come and go without misfortune. But even the most cursory study will show that the student in his second year is considerably perplexed about course selection, course achievement, the decisions about a major and minor, and so on. Most institutions recognize the fact that some kind of faculty advisement is necessary even after the first year. A variety of practice exists within institutions concerning the provisions made for upper-class advisement, four examples being cited as follows:

TRANSYLVANIA COLLEGE: After the freshman has been in residence for two quarters, the freshman adviser will call in his advisees to determine if each is ready to choose a permanent adviser who will work with him in the remaining three years. The student may choose any person who does not at the moment have a full load of advisees. Care is exerted not to persuade the student away from or toward a particular faculty member as well as to impress upon him the permanency of his choice.

ARIZONA STATE COLLEGE: After the freshman year, advisement will not be compulsory nor will students be required to have approved programs of studies signed by their advisers. Every effort will be made, however, to continue adviser-advisee relationships throughout the four years. If the proper relationships have been set up, students who need help should feel free to go to their advisers for help.

COLUMBIA COLLEGE: Although a student normally stays with the same faculty adviser throughout his four college years, the need for specialized guidance arises in the junior and senior years, which are designated as the Upper College. For this purpose, a number of Upper College consultants have been named—men who are available to students for consultation regarding their elective studies in the upper years. The departmental representatives who are heads of the various departments of instruction in the college are also available for counseling service.

STATE TEACHERS COLLEGE, NEWARK: Each student, upon entrance, is assigned to a faculty member who serves as his adviser for the four years of college. Approximately five freshmen are assigned to the counselor each year. Thus each counselor has, within his counseling group, students on all four class levels, with a total of about twenty students. Counseling groups have several social experiences which include parties, trips to the theater, picnics, and the like. One hour a week is set aside for group meetings and counseling interviews, with no classes scheduled in the entire college during that hour.

The most optimistic faculty members hold out hope that the maturation of the student will be accomplished in a single year and that the salvo of counseling—loud in the beginning—will become only an echo at the end of the student's college life. It is probably true that the best programs of counseling make provision for (1) the student who reaches maturity early and has only occasional and temporary upsets, (2) the student who reaches maturity later, much later, and has frequent complications all along the way, and (3) the students—and their name is legion—who range all along the continuum and about whom a judgment concerning "from here to maturity" is most difficult to make.

It is increasingly evident that some graduate students, young in years, with little or no work experience, struggling with deep emotional problems, need counseling. Studies like that of Strang [5] point to these areas of real need for the graduate student.

HOW FAR SHOULD FACULTY COUNSELING GO?

A program of faculty advisement becomes concerned at some time or another with the question, "How far should the faculty adviser go in counseling students on personal problems?" The answer is not always to be found by reading job descriptions of counseling personnel nor by scanning the organizational chart of an institution. While the area of personal-social adjustment is oftentimes designated as the responsibility of administrative officers—dean of students, dean of men, dean of women, and professional counselors in the counseling center—problems of a personal nature, nonetheless, are carried to faculty counselors by troubled counselees. One investigator sums the problem up ably: [6]

In every college there are a number of students whose academic success is enhanced rather than hindered by aspects of their personality which seem likely to result in great ultimate unhappiness. There are students who use preoccupation with abstract theoretical material to distract themselves from personal and social inadequacies. There are students who seek academic distinction in order to flaunt it in defiance of a culture which they believe to disparage it. There are students who are convinced that they can only be valued because of their scholastic achievements, and who are ceaselessly driven to seek grades

[5] Ruth Strang, "Personnel Services for Graduate Students in Education," in *Graduate Study in Education*, Fiftieth Yearbook of the National Society for the Study of Education, University of Chicago Press, Chicago, 1951, pp. 83–113.

[6] Edgar Z. Friedenberg, "The Measurement of Student Conceptions of the Role of a College Advisory System," *Educational and Psychological Measurement*, 10:548, pt. II, autumn, 1950.

as copper tokens to exchange for affection at a very unfavorable rate. What is the responsibility of the adviser for the welfare of such students? If he can recognize them, should he seek to initiate personality changes which will probably make the student's academic record less spectacular, even if they also result in happiness and ultimately greater productivity and creativeness?

Contending that the answer to such questions depends upon a complex hierarchy of values, the investigator proceeded to develop an instrument which would measure four things relating to the college advisory system of the University of Chicago, as follows:

1. Student opinion of the *scope* desirable in the advisory system

2. Student information about the *system* as it actually exists, to permit an estimate of the degree to which criticism and opinion might be regarded as informed

3. Student evaluation of the *effectiveness* of the system in solving certain problems which it recognized as possible sources of weakness in itself

4. An indication of the kind of *role* with respect to themselves which students believe an adviser should play in assisting in the solution of certain complex problems

The instrument as constructed consisted of a group of five batteries of objective questions, with space provided for additional focused written comment by students. The instrument required something under two hours for students to complete. Summarizing the completed study, Friedenberg writes: [7]

If the results obtained by applying the instrument described at the University of Chicago are representative, then it seems that, while students feel that they need warmth and understanding and that the university is obligated to provide help with personal problems, they are not likely to misuse or overburden the source of such help. They will, in general, take as much as can be given of what they need. The more psychological insight which the advisers in a system possess, and the more clearly the system defines its scope to include service with personal problems, the more students will expect of it and use it. Some, however, will become frightened and hostile, and most expect enough initiative to be left to them to permit them to feel respected rather than manipulated.

The findings as stated apply to the College of the University of Chicago and the particular student therein enrolled. Student expectations of faculty counseling in other institutions probably cannot be "guessed at"; instead they merit a similar investigation. Once the expectation of students is determined, the responsibility remains for studying the expectation of faculty counselors of their role. The selection of faculty members to do the job expected of them and the adequate in-service

[7] *Ibid.*

training of those selected follow. No director of faculty counseling or committee charged with its direction can vouchsafe the function of the adviser without study and investigation.

WHAT IS FACULTY COUNSELING WORTH?

It goes without saying that those who invest in an enterprise are vitally concerned with the outcome. A college or university, having invested in a system of faculty advisement, seeks to determine what the investment, made in time, energy, and money, is producing. Necessary for the ongoing program of faculty counseling is a plan of systematic evaluation relating to the organization of faculty counseling, the procedures used in counseling, and the coordination of faculty counseling with the total institutional program. Necessary as well is the appraisal of the performance of the individual faculty member—his or her effectiveness as a counselor.

All too many programs of counseling can be chronicled as most folklore: "Once upon a time there were some faculty members who were told they would counsel students the next fall. So the next fall they counseled students. After that, they were told they would counsel students the following fall. And they did. (The monotony of repetition without constructive change goes on for a series of falls.) After a while nobody even reminded them that they would counsel the next fall. They just did it." Therein lies the clue as to why the programs of faculty counseling, beginning with faltering faculty flutists, end with the same or increased falterings. Not many institutions, it appears, have devised means for doing more than designating counselors.

Evaluation of programs is a time-consuming activity demanding the energies, creative and purely slavish, of the program director and persons serving on various committees. In addition, thorough evaluation is costly in materials. In lieu of systematic evaluations, too often the "off-the-cuff" comment of one or another observer or participant is used as the index of worth, and this is usually to program detriment. Commenting on this, one writer suggests: [8]

Obviously, the busy administrator or teacher-counselor rarely has the time, energy, or money to conduct research. . . . He can employ a method which the writer likes to call the "straws-in-the-wind" approach. It consists of the collection, over a period of time, of data which answer questions such as these: What are the attitudes of students, colleagues, and parents toward a given faculty member's counseling activities? Is there evidence of antagonism, of indifference, or a feeling of respect and confidence? As the counseling program

[8] Nelson, *op. cit.*, pp. 354–355.

has developed over a period of years, has there been a gradual decrease in the number of misfits in various courses? A decrease in the number of drop-outs from college? A gradual increase in the number of students who voluntarily seek conferences with their counselors? The answers to questions such as those suggested will not constitute precise, objective, conclusive indications of the effectiveness or the ineffectiveness of counseling. The data will have to be regarded as incomplete and indirect evidence. . .

Any consideration of worth of program will, at some point, take into account the matter of financial outlay. All too little has been written about the dollars-and-cents investment in the program of faculty advisement. Such questions as these continue to perplex program planners: If the institution is unable to afford a corps of professionally trained counselors to dispatch the functions assigned to faculty advisers, how can it afford the latter functionaries? For the faculty member's assumption of the advisement function, is there no additional financial reimbursement? Is there no released time from teaching given to faculty advisers? If not, is it thought that teaching faculty are not "busy" with their teaching, committee assignments, and research commitments, that they have ample "time on their hands" in which to counsel and advise students assigned to them? Or is advisement recognized as a legitimate part of the individual's total service in the institution?

If there is additional reimbursement given to faculty advisers, what is the amount of pay and who pays it? If there is released time from teaching, who is employed on what funds to take over the classwork from which these advisers are freed?

Other monetary considerations relate to the materials used in faculty counseling—the counseling folders, the forms used in reporting and in coordinating the counseling activities. There is the cost of clerical help in preparing and distributing the counseling folders, together with the other materials necessary for the advisement of students.

All in all, there is a sizable investment of funds in a program of systematized faculty advising. A clear explanation of from where the "manna from Heaven" comes is eagerly sought by those who are initiating programs. In Chapter 4, the account of the program at the University of Illinois poses interesting possibilities in financing. The program at the University of Iowa described in the same chapter was originally operated under a subsidization plan, with assistance from the liberal arts advisory subsidization fund. This was eliminated in view of the extra bookkeeping needed in allotting additional funds to a department for counseling purposes. At the present time, the separate department takes cognizance of the advisory load of the faculty member when teaching schedules are prepared.

Occasionally the matter of comparative cost studies comes up for discussion in professional meetings. It was observed in a recent meeting [9] that students are being trained in counseling supervision in order that the costs of hiring a professional be cut. This trend, if it may be termed one, is discussed somewhat more in detail in Chapter 14. In Chapter 18, the question is posed in view of the difficulty in obtaining teachers *to teach*, as well as to assume advisory responsibilities. The advisory function would need to be made exceedingly attractive to secure the numbers of faculty advisers needed in the face of rising enrollment figures!

Some years ago, Bergstresser [10] made the following proposal which to date has been implemented all too little, in so far as the author can determine:

...I would recommend (1) that those selected as faculty counselors be relieved of from one-quarter to one-half of their teaching loads; (2) that their pay for the counseling part of their work be a stipulated amount paid from a special budget set up to cover the cost of this counseling, and (3) that faculty and administrative sanction be given, publicly and in definite terms, to the policy of recognizing excellent service in counseling on a par with excellence in teaching and research in granting salary increases and promotion in rank. If faculty counseling is as important as everyone, even presidents, say it is, why not find out what it costs to do a good job by proper cost accounting and budgeting? And why not claim for successful counseling the same material rewards of good pay and increased status that are given for successful teaching and research?

Chapter 17 of this book deals with ongoing studies which need to be made of aspects of institution-wide counseling, including faculty advisement. Worthy of consideration at this point are these suggestions:

1. Colleges or universities engaged in a program of institutional self-survey need to study the program of counseling in relation to the educational philosophy of the institution. The effectiveness of the program of faculty advisement should therefore be viewed by appropriate committees numbering administrators, teaching faculty, and personnel workers.

2. Institutions with graduate programs have the opportunity of attracting advanced students who are willing to participate in projects evaluating the program of faculty counseling or advisement. (See Atherton study, App. T.)

3. Any evaluation of the program of faculty counseling should be

[9] John P. Gwin, Katherine Warren, and others, "Cost Studies Applicable to Student Personnel Functions," *Personnel-O-Gram*, 11:38–39, June, 1957.

[10] John L. Bergstresser, "Issues in Faculty Counseling," in E. G. Williamson (ed.), *Trends in Student Personnel Work*, University of Minnesota Press, Minneapolis, 1949, p. 318.

made from a number of points of view: appraisal of the program (*a*) by the counselee, (*b*) by the faculty adviser, (*c*) by the parents of the student, (*d*) by administrators within the institution, (*e*) by colleagues in counseling—residence-hall personnel, clinicians in special areas—and (*f*) other observers on or off campus.

4. Not only is this proof of the worth of the program of faculty counseling sought by administrators within the institution but also by parents, legislators, and governing boards. This comment of a board member deserves attention:

> We are somewhat wary of much of the counseling that is being done in many institutions. We believe that it is a form of busy work that gives an outlet for the energies of a larger staff without comparatively greater service to students. We could hire a dozen persons who would be buzzing around like dervishes getting information that is none of their business and making decisions that should be made by the students themselves. It seems to us that, by the time a student has reached college age, he should be capable of walking alone to a considerable extent and that overzealous counseling should be kept at a minimum.

SUMMARY

Defense for current counseling practice which requires time and energy of faculty members can be rallied when convincing answers to these questions are found: What is the program worth? Is faculty counseling largely busy work? Does it eventuate in relatively little service to students? Do faculty counselors make decisions for students? To what degree does faculty counseling "disable" the student? What is the minimum to which faculty counseling should be kept? What are the evidences of overzealous, inquisitive, incapacitating faculty counseling on campus?

Chapter 7 reports the ideas of faculty advisers who discuss as members of a panel their conception of assistance to the student with reference to decision making. Counseling or advisement which incapacitates the student deserves to be "outlawed" in the legitimate business of advisement. Counseling which contributes to the individual's growing self-reliance is the admitted true objective.

CHAPTER 7 *Decision Making in Faculty Advising*

The suggestion in the foregoing chapter of the existence on college and university campuses of "a dozen persons buzzing around like dervishes ...making decisions that should be made by the students" is likely to be more fiction than fact. The faculty flutist resembles little, if at all, the fabled Pied Piper heading a procession of the young in heart who regard him and his pipings as infallible.

In an effort to depict the faculty adviser as one who assists students in making decisions (as contrasted with one who dictates a decision which the student will follow unquestioningly), five faculty advisers presented the following panel in a Fall Seminar for Educational Counselors. The seminar was presented as an in-service training activity for the 150 faculty advisers and was attended by a sizable number of academic deans, department heads, and residence, vocational, and other specialized counselors (see App. F-3). Participants on the panel were as follows:

Miss Audrey Atherton, Coordinator of Upperclass Counseling, School of Education

Miss Inez Frink, Faculty Adviser, School of Business

Mr. Dean Johnson, Faculty Adviser, School of Social Work, and Director, Human Relations Institute

Dr. Vincent Thursby, Faculty Adviser, Department of Political Science, College of Arts and Sciences

Mr. George Spencer, Assistant to the Coordinator of Counseling, Department of Psychology

Chairman, Coordinator of Counseling

CHAIRMAN: [Opening remarks to the seminar.] It is a healthy sign when faculty advisers question their role in the total educational process. Preliminary to this meeting, several new counselors asked if the program might include some suggestions on the matter of decision making, that is, the responsibility of counselors for furthering decisions of students.

Now, our office can do, reasonably well, a job of organizing and assembling

124

counseling materials, aids, and informative notes—packaging them up for you. But we are not able to prescribe just what you ought to do in every interview. We cannot know the particular counseling situation; we cannot anticipate all the variables; we cannot predict the kinds of intrapersonal relationships which develop in the counseling process. These things are known and understood best by you, the faculty adviser.

There are, however, some general observations which can be made on the matter of the counseling relationship. These faculty advisers on the panel will make such observations, recognizing this definition of *counseling:* [1]

Counseling is a personal and dynamic relationship between two people who approach a mutually defined problem with mutual consideration for each other to the end that the younger, or more troubled, of the two is aided to a self-determined resolution of his problem.

These five faculty advisers have agreed to discuss some of their points of view about the following: (1) the personal and dynamic relationship, (2) the mutually defined problem, and (3) the self-determined resolution. We hope to cover these problem areas of our students:

1. The decision regarding choice of major or field specialization
2. The decision regarding choice of subjects
3. The decisions relating to ways for improving an unsatisfactory grade

This year we communicated with parents of enrolling new students. In your counseling folders you may find a letter which the parent has written in answer to our request for information.

One of the first letters to reach my desk came from a parent who expressed himself as follows:

We feel Jerry should take up engineering, for in his youth, and even now, he takes great pride in building things such as model planes. He can fix almost any gadget and loves to work with his hands and do blueprint reading. We hope and pray you will impress on him that he should take engineering.

Upon reading the letter from the parent, I checked the student's educational aims as he stated them in part III of the application form. I was interested to find that Jerry had listed not *engineering* but *marketing* and *retailing* as his interest. This poses a problem for the faculty counselor. In fact, one of the advisers on this panel will have Jerry as his counselee this fall.

CHAIRMAN: [To panel.] Inez, assuming that Jerry is your counselee, what will you attempt to do in the initial interview? May we assume that Jerry tells you that he has *both* engineering and marketing as interests?

MISS FRINK: [The adviser gives information about a study plan and work experience.] Since Jerry is undecided as to whether he should study engineering or marketing, I would explain to him something of the actual course work required in each field so that he might have a better understanding of the preparation each would involve. Then, too, since quite a few students do not seem to have a clear conception of the work leading to certain areas of specialization, I would try to give him information about the actual work he would be doing in each field. This

---

[1] C. Gilbert Wrenn, "Counseling with Students," in *Guidance in Educational Institutions,* Thirty-seventh Yearbook of the National Society for the Study of Education, Public School Publishing Company, Bloomington, Ill., 1938, part I, p. 121.

would perhaps further clarify his thinking along the line of a choice of a major.

MISS ATHERTON: [The adviser considers the emotional aspects of the problem.] Inez has pointed out one important aspect of counseling—the information-giving phase, which calls for a discussion of job opportunities, requirements for the job, and remuneration. However, there is another angle which is also important. It is the emotional, or feeling, aspect. We need to consider how Jerry would *feel* about dissension in the family if his mother and father were upset about his following a vocation which was not their choice. I should think that we might encourage Jerry to talk about alternatives. Our question might be, "Would you be able to study effectively if you knew your family was opposed to what you were doing?"

CHAIRMAN: What might you suggest on this, Vince?

MR. THURSBY: It occurs to me that Jerry might advantageously postpone his vocational decision. Do you agree?

CHAIRMAN: By postponement, would you mean for the student to stop thinking about the choice of major for now?

MR. THURSBY: [The adviser suggests exploration of several fields.] No, I do not mean that he should be inactive. Rather I think that he might advantageously hold his decision in abeyance, taking some exploratory course work, scheduling his general-education course work, and consulting the counseling office to ascertain his aptitudes and interests. After all, his parents might be correct in their assessment of his potentialities. At any rate, pursuance of such a course of exploratory action would do justice both to his and his parents' wishes.

MISS ATHERTON: [The adviser refers the student to others who can assist.] That's good, Vince, because it shows another function of the faculty counselor —that of serving as a referral agent. It stresses the importance of the adviser's familiarizing himself with other student personnel services on the campus. The adviser becomes "a little coordinator" who keeps all information about a student in one central place. As the student visits various offices and talks with other staff members in student personnel, he reports to his faculty adviser who then aids him in thinking through the referral.

CHAIRMAN: So far, you've been very convincing about the matter of your relationship with the student, but remember that this parent is actually *praying* for you to direct the boy into engineering. Dean, as faculty adviser, haven't you some obligation to this parent who puts his trust in you to this degree?

MR. JOHNSON: [The adviser "feels the feeling" of parents.] I think this: We cannot forget our dual responsibility to the student and to the parent. In this case, the faculty counselor is aware that the parent has certain wishes with regard to the future vocation of his son. The counselor will do well to keep in mind the fact that the parent has written a letter urging the counselor to guide his son into engineering. However, the counselor is not dealing directly with the parent. *He is dealing directly with the student and must, therefore, help the student as best he can.* In this instance, it seems to me that what is most needed is some clarification of the student's own wishes. After all, in the final analysis, our goals and the goals of the parents are probably the same for the student. Most parents are vitally concerned about the welfare and happiness of their children.

[The adviser assists the student in gaining insight into the problem.] I remember one instance in which the student came to her faculty adviser saying that she would have to major in music because her mother wanted her to do so. She knew that her mother had always wanted to be a concert pianist but never achieved this ambition. It was necessary to help the girl clarify her own wishes. The daughter really wanted to major in home economics and was looking forward to a career as a housewife rather than as a concert pianist. The mother wanted, basically, to see her daughter happy, doing what she really wanted to do. Consequently, the mother accepted the wish of her daughter as to her real choice of vocation and major.

[The adviser regards as paramount the integrity of the student.] I know that this solution might not work out so happily in all cases, but I am convinced that parents are basically concerned about the happiness and welfare of the child. So I think, probably, the dual responsibility of the faculty adviser to student and parent is not a divided responsibility. I should like to point out also that, in our counseling, the student who is before us at the moment is the *most important individual.* Our work must be carried on within the framework of this close relationship.

CHAIRMAN: What the members of this panel have said so far assumes that our new freshman, Jerry, admits in the first interview that he has two conflicting vocational-educational goals. What if Jerry told you, Inez, that he wanted *marketing,* not mentioning the parent's preference for him?

MISS FRINK: [The adviser provides an "atmosphere" of permissiveness.] I have found, usually, if a student is given a chance to talk quite freely that a difference of opinion or conflict of goals reveals itself during the conversation, perhaps not so much in actual words as by an attitude pointing toward a difference.

MR. SPENCER: I need to remind you that many students will not have letters from parents in their counseling folders. There will be a number of students whose parents have not written us. Even without the letter, the parent and the student may be in conflict as to the student's major interest. Perhaps this requires that faculty counselors should do considerable listening in order to give the student an opportunity to bring into the light factors which might be overlooked.

CHAIRMAN: Would you, as adviser, indicate to Jerry that you had received a letter from his father?

MISS ATHERTON: Since the letter to parents was part of a general plan for all freshmen, it might be advisable to mention to Jerry the receipt of the letter. The counselor would avoid commenting on the parent's choice of vocational goals. This would give the student free rein to state or to avoid mentioning any conflict involving him and his parents. In this permissive atmosphere, perhaps the whole problem could be brought into the open.

CHAIRMAN: That's true. Now, if Jerry brushed aside his father's idea of engineering as not interesting to him and went on pursuing the idea of the marketing major, would you feel that you should represent the parent in the conference, Vincent?

MR. THURSBY: I concur with Dean in his idea that we faculty counselors have a threefold responsibility: to the student, to his parents, and to the university. Yet, in a real sense, we operate in place of the parents, and in representing them, we should recall that it is the student who will have to lead his life and make his own decisions.

CHAIRMAN: Well, Vince, would you feel it your duty to write the father in order to explain why you cannot promote his wish?

MR. THURSBY: I just don't know.

CHAIRMAN: Perhaps the counseling office having access to information from a number of counseling sources could cooperate with faculty advisers in corresponding with parents on points such as this.

Now, suppose that Jerry puts the question of his vocational choice directly to you, saying, "What do you think I should prepare for, Miss Atherton?" What would be your rejoinder?

MISS ATHERTON: [The adviser makes use of objective data in aiding the student in his self-analysis.] This is rather a touchy situation, for I see two aspects. The counselor may make Jerry feel that he is avoiding his question and that he has no interest in Jerry's choice. On the other hand, there is real danger in giving Jerry an opinion—danger that he will accept it as "the law." Perhaps this is the time for the counselor to introduce into the conference the subject of Jerry's grades in high school and his achievement in course work. By throwing the decision back to Jerry and encouraging him to analyze his own abilities in terms of what he has achieved in school, wherein he is weak or strong, Jerry may be motivated to think through the solution for himself.

CHAIRMAN: Dean, what do you think? What is the frame of mind of the young modern? Is he so used to being told what to do that he considers it a weakness of the faculty counselor *not* to decide for him?

MR. JOHNSON: [The adviser aids the student in taking responsibility for his decision.] It may be that some students will consider the counselor's reluctance about making decisions for him as a weakness on the counselor's part, but I think the majority of college freshmen are struggling with the matter of dependence versus independence. They want to decide for themselves. They need to be mature in order to do this well. At the same time, they probably wish to be somewhat dependent. They demonstrate an ambivalence in their desires. Moreover, many of them are not quite certain as to how dependent they *can* be. They may think that the counselor is supposed to make decisions for them. In the event a counselee asks us directly what we think he should do, it would be reasonable for us to say something like, "Well, I have only known you a very short while and I am really not in a position to make an accurate judgment at this point. Suppose we consider it together?"

CHAIRMAN: So you faculty counselors feel that you can give a counselee support on a plan of action without necessarily telling him how and when and what to do?

MISS ATHERTON: [The adviser explains his function as a faculty friend.] Yes. Perhaps in high school Jerry did not have a faculty adviser. There may not have been anyone working in a similar capacity in his school. He might have had a home-room teacher or maybe a dean of boys or girls as do some of our high schools. However, even if this were the case, these teachers or counselors may have taken the point of view that Jerry was an adolescent and should be told what was best for him. His concept of a counselor might be that of a person who is prepared to solve his problems. He may feel his role as student is that of merely asking what he should do. In this event, it may be wise for the faculty counselor to explain to the student what his functions are.

MR. JOHNSON: [The adviser exhibits interest and enters into the dynamic relationship.] This reminds me of a student who, when he first came in to see me, found it extremely difficult to talk because of his hesitation. Going on a hunch, I tried to make the atmosphere as comfortable, casual, and relaxing as possible. For some time we chatted about football—the coming games, some of the players, and about other matters not directly concerned with the student's academic program. At the close of this interview, the student was able to talk without faltering. Apparently this young man had a preconceived idea that the academic counselor was an authoritative person. When the counselor turned out to be "human" and fairly permissive, the student became comfortable.

CHAIRMAN: Let me propose another idea, before we leave the case of Jerry. Suppose that he visits the counseling office, takes supplementary tests, and has these interpreted to him by the vocational counselor. It would be well for you as his faculty counselor to discuss the results with him also.

Let's assume that the interest patterns point to his ability in the scientific area and that the abilities he demonstrates on the tests are similar to those of successful engineers. Vince, could you then begin to promote his going into the field of engineering?

MR. THURSBY: [The adviser views test results as only one piece of evidence to be used.] I still would refrain from making his decision for him. But I would point out that his test results showed an aptitude in the scientific area and that he ought seriously to consider this in making his decision. A comparative analysis of scores might lead Jerry to the conclusion that he preferred engineering rather than business.

CHAIRMAN: Apparently you are pretty much convinced that the decision is the student's. Now a final question—suppose that Jerry decided to try engineering, pursued it a semester or so, and became discouraged with low grades in mathematics and science. Is it your responsibility to counsel him out of pre-engineering, Dean?

MR. JOHNSON: I may not be the right person to talk about this subject because I am not a good "counsel-outer." I prefer to talk it over with the student and to be sure that we are seeing all the factors that are involved in his choice of vocation and major.

CHAIRMAN: Up to now, we have discussed Jerry whom one of you on the panel will meet on Wednesday. I would like to suggest that the faculty counselor keep notes on the initial interviews with Jerry and that we follow his case closely, reporting to the faculty advisers later in the year on some of the self-determined decisions which he will make.

Can we turn now to the question of choice of course work in terms of total load and of balance in the selections? George, you talked the other day to a new freshman who is interested in restaurant-hotel management. I overheard enough of the conversation to know that he felt a little "cagey" about taking what he called "liberal arts" courses. What was his problem?

MR. SPENCER: This student was, as he put it, "hot" on the idea of taking the restaurant and hotel management course work but didn't quite see why he had to have such course work as philosophy, literature, and humanities. He just didn't think these courses would be of any value to him. Underlying all he said seemed to be a real fear of some of the requirements in these courses.

CHAIRMAN: I recall that the student asked you if he might postpone these courses, humanities particularly, to the third or fourth year. When a student expresses a feeling of fear or distaste for an area of work, what is your procedure, Inez? Do you humor him or argue against it?

MISS FRINK: [The adviser operates within the framework of the institution, its requirements.] This isn't an answer to the question, exactly, but I would like to say that I am planning this year to discuss the general-education requirements in my group session which is held before the individual conferences. I would hope to elicit questions from different students about general education. It seems to me that it would be well to explain the purpose of the general-education courses and something of why these courses are of benefit to the individual. Particularly *why*, for if a student understands *why*, his attitude is often more favorable.

MR. THURSBY: [The adviser relates subject fields to life pursuits.] I would include in the "why" the observation that a student in a democratic society has a responsibility to prepare himself not only for a specific profession or vocation but also for making intelligent policy decisions, for intelligent voting, in short, for the role of a generalist in society. Every type of society requires specialists but only the democratic ones put so great a premium on generalists.

MISS ATHERTON: [The adviser reviews the institution's policy and philosophy.] That's a good speech from a political scientist. My presentation to the student isn't so scholarly, but in it I make use of our general-education pamphlet in which there is a picture of a clock. This clock is divided into three equal parts, of eight hours each. This is to represent the twenty-four-hour period in the life of an individual. One eight-hour period represents the working hours in which the individual is pursuing his choice of vocation. The remaining sixteen hours represent the person in the role of citizen, neighbor, parent, human being. The illustration graphically points out the need for general education as a part of the education of all people, no matter what their chosen occupations may be. Many times I use this example with some of my counselees when they can't see any need for taking course work other than their special field.

MR. SPENCER: That's a good suggestion, Audrey. Here's another aspect: This same student in restaurant hoped that he could take a moderate course load, rather than a heavy load, his first semester. We called the head of the restaurant and hotel department, who arranged to speak to the student on that score.   .

CHAIRMAN: What about course load? Would you say, generally speaking, Dean, that when your student requests a twelve- or fourteen-hour load, you agree and assist him in making out such a schedule?

MR. JOHNSON: [The adviser cites information which the student may need to consider.] Under the Selective Service regulations, students will need to consider carefully the course load for which they register. I do not think this fact needs to change our basic concept with regard to helping the student to a self-determined resolution to his problems. I believe that most students have a pretty good idea of their own ability to study and carry on their academic work successfully.

CHAIRMAN: By the same token, would you honor a student's request to take seventeen or eighteen hours the first semester? That's maximum, you know, Dean.

MR. JOHNSON: I think such a request should be carefully talked over with the student in order to make certain that the student's self-assurance in this matter is well based. After ascertaining this, I probably would honor the student's request. I think it should be pointed out in this regard that some major areas almost necessitate the student's taking a heavier-than-average load.

MR. SPENCER: As an example, let's take into consideration the heavy load required of preengineering majors. They have to take around nineteen hours of work. Music majors and nursing majors are also heavily scheduled during their first semester. In these fields, as well as in other majors, the student has to carry a pretty full course load and some of this work is noncredit.

CHAIRMAN: What about learning and earning simultaneously? A student who must work half-time downtown or on campus should carry what kind of hour load?

MR. THURSBY: [The adviser considers the case of each student on its own merits.] I think it's impossible to generalize on this. It depends upon the student. If a student is sufficiently interested in a college education to expend the double effort to carry the course work and the work load necessary to underwrite college expenses, we owe him every consideration which is consistent with high academic standards in such things as the adjustment of schedule, deferment of some courses, and so on.

CHAIRMAN: I talked to a bright student this summer who is a science major and who is employed more than half-time. He has excellent grades from the local high school, is preparing for West Point exams, has been studying code to pass an examination, has as a hobby auto mechanics. He asks, "How many hours do you think I can take?" He reports that his health is fine, and he has a good place at home to study. He wants a course load of eighteen hours, which is heavy for a freshman. Here is a case in which the mutual deliberation of student and counselor is needed.

Our third point of consideration is on the matter of counseling students on problems of achievement. Inez, do you find at mid-semester that most of your students doing unsatisfactory work are aware of their status?

MISS FRINK: As a general rule, yes. When you see them on campus and ask them how they are getting along, they will stay quite frankly that they are not doing very well in certain subjects.

CHAIRMAN: When you discuss with them the matter of improvement, as we are required to do in the freshman counseling program, do you suggest what to do?

MISS FRINK: [The adviser aids the student in defining the problem.] Emphatically, no. I usually ask these counselees if they have talked with the instructor of the course in which they are doing unsatisfactory work. If the answer is "yes," the student discusses with me the suggestions made and how he plans to use them. If the answer is "no," I suggest that the student see the teacher and ask for specific information, such as (1) why his work is falling down (lack of preparation, late work, failure to do parallel reading, etc.) and (2) what the instructor would suggest by way of improvement. In either case, I might make several suggestions which the student could utilize if he wishes to do so. For example, I had a counselee who felt that reading her history assignment before class was a waste of time "because the teacher lectures about it in class anyway." It was suggested that she might study her assignment before class, making an outline of the main topics and filling in the details during the class lecture.

MR. THURSBY: I follow roughly the same pattern as that outlined by Inez for the conference with students on their unsatisfactory status. At times the results are not satisfactory, of course. One of my counselees who was having difficulty with a modern language succeeded, in the course of our consideration of her study techniques, in convincing me that she shouldn't be in a university! [Laughs]

CHAIRMAN: Did she convince *herself?* That's the more tender point, isn't it? As faculty counselors, you may see the students rather infrequently. They may not be in your classes—in fact, they usually aren't. You have little chance to observe them. How can you understand the achievement problems of your counselees?

MISS ATHERTON: [The adviser solicits information from other counselors who know the student well.] Perhaps one important source which we overlook is that of our residence-hall counselors. They see students in the dormitories where they study, and they observe students' study habits. So many times we faculty advisers see counselees only in a rather formal setting. We have very little opportunity to observe their study habits. We should utilize the help of residence-hall counselors who can give us information about this area of the student's life.

MR. SPENCER: That's right. We have found that the student is best assisted when the faculty counselor and the residence counselor work together. The letters which the counseling office has received from parents have been made available to both the faculty counselor and the student's residence counselor.

CHAIRMAN: Now to conclude—we have sought to discuss something of the faculty counselor's role in the matter of making decisions *with* a counselee. We have agreed that our role is to aid the students in gaining insight and understanding and not to control the thought of counselees. We in counseling cite alternatives and consequences, and within the structure and limits of university regulations and departmental requirements, we point out a path or paths which students may take. We can expect, as our students grow in self-reliance and self-determination, that they will use our services less and less—in fact, that were it not for oncoming new seventeen-year-olds, we might work ourselves out of business.

These faculty advisers on the panel admittedly don't give *advice* to their counselees, but they have told me they would like to indulge themselves by giving advice to their colleagues. What's your parting word, Audrey?

MISS ATHERTON: [The adviser provides information, factual in nature.] I'd emphasize that one function of the counselor is that of giving information. Perhaps we have given the impression that faculty advisers beat around the bush, never answering any question, and throwing the conversation back to the counselee. We do feel that decision making is the responsibility of the counselee; however, there are obligations which the counselor must accept for knowing certain facts and information. For example, the faculty counselor must be familiar with the number of hours required for graduation, the number of quality points necessary, the difference in course work required for an A.B. or B.S. degree. This requires familiarization with the college catalogue. Perhaps this serves to point out what I consider an important phase of counseling.

CHAIRMAN: What is your famous last word, Inez?

MISS FRINK: [The adviser familiarizes himself with descriptive information concerning the student.] I think it is important for the faculty counselor to study the materials in the counseling folder which the counseling office prepares in conjunction with the office of personnel records. A knowledge of family background, high school test scores, high school grades, and college test scores is *a must*.

MR. SPENCER: [The adviser uses materials provided.] My advice is that we should make use of the general-education check list provided in each student's counseling folder. If the faculty counselor and the student will keep this up to date, there will not be cases of senior students with course work in general education incomplete at graduation time.

CHAIRMAN: As next to the last man, what do you say, Dean?

MR. JOHNSON: I think that we need always to remind ourselves that we are dealing with total persons and not merely with the academic desires, ambitions, problems, or shortcomings of the student. The student has concerns which are not academic. Sometimes these are related to his own personality—how he gets along with others, the girl he dates, the folks at home, money problems, the selective service, and many other things. It seems to me that to perform adequately our duties as faculty counselors we need a basic attitude of acceptance, understanding, and permissiveness which allows us to be approachable from the student's point of view.

CHAIRMAN: Yours is the last word, Vincent.

MR. THURSBY: [The adviser views the student as a changing and changeable entity.] I would like to stress the desirability of an open-minded approach. Albeit it is correct that many of our freshmen have decided their professional objectives, it is also true that a goodly percentage of those decided students will reconsider and change their decisions by their junior year. We can help by keeping open as many avenues as possible to render such changes less catastrophic.

CHAIRMAN: Thank you, panel members, for your erudition. The last minutes of this hour have been promised to members of the audience for use in discussing any of the points we have covered in the three decision-making areas which we presented this morning.

SUMMARY

In the preceding pages, five faculty advisers representing as many major fields or disciplines were "overheard" discussing their views of giving "assistance to students" in several aspects of decision making. Certain ditches between disciplines were bridged as these practitioners in the fields of political science, education, sociology, psychology, and business viewed the needs of individual students. In so doing, they approached an interdisciplinary role described by Gillin: [2]

From one point of view the student personnel officer or adviser serves as a link between the student, on the one hand, and the rest of the university on the other hand. But in order to carry out his duties properly he must not only be able to see personalities as wholes, but he should be enough of a social scientist to see the university community as a functioning whole—the administration, the faculty, athletics and other extracurricular activities, town and gown relationships, fraternity and sorority life, and so on. Thus, it seems that the counselor must be something of a psychologist, psychiatrist, sociologist, cultural anthropologist, economist, and perhaps political scientist (at least when his advice is sought, say in campus politics). Furthermore, he presumably should know his way around the curriculum sufficiently well, at least, to point out to students that histology and history are not the same thing, that there is usually a difference between sociology and socialism, and that entomology and etymology are not only distinct words but quite separate subject matters. The counselor must do all this mainly on the basis of experience with the situation, common sense, and a personal background of courses in a variety of fields, for there are not, so far as I know, any well-integrated courses on the university or college as a community.

With the interdisciplinary disposition of the faculty counselor assuming such great importance, one questions the means by which this point of view is achieved. Through preservice or in-service training, such as described in Chapter 5? In day-to-day experiences which contribute to the faculty member's growing self-reliance? What is the formula—with its equal parts of training, experience, and common sense—which will produce the interdisciplinary counselor or faculty adviser? These are questions not easily answered. Some additional consideration of the interdisciplinary role is given in Chapter 9. At this point, however, it is important to point out that to a considerable degree the interdisciplinary disposition applies not only to faculty *advisers* but also to faculty members who do not carry advising responsibilities and to nonacademic personnel.

In the chapter to follow, the dedication of these two groups to the educational philosophy of the college or university is viewed.

[2] John Gillin, "The Role of the Interdisciplinary Faculty Member," *Personnel-O-Gram,* 10:32–33, June, 1956.

CHAPTER 8 *The Noncounseling Faculty Member and the Staff Employee in the Program of Counseling*

If the foregoing pages would seem to imply that the "ordinary" faculty member—one to whom no special counseling responsibilities are assigned—has no place or only a minor place in the "whole institution," this chapter is intended to correct that notion.

One student personnel administrator graphically portrays the role of the extra-ordinarily important "ordinary" teacher: [1]

It came to pass that a certain student fell among evil companions. They stripped him of his allowance, induced him to forsake his studies, left him outcaste by his elders, wounded of pride, and fallen by the wayside.

And by chance there came that way a Keeper of Records who saw that the student had fallen. And, as is the custom of record keepers, he recorded it. And he said unto the student, Every student who falls by the wayside should be helped. There should be no partiality. Would that I could help all students, then I could help thee! And so saying, he consulted his book and found that it was so written, and he passed by on the other side.

And there likewise came that way a Test Maker and he looked upon the student and it appeared that he was sorely beaten. He examined his allowance and found that it was 98 per cent empty. He consulted his companions and discovered that seven out of ten of them were evil. He talked to the elders and learned that they had all rejected him. He devised an ingenious method of measuring the extent to which the student's pride had been wounded. He at last became convinced that here, indeed, was a student who had fallen by the wayside!

And the Test Maker assembled paper and pencils and wrote a mighty dissertation recommending that help be provided. And he filed his dissertation and passed by on the other side.

And there also came that way an Interviewer. And he looked upon the fallen student and said, How feelest thou? And the student answered saying,

[1] George A. Pierson, "The Parable of the Teacher-Counselor," *Personnel and Guidance Journal*, 33:443, April, 1955.

My pride is wounded, my companions were false, the elders have forsaken me, there is no hope! And the Interviewer said, Thou feelest, then, that there is no hope! And the student cried, Woe is me, my mistakes are grievous, I have been false to my heritage, leave me that I may mourn alone! And the Interviewer said, Thou wouldst have me go. And the student answered, Thou sayest. And the Interviewer made note of it and passed by on the other side.

But there also came that way a certain teacher. And when he saw the fallen student, he had compassion on him. He found linen and oil and helped the student bind up his wounded pride. He directed him to an agent who found work to replenish the misspent allowance. He helped the student rediscover his studies. And he assisted him in convincing his elders that he should no longer be rejected.

Which, now, of these four, sayest thou was counselor unto him who had fallen?

The faculty member whose compassion for the student is shown in assistance such as this is counselor nonpareil! The same can be said of nonacademic personnel—secretaries, clerks, and other campus functionaries—in the offices of deans, department heads, counseling units, and elsewhere. Writing of the college student with a problem of vocational-educational uncertainty, Morse declares: [2]

The student who has gnawing doubts about whether or not he has chosen the right track will often, in seeking guidance, wander unhappily from department to department, rebuffed by crisp and busy secretaries. He may occasionally find a professor who will bend an ear to his troubles, but often with the detached attitude of one who is convinced that any student who lacks the ability to solve his own problems does not have the gray matter to deserve to occupy a seat in the halls of higher education.

Perhaps the number of crisp and busy secretaries and of detached or judgmental professors is small, but even *one* impatient secretary and *one* indifferent professor are too many for institutions of truly "higher" education. An early identification of these uninterested staff members should be made, their lagging samaritanship being pointed out to them. Conversely, those staff members who demonstrate good human relations in contacts with students deserve to be commended and encouraged to continue their good work.

THE NONCOUNSELING FACULTY MEMBER

One might ask why, if a faculty member is truly interested in the student, he or she is not serving in the program of organized faculty counseling? (See Chapters 3, 4, and 5.) The question is answered by one respondent in the polling of 218 institutions cited earlier:

[2] Horace T. Morse, "General Education and Individual Guidance," in Melvene D. Hardee (ed.), *Counseling and Guidance in General Education,* World Book Company, Yonkers, N.Y., 1955, pp. 10–11.

Obviously not all college teachers care to or are competent to serve as faculty-counselors (dons). Some teachers believe that the college professor's function is to impart to his students as much knowledge of his subject as they can assimilate and that his responsibility to the student ends there. It is certainly true that in any institution there will be gifted teachers whose range of interest in students is limited to what students can learn about the subject.

Yet the responsibilities incumbent on the teacher for counseling, despite his or her noninclusion in the program of organized counseling, are obvious, as affirmed by institutional planners at Ohio State University: [3]

In any discussion of counseling in a university setting, the question always arises as to who will counsel. Is it to be the teacher or the nonteacher? Are a teacher's responsibilities completely discharged by fulfilling his duties in the classroom? Is he to decline to talk with students outside the classroom? If he does talk to his students, must the conversation be kept entirely within his teaching field? In case some question is raised outside his special field of study, must the student be referred to some counselor who will know the answers or know where to get them? Must there be two sets of teachers—one in the classroom and one outside? How far shall such a division of functions go? Most educators take the position that it is impossible to separate teaching from counseling. Every act and word of a teacher may have some influence upon his students. His position in the university gives him great prestige. His knowledge and experience extend to areas other than his teaching field. No wonder students seek out their teachers for conferences and ask their opinions on many varied topics. In some cases it can be seen that a teacher's influence outside the classroom is greater than his influence within. It is difficult to see how the teaching and counseling functions can be separated.

If the "ordinary" teacher assumes a role of such importance, what are his specific functions with reference to the individual student? Among the most important of these functions are the following:

1. The faculty member serves as an adult friend to the student.

2. The faculty member aids in the identification of students who need particular help, referring them to the proper person or office.

3. The faculty member shares information about a particular student with professional counselors who are able to assist the student in resolving a problem. In addition, the faculty member recommends to the proper officer or agency that a student be encouraged to follow a particular course of action or be cited for certain activities.

4. The faculty member confers with professional counseling personnel on student problems, with decisions being made on the wisdom of a particular course of action, such as (*a*) continued contacts of the student with the faculty member, (*b*) referral of the student to a specialist, or (*c*) both.

[3] *Counseling and Guidance,* Ohio State University, 1951, p. 6.

The Faculty Member Is Adult Friend of the Student

In Chapter 1 the quest of the student was discussed, with the faculty member pictured as a guiding craftsman and more experienced comrade to whom the student gravitated. The unfulfilled quest of one college graduate is narrated thus: [4]

... Doubtless among the many professors and instructors whose classes I attended in the four years, there are at least a few men of vast knowledge of world affairs, literary trends, and social, economic, and political philosophy. An acquaintance with those men should have been a stimulating experience; their example should have guided me and shown me the way to culture. But how was a student to become acquainted with these men, or with any other of his teachers? My contacts with the instructors were limited to the three hours a week in which they gave lectures on the subject of their courses, cut-and-dried lectures which they had been giving for years. If they had something more to offer, they didn't offer it. There was nothing in their contracts with the university to compel them to regard me and the other students in their classes as anything more than the occupants of chairs arranged in rows in front of them; and occupants of chairs we were. Their job was to teach us the subject matter of their courses, not to worry about how we were going to fit that subject matter into our lives.

Friendship is compounded of many things, and the elements of mature enduring friendship of teacher and student are in need of thoughtful analysis. In a seminar session for faculty advisers, a panel of teachers and students considered the topic "The College Student: His Nature and His Nurture." One aspect of the discussion dealt with the building of friendships among faculty members and students. From the panel the following excerpts are taken to illustrate the discussion. The discussants were Dr. Graydon S. DeLand, professor of modern languages; Dr. Meyer Nimkoff, head of the department of sociology; Dr. Ralph Witherspoon, professor of psychology; and three undergraduate students.

DR. DELAND: We have been speaking about counseling folders and records of students—none of which are substitutes for getting to know the student from the faculty man's viewpoint. As I look back upon my undergraduate years in college, I recall that we had no counseling folders—nobody had much of any record on anyone. But the faculty did get to know us because we got into the faculty people's families!

DR. NIMKOFF: Do you suggest, Graydon, that we take students into our homes?

DR. DELAND: Yes, I do. As a teacher of five courses, I can rather honestly say that I don't know my students as well as I should like. Of course, this is a large university, and it is easy to say that we live on a bus line where the bus

[4] Ernest Havemann and Patricia Salter West, *They Went to College*, Harcourt, Brace and Company, Inc., New York, 1952, pp. 260–261.

runs only once an hour and that it is hard for students to get to our homes, but those are not real excuses.

DR. NIMKOFF: I shouldn't say that having students come into our homes would negate the value of the counseling folder or the cumulative record of students.

DR. DELAND: No, I did not mean to imply that it did. I would use the verb "augment."

DR. NIMKOFF: I will agree that it is important to know something about the kind of student who comes to this university. For instance, the student body here is very different from that at B— — where I formerly taught. There, when I asked my students—as I always do during the first week—for a little biographical information, they would say: "My father is vice-president of such-and-such a corporation or the head of so-and-so utility." At this university, however, the freshman student may say, "My father has a filling station or he is a carpenter or a salesman." The economic level is quite different. If I am to take them from where they are, from A to B as it were, it is very important for me as a teacher to know their background.

DR. DELAND: Yes, but more than that . . . for instance, in my own class I try to put on a little card some information which makes each student distinctive. But before I do that, I tell the class in a résumé where I have taught, what I have done in the past. Invariably, in every class there is somebody who has known people our family has known. This personal review helps in building what the French call *rapport* between the teacher and the student. . . . The only reason in the world why I am teaching foreign languages is because teachers I had at C— — took me into their homes and sold me on the idea. (I was supposed to be a railroad man. My wife tells me I got "sidetracked.")

DR. NIMKOFF: I know that a case can be made for inviting students into the faculty members' homes. But the home is a very precious place—a place where one gets some rest from the hectic world outside. I well remember a renowned professor at the University of C— — who balked at entertaining all of his students in his home or even one or two sons or daughters of wealthy donors. He said, "My home is for my friends. We have people in our home—planned teas every Sunday afternoon. But friendships and professional life cannot be mixed." I think this viewpoint needs to be considered. I must admit that I have had some students in my home when I have regretted it afterwards. I think a strong case could be made out for having *selected* students in the home but not all of them.

DR. WITHERSPOON: Do you think students like to go to faculty homes? The reason I ask is that a couple of years ago the Student Christian Association had a project which consisted of the faculty members' holding open house for students on a given night. On this particular night I went to the dormitory where I was to get a load of students to take to our house, and the president of the student body came stomping in and declared, "Who is this guy Witherspoon anyway? Doesn't he know that students are too darned busy to bother with going to their homes? If they want to get to know us, why don't they come up here to campus?"

DR. DELAND: In that instance, I think the approach may have been wrong—

to call it an "open house" would not be the same thing as a personal invitation. Perhaps there should have been a more "natural" approach, one growing out of a normal student-faculty situation.

MISS CHARLOTTE PATTEN (STUDENT): You probably know that certain faculty members are invited to the residence halls for tea each week. We had such a tea in my dormitory two weeks ago. It was more like a "bull session" in the dormitory. The teachers looked and acted like my mother and dad's friends.

MISS PHYLLIS PATTEN (STUDENT): Do they have anything around here like faculty-student picnics or baseball games? Where I went to prep school, I recall that there were teachers I didn't think I would like until I saw them out playing baseball. Then they seemed to be human. A free atmosphere like that seems so much better than a formal tea.

MISS HILDEGARD WAGNER (STUDENT): It is hard for me to see this matter as the twins do because I have a different educational background—European. We did not go to school to have fun and nobody had to make me like a teacher. We experienced enjoyment in our studies and respected all our professors highly.

The foregoing verbatim comments of teaching faculty members and students serve to point up the fact that the quality of student-teacher relationships in small institutions and in large is not totally understood. Means for effecting such rapport have not been tried generally on an institution-wide scale. A great deal more deliberation by students and faculty members is needed.

Among the experiments of merit under way in various colleges and universities is that termed the freshman-faculty week end at the State College of Washington:

Every dormitory, sorority, and fraternity is asked to choose one or more freshmen as a representative from their house. It is suggested that the choice be based on potential leadership. Late in October, approximately 120 faculty and freshmen spend two days, from Friday evening until Sunday evening, in a large lakeside camp. Transportation must be effected entirely in faculty cars. Each faculty member with his passengers is humorously designated as a "family," and this "family" becomes the organizational unit for all activities in camp. These activities include everything from preparation of meals to discussion groups. Each of the latter is composed of two families. There is much recreation, including group singing, and the discussion periods are carried out informally. The faculty member asks each student in effect—Now that you have been here for a month, what have you to say? What experiences have you found significant? What puzzles you? What has been most difficult? What has been most satisfying?

The conclusions reached by each group are recorded by freshmen secretaries who report at a plenary session on Sunday. During the subsequent week, the freshmen secretaries meet to combine their reports into one. Original copies are sent to all participants. The dean of faculty, who is a regular "family head," passes on pertinent information to certain responsible agencies on the campus and sends an edited version of the report to all faculty. The most significant result is the high degree of faculty-student rapport, and it is hoped that much of this is "caught" by other members of the campus community, both students and faculty.

The Faculty Member Aids in Referral of Students

The faculty member, through contacts with the student daily, twice, or three times weekly, is in an excellent position to identify students who need help of a specialized nature. Three institutional representatives comment as follows on the matter of faculty referral of students for special help:

ALABAMA POLYTECHNIC INSTITUTE: The teaching faculty refers cases in which (a) the student deviates from the normal pattern of behavior or performance or (b) the professor feels inadequate to meet the needs of the student. Cases are referred to the academic dean, to the student guidance service for special testing and vocational counseling, to the dean of women or the director of student affairs, to the college physician, or to a local minister.

UNIVERSITY OF ILLINOIS: [5] The question is often voiced by staff members: "I have a student in class who needs to come to the bureau, but how am I going to get him to go?". . . Most any student seems to feel grateful to an instructor who shows enough interest in him to ask him into his office and then to ask him why he thinks he did so poorly on the last exam; why he thinks he does well on his home work and quizzes, but poorly on hour exams; why he is absent from so many classes; why he thinks he has trouble in understanding the course, and the like. If these questions are asked in a kindly fashion, most students will do their best to answer them and, in doing so, will explain their difficulties as they see them.

SACRAMENTO STATE COLLEGE: The reasons for referral should be discussed so that the student convinces himself that he will benefit by the additional service; otherwise he will consider the suggestion an imposition. Instead of saying, "I think you ought to see the dean about this," it would be more effective to say, "The dean might be able to help you with this problem. Would you care to make an appointment with him?" Thus, the student feels that he is making the decision, yet his hopes for a solution are not overexpanded.

(See App. M-1 for the student referral sheet which provides space for information sought as well as for indicating whether the student should be referred back to the referrer.)

Proper referral of students by a faculty member to specialized counselors assumes a knowledge of these services and an acquaintanceship with persons who function in the service. Much of the same "publicity" of student services provided to faculty advisers (Chapter 5) should

[5] From *Faculty Bulletin,* University of Illinois, vol. 1, no. 7, September, 1948.

reach the faculty at large, with distribution being made of directories which list campus offices or agencies, their location, and telephone numbers. (See App. K for Ohio University referral guide.)

In addition, personal acquaintanceships effected through informal meetings are decidedly helpful. At the University of Texas a letter is written to each new member of the instructional staff, inviting him to come in to the office of student life for a visit.

Rallying faculty members to this kind of task, one writer declares: [6]

Get to know the various student personnel functions and people on your campus: the deans; the infirmary; the testing service; the vocational, academic, and personal counselors; the psychiatric resources, if available; the chaplains and student ministers; the dormitory counselors. Visit them, find out what their special competences and defined roles really involve, size them up (if you find them all quacks, take another good look at yourself!). Successful counseling (by the faculty member) can frequently involve just guiding the student to the right source of such specialized attention.

The Faculty Member Shares Information with Professional Personnel

Information of importance to those who counsel with students is obtained by the faculty member through observation of students, through student recitations, through papers submitted by students, as well as from the comments of other students, classmates, and friends. If the information is of importance to the central records office, the dean of women, dean of men, director of counseling, etc., the faculty member may move to share it, with the understanding that its use will be for the good of the student—his better adjustment to the college or university.

Among the institutions which make special effort to provide for the sharing of information on the part of teachers and professional counselors are the following:

CENTRAL MICHIGAN COLLEGE OF EDUCATION: Through the extensive use of Form SP38 [see App. N], the faculty makes frequent recommendations to the dean of students regarding the activities of students in his courses. These recommendations range all the way from extreme criticism of the student by the teacher to high commendation for unusual educational achievement. All the forms are classified and turned over to the personnel counselor of the student who then works with him to organize a program in harmony with the recommendations of teachers. Through this interchange between teachers and counselors there grows up an increasing understanding between the two staff members.

ORANGE COAST JUNIOR COLLEGE: Counselors propose to keep reminding faculty of the need for gathered information by use of a standard-sized slip

[6] Junius A. Davis, "The College Teacher as Counselor," *Journal of Teacher Education,* 6:284–285, December, 1955.

of a distinctive color (not mimeographed). These are placed in boxes as a reminder for the faculty member to jot down any pertinent information. The instructor drops the slips in a locked box in the mail room, and the counselor's secretary distributes them. Counselors use the same slip to convey information to the instructors.

SOUTH GEORGIA COLLEGE: An effort is made to maintain an atmosphere of informality and cooperativeness so as to encourage a maximum flow of information, advice, and assistance from faculty member to faculty member, from them to the dean of students, and return. Faculty members are furnished with (1) a summary of freshmen test results, (2) a compilation of grades at mid-term and at the end of the quarter, (3) health reports on individual students where advisable, and (4) any other information which would be either necessary or helpful.

ALLEGHENY COLLEGE: As far as our working relationships with the faculty are concerned, we rely primarily on the discussions of specific problems. Members of the staff of the counseling center will talk with Teacher A about John Jones who is a student in his class or with the faculty as a whole about a group feeling, such as a student evaluation.

The kind of information which is welcomed by the faculty adviser or other counselor is such a statement as this sent by the English teacher of a freshman student who appears not to be producing up to his capacity academically or on the athletic field:

This boy has been fighting a problem of adjustment. In private conference, I found that a child's fear, rebellion, and homesickness were hidden within a man's body. I suggested that he talk with his faculty adviser and with the head coach. The boy is physically tired, behind in all his class work, confused and discouraged. Since that first talk, I have conferred with Arthur twice, and I feel that he has greatly improved in attitude and settled down.

The sharing of information among teaching faculty and professional counselors takes place also in the case conference described in Chapter 15. Whether the information is shared in casual conversation, in informal case-conference arrangement, or in writing, the *sine qua non* is its professional, ethical sharing, devoid of gossip and the maligning of students.

The Faculty Member Is Guided by the Professional Counselor on Problems of Students

In institutions where the working relationship of teaching faculty and professional counselors is good, the professor of military science, head of the humanities department, teacher of restaurant and hotel management, and others will seek the professional counselor who he or she feels can help with the problem of a student. The preface to the conference is often a telephone call beginning, "When can I come by to see you about a student I have in class?" On occasion, the overture is, "I have a student in class who needs help." The professional counselor may reply by offering to drop in at the teacher's office for conference. This flexible arrangement is often desirable, allowing the counselor to get out of his office and into the academic environs, and permitting the faculty member, on occasion, to observe the counseling area.

Frequently the word from the faculty member is, "I am sending Jerry Genesis in to see you. He has a problem that is beyond me." In this instance, the counselor may inquire if the faculty member would like an immediate report on the referral, in writing, by telephone, or through a follow-up conference of the faculty member and the counselor. Frequently the follow-up is requested; other times it is enough for the faculty member to know that the problem has been transferred to the professional counseling staff.

Paying real dividends in the matter of effecting good working relationships between academic personnel and the counseling program is a procedure such as this:

GETTYSBURG COLLEGE: I visit the various department heads periodically and from these conferences comes the acknowledgement of individual cases which can then be channeled to the proper personnel for guidance. One of the more lucrative sources of information about those who need help is the athletic trainer's "rubdown room." I believe many trainers are quite wise in the necessities of personality.

Several of the functions of noncounseling faculty members can be seen operating in the arrangement at Boston University Junior College,[7] which is designed to facilitate integration among the various subject-matter areas in the curriculum (see also Chapter 9).

Described as the "team approach," the plan requires the designation of five instructors, one from each of the areas of humanities, social relations, science, guidance, and communications, with one member of the team elected as chairman or coordinator. In the arrangement, three members share one large office, while the guidance counselor and communications instructor occupy private offices for the purpose of having personal interviews with students.

Classroom sections in each of the subject-matter areas consist of twenty-five students, with each instructor teaching the same sections and the same students as the other four. Formal meetings of the team are held once a week for a two-hour period, with many informal meetings taking place spontaneously in between. Each team maintains a file containing a record of its activities. Among the functions of the team are these:

[7] Vernon A. Anthony, Colin Livesey, Peyton E. Richter, and Charles H. Russell, "The Team Approach to General Education," *Junior College Journal*, 26:319–410, February, 1956.

(1) to prepare end-of-year evaluations and recommendations for transfer of students or their placement; (2) to render service to the student who may be in difficulty because of attitudinal problems; (3) to function in instances of unethical procedures such as plagiarism or cheating; (4) to detect student problems at an early stage; (5) to communicate with members of the administration with reference to students in difficulty, etc.

Extending "corporate guidance" to the student, the team of teachers and guidance counselor adopt a "guidance frame of reference," with the teacher's role delineated as follows:

1. The teacher should attempt to visualize the world of the student as perceived by him in order to render the most effective service.

2. Each teacher should realize that he does not *become* a counselor but rather that he *is* already a counselor in the eyes of many of his students.

3. The teacher's duty to his students is not fulfilled by competent classroom teaching alone but necessitates the teacher's concern with the student as a human being with a past, present, and future.

4. While the teacher should make every effort to present the subject matter to the student in a comprehensible and meaningful form, he must recognize that the ultimate integration of subject matter must be made by the student himself in relationship to his unique total life experiences.

The exponents of this approach at Boston University Junior College contend that growth as a faculty member can be initiated and sustained through the interpersonal context of the team.

Summarizing the whole matter of the performance of noncounseling faculty is this statement: [8]

They (the students) would profit more from counseling if there were a proper working relationship between teachers, designated as counselors or not, and the professional counselors. Such an understanding would prevent the student's being the object of two separate programs on the campus—one of instruction and one of guidance.

THE NONACADEMIC STAFF MEMBER

Much of what has been said in the foregoing pages concerning the noncounseling faculty member also applies to the nonacademic staff member—the administrative assistants, executive secretaries, senior and junior secretaries, clerk typists, campus police, and others. Guidance and counseling are where they (the students) find them; oftentimes the source of this aid is not dignified by an administrative title, a comfort-

[8] Marjorie Carpenter, E. H. Hopkins, and M. Eunice Hilton, "College Guidance—Whose Job Is It?" *NEA Journal*, 42:272–274, May, 1953.

able reception room, or a set of counseling records. The curbstone conference with the campus guard, an "off-the-cuff" conversation with the Number 3 file clerk, or the hurried telephone call to the receptionist of a given service may constitute the direction—vocational or academic—which the student needs and seeks.

Speaking about the importance of the nonacademic staff member are these representatives of colleges or universities:

DARTMOUTH COLLEGE: An often forgotten and misunderstood factor in the maintenance of a good student personnel administration is the secretarial staff. These personnel represent the front door to the service and hence can control the "open door" policy which we all would like to maintain. Since these people, in the main, female personnel, are in close daily contact with the male members of the staff, it seems basic to me that their selection be made with care and insight. How my secretary discusses a situation with a member of the faculty is perhaps more important than whether or not I can help him with the problem he has. I have found that one of the greatest ambassadors a person can find for a student personnel program is the lady who sits behind the reception desk.

DRAKE UNIVERSITY: I feel that it is important that, wherever possible, a meaningful job title be given. For example, in the clerical area, if a secretary is doing a special job (let us say, doing placement work or administering loans and scholarships), a title such as "Assistant in Placement," etc., might be given.

SAVANNAH STATE COLLEGE: Our personnel secretary works harmoniously with all members in the department. Her techniques of working well with people, organizing work, meeting and delegating responsibilities have created an excellent atmosphere in which to work.

SUMMARY

The wish to be of service to mankind resides in almost all individuals in some degree. To capture this measure of altruism in individuals who serve in institutions of higher education is the assignment. To provide them with the best and most accurate information about the specialized services, skilled counselors, sympathetic teachers and administrators—this is essential. To reward the efforts of classroom teachers and nonacademic personnel with encouraging words and suitable recognition is equally important.

In this chapter, the role of the noncounseling faculty member was pointed out. It was indicated that this teacher who does not carry assigned counseling responsibilities will (1) serve as an adult friend to the student, (2) effect referrals to specialized personnel, (3) share information with professionally trained counselors, and (4) be guided by suggestions made by specialists in counseling and student personnel work. The nonacademic staff member, serving often as the student's first contact, will likewise need to be apprised of specialist services and of referral procedures.

Contributing to the institution's wholeness, to the atmosphere of good working relations between and among teaching faculty, advising faculty, professional counselors, academic administrators, and nonacademic personnel is the administrator of the program of counseling. This individual's attitudes about cooperative working relationships together with his skill in effecting cooperation are reflected in daily routine. At this point, attention should be given to the actual work assignment of the director or coordinator of counseling.

CHAPTER 9

The Coordination of the Program of Counseling: The Function and the Functionaries

Despite some "shadowboxing" with the term in earlier chapters, the detailed discussion of the key word—coordination—has been postponed until now. To have placed this discussion earlier would have been presumably to cut off the early view of the many possibilities for coordination of effort. On the other hand, to have placed this chapter last would have left no opportunity for illustration of specific procedures or summation. It is fitting, therefore, that the discussion of coordination which aids in the process of integration and which is central to this book be placed in the approximate, if not exact, center.

Viewing in retrospect his experiences in top management and government, one writer states: [1]

Last among this partial list of problems comes that terrible matter of coordination. I had hoped to avoid the word because "coordinator" became an epithet rather than a title. Men who were otherwise patient and reasonable and who would readily admit the need for coordination in a machine so huge, so complex, and so divergent in interests and objectives, would roar with frustration when subjected to it. In fact, one of these bitter and now familiar definitions which helped blow off steam ran something like this: A coordinator is a man who brings organized chaos out of regimented confusion.

Well aware of the fact that similar strong feelings are likely to be held by certain educators, the author included the following questions in the survey of counseling practices among the 218 institutions of higher education (see Table 13): How is the work of counselors, administrators, faculty, and students coordinated? How successful is it? What are the

---

[1] Robert A. Lovett, "A Business Executive Looks at Government," in Joseph E. McLean (ed.), *The Public Service and University Education,* Princeton University Press, Princeton, N.J., 1949, pp. 74–75.

evidences of good working relationships? What factors prevent good coordination? What changes in the foregoing do you see in the near future?

The summary of replies from these 218 respondents indicated that the work of counselors, administrators, faculty members, and students was coordinated chiefly through the following means:

1. The efforts of a single individual—dean of students, dean of men, dean of women, director of counseling and guidance, or one of similar designation

2. The work of a committee variously named as counseling and guidance committee, committee on student affairs, student personnel committee, etc.

3. The case-conference activity which brings together a number of teachers, counselors, and administrators to consider a student's problem

4. Informal conferences between the administrator of the program of counseling, the faculty counselor, the student counselor, the non-counseling faculty member, and others

5. Seminars and workshops proceeding under the direction of the person charged with directing or coordinating the counseling program

Respondents cited as evidences of good working relations among persons in the counseling programs the following as shown in Table 14:

1. The belief shared by the faculty that counseling is a joint effort

2. The greater acceptance by faculty of counseling duties, as shown by their participation in in-service training activities, their wider use of referral, and so on

3. The improved behavior of students, evidencing better academic achievement and a willingness to accept help in solving problems

4. The evaluative statements of students denoting satisfactory experiences in counseling

From the replies, however, it was readily seen that respondents tended to give greater expression to the *adverse* factors relating to coordination of effort (see Table 15). Heading the list of adversities on campuses were these:

1. The lack of understanding and sympathy on the part of some faculty members for the over-all program of counseling

2. The lack of adequate time for developing a program of coordinated counseling services

3. Competing departmental interests and demands

4. Budgetary shortcomings resulting in too little space, too few counselors, and limited facilities for counseling

5. The need for better training of those who counsel

6. The need for better communication among those working with students

7. The need for administrative leadership—a single individual to head up the program of counseling

Among the proposals for improving institution-wide programs of counseling were the better coordination of the parts of the program through *designation of a single administrator;* the *clearer definition of duties of all individuals in the program of counseling;* and the *improvement of communications throughout the whole institution* (see Table 16).

This chapter aims to clarify some of the questions relating to coordinative planning: What is the need for coordination? What is meant by coordination of counseling? How is coordination effected? What are the functions of the program coordinator?

THE NEED FOR THE COORDINATION OF EFFORT

In two preceding sections of this book, attention was directed to certain aspects of coordination. In Chapter 1, some ten questions were cited as those likely to be raised by students, their parents, or the faculty. In Chapter 2, another set of questions was posed, calling attention to intra-institutional policies and procedures.

That there is need for administrative planners to look more searchingly at the matter of organization and administration of counseling services is evident from such statements as these:

One of the most important things we need to know in our institution is how to increase general knowledge of what people in different offices are doing, as well as of ways in which students can be led to make the maximum use of the facilities we have.

We need to chart more clearly and carry out more completely the communication between the groups charged with personnel work and the instructors who serve as counselors for individual students.

A summary statement confirming the need for coordination of services is the following: [2]

Each institution faces the problem of coordinating the work of the many different services. This coordination is necessary if each service is to make its maximum contribution, if overlapping is to be avoided, and if decisions affecting students are to be made after consultation with all individuals able to make a contribution. It also is necessary to avoid a feeling of competition between the various services.

Throughout this discussion, it will be seen that the need for coordination of counseling exists in many quarters—within a given service, between and among specific counseling services, among counseling services

[2] Donald J. Shank and others, *The Teacher as Counselor,* American Council on Education Studies, ser. 6, no. 10, Washington, October, 1948, p. 35.

and the several academic units, between the college counseling services and those of the community, region, or state.

WHAT IS MEANT BY COORDINATION OF COUNSELING?

Of the term, one writer says, "Coordination involves unification of information, decision, and action—upwards, downwards, and cross-wise." [3] One might then ask, For what purpose is this unification of information, decision, and action undertaken? The proper answer to that would be to keep intact "the central design, the operating relationship and the imprisoned idea." [4] The idea in this instance is that of utilizing the whole institution for the whole student. Certain relationships are built in order to facilitate this operation. The central design is that pattern envisioned by the institutional planners for accomplishing this wholeness of operation.

Coordination, if effective, should (1) promote and maintain a spirit of unity or "oneness"; (2) build understandings among professional staff; (3) weld groups of the instructional staff with professional counselors; (4) decrease or eliminate duplication of effort among the various offices in the institution; and finally (5) facilitate communication between individuals and groups working together on common tasks for the good of students, within the total institutional setting as well as in the community.

It is believed that effective coordination of a program of specialized counseling is facilitated when these conditions obtain:

1. When the *philosophy* basic to counseling is *analyzed* and discussed by those who counsel

2. When *specific functions and responsibilities are defined* and the duties of each officer understood by the other officers

3. When the *functions* and responsibilities as defined *are accepted* by each officer and regarded as important and worthwhile

4. When individuals who counsel *are given opportunity to participate in policy formation*

5. When there is an *accounting made of the resources of counseling* and the findings made known to all who counsel

6. When a *means for communication* of ideas among persons responsible for counseling *is provided,* and when these channels of information are used

[3] Henry E. Niles, "Principles or Factors in Organization," in Catheryn Seckler-Hudson, *Processes of Organization and Management,* Public Affairs Press, Washington, D.C., 1948, p. 90.
[4] Luther Gulick, "Notes on the Theory of Organization," in Luther Gulick and L. Urwick (eds.), *Papers on the Science of Administration,* Institute of Public Administration, Columbia University, New York, 1927, p. 3.

7. When there is *mutual deliberation on problems of individual students* by those who counsel

8. When there is a *systematic evaluation* of the counseling opportunities offered to students

A program of counseling coordinated in the eight ways suggested is almost certain to provide more satisfactory answers to the basic questions than can a program which lacks centralization of policy—which delegates responsibility but fails to unify efforts. The criteria furthermore would seem to hold true (1) for the program of counseling which is organized by means of a single central agency and (2) for the program characterized as "decentralized but coordinated." (See App. F-6 for suggested topics for discussion among personnel.)

EXAMPLES OF COORDINATION

Administrators in higher education, in describing the pattern of the counseling program, tend to identify it often as "centralized" or "decentralized." The implication in the first instance is often that, with the existence of a counseling bureau or center, the total responsibility for the guidance and counseling of the whole student rests with this unit. The impression is thus given that the center is the coordinating unit for all counseling taking place on campus.

On the other hand, the designation of a program as "decentralized" tends often to indicate that a number of offices or agencies are given the responsibility for counseling and that the arrangement lacks centrality or singleness of control.

Actually, one needs to examine each program of counseling to judge its components before a true understanding of "centralized" and "decentralized" is obtained. A program of disparate or decentralized counseling services may have a high degree of centralization as effected through the work of a coordinative office or committee. Similarly, the work of a counseling center may not be directed toward the coordination of effort of other agencies, with the result that the degree of centralization is considerably less than that of the decentralized but coordinated program. Points of view concerning the "centralization" of organization are expressed here:

FORT HAYS, KANSAS, STATE COLLEGE: We have not been sold on the idea of establishing a highly centralized office of counseling. It has been our observation that, where such fine paper setups have been established, there is the tendency on the part of the faculty to presume that all counseling should be done in this specialized arrangement. On the other hand, we believe that a thorough job of academic counseling can be done by the instructional staff better than it can be carried out in a centralized office.

ALBRIGHT COLLEGE: The administrative pattern of student personnel work is so organized at Albright College that everyone on the campus—student, faculty, and administration—participates in some phase of the personnel program. Our decentralization of functions (as opposed to centralization in one department or completely in one person) tends to increase the direct effectiveness of our services to students only so long as coordination produces the exchange of information and freedom of communication that avoids conflict of service and provides help to students who so badly need the combined services.

Once a point of view is reached within an institution on how services shall be combined, experimentation with methods for integrating the work of these services must proceed. The following institutions state their beginnings of *work in combination:*

Teaching faculty and professional counselors combine efforts

LONG BEACH CITY COLLEGE: We have sought to approach the values of a decentralized service without losing the values of a centralized program. We believe that classroom teachers should be involved in a guidance program as rapidly as they can develop adequate competence in such an assignment. In our liberal arts division, for example, we now have five full-time guidance specialists working with eighteen or twenty teacher-counselors who teach regular subjects the larger proportion of their time. Our present task is to define the functions of full-time counselors, part-time counselors who teach half time and counsel half time, and teacher-counselors who counsel a small proportion of their time.

BRIGHAM YOUNG UNIVERSITY: We have established counseling on a technical basis with a counseling staff trained specifically for the work and supplemented by the contributions that can be made from faculty members in the subject-matter areas. These technically trained counselors meet on occasion with faculty members of the academic departments, discuss with them fundamental problems that affect both academic and nonacademic life of the student, and assist faculty members in obtaining an understanding of student capacity and achievement.

Frequent meetings of those who work with students

BOB JONES UNIVERSITY: Every morning, all the administrative and personnel staff including dormitory supervisors, the director of religious activities, the deans, etc., meet for an hour's conference in which they discuss any problems which may have come to their attention in connection with a certain student. Each member of the conference brings to the group's attention any symptom or evidence of unsatisfactory adjustment or personality difficulties which he has noticed.

Central housing for student personnel staff

SACRAMENTO STATE COLLEGE: We have new buildings on a new campus, and the physical arrangements facilitate good staff relations. All parts of the personnel program are centered in one end of the administration building with the exception of the student health center. The admissions and registrar's offices are on the ground floor, and the guidance center, placement, and housing are on the second floor, with a dumb-waiter arrangement to control any transfer of records between offices. Several small interviewing rooms are used interchangeably according to peak loads in testing, placement interviews, counseling, and reading accelerator practice. The clerical staff as well as the professional staff serve as a team as a result of physical arrangements.

Frequent check of student experiences

BUCKNELL UNIVERSITY: A technique to improve communications and personnel on our campus is to place a student on "dry run" through the different offices and departments of the university from the time he enters as a freshman student to the end of his freshman year. The aim is to study the problems he encounters in the different offices and departments and how, through better communications, these problems might be solved. Another technique used is to check a list of the students who have been dropped by the university and trace the path they followed in college back through the different activities, trying to determine why failure occurred and if it occurred because of the failure of any office represented on the student personnel services committee.

Coordination through merger of functions

TEXAS AGRICULTURAL AND MECHANICAL COLLEGE: [5] In the interests of achieving a higher degree of coordination in the total guidance effort of the campus, the duties of the dean of student personnel were extended to include those of the dean of the basic division. This latter includes four areas of emphasis: (1) educational supervision (serving as the office of "academic dean" for all basic-division students), (2) remedial and improvement services, (3) group work and counseling, and (4) testing, research, and evaluation.

Although the basic division is that administrative unit in which freshmen enroll, the various special services offered are available to all students. . . . Although the basic division personnel have not traditionally had responsibility for the faculty advisory program for upperclassmen, we are branching out in this respect and hope to have a meaningful program in operation. . . . To be sure, the basic division staff personnel are not in direct contact with upperclassmen; yet, through a program of "cultivation," dormitory counselors and upperclass faculty advisers are doing more in the way of referral.

Coordination through designation of an administrator

IOWA STATE TEACHERS COLLEGE: [6] The coordinator of student counseling is administratively responsible to both the dean of students and to the registrar. In this position, the duties of coordinator include (1) coordination of the guidance services, (2) supervision of the academic advisory program, (3) voca-

[5] Letter directed to the author by Robert Kamm, Dean, June 1, 1956.
[6] *Personal Guidance for the Prospective Teacher,* prepared for the American Association of Colleges of Teacher Education, 1957.

tional and personal counseling, (4) chairmanship of orientation activities for new students, (5) membership on the professional screening and admissions committee and board of health, (6) interviewing prospective students, (7) initiating case conferences, (8) making referrals for specialized counseling, (9) reviewing applications for student teaching, and (10) developing and maintaining an official centralized student personnel file.

After a student is admitted, his records are sent to the coordinator of student counseling, who initiates a cumulative folder. The coordinator assigns a faculty adviser and notifies the student of this assignment and of the date to report for orientation-week activities. He also writes a letter to the parents of each new freshman requesting information about health, hobbies, interests, personality, and potential problems of the student. Excerpts from the parent's letter, together with the high school rank, standardized test scores, speech and hearing check card, and other available information are sent to the faculty adviser and to the residence-hall director prior to the registration of the student. In the residence hall, every new student is assigned to a student counselor who is responsible for knowing him as a person. Two student counselors work with a group of twenty to thirty new students, aiding them in the orientation process, in learning college policies and regulations, in achieving proper study habits, and in adjusting to group living. The student counselor frequently makes informal referrals of students needing additional help to the residence counselor, dean of students, coordinator of counseling, director of the health service, academic adviser, or an instructor. Finally, in the coordinated program at Iowa State Teachers College, the classroom instructor assumes considerable responsibility. He observes special talents of his students and aids students in using these talents wisely. He frequently consults with the coordinator of counseling, residence-hall director, and the student's faculty adviser, seeking further information or relating observations.

BROOKLYN COLLEGE: [7] The dean of students is responsible for (1) all relations with high schools; (2) admissions to the college as a whole; (3) intensive freshman counseling; (4) integrated program of counseling including the personal counseling of freshmen and of upperclassmen when requested, curriculum counseling of freshmen and sophomores, and extended counseling in special cases—handicapped, vocational, psychological—as indicated; (5) conditions pertaining to student health and safety; (6) administration of college policies regarding individual discipline; (7) development and coordination of all college records on individual students; and (8) coordination in all the preceding areas.

The dean of students is assisted by an associate dean of students (coordinator of counseling) whose duties are extended to include the coordinating of freshmen-sophomore counseling, conducting of panels of counselors, programs of in-service training for part-time and full-time counselors. In the general counseling program, forty-two faculty counselors are assigned a group of fresh-

[7] From a letter and enclosure directed to the author by Herbert Stroup, Dean of Students, Sept. 21, 1955, and from an article by Norman Kiell, "Freshman Evaluation of Faculty Counsellors," *Personnel and Guidance Journal*, 35:261–264, February, 1957.

men whom they would carry for the full four college years. The counselors participate in the freshman orientation program, meet monthly as a group for staff business, and engage in frequent but informal in-service training sessions. These are led, in one phase, by members of the department of personnel service, whose chairman is the dean of students, the majority of whom hold doctoral degrees in clinical or counseling psychology or in education. The in-service training meetings have included case conferences, tape recordings of interviews held with students, interpretation of the ACE, etc. An in-service training program is held for the professional counselors which, in turn, is led by the faculty counselors, with the time being devoted to curriculum matters. The two groups function as a team, each respecting the other as resource people.

BOWLING GREEN UNIVERSITY: [8] The major purpose in the establishment of the office of coordinator of counseling services is to bring about effective coordination and extension of these services. The coordinator convenes meetings of those engaged in the various kinds of counseling activities for the purpose of bringing about better integration and improving procedures and practices. Services of the coordinator will be available in a consulting or training capacity. Development of a system of central records will be begun for the housing of significant information and reports. The office of coordinator of counseling services seeks to coordinate academic counseling by deans and faculty members; residence-hall counseling by head residents and student assistants; general counseling on personal problems by student personnel officers; health counseling by university physicians; counseling on financial problems by the student financial aid counselor; counseling by clinical specialists in the departments of education, psychology, and speech; general counseling on academic and personal matters by faculty advisers especially designated for groups of advisees; religious counseling by local priests and ministers; precollege counseling by the director of admissions, the registrar, and members of their staffs; and other informal types of counseling.

Coordination through the "team approach" of academic personnel and guidance counselor (See also Chapter 7 for descriptive information)

BOSTON UNIVERSITY JUNIOR COLLEGE: [9] Five instructors, representing all departments of the college (guidance, communications, humanities, science, and social relations), cooperatively teach and work with five sections of students (125 to 149 total). These five instructors, including the guidance counselor, meet for two hours per week, share the same office (except for the counselor and communications instructor), and serve many functions in the program. Among these are integration of subject matter, coordination of teaching methods, administrative implementation of the educational program, in-service training, and individualized instruction.

The major function of the team, however, is in the counseling and guidance area. Individual conferences, diagnosis, advising, listening, counseling, particularized remedial action, and weekly case conferences allow the team to become a truly equal partner in the counseling and guidance process with the

[8] From a letter and enclosure directed to the author by Frank C. Arnold, Coordinator of Counseling Services, Sept. 30, 1955.

[9] Edward C. Glanz, *A Guidance Program in Action*, pp. 26–27. (Mimeographed.)

regular counselor. The team fulfills the responsibilities usually undertaken by faculty advisors, "released-time faculty counselors," educational orientation advisors, and virtually every known role that regular faculty members can play in a guidance program.

Teams consider and deal with the student from entrance to college until after graduation. Recommendations for dismissal, transfer, special action, or administrative action always originate with the team. The "whole student" becomes more than a hackneyed cliché.

FUNCTIONS OF THE COORDINATOR OF COUNSELING

Wrenn,[10] in discussing attempts which have been made at coordination, labels as "superficial" two types: The first consists of giving an existing administrative officer additional duties. This results when the dean of the college, dean of men, or dean of women is asked by the president to "look into" one or another matter or to assume responsibility for seeing that something is done about it. The second sets up a committee to study a situation and make recommendations. This eventuates in a report which may call for coordination without reorganization, with persons shuffling titles but continuing to perform the same segregated functions, or with recommendations for new organization and personnel but with the implementation being delayed and finally dropped. Adequate coordination, in the opinion of Wrenn, means placing certain student personnel services under a director, as well as developing appropriate staff relationships with other services and other departments of the institution.

The over-all functions of the coordinator of counseling are seen to be (1) that of architect and engineer for the program of counseling; (2) that of observer; (3) that of appraiser or critic; (4) that of student of and expert in human relations; (5) that of strategist or ethical promoter; and (6) that of interdisciplinary faculty member.

Architect and engineer

It is in the role of architect that the coordinator of counseling has opportunity to use powers of imagination and creation. After the fashion of the artist-technician described by Gropius, the coordinator of counseling "must use the powerful tools of his time and learn to coordinate with broad vision the work of many specialists and special pleaders." [11]

---

[10] C. Gilbert Wrenn, "Counseling with Students," in *Guidance in Educational Institutions,* Thirty-seventh Yearbook of the National Society for the Study of Education, Public School Publishing Company, Bloomington, Ill., 1938, part I, pp. 36–48.

[11] In a review by Peter Blake, *The New York Times* Book Review, Nov. 28, 1954, p. 5, of S. Giedion, *Walter Gropius: Work and Teamwork,* Reinhold Publishing Corporation, New York, 1954.

Observer

As an observer, the coordinator of counseling will spend many hours studying the general aspects of the program as well as its detailed, specific workings. Each new innovation will be approached with these questions:

How will this suggestion affect students on all levels in the academic program? How will this idea be regarded by the teaching faculty? How will this fit into the plans of the top-level administrators? Is this idea pertinent to the work of standing or *ad hoc* committees?

Through observation, the coordinator of counseling is able to anticipate the outcome of events with some of the accuracy of the meteorologist who predicts weather. One may be constrained to ask, "How can one individual (the coordinator) know the feelings of all groups?" The answer lies in the fact that frequent opinion polls, casual as well as formal, are undertaken by the coordinator, these results being recorded and analyzed. A sensitivity to people, both as individuals and in groups, and to situations is essential.

Appraiser or critic

The coordinator of counseling as appraiser or critic is able to detect in his observation the harmonious workings of the counseling process as well as the points of imbalance, overlap, omission, and friction. In the evaluation of the effectiveness of counseling, the coordinator will enlist the help of others—faculty, administrators, students—who are themselves involved in the particular aspect of counseling under surveillance (see Chapter 17).

Expert in human relations

As a professionally trained person, the coordinator of counseling can be expected to demonstrate an understanding of persons—their needs, motives, and personal goals. The caution in the assignment is that oftentimes the pressures of planning, organizing, and coordinating *things* become so heavy as to cut into time which is needed by the coordinator for dealing with the personal problems of *people*. For this important aspect of his work, the building of good spiritual resources and the maintenance of proper mental health are paramount.

Strategist or ethical promoter

The coordinator of counseling as a strategist or ethical promoter senses and secures opportunities for moving the program of counseling forward. The term "strategist," however, possesses a military flavor, smacking of direction, command, and maneuvering. Similarly, the word "promoter" may connote high-pressure dealings, steam-roller tactics, and overselling. The coordinator will, through study and experience, decide when to push an issue concerning a program innovation, how to push, whom to enlist to help, and when to accede. A daily (or nightly) pause for meditation, to consider the extent and quality of the counseling program, is prerequisite to any move on the part of the coordinator of counseling.

Interdisciplinary faculty member

The coordinator of counseling operates most effectively as a member of all faculties, even though the assignment may be to one. The coordinator needs some academic "know-how" with reference to all disciplines. The assignment to teaching, if there is one, may be to the area of psychology or education. Nonetheless, this assignment should not prevent the coordinator's interdisciplinary performance.

Attendance at special art showings, departmental teas, musical events, dramatic presentations, scientific lectures, seminars in the social sciences, short courses for health and physical education, and similar events on campus tends to "educate" the coordinator of counseling to the interdisciplinary role. The reading of departmental newsletters, books, or magazine articles suggested by members of a given department constitutes another way of learning about these disciplines.

The coordinator of counseling may find it possible, on invitation, to teach a given unit in personal adjustment, personality appraisal, or interviewing for the school of education or for the departments of nursing, psychology, sociology, anthropology, business management, or home and family life. He may appear as speaker or member of a team of speakers before business majors or professionals in nursing, home economics, social work, and related fields. Finally, if a program of practicum training can be arranged in conjunction with the departments of education, psychology, social work, home and family life, business management, etc., the graduate student from these disciplines can conceivably profit from the opportunity for applying the techniques of his major discipline in a counseling setting.

Commenting on the need for unifying the disciplines relating to individuals, Gillin writes: [12]

The difficulty is that much of this knowledge is split up and fractionated among a series of disciplines, in such a way that the experts are often unable even to talk to each other intelligently about their respective bodies of knowledge. What is desperately needed is a single discipline dealing with *social man*, a single discipline containing, of course, as many specialties as are required for advancing knowledge. What we have now, however, is a series of

[12] John Gillin, "The Role of the Interdisciplinary Faculty Member," *Personnel-O-Gram*, 10:27–36, June, 1956.

disciplines dealing with man in his social aspects, each to some extent fenced off from the other and each containing competent specialties.

Concluding his discussion, this writer comments: "We need students who are able to seek situations as wholes and faculty who are able to help them do so."

The rejoinder to this comment is, of course, that faculty members themselves must be able to see the institution as a whole entity and their students as whole beings. It is the task of the coordinator in the program of counseling to assist in this objective. In order to promote the inter-disciplinary concept, it is requisite that he be exemplary in the role.

SUMMARY

In the foregoing pages of this chapter, the following questions were considered: What is the need for coordination? What is meant by co-ordination of counseling? How is coordination effected? What are the functions of the program coordinator?

By way of summary it can be said that coordination is a theory of administration. It is an idea which makes use of the abilities of a generalist who possesses knowledge about using the talents of specialists and experts. It is an idea which seeks to keep intact a central design or pattern—in this instance, a pattern of counseling. It is a concept which seeks to promote an operating relationship by welding the workers together by their recognition of a dominant idea. Coordination is not a system of authority; it is rather a method of cooperating. As a theory of administration, coordination comes about "not by accident but by intel-ligent, vigorous, persistent, and organized effort." [13] Once a coordinative plan is outlined, it must be carefully followed, its effectiveness checked, and its efficiency tested. The "price" of effective coordination is eternal vigilance, and this assumes continuous evaluation.

Turning to related aspects, the reader will likely agree that an in-dispensable part of the program of coordinated counseling services is that of record keeping. If the student is to be viewed in total, then the bits and pieces contributing to the whole picture must be marshaled. The student's academic performance, health status, vocational interests, and personal adjustment as reflected in classroom, extraclass, counseling, residence living, and other operational areas must be noted.

The chapter to follow attempts to place emphasis on the need for a system of central records designed to contribute to the improved integra-tion of instructional programs and student personnel and counseling services.

[13] Gulick, *op. cit.*, p. 3.

CHAPTER 10   *Central Records: A Key to*
Coordinated Counseling Services

Record keeping has been or is sure to be the concern of nearly every individual, with recording activities ranging all the way from the entering of dates of birth and death in the family Bible to the more complex setting forth of income and outgo in the ledger used for the family budget. But whether it be Bible or budget that is being annotated, the purpose is the same, namely, the communication of information in writing between and among *those who know the facts* and *those who need to know them.* As a communicational act, record keeping assumes a system, an organization, and a utility.

Thomason [1] contends that the philosophy of records is related to the philosophy of education held by the college or university: If the institution is committed to the promotion of the individual's good and to the stimulation of a continuing process of his development, the records must tell the story of the student from his earliest arrival to the end of his time in the institution.

In programs of counseling in institutions cited in this book, the story of the development of the student is told in such areas as the admissions office, the offices of faculty advisers, the counseling services, the classrooms and offices of administrators, the health service, the residence halls, etc. The necessity for the various parts of "the story" to be brought together [2] is emphasized in the following statement:

Key data should be readily available for use by appropriate academic officers, teaching faculty and personnel workers for the purpose of assisting individual students directly or through intelligent referrals to make wise decisions in educational, vocational and personal adjustment. Due caution, of course,

[1] R. Fred Thomason, "A Registrar Looks at Records," *College and University,* 30:186–193, 1955.
[2] *Future Needs in Student Personnel Work,* American Council on Education, Washington, 1950, pp. 10–11.

should always be exercised in safeguarding data of a confidential nature. Where a central records office is not considered necessary or desirable, some system of assembling records quickly for a given use should be developed. An unwieldy or inadequate system of records tends to discourage referrals and the exchange of important data among the people who should be concerned. Furthermore, the most elaborate and perfected system of records is worthless if it is not in constant use on behalf of the better understanding and adjustment of the individual student.

The strength of the foregoing statement lies in such words and phrases as key data, readily available, appropriate academic officers, faculty and personnel workers, assisting students directly, intelligent referrals, safeguarding data, central records—all of which deserve consideration in this discussion.

BASIC CONSIDERATIONS

Key Data

A working definition of key data might be as follows: that information which characterizes an individual as one of a class and yet different from others within the classification. Age, grade level, family background, personal health index, measured abilities, aptitudes, personality traits, observed behavior and manner, expressed goals and aspirations—all these tend to classify the individual but also to give him special designation within the class. Conceivably, the narrative reports of parents, high school counselors, admissions personnel, residence counselors, faculty advisers, teachers, clinicians, and others, together with the objective indexes, such as course grades, test scores, and other citations of creative output and fitness, constitute the key data about a student which are communicated from those who know to those who need to know. Humphreys [3] enumerates those particular items of information and identifies them as deriving from personal interviews with prospective students, their parents, high school principals and teachers, from admissions officers, and from the various forms submitted to the admissions office.

Availability of Information

That this information must be readily available to those who need to know is understandable. The rather frequent student emergency dictates a "ready-to-go" policy concerning records, in contrast to a "we'll-try-to-get-the-information-soon" policy which delays action and decreases confidence. Hours of valuable administrative time, parent anxiety, and stu-

[3] J. Anthony Humphreys, "Potential Contribution of Admissions and Registrars Offices to the Student Personnel Program," *Personnel-O-Gram*, 12:7–9, December, 1957.

dent frustration can be circumvented through investment of minutes by a records expert in planning ways to gain optimum record utility.

Who Are "Appropriate" Users of Data?

Use of readily available key data by appropriate academic officers, teaching faculty, and personnel workers should be the working pattern. Just as some recorded information about one's family—instances of birthright and budget—is withheld from the "folks outside," so, too, are records of students reserved for the scrutiny of the appropriate and designated faculty personnel. These latter include, conceivably, individuals in the institutional "family" who (a) have an understanding of sociological-economic information, test data, measurements of personality, dynamics of human relations, (b) see the relationships which exist among these data, and (c) appreciate their relevance to the behavior, past and predicted, of students.

Confidentiality

The limitation of the use of key data to appropriate persons tends to safeguard the confidentiality of records. It is obvious that the practice of allowing key data to be used by students and staff indiscriminately will result in the eventual refusal of medical officers, counselors, parents, high school personnel, and others to contribute to the collection of data. The head of a clinical or counseling service must be assured that his report on a given student will be read only by those who have the knowledge and understanding required for reading and subsequent relating of the facts or observations to the problem at hand. Under these conditions, the report will be more fully and more willingly supplied.

The matter of safeguarding materials in the central records office should be studied by each college and university. Among sources helpful for review in an analysis of practice are writings of Omer and Shepard,[4] Shrewsbury,[5] Wrenn,[6] Gilbert,[7] Hahn and MacLean,[8] Stroup,[9] and a series of published statements of ethics by the American Psy-

---

[4, 5] Mary I. Omer and Eugene L. Shepard, "How Records Contribute to Deeper Teaching," pp. 63–83, and Thomas B. Shrewsbury, "Legal Implications for Student Personnel Workers," pp. 299–301, in Esther Lloyd-Jones and Margaret Ruth Smith (eds.), *Student Personnel Work as Deeper Teaching*, Harper & Brothers, New York, 1954.

[6] C. Gilbert Wrenn, "The Ethics of Counseling," *Educational and Psychological Measurement*, 12:161–177, summer, 1952.

[7] William Gilbert, "Relationships Between Counseling Organizations and Other Divisions," in Ralph F. Berdie (ed.), *Concepts and Programs of Counseling*, University of Minnesota Press, Minneapolis, 1951, pp. 45–46.

[8] Milton E. Hahn and Malcolm S. MacLean, *Counseling Psychology*, McGraw-Hill Book Company, Inc., New York, 1955, p. 94.

[9] Herbert Stroup, "Letters to the Editor," *Journal of Counseling Psychology*, 4:248–250, fall, 1957, and a rejoinder by Leona Tyler, "Letters to the Editor," *ibid.*, 4:324, winter, 1957.

chological Association.[10] In discussions relating to confidentiality of records, the members of the staff will come to grips with questions of responsibility to the individual student, the campus community, the national welfare, and society in general. A firm policy with no exceptions to be allowed or a flexible policy with each circumstance to be decided on individual merit—these may be the choices.

Access to Data by Students

The matter of assisting students directly by means of a system of records gives added pause for reflection. Some "great debates" have been staged on the premise that is supported by Omer and Shepard: [11]

> ... the personnel record belongs to the student. He not only should have a part in the building of it but he should have access to the data (since it is about him) in order to be able to use it in the solution of his life problems.

Granted that self-direction and self-reliance are the ultimate educational objectives toward which students strive, *is* the student aided in achieving his goals through recourse to his records, the examination of which may present clues for making a decision of one kind or another? How can a student be helped directly if he is not allowed to review the collected key data? Does this ban upon his viewing the details of his own record create a suspicion on his part of the institutional philosophy? Of counseling aims and objectives? These, too, are questions for staff review in colleges and universities.

It is conceivable that the student may be helped directly if personal data concerning him is used skillfully and judiciously by a professionally trained counselor or an appropriately trained teacher or administrator. Having studied the needs of a group of graduate students in a large metropolitan university, Clark [12] reveals that a comprehensive records system is needed to provide rich and meaningful information which faculty advisers may use in aiding the graduate student in his program planning and the selection of his professional objectives. The establishment of such a system of comprehensive records was visualized as one means for improving the quality of students' contacts with advisers.

The useful information provided for faculty counselors of undergraduates at the University of Connecticut [13] is typical of good record prac-

---

[10] *The American Psychologist,* 5:620–626, November, 1950; 6:57–64, February, 1951; 6:145–166, May, 1951; 6:428–452, August, 1951; 6:626–661, November, 1951; and 8:425–455, August, 1952.

[11] *Op. cit.,* p. 72.

[12] T. C. Clark, "A Plan for Improving the Student Personnel Program of the Department of Educational Administration, Teachers College, Columbia University," a thesis submitted in partial fulfillment of the requirements for the Ed.D. degree, 1953.

[13] *Manual for Academic Counselors,* p. 9.

tices conducted by some institutions. The counseling folder for each student contains the following:

1. Summary of high school courses taken by each entering student
2. If a transfer student, an evaluation of the courses previously taken, including a list of the university equivalent courses, and the freshman-sophomore requirements completed, as well as those still to be completed
3. A check list of college freshman requirements
4. Scores made in the freshman testing program
5. Copies of mid-semester and semester scholarship record
6. Copies of administrative actions pertaining to the student
7. Student interview record for academic counselors on which are recorded notes about conferences with the student
8. Student information sheet for faculty counselors which the student fills in during his first interview with the faculty counselor

Similarly, in the discussion in Chapter 5, the reader will recall that much of the information provided to faculty advisers to facilitate their work was extracted from or was a duplicate of information in the central files. On this score, Humphreys [14] comments:

Fortunately there is available a variety of mechanical and electrical devices for copying materials. Thereby the task of duplicating summaries and transcripts of records is not too difficult and not too expensive. Whatever the cost may be, it is justified by a better quality of student personnel service and by increased efficiency in the operation of the program.

So it is that, through the best possible professional demonstration of the use of student records *for the benefit of the student,* wariness about the misuse of personal data may be diminished. A trust in the system on the part of students and faculty members who contribute information to central records is more likely to be ensured.

Referrals

In possession of key data and enabled to make judgments in conference with the student, the counselor may see good reason for referring the student to another counselor, administrator, member of the teaching faculty, or off-campus agency. That such referral is a part of the counseling process and not merely a "detour," "brush-off," or "sidetrack" is understood by most individuals who work with students. Students themselves can be helped to regard the referral as an aspect of counseling, which, when systematized by means of coordinated procedures, aids them in making a decision.

[14] Humphreys, *op. cit.,* p. 8.

Faculty advisers, for example, will make frequent referral of students to remedial services—reading and speech units.[15] The availability of personal data about the student referred to these units is essential. Time of the student and of the clinician may be saved if background information is transmitted by the faculty adviser together with the statement of the problem as seen by the adviser.

The follow-up report of the clinician, transmitted to the central records unit, will add new information to the growing dimension of the student. The report becomes available for review, as needed, by personnel appropriately trained in methods of interpreting the data.

Where Should Data Be Kept?

In order that appropriate persons in a given college or university have ready access to key data concerning students, consideration should be given to the value of initiating and maintaining a central records office. This is the thesis of the present chapter, and questions such as these, raised earlier, were intended to stimulate thinking relative to the proposal:

Is there, within the institution, an established channel of communication between the various persons who counsel? Is this channel used? Can it be used more effectively?

With whom shall the most personal items about the student reside? Where shall results from tests and examinations be kept?

Shall there be a report of the progress of the student as he works toward a solution of his problem? To whom shall this report be made? At what intervals shall it be made? To whom shall the report be available?

It is the belief of the author that a system of *central* records is decidedly necessary if the aim of the institution is to keep the student *whole* and the persons who work with him fully informed.

THE CENTRALIZATION OF RECORDS

As a result of the consideration of a group of educators as early as 1941, the matter of desirability of central records was viewed as follows: [16]

If the avowed purpose of personnel work with students is to consider them as unified organisms and to see them whole, then it is the responsibility of such a program to make some provision for gathering in one place all the various items of information concerning the individual. There should be kept in the

[15] Albert T. Murphy, "Counseling Students with Speech and Hearing Problems," *Personnel and Guidance Journal*, 33:260–264, January, 1955.

[16] Mrs. Herbert Hawkes, "Importance of Student Personnel Services," Report of Conference Group X, Department of Higher Education, *Current Issues in Higher Education*, Washington, D.C., 1941, pp. 117–118.

personnel office a folder which is as complete a dossier as it is possible to make. Test data, records of interviews, information from the academic office, the health service, the residence halls, and other sources should be assembled and recorded in meaningful cumulative form. There is little disagreement as to the value of a centralized record in the personnel office.

What does centralization of records, as opposed to decentralization, gain? What are the benefits of a central repository? If the attempt of those who work with students is to deal with the whole individual, then information in fragments scattered over one or more acres of campus is not contributing to the aim. The bringing together of well-organized key data constitutes a first step in constructing the picture of *wholeness*. Such centralization would impose the following functions upon the supervisor of the bureau of centralized records and his staff: (1) the collection of data, (2) the organization of data, (3) the preservation of data, and (4) the distribution of data. To carry out each of the functions adequately, the administrator of the central records unit would set his objectives as follows.

Collection of Data

The purpose of collecting data is to develop a working relationship with all college or university personnel who have information about students. These sources of information are, conceivably, admissions office, health service, housing department, business office, areas of the dean of men and dean of women, testing bureau, academic divisions and departments, counseling office, office of placement and financial aid, and other off-campus agencies, such as the Veterans Administration, Vocational Rehabilitation, Council for the Blind, Mental Health Institute, and other community agencies. To effect good working relationships with personnel in these offices, it is essential that the objectives of the central records bureau be understood by those who contribute information. Mutual confidences must be gained particularly with respect to protecting the cumulative reports from the eyes of the prying.

A system for collection of data at definite periods in the academic year should be devised in conferences between the supervisor of records and the officers in cooperating areas. Such questions as these will be raised:

1. What type of information shall be contributed? What items are considered to be of little worth for reporting to central records? What aspects are of very considerable worth? What information is highly confidential?

2. At what time shall the various reports be sent to the office of central records? When is the information most needed by other personnel?

3. In what form shall a given report (test results, health record, residence counselor's evaluation, etc.) be made? Can report forms be devised with a view to try-out?

4. Shall a copy of all information sent to central records be kept by the contributing officer? Does this constitute a duplication of records which is both costly in time and space?

Organization of Data

In organizing collected data, the use to be made of each piece of information should be considered from the point of view of both user and utility. A consideration of such items as these will proceed:

1. The filing system
2. Arrangement and location of files within the room
3. Type of individual cumulative folder
4. Variety of reporting forms within a student's folder
5. Use of a sealed envelope to contain confidential materials
6. Filing of miscellaneous reports and records (original or duplicate form)

These and other considerations are necessary if information is to be communicated between and among (1) those who know the facts about a student and (2) those who need to know them. It is particularly important that all information received be checked for proper source, value to the student's record, general or confidential nature, and immediate or long-term use.

Preservation of Data

The future use of the recorded data as well as their present utility must be considered. In this connection, the director of records, like the librarian, will need to estimate the proportions to which a dossier on a student may grow. This collection of information (multiplied by the hundreds of others on whom folders are being made) will point to the need for a thorough study of the possibilities for housing the records. Limitations for storing the records of students formerly enrolled will surely be felt, since competition for space is spirited in most institutions. These questions must sooner or later be faced by the director of records:

1. What portion of a student's record should be kept after his withdrawal or following his graduation?
2. What are the possibilities for keeping a part of the original record? What is dispensable?
3. What are the possibilities for microfilming the records of those withdrawing or graduating or, in fact, of all students? What are the savings with respect to space in adopting a system of microfilming? Do the space savings make up for the expenditure in microfilming? With microfilming, are the records of students as easily obtainable and usable?

These and other questions deserve review as student enrollments rise, as the use of records increases, and as the space factor looms larger in institutional planning.

Distribution of Data

Another question to be considered is that of the best methods for the use of collected information concerning students who are referred for help. A purely *custodial* concept of records is not reasonable if records exist for the benefit of students. Fundamental to the operation of an office of personnel records is a concept of *service*. Aspects to be considered with respect to serving faculty counselors, administrators, and other qualified personnel are as follows:

1. How shall key data on students be transmitted to appropriate personnel? By face-to-face contact? By telephone? In writing?

2. Who shall be privileged to check out a student's record? Under what conditions? For how long?

3. What information shall be withheld from what members of the faculty and staff? From prospective employers? From governmental or military personnel?

These and other questions are worthy of consideration if there is to be implementation of the policy of supplying accurate information to those persons who are responsible for assisting students in their academic, vocational, and personal-social planning.

In performing the functions of collecting, organizing, preserving, and distributing key data, the director or supervisor of the office of centralized records must (1) effect good working relations with those persons, both on campus and off campus, with whom he works; (2) inspire confidence in those who contribute to the records as well as in those students on whom records are kept; (3) allow the use of the data to dictate the organization of information; (4) consider the custodial aspects of keeping the student's record while he is actively enrolled and after he has left the institution; and (5) experiment with methods of disseminating the information to those whose use of it is legitimate and justified.

THE WORKING RECORD

If a system of centralized records is adopted by an institution, it does not necessarily follow that no records can exist outside the central office. Jottings, notations, and reports in systematized form *are* necessary to the work of counselors. Not all "bits and pieces" of information about a student deserve to be placed in the central cumulative file. There is, then, the need for auxiliary or working records of one or another kind to be kept within easy reach in the office of a counselor, an academic dean, residence counselor, or others. Some duplication of reports, particularly of admissions information and grade sheets, will exist, for understandable reasons.

The counseling folder, prepared for the use of the faculty adviser or counselor and transmitted from one adviser to another as the student progresses in his program, will contain some items which may likewise be found in the cumulative record of the student. The counseling folder is a working record of the type conceded to be indispensable to the counseling process, not a planless duplication of materials in the central records unit. (See App. F-5 for sample work sheet.)

THE PROGRAM OF CENTRALIZED RECORDS AT FLORIDA STATE UNIVERSITY [17]

The office of personnel records at Florida State University was established with these aims: (1) to provide an adequate system of permanent cumulative personnel records which will include pertinent information relative to all aspects of student life and (2) to make such records readily accessible to student personnel officers, to administrative officers, and to members of the faculty. Specifically, the objectives of the office are as follows:

1. To assist faculty counselors, professionally trained counselors, academic and general administrators, and faculty members as they aid the student in the selection of proper curriculum and in adjustments to the university

2. To assist the office of placement in placing the graduate in an appropriate position

3. To encourage broader contributions to the records by those having information about students

4. To assist the supervisor of personnel records in answering confidential inquiries from outside agencies about students

5. To aid faculty members and graduate students in conducting appropriate research in the area of student services

6. To provide information as rapidly as possible concerning any student to those persons who need information about him

Functions of the Office of Personnel Records

Securing information

The task of securing information continues daily, weekly, monthly, and annually. It is necessary to follow up each source of information con-

[17] Contributed by John T. Flournoy, Supervisor of Personnel Records. This unit at the Florida State University has attracted considerable attention both regionally and nationally. Organized in 1947 under the leadership of Dr. J. Broward Culpepper, then Dean of the Division of Student Welfare, this unit has been an important factor in the coordination of a system of decentralized counseling services.

tinuously so that the normal turn-in will not be delayed. Sources of information must be contacted regularly to make certain that the information is in a form that may be readily recorded and interpreted. Information is secured from the office of the president, dean of student personnel, dean of men, men residence counselors, dean of women, women residence counselors, faculty counselors, placement and student aids, test service bureau, registrar, admissions office, veterans unit, academic departments, health services, fraternities, sororities, Florida state-wide testing program, State Department of Education, and other sources that may offer information of value to the records.

Assembling information

Information begins with the receipt of the student's application for admission (see App. F-5) and continues through the date of graduation. The assembling of information requires a special interest in and aptitude for this type of work among the members of the staff. A constant check must be made for accuracy in recording and filing. Information received, confidential or general, is not discussed among office personnel and is not divulged except to certain members of the faculty and administrative staff. Original copies of all information received are permanently filed. All information received is checked for proper source, value to the record of the student, approval of the department head from whose area the information comes, type of information—general or confidential— and immediate value to the faculty and staff with reference to their work.

Disseminating information

Every effort is made to see that all information secured and assembled is readily accessible to those who need such information at the time they need it. The following steps have been taken to render such service:

1. Special forms are provided to give basic information on all incoming students to the coordinator of counseling.

2. Special forms are provided for use of the chaplain, psychiatrist, foreign-student adviser, vocational counselor, etc., in summarizing their student contacts.

3. Special reporting forms are used to give requested information to faculty members making student surveys.

4. Office hours are continuous through the lunch hour to allow extra time for use of information by faculty and administrators.

5. A record check-out system is provided for deans and members of the student personnel council.

6. Sufficient desk space is provided to allow study of the records by the faculty and administrative staff.

7. Manuals for interpretation of all recorded information are available.

8. General information on students (address cards, schedule cards, etc.) is so filed that individuals may have ready access to it.

9. The supervisor of records is available for conferences concerning the records.

10. If particular information is needed and not available, arrangements will be made to secure such information.

11. Information transmitted over the telephone is not encouraged, because of limited personnel and the limitation of telephone facilities. Confidential information will not be given over the telephone.

12. Trained personnel are available to locate records for use of counselors and administrators.

13. Assistance to graduate students conducting research is available when approved by their department head and the dean of the graduate school.

Types of Records

Cumulative personal data card

This card is of heavy material, and all entries are made in ink. The following information is given in easily readable form: name, sex, class, date of birth, home address, birthplace, church affiliation, family background, high school attended, other colleges attended and reasons for changing, vocational plans at the time of admission, course work at Florida State University, extracurricular activities, financial aid, health record, test data, preuniversity-work history, dates of admission and withdrawal, and space for general remarks.

Cumulative folder

This is an expansion-type folder made of heavy, durable material with a tab insert bearing the student's name. In this folder the following information is filed: cumulative personal data card; grades; evaluation of high school credits; health summary; reports from vocational, residence, and social counselors and faculty advisers; letters from parents; other general information. Special sealed envelopes are used for protecting confidential information. (For other types of records, see listing in App. F-5 and F-8.)

Confidentiality of Records

At Florida State University a check-out system for releasing the cumulative folder of the student has been adopted. The entire cumulative folder of a student may be checked out by the president, a dean, or a member of the student personnel council such as the registrar, university physician, coordinator of counseling, director of student aid, or chaplain. A folder must be returned within a twenty-four-hour period unless unusual circumstances dictate that it should be held longer. Highly confidential information is kept in a sealed envelope which may be opened only by the dean or a member of the student personnel council.

A member of the faculty who is neither a dean nor a member of the student personnel council may view the cumulative personal data card only upon request made to the supervisor of the office of personnel records. (See information on an earlier page concerning content of this card.) Other collected key data such as letters from parents, student autobiographical statements, and narrative reports from residence, faculty, or vocational counselors are withheld from the view of general faculty.

To assist the general faculty member in his understanding of test scores, the office of personnel records provides a desk and materials which enable the faculty member to sit down and study materials relating to the purposes of a given test and the implications of the test scores. This preparation assists the faculty member in learning about the test before he or she views the percentile ratings of a particular student.

Should more information be needed by a residence counselor or faculty adviser than is given on the cumulative personal data card, the faculty member is referred to his dean (in the case of a residence counselor) or to the coordinator of counseling (in the case of a faculty adviser).

Coordination of Decentralized Counseling Services through a System of Central Records

The reciprocal activities in building and maintaining a central records system and of using records to effect better communication among those who counsel students can be seen as follows:

1. At the time a student applies for admission to Florida State University, his application is received by the office of admissions and is transmitted directly to the office of personnel records where the cumulative record card is begun. In this file are put health reports as soon as they are received from the health service.

2. Thereupon, the staff in the office of personnel records sends to the coordinator of counseling (on a form devised by the two offices) information which enables the latter office to begin the preparation of a master card, counselor card, and a counseling folder to be used by the faculty adviser. (This counseling folder is not to be confused with the expansion-type cumulative folder housed in the office of personnel records. The

counseling folder is a working tool which is transmitted to the faculty counselor by the coordinator of counseling at the beginning of the new semester when incoming new students are initially counseled.)

3. As a part of the preparation for incoming students, the staff in the office of personnel records begins the annotation of a three-page personal data summary (see App. F-5) which bears information about the student's home address, high school, high school grades, and test scores from the state testing program. The personal data summary is completed immediately after the testing period at the beginning of each new semester when results of the college entrance tests are transmitted to the office of personnel records. This sheet on each new student is transmitted to the coordinator of counseling, who assembles the information in the already prepared counseling folder which is given to the faculty adviser for use in the counseling and advisement process.

4. Pages two and three of the personal data summary are blank at the time of transmittal from the office of personnel records to the coordinator of counseling. It is expected that the faculty adviser will obtain information in the initial conferences concerning the student's educational plans, work history, and other goals. Accordingly, advisers are asked to reciprocate by sending directly to the office of personnel records, after counseling and registration, the completed pages two and three of the personal data summary. Upon receipt of these pages from each counselor, the clerical staff in the office of personnel records makes note of the data on the cumulative personal data card. Pages two and three of the personal data summary are returned within a forty-eight-hour period to the faculty counselor in order that he may have continued use of the material in his counseling.

5. At the end of each semester, the residence counselor supplies the office of dean of men (for men's residence) or office of dean of women (for women's residence) with reports on each resident student. These are transmitted to the office of personnel records for filing in the student's cumulative folder. Reports on day students are submitted by day-student advisers.

6. At mid-semester, the faculty adviser confers with each freshman who has received an "unsatisfactory" warning in his course work. A report of this conference is transmitted to the coordinator of counseling who, after reading it, sends it to the office of personnel records for filing in the cumulative folder of the student (App. F-7).

7. Reports of all case conferences, disciplinary action, and health committee action are sent by the appropriate officer in the division of student personnel to the office of personnel records.

8. All correspondence with the family of the student is filed by the receiving officer in the office of personnel records.

In this connection a questionnaire, completed by the parents of a student, covering matters of educational-vocational choice and sent to the office of coordinator of counseling, is handled in the following coordinative fashion:

a. The information is read by the staff in the office of coordinator of counseling. Notations are made on the *master card* of the student.

b. The form containing the information is put in the counseling folder of the student for the use of the faculty adviser.

c. The faculty adviser retains the parent's statement for approximately four days of initial counseling during the orientation period. Thereafter this statement, together with the personal data summary, second and third pages, is sent to the office of personnel records.

d. The statements from parents are sorted by the office of personnel records and sent to the respective residence counselor or day-student adviser of the student for his or her information.

e. After perusal by the residence counselor or day-student adviser, the parents' statement is returned to the office of personnel records where it is filed in the cumulative folder of the student.

9. An autobiographical sketch of the student stating his aims in coming to college, devised by the coordinator of counseling and appearing as Part III of the application form, is viewed in turn by the faculty adviser, residence counselor, or day-student adviser before its return to the office of personnel records.

These and other working relationships set up between the office of personnel records and cooperating agencies on campus serve to provide a means of communication between and among personnel who know or who need to know key data concerning the student. In the opinion of Omer and Shepard, this type of communication is essential to the coordinative process: [18]

> Coordination of the efforts of the various specialists with whom the student may be working, prevention of duplication of counseling and "clinic-hopping," and prompt referral of students to appropriate sources of help are possible only when there is a central cumulative personnel folder for each student easily accessible to the coordinator.

A central records system, well planned and efficiently organized, provides opportunity for the following:

1. Sharing of admissions information, including health examination, about incoming students among personnel in the office of registrar, offices of dean of men and dean of women, and office of coordinator of counseling.

[18] Omer and Shepard, *op. cit.*, p. 77.

2. Sharing of information submitted by parents of the student among personnel in the office of coordinator of counseling, faculty advisers, and residence-hall counselors.

3. Sharing of high school grades, high school test scores, college-entrance test scores, and college grades among personnel of the test service bureau, faculty advisers, and residence counselors, as well as among members of the student personnel council.

4. Sharing of narrative end-of-semester reports of the residence counselors, as well as mid-semester and end-of-year reports of faculty advisers, among members of the student personnel council.

5. Sharing of case-conference reports and reports of committees on discipline and health (as an individual student is involved) among members of the student personnel council.

6. Sharing of all the foregoing information with the president, the dean of students, director of personnel records, dean of men or dean of women, coordinator of counseling, and with representatives of the government or military services as needed and requested.

7. Sharing of some aspects of the foregoing information by the director of placement with prospective employers of the student.

8. Sharing of certain "distilled" aspects of the information with the parent of a student or the student himself, particularly as respects college grades and predictions of probable achievement in college work. This interpretation of the student's ability and achievement is done by personnel in the office of coordinator of counseling or the office of admissions in a conference setting or in correspondence with the parents.

9. Sharing of certain aspects of the foregoing with trained counselors and with qualified graduate students majoring in guidance and personnel who are conducting studies on a particular aspect of student life or student counseling. A committee set up by the dean of students and numbering the director of personnel records, the coordinator of counseling, dean of men, and dean of women review all requests for use of data by graduate students and make appropriate recommendations regarding such use.

The Expanding Service

With the increase of numbers of students as well as of student services and with the change in personnel in the various offices on the campus, there is need for periodic review of the functions of the office of personnel records. Opportunity for this review comes about at Florida State University through reports given by the supervisor of personnel records to the student personnel council in weekly meetings. In addition, frequent conferences are held by the supervisor of records with the dean of students, coordinator of counseling, the registrar, dean of men and dean of women, university physician, director of test service bureau, and other officers who cooperate in the collection of records. Further to systematize the program, a committee has been appointed to study and make recommendations concerning the kinds of testing being done in all areas of campus activity and the recording of these scores. If record keeping is basically a communicational activity, then frequent review of the functions of collecting, organizing, preserving, and distributing the key data should be made.

An efficient records service will anticipate the needs of a growing student body and of expanding student services. Present practice should be examined in the light of demands of the coming year and decade. Plans for improving the system of centralized records described in the foregoing are seen in these aims:

1. To make a study of the types of information requested by university personnel and how such information is used

2. To encourage a broader use by qualified personnel of information which is available, thus increasing the cooperative aspects of record collection

3. To encourage broader contributions to the records by those having pertinent information to give, this resulting in the more nearly whole picture of the student

4. To continue to improve the program of in-service training concerning records for all personnel who contribute to central records

SUMMARY

In the interest of coordinating better the efforts of all those who work with students, the exploration of a system of centralized records is recommended by the author. Greater economy in space utilization, in avoidance of unnecessary duplication of effort and materials, and in more efficient use of faculty time is achieved when the student's record can be located in a matter of minutes and his progress in the institution viewed in materials systematically arranged. A system of centralized records gives evidence of an institution's belief that a whole picture of the student is exceedingly more to be desired than a partial picture. It gives evidence, too, of an educational philosophy which denotes that administrators, counselors, and faculty are in agreement as to the importance of sharing key data in a professional enterprise.

In this day when staff members wince at extra clerical work and academic jokesters portend that the nation's forests are being critically denuded by administrative paper pyramiding, the author pauses to reflect the sane view of records given by Wrenn: [19]

[19] C. Gilbert Wrenn, *Student Personnel Work in College*, The Ronald Press Company, New York, 1951, p. 447.

Records are a means to an end—that of assisting in but not determining the judgment of the user. They have no sacred significance in themselves.

Up to this point, major consideration has been given to the integration of effort of on-campus personnel—teaching faculty, advising faculty, general and academic administrators, directors of counseling, and nonacademic personnel. There are other integrative concerns, and a chief one among them is a concern for better articulation of programs in the secondary school with those of the college or university. Emphasis upon the whole student demands that an accounting be made of the coordination of high school and college-university counseling. Such consideration is made in Chapter 11 to follow.

The Articulation of High School and College Counseling

THE STUDENT IN TRANSITION

Along with his wardrobe, room furnishings, and items of sentiment and treasure, the new freshman brings to college his most personal possessions—motives, abilities, aptitudes, habits of work, manner of expression, and other marks of his individuality. The interim of three summer months following high school graduation does little to alter these trappings of self. The mere transplantation of the young adult from home to the college campus effects no great changes in him. As was true in his transition from junior to senior high school, he carries with him to the new environment patterns of behavior reasonably well set.

Accordingly, a picture of what the new student is like, what his previous school performance has been, and what his expectations of the new college experience are—all these are of paramount importance to those who counsel him. The expectation of the new college student for himself and the expectations of others concerning him are of interest not only to the college counselor but also to the high school teachers, his college instructors, his parents, and himself. One writer [1] has graphically portrayed the picture of the high school graduate with his newly acquired possession:

IT DOESN'T LOOK HEAVY

It doesn't look heavy, a high school diploma: only a bit of paper (it isn't really sheepskin), a few drops of ink, a bit of colored ribbon from Woolworth's. It doesn't weigh much; nevertheless, a high school diploma is heavy. It is heavy with expectations.

There is the expectation of teachers that the diploma bearer will be willing to use the dictionary and the encyclopedia, the expectation that he will think clean and clear and straight and frequently.

[1] Kenneth I. Brown, *Not Minds Alone*, Harper & Brothers, New York, 1954, p. 63.

There is the expectation of both teachers and parents that he will be teachable, and being teachable is essentially wanting to grow in wisdom and understanding.

There are the citizens who expect him to be a good citizen, informed about the world with its variety of governments but loyal to America.

There are the neighbors who expect him to be dependable, able to carry routine for a succession of days.

And there are those friends who expect him to have a special ability of understanding and caring for people, any people, all people.

The high school diploma is a heavy bit of luggage when the proud graduate sets out for college.

At what points are the expectations of others and the expectation of self identical, somewhat similar, totally dissimilar? In what direction will the student, new to college, go? What are the forces which will change this "set of sail"? How can the expectation of himself, of his parents, high school teachers, college teachers, and counselors be brought into closer alignment? (See Chapter 13 for some discussion of this question.)

In an effort to determine the views of "students in transition" concerning general high school–college articulation, Dr. Marjorie Carpenter [2] interviewed six Stephens College students. Some individual comments were these:

During my freshman year in high school everyone filled out a form telling whether or not he was going to college and what vocation he planned to follow. I was sure then that I wanted to major in dramatics. But each year that's passed has made me less sure.

I'm transferring next year to a university where science courses are required. I'm not interested in science. If I had known I needed science in senior college, I would have taken the courses in high school.

In our high school the teachers did too much for us. However, in our junior year we could elect junior-college work, such as art history, which helped us to think. I wish a course in psychology had been available.

A summary of comments from the six discussants, new to college, indicated that they felt that (1) they needed English skills which could be counted on to assist them in college course work, as well as a background in history and American government; (2) they should like to have known in advance the courses required in college; (3) they needed competent guidance in high school but felt that this should be directed toward a development of self-reliance; (4) they preferred somewhat more freedom in college, feeling resentful of having to take certain required course work, and (5) they agreed that the high school curriculum (or instruc-

[2] Marjorie Carpenter and students, "High School–College Articulation," *NEA Journal*, 44:172–173, March, 1955.

tional methods) should have included more training in how to study effectively.

At another level, a group of educators studying pressing concerns in student personnel work affirm that there is a need as follows: [3]

To achieve a better degree of integration between the student personnel programs in secondary schools and institutions for higher education. Pread-missions counseling and selection procedures may become more useful both to the student and the institution if what has gone on in the secondary school is recognized as a part of the process. This principle involves not only utilization by the admissions office of available high school data but also a recognition and encouragement on the part of the higher institution of the incidence, growth, and development of student personnel practice in the high schools.

In order to assess the kind of integration which needs to be achieved between the high school and institutions of higher learning, the following questions should be reviewed:

1. Is there *preadmissions counseling* offered to prospective college students by (*a*) the high school, (*b*) the college or university, or (*c*) by both? Is the counseling fair, without bias, and individualized?

2. Are *selection procedures* of the college or university well defined and understood by high school teachers, counselors, and administrators? By college teachers, counselors, and administrators? By prospective college students and their parents? Are *retention regulations* equally well understood?

3. Are data on high school graduates transmitted by the secondary school administrators to officials of the college? How will these data be used?

4. Are there *recognition* and *encouragement*, on the part of college personnel, of good student personnel practice, including counseling, in the high schools?

5. Is there a *working relationship*, professional yet friendly, among those who teach, counsel, and serve administratively in the secondary school and those who teach, counsel, and serve as administrators at the college and university level? If such a relationship exists, what is its *quality?*

WHO IS THE NEW STUDENT?

As has been indicated, the average student new to college carries with him the cumulative educational trappings of his seventeen or eighteen years. To consider that his life "begins with college" is to discount the

[3] *Future Needs in Student Personnel Work,* American Council on Education, Washington, 1950, p. 7.

continuity of human experience. He is "a part of all that he has met," which gives rise to the questions: What *has* he met? What *is* he physically, physiologically, psychologically, mentally, spiritually, socially? What are his purposes in coming to college? What are his hopes and dreams and aspirations? What have been his failures, frustrations, and faults?

The task of those who counsel is to determine who and what the new student is and, in view of this knowledge and understanding, to assist him in finding his place in the educational program of the college or university.

Who knows the newcomer and who knows him best? Without doubt, he is known by twenty or more teachers who have worked with him in grade and secondary school and by a sizable number of public school administrators, supervisors, and specialized personnel. The knowledge possessed by these educators has very likely been reflected in grade reports, narrative or anecdotal records, rating scales, and letters of recommendation, with copies of these residing in the student's cumulative record.

If the precollege information, objective and subjective in nature, is collected and recorded, then a very important means for improving the integration of high school and college counseling may exist. High school administrators customarily send information relating to students' academic achievement to the registrar of the college or university. In addition, there is the possibility of the high school guidance counselor's forwarding to the director of college counseling additional information which reflects particular guidance given to the student. This transference of record will probably take place only when the high school administrator has complete confidence in persons who use such records in the institution of higher learning. This practice makes necessary the establishment of good working relationships between the high school and the college and among counseling personnel in both. One expert in the area of student personnel contends: [4]

The method whereby all of the information that is available within an institution concerning its students may be brought together in usable form is really the crux of the coordination of personnel services.

The real challenge in interinstitutional coordination lies in perfecting methods and procedures whereby all the information that is available within a given institution concerning its students, *and likewise within institutions or agencies cooperating with it,* can be brought together in usable form and oftentimes at fairly short notice.

[4] A. J. Brumbaugh, "Issues in the Administrative Organization for Student Personnel Services," in John Dale Russell (ed.), *Student Personnel Services in College and Universities,* University of Chicago Press, Chicago, 1941, p. 124.

WHAT HAS THE NEW STUDENT BEEN TAUGHT?

The view of the new student's previous academic achievement (grades, test scores, etc.) is important, but these are more meaningful if college and university personnel have knowledge of the total curriculum of a given high school and of the teaching of specific courses. As college personnel in the areas of admissions, records, testing, and counseling review the transcripts sent in from the high schools, such questions as these are raised:

What is the course in college-preparatory English offered by the high school? What is its emphasis? In what ways does it prepare the student for the beginning course in college?

What is the first-year course in algebra in this particular high school? The sophomore courses in geometry? What offerings in high school mathematics are intended to prepare the prospective collegian for advanced mathematics, college physics, chemistry, or other science areas?

What is the ninth-grade government or civics course? Is its aim to prepare for the college course in American problems, social problems, current social issues?

To the extent that high school and college teachers can communicate with each other about their teaching areas through printed materials, in professional meetings, and in informal gatherings, some understandings about the educational experiences of high school students can be shared. In many instances, the communication falls short of the best expectations. Teachers of core subjects in high school are not always conversant with the recent developments in programs of general or basic education at the college level. The college teacher, in turn, is not apprised of developments in core curricula in secondary schools of the area. The pre-college preparation necessary for a prospective nurse, home economist, or scientist is oftentimes not known by the high school student or his counselor. The college counselors may have failed to transmit this information to guidance personnel in the high school. The segmented student with compartmentalized learnings from secondary school contemplating the prepackaged and discrete learnings of higher education is too common. More frequent and more accurate communication between and among high school and college teachers and administrators about course content on both levels is necessary for the effective coordination of counseling.

Knowledge is needed, too, of the methods used by teachers of courses in the high school core curriculum and in the special subjects. Analysis needs to be made of the certification requirements which apply to teachers in the various subject-matter areas, of the provisions of the temporary teaching certificate, and of the degree to which the accreditation standards are being met by the particular high school. The student new to college is helped or hindered by "all that he has met" in relation to the breadth or limitations in content of his high school courses, the excellence or mediocrity of method employed by his instructors, and the general accreditation rating of his school.

How can an institution of higher learning—its teaching faculty and its counseling staff—learn how a student has been taught? One of the obvious means is through the professional activities, statewide or regional, in which high school and college personnel join. In addition, understandings are built through the visitation of high school teachers and counselors to the college campus and the reciprocal visitation of college personnel to high schools. Cooperative action of the two groups in preschool planning workshops, seminars, and conferences also produces results. A combination of activities such as these deserves to be tried.

WHAT WILL THE NEW STUDENT BE TAUGHT?

To require that college personnel be acquainted with the curriculum and teaching in high school is to view only one phase of reciprocal activity. As indicated, high school administrators, curriculum supervisors, and guidance counselors need to know about the curriculum of the college or university into which high school graduates will enter. Such questions as these will surely be asked by high school administrators and counselors about the alphabetic gamut, A through Z, of colleges and universities:

Is there a core curriculum or program of general or basic studies in Utopia University? Of what is it composed? Where in the various subject-matter areas is there a duplication of the basic or core program in high school? At what points is reinforcement needed?

What are the areas of educational specialty in the program of Celestial College? For what specific professional areas is training given? What preparation, for instance, is given in fields in which women can major? What technical training is offered for a prospective two-year student?

In Nonpareil University, is there a program of work-study for the student with financial problems? Is correspondence or extension work open to the undergraduate? Is there the possibility of effecting an interdivisional program of studies? What are the possible combinations in major and minor course work and in supporting areas?

As was pointed out in Chapter 1, the program of personnel services, and of counseling specifically, is an integral part of the educational experience. As important as it is for high school personnel to learn of the course offerings of the college, it is equally important to inform them about other educational opportunities. In this connection, these questions deserve answer:

What kinds of counseling does Superlative College offer to students? What induction will the new student receive as he enters upon his program of studies? In selecting his course work will he be aided by a faculty adviser? A professionally trained counselor?

What does Exemplar University provide in the way of residence counseling? Is there an experienced and understanding person in the residence hall to whom the new student may turn for help in solving a personal problem?

Does Peerless College provide vocational advisement? Financial counseling? Opportunities for individual testing and for interpretation of the results?

Is there adequate health advisement in Quality College? Are consultations with specialists in physical and mental health possible?

At Paragon College, is it possible to discuss a problem of religious nature with a trained counselor? To obtain counseling on a marital problem?

How can information about the total educational program of the college and university be transmitted to the high school teachers, counselors, and administrators who are responsible for counseling college-bound youth? Perhaps the most-used method is that of publication—a brochure explaining general education; a series of pamphlets dealing with the preprofessional, technical, terminal, or specialty preparations; a section of the college or university catalogue reserved for the description of major and minor course work; or bulletins issued once a year (or oftener) devoted to the expanding college cafeterium of offerings. Educational radio and television can help to portray the life and times of a college or university by means of selected incidents. Sound movies are another useful means of communication, with numbers of institutions experimenting in producing an aesthetically pleasing version of "campus life on celluloid."

The "live speaker" is most often used to communicate information to high school students about the college. Frequently, high school students and guidance counselors request that upperclass college students be sent to speak about the curriculum as they have experienced it. These young college ambassadors appearing before high school groups on career- or college-day programs or engaging in interviews with students and their parents help the high school student "project himself" into the role of the collegian. This choice of speaker does not rule out the possible effectiveness of a faculty member who is selected to speak about the curriculum or offerings of his institution. If his explanation is made graphic and functional for the high school audience, the faculty emissary has similar appeal. Oftentimes the "student-faculty team" is effective, with the faculty member giving a total picture of the institution and the student representative speaking about his particular curricular experiences.

It is obvious that, in the planning for publications, visitations to high schools, participation in college day, and in dramatization through radio, television, and movie media, those persons who are actually engaged in teaching and in counseling deserve to take part. In this latter instance, the service of the director of counseling on the high school relations committee is especially desirable. When high school students select colleges, and high school counselors recommend them, on the basis of individualized attention given and personalized learning experiences provided, then the activity must be accurately described.

WHAT ARE THE OPPORTUNITIES FOR COOPERATION BETWEEN HIGH SCHOOL AND COLLEGE?

If integration of effort between high school and college is to be effected, it will probably devolve upon some group of teachers, counselors, and administrators in the high schools or the colleges to do systematic and concerted planning. The "higher-level" institution has, historically, been in the position of "playing the tune and calling the dance." In some instances, college administrators have had greater opportunity for giving attention to the theory and practice of integration of this type, possessing the financial means for experimenting with methods of integration. Whether it be tradition, timidity, time, or dollars which have retarded the efforts of the high school group, the fact remains that it is most often the college or university which has encouraged coordinative moves. In this day of selective and competitive admissions to college, the ingenuity of high school educators should be challenged in the search for solutions to problems relating to improved articulation.

What are some heartening moves of high school and college personnel toward integrative action? The following review of some present practices is given with the admonition that the reporting institutions have singled out a special type of integration effected by them, although a combination of practices may exist. Hence, the categories are not strictly descriptive of all that is being done.

Integration through cooperation with admissions personnel

HARPUR COLLEGE: Our admissions counselors keep in touch with the high school guidance officers. Each year we have a dinner for these counselors and invite certain members of the faculty to attend. Our admissions counselor personally takes transcripts of grades for each college student to the local high schools at the end of the first semester.

CASE INSTITUTE OF TECHNOLOGY: Our admissions office makes it a point to contact the high school concerning each applicant for admission who is rejected, giving the reasons for rejection. One of the objectives of this procedure is to enable the high school guidance counselor to gain a better perspective of our requirements in order to increase his effectiveness in counseling students about our educational program.

HOWARD UNIVERSITY: Our program of precollege guidance and the Howard University national competitive scholarship examination is centered in the office of admissions. In this office there are a director of admissions and two assistant directors of admissions who spend a large portion of their time in the field, visiting high schools for the purpose of conferring with high school counselors, prospective students, and their parents. These officers are joined by other officers in the student personnel division who spend approximately four weeks during each academic year visiting high schools, holding conferences with prospective students and their parents. Our precollege guidance is not primarily a promotional program; it is a guidance program, focusing upon the individual student. We find that we have excellent working relationships with high schools for the reason that we endeavor to offer the high school and its students *a service* rather than to seek entrance to the high school for promotional reasons only.

Integration through exchange of recorded information between institutions

Every high school administrator makes available to college personnel some kinds of information concerning graduates, but more emphasis could be placed upon this type of cooperation. Chico State College states that cooperating high schools share reports on student ratings and activities at given intervals during the year. South Dakota State College indicates that cumulative records from high schools come to their institution. By way of experiment, the principal of Miami Jackson High School is working cooperatively with the supervisor of personnel records at Florida State University to determine the uses which can be made of the cumulative records of graduates of the high school who enter the university. Some questions to be considered in the process are these: What kind and how much information in the student's cumulative folder will be of use to the faculty adviser in the university? To the residence counselor? To the university physician? To the admissions office, offices of academic deans, and so on? What information shall be retained by the high school for its purposes?

The University of Toledo cites this attempt to improve articulation of high school and college through the exchange of recorded information:

As part of our orientation course, students deliver rating blanks to their high school teachers who return them directly to the student's orientation instructors at the university. In this way, during orientation interviews throughout the first semester of college, high school teachers, college instructors, and the students have an opportunity to contribute to the fund of centralized information about the students. In a city the size of Toledo, it is easy to contact the high school by telephone.

Integration through direct contact of high school and college personnel

ALABAMA POLYTECHNIC INSTITUTE: Our working relations are aided by a program of high school visitation where faculty members from the college instructional staff each year in the spring visit each high school in the state. These faculty members are given brief information about the student guidance service at our institution for use with high school seniors.

TYLER JUNIOR COLLEGE (TEXAS): Permission has been granted for several years now for a "caravan" of faculty members and administrators to visit in each high school in the Tyler Junior College territory to counsel with members of the senior class concerning their plans for college. The "caravan" consists of the dean, the registrar, one or two members from the counseling committee, and one or two faculty members who have a day available. Students are counseled along the lines of how their future in Tyler Junior College can blend with their choice of senior college. This counseling is carried on throughout the year, mainly in the spring, by appointment with the superintendents of the local schools.

Integration by means of a committee

SAN FRANCISCO STATE COLLEGE: We effect a working relationship with the high schools by means of a school relations committee which sponsors visits to high schools, college–high school conferences, and similar activities.

SOUTH DAKOTA STATE COLLEGE: Our institution maintains a committee on high school relations. Members of the committee include the chairman of the admissions committee, the dean of student personnel, the director of testing, and several others. The committee maintains continuous contact with high school officials by mail. Cooperation is given in all testing and guidance programs and through a series of college-day programs sponsored by the State High School Principals' Association.

KENT STATE UNIVERSITY: We have an area guidance council which is composed of high school counselors and directors. They meet periodically on the campus under the general leadership of our director of guidance testing who also teaches some of the courses in the graduate program.

As can be seen, the possibilities for conveying information accurately and graphically to the high school student and his counselor have by no means been exhausted. Increasing demands point to the need, in some large institutions, for a special officer or a permanent committee to devote full time to the matter of articulating high school and university. At Michigan State University such an officer is designated as director of high school relations. Among the activities sponsored by his office is the high school principals' conference which brings to the campus each fall a number of principals who discuss with freshmen their adjustment to campus, their progress in academic subjects, and their particular problems or reactions to the program of general education. Participating in the conferences, in addition, are counselors from the counseling center, teachers of general-education courses, and personnel from the office of dean of students.[5] In institutions in which the appointment of a special officer is not possible, the creation of a committee of administrators and faculty to work on methods for better articulation of high school and college is desirable.

WHAT ARE THE OPPORTUNITIES FOR CONTINUING COOPERATION?

The choice of the "right" college or university and the launching of the new student on a suitable program of study in an environment conducive to his best all-round adjustment make obligatory good working relationships between high school and college counselors. Once launched, the new student, like any small craft on the sea, may be buffeted by emotional tempests or caught in the academic crosscurrents. To right himself before capsizing, the new student may do any one of several things:

He may, if the relationship is a strong and continuing one, write to his high school counselor for advice. Not on the scene and not apprised of all the details, the high school counselor may recommend that his former student seek out the director of the counseling center or a member of the staff. The student will in all likelihood follow through on the suggestion since he places confidence in the advice of his former high school counselor.

Or, the student, finding himself in the academic doldrums, may seek help on campus first, relating to the college counselor the name of his former high school counselor. The professional working relationship enjoyed by the high school guidance counselor and the college counselor generally paves the way for a good counseling relationship to be effected between the new student and his college counselor. That the high school counselor is a member of "the team" of counselors on campus is evidenced by the following case.[6]

Joy, a junior student, was referred to the counseling center for a reevaluation of her plans to enter the field of teaching. Through a case conference, a review of her case was made. Taking part in the case review were the residence counselor, faculty adviser, speech clinician, university physician, and various teachers. It was the opinion of the conferees that

[5] For further explanation, see Melvene D. Hardee (ed.), *Counseling and Guidance in General Education*, World Book Company, Yonkers, N.Y., 1955, Appendix, pp. 417–418.

[6] Related by Audrey Atherton in a panel presentation, American College Personnel Association, Buffalo, N.Y., 1954.

Joy was decidedly handicapped for teaching because of a speech impairment resulting from malformation of her teeth. The speech clinician felt that progress in speech clinic would be great facilitated by dental aid.

After investigation, it was found that Joy's family would be unable to contribute funds for the prosthesis. Accordingly, the director of counseling communicated with the dean of girls in the high school from which the student came. The high school dean consulted with the school nurse who was able to enlist the help of the county health office in obtaining braces and dental treatment for Joy. As a result of this working relationship between the college and the various agencies in the home community, Joy was able to get dental treatment which enabled her to be accepted for teaching internship and later to be employed as a teacher.

The key to this type of working relationship is probably best expressed in the words of one writer: [7]

In any area of social endeavor in a democracy, coordination reduces itself in its simplest form to problems in establishing and maintaining friendly, working relationships among specialists who are essentially human beings first and specialists secondary. Coordination is, therefore, to an appreciable extent, a phase of administration which calls for leadership in the area of human relationships.

The quality of such a working relationship is evidenced by the following communication between a high school counselor and the director of a program of college counseling:

Dear Dr. _____:

We have a girl, Jane B., graduating in June, for whom I am very anxious to make some scholarship arrangements. The girl is almost a straight A student, IQ 126 (at least), and a thoroughly resourceful individual. She has planned all along to major in languages with an idea of entering government service in some field. She has succeeded in two years of Latin and is currently enrolled in Spanish 2 and French 1, showing remarkable aptitude in all.

Jane is not a pretty girl—red hair that needs styling, freckles, and a bit overweight, but lovely brown eyes, a good sense of humor, and an intense desire to go forward in her chosen career. When she moved to our town shortly after the beginning of her ninth grade she had quite an adjustment to make to our rather overprivileged student body. Her father bought a small business and was just getting started when he died very suddenly last summer. Her mother is trying to keep the business but will be able to offer very little help toward college expenses. Jane is willing to take any type of work, even mentioned dishwashing, that would make it possible for her to get her education.

I know how many similar calls you have, but would appreciate any information you could give me about any possibilities for help for this girl.

S/ Dean Katherine Smith

[7] E. G. Williamson, "Coordination by the Administrator," *Journal of Higher Education*, 19:306, June, 1948.

Dear Dr. _____:

Thanks for the copy of Dean Smith's letter to you concerning Jane B. The girl seems to be a high-caliber student and worthy of every effort we can expend in her behalf. I have asked Mrs. Blake of the scholarship division to communicate directly with Dean Smith regarding available scholarships at our university, and I have written to offer a possible undergraduate student assistantship to Jane in the modern language department for this year. Enclosed with my letter were copies of our departmental bulletin and a brochure on language study.

I certainly appreciate your calling my attention to this case. Such suggestions are always most welcome and, as you already know, you can count on this department for cordial, full cooperation with your office and program.

S/   Dr. Victor Olds, Head,
Department of Modern Languages

Dear Dean Smith:

I learned this morning, through the director of counseling and the head of the department of modern languages, that you are interested in securing some assistance for Miss Jane B., a senior in your high school. I understand that Dr. Olds, the head of the department of modern languages, plans to give her every consideration in securing employment for her, and I am writing to bring to your attention any services which this office may give in the way of financial aid. Incidentally, we do not have very much in the way of cash for gifts; however, it may be that in the booklet on scholarships, loans, and student employment, which I am sending under separate cover, Jane may find some suggestions which will result in aid.

Please do not hesitate to write me if I may be of further assistance. With best wishes, I am

S/   Mrs. M. Blake, Acting Director,
Placement and Financial Aids

Dear Dean Smith:

I note that Jane's application to work as a student assistant is already on file in the placement office, which handles student employment. This is all that needs to be done at this time, and we feel that her student assistantship is assured. Perhaps Jane might write Dr. Olds, telling him that she has filed application and that she awaits further instructions from him.

It is well to bear in mind that a student can hold only one campus job at one time. If further funds are needed, you might contact your local Panhellenic, PEO, Women's Club, Eastern Star, Altrusa, Pilot Club, or other organizations of this nature which frequently help students when their need is made known.

The assistantship would certainly cover her food expenses, but there would be the additional cost of the registration fee each semester, books, and extras.

We are very much interested in Jane and hope you will keep in touch as she prepares to enroll.

S/   _____
Director of Counseling

This and other correspondence between personnel in both high school and college resulted in Jane's enrollment as a college freshman. It was the beginning of a working relationship which was to include Jane herself, her faculty adviser, residence counselor, and others who figured in the preliminary correspondence.

Such a case as this points out the manner in which counselors in secondary school may take an active part in the selection of students for college. There is further need for counselors in high school and college to continue cooperation as the student progresses in the curriculum of study. One administrator has stated that, once the high school personnel ascertains where its graduates are enrolled, it must share the burden of follow-up which is needed to improve articulation between high school and college.[8]

In a conference for counselors sponsored by Morgan State College and titled "Articulating the Guidance Program of High School and College," some specific recommendations were stated as follows:

RECOMMENDATIONS FOR COLLEGE AND HIGH SCHOOL

1. Find ways and means to develop some sensitivity to the personnel point of view and definite counseling skills among a larger number of the college instructional staff to the end that "they will realize that freshmen are human."

2. Prepare a handbook designed for high school counselors (formulated jointly by high school and college counselors) and for use especially by the "feeder" schools. This handbook should be in part based on a job analysis aimed at identifying the basic tools necessary for success at the particular college.

3. Work to articulate the testing programs of high school and college—to the extent of working out measures whereby the high school might be better able, using the results of its testing programs, to appraise the student in terms of the likelihood for success at the college level. This would enable the high school to establish the validity of its testing instruments.

As for the summaries from the poll of the fifty colleges and universities cited earlier, the author noted a number of trends toward increased integrative effort in high schools and colleges:

1. The belief on the part of some colleges and universities that ideas for the integration of effort should originate *in the high school* rather than in the institutions of higher education.

2. The tendency of several universities to center responsibility for high school relations with one individual who is able to devote full time to these activities.

3. The sponsorship on the part of the college or university of regular,

[8] Herold C. Hunt, "Problems of Articulation Between High School and College," *The Educational Forum*, 18:285, March, 1954.

carefully planned training programs in guidance for the high school personnel.

4. The inauguration of a series of meetings among high school, junior college, and senior college administrators for discussion of common problems.

5. The move on the part of college personnel to obtain more information on the personality and character of prospective students. In some instances, there was the wish to obtain a report on every student, this leading to the establishment of a central records bureau and to continued in-service training of staff members who would use the records wisely.

6. The sponsorship of more activities on college campuses, such as workshops, seminars, and graduate-course offerings in guidance, designed to attract high school counselors for a period of study, with advanced credit given. (This would afford opportunity for these high school counselors to interview, while on campus, their former students in an effort to obtain information helpful to both the high school and the college in improving articulation.)

7. The improvement of programs already under way which are aimed at coordinating the efforts of high school and college personnel. This would mean the refinement of some ideas, the expansion of others, and the elimination of those which have not worked sufficiently well.

To these might be added the intensification of the search for individuals to fill high school and college counseling posts who see the value of cooperation and who, as Williamson affirms, are specialists in "establishing and maintaining friendly working relationships." [9]

SUMMARY

This chapter has attempted to depict the student in transition from high school to college, centering upon who he is, what he has been taught, and what he seeks to learn in the new environment. Some examples of effective working relations between high school and college were cited, denoting possibilities for increased and improved articulation.

In the chapter to follow, the student in transition is viewed at the point of entry into the college or university. Emphasis is placed in this chapter on the process of coordinating the orientation activities—of utilizing the efforts of teaching faculty, advising faculty, general and academic administrators, and nonacademic personnel. Coordination *in action* with the faculty member in the foreground is the focus of the discussion.

[9] Williamson, *op. cit.*, p. 306.

CHAPTER 12 *The Faculty Member in Programs of Orientation* [*]

In the preceding chapter were discussed both the need and the means for establishing effective channels of communication between the secondary schools from which collegiate neophytes emerge and the colleges which are their destinations. The effort expended to achieve such aims is justified only when the result is put to work for the benefit of students. There is probably no period of greater need for this good working relationship than the period in which students make their initial venture into the life of the college or university. It is at this time also that there is opportunity for interested members of faculty and staff to contribute to a worthwhile endeavor which properly concerns every department and division of the institution. The orientation of a class of new students, when adequately planned and effectively carried out, is a sizable undertaking, and the purpose of this chapter is to review such programming, with emphasis upon the role of the faculty member in its planning and execution.

The members of a new class of college students face their new adventure, for the most part, with both anticipation and some misgivings. As they set out on their golden quest for a college education, they, like Jason's company in that classic earlier quest, know little of what lies ahead. Those famous Greek voyagers, however, were singularly blessed in that their success was assured by means of many mystic devices. From the beginning of their voyage, when Jason poured his libation of magic wine upon the sea, they were protected by all manner of magic and prophecy.

But, unlike Apollonius, the modern educator has no powers of prophecy, no sacrificial libations, and no magic processes upon which he can rely for help in charting a safe, sure course for his youthful voyagers. Lacking a mystic libation, he attempts to bolster the yearly academic launching

[*] By Orrin B. Powell.

194

by means of a well-planned program of orientation. His prophecies are limited to the predictions he is able to obtain from his files of test data and personal information, and in the stead of magic to ensure the success of the venture, he depends upon his ability to achieve the effective co-ordination of all the interests, ideas, plans, and efforts so essential to his enterprise.

The members of almost any freshman class at almost any American college or university lack the homogeneity of background and interest that was enjoyed by the mythical company of the Argo and may be almost as foreign to each other as they are to their new environment. If left to their own devices in this period of newness, they would attempt to adjust to the new situation in many different ways and with more widely varying degrees of success than is now the case. The need for help in this critical period is widely recognized, as may be seen in the efforts of nearly all institutions of higher education to plan and carry out helpful, effective programs of orientation for their new students.

In its simplest sense, orientation is a process of determining where one is with respect to his environment, or to some aspect of it. In its application to helping new students, orientation is a much broader concept. It has implications for the process by which students are helped, not only to find a familiarity with their new environment, but to adjust to it and to realize its potentialities for contributing to their own best interests. It represents a meeting of individuals of widely varying backgrounds and interests and the means by which it is attempted to help them to achieve a feeling of unity, satisfaction, and belongingness within the group and to foster adjustment and security for the individual. At the same time, the educational institution upon whose campus and under whose sponsorship this giant human reaction is taking place has needs of its own which must be met.

Before the institution can begin to function in its traditional role, its new students must be brought to the campus at the proper time, helped to furnish necessary personal information, adequately housed, and accurately registered.

TYPES OF PROGRAMS

In order better to illustrate the nature of the undertaking and the need for the faculty member to leave his classroom or laboratory to participate in this yearly project, it might be helpful to consider some of the most widely adopted kinds of orientation programs and practices. The following descriptions of what are believed to be typical elements of orientation programming are based on data from returned questionnaires, printed programs, correspondence, and other materials obtained from a recent survey by the author and reflect the orientation procedures of some 125 institutions, varying widely in size and geographical location.

The Short Program

The most widely adopted plan of orientation appears to be the somewhat intensive "orientation-week" type of program held on campus just prior to the beginning of classes and covering a period of two days to a week in duration. For this type of orientation program new students are required to arrive on campus in advance of the upperclass student body for a planned series of activities which may include convocations, testing, meetings with deans and faculty personnel, health checks, social events, and registration. Each day's activities are closely scheduled in order to meet the needs of this initial period.

In many institutions the orientation week represents the first direct organized contact with new students and may be terminal in that there is little continuation of planned procedure having as its primary purpose the promotion of good early adjustment of new students to college.

In such instances any necessary continuity of help for and interest in the student's early progress and welfare appears to be largely dependent on the contacts and relationships that he may have been able to establish with his adviser or other faculty members during the brief orientation period.

The "orientation-week" program is a relatively new process in higher education, having made its first appearance about 1923 on the campus of the University of Maine. Such programming, however, has received wide acceptance and now appears yearly on the campuses of institutions of every size and type in almost every part of the nation. Even colleges of the "day-school" or "streetcar" variety that have no housing facilities report holding short orientation programs to aid in meeting the complexities attendant upon the incorporation of new members into their student populations.

Because of the extensive adoption of this kind of program and because of the necessarily considerable contributions of the faculty in its planning and execution, some of its major elements are considered briefly here.

Objectives

The stated objectives of the various orientation-week type of programs investigated by the author appear to fall largely into three general categories:

1. To help the student become acquainted with the institution, its physical facilities, rules, traditions, and opportunities, and with other students

2. To help the student in his initial adjustment to the college environment so that he may achieve a feeling of satisfaction and belongingness in the college community

3. To implement and facilitate the fulfilling of administrative needs related to receiving and enrolling new students

Testing

One of the most widely utilized practices of the orientation process is that of administering tests to the new student group. Inasmuch as it is hardly possible that faculty advisers, deans, and others can know the proficiencies, academic needs, and levels of achievement of new arrivals, and because of the recognized need for a useful, objective basis for early planning, referrals, and general counseling, tests of many kinds are administered.

The kinds of tests most frequently said to be required of new students were psychological or intelligence tests, English placement tests, mathematics placement tests, and tests of reading skills. Other types of instruments not infrequently named were speech and/or hearing tests, interest inventories, personality tests, and achievement tests in a variety of specific academic areas.

The number of tests utilized in individual programs was found to range from as few as a single test to as many as seven, with a majority of institutions reporting three to five such instruments. In a few instances batteries of tests were named. Time requirements for test administration were said to vary from two to twenty hours, although most respondents reported testing periods fairly close to the average requirement of approximately five hours.

The process of scoring tests was said to require as great a period as several weeks in a few institutions, while others reported making them available within twenty-four hours. With a majority of larger institutions and others having machine scoring facilities, test results were said to be ready for use by faculty advisers in the first planning conferences with new students. In this early period, test data were reported to be of greatest value to faculty advisers in providing a basis for schedule planning and sectioning of new students. Test results also were said to aid the faculty adviser in an early detection of need for referrals for remedial help, personal, vocational, or other counseling.

The role of the faculty member in the psychological testing of students is usually considered to be one of applying test results. In some instances faculty members apparently accept responsibilities for their administration as well. An account of the freshman guidance testing program at the Agricultural and Technical College of North Carolina in the second year of the testing program finds tests being administered and processed by faculty members on a voluntary basis.[1]

Counseling-advising

It might reasonably be anticipated that newly enrolled college students could profitably receive individual help in achieving early adjustment, planning schedules, reading the college catalogue, and finding their way through the intricacies of a first registration. Almost every institutional program studied indicated that help of this kind was given in registration-advising. The greater part of counseling in the orientation period was said to be concerned with academic planning and the scheduling of courses for new students. Most prominently named as the persons employed in counseling in this phase were faculty advisers, academic deans, departmental counselors, and counseling-center personnel. A few responses stated that no counseling was required but that such services were available to the student at his own discretion. Only two respondents stated that they did not offer any preregistration counseling, and a third declared it unnecessary, inasmuch as all new students enrolled in the same core curriculum.

Providing for each of these numerous new students an opportunity to talk and plan with a faculty person is no small task. In many cases there are individuals who need to confer with a counselor or adviser a second or even a third time before completing registration with a program befitting his purposes and abilities. The faculty adviser is discussed elsewhere in this book, and it is sufficient to point out that the period of orientation is a point of peak work load and of major contribution. (See App. J for sample program.)

Social activities

Social activities were also seen to play a major role in the orientation programs studied. The majority of printed programs listed a sequence of social events which were scheduled largely in the late afternoon and evening hours. Only a small number of institutions, for the most part junior colleges and day schools, indicated the omission of social events from their programs. Dances, Coke parties, informal mixers and "at homes," student talent shows, picnics, swimming parties, residence-hall parties, and fraternity and sorority rush parties were the events most frequently named. Many programs also listed a special tea, dance, or reception sponsored by the president of the institution. Only a small number of programs included overnight camps, hikes, or other activities

[1] "Utilization of Faculty in Guidance Programs," *SCPA Newsletter*, vol. 6, no. 2, May, 1956, pp. 1, 6.

utilizing local features offering good social or recreational opportunities separate from, but adjacent to, the college campus.

The role of the faculty member varies widely in the social aspects of orientation. In some institutions events of a social or recreational nature were said to be planned and carried out almost entirely by students. On other campuses the social activities were seen being utilized to bring together all the levels of the college community. Some activities attended by both faculty and new students were dances, picnics, field day, hikes, a Dutch-treat luncheon, and others. In this respect the smaller institutions would appear to have some advantage. When new-student classes were small, there seemed to be more opportunities for faculty and new students to share social and recreational activities.

In one such institution where adviser-advisee loads were small, all new students were, on occasion, dinner guests in the homes of their advisers. In another, faculty and students share a talent show. One example of such a relationship is the program of Adrian College where all new students and faculty, including the president and coaching staff, go camping for three days following completion of such necessary activities as testing. In this situation the faculty member is able to accomplish a good deal of counseling and teaching in both group and individual settings.

Assemblies and convocations

Almost all programs investigated scheduled assemblies and convocations for their new students, bringing them together as a whole or in some division for the purpose of bidding them welcome, introducing key persons, and offering information and explanations. Meetings of this kind were reported to present to new students such considerations as the significance of higher education from a personal and/or vocational point of view, the opportunities and facilities available in the institution they have chosen, the prerequisites for success in college, and the standards and traditions of the college or university. A welcoming assembly for new students was the opening feature of the great majority of programs investigated.

Registration

Many programs of orientation listed registration among the activities of the orientation period. However, a number of respondents stated that registration, while taking place within the time and general framework of orientation, was not a part of it. Whether registration is considered a part of orientation or as "something" else, it would appear to have implications affecting the planning and function of the "orientation-week" type of enterprise in that duties attendant on registration usually become the responsibilities of faculty members to some degree, this often depending upon the adequacy of the clerical staff available and the procedures employed.

Only a small number of respondents reported registration of any kind carried out off campus or at some time during the preceding summer. Registration by mail was said to be offered by a few institutions. Respondents were fairly evenly divided with respect to the separation of old and new students for purposes of registration, with approximately half reporting a period for registering new students only.

The Precollege Program

In view of growing enrollments and increased demands on available time, space, and facilities, orientation planners in some institutions have devised procedures for meeting a portion of their orientation needs before students arrive on campus to begin their first period of enrollment.

Summer Programs

In a number of institutions a summer program has been initiated to relieve some of the problems of the crowded orientation period. In programs of this type prospective new students, in most cases already accepted as entering freshmen, travel to the campus for a short stay during the summer months at a time previously scheduled. For several days new-student groups are housed at the institution of their choice while testing, counseling, and often registration are carried on.

The place of the faculty member in such supplementary orientation may best be illustrated by some specific examples of this type of programming.

1. The University of Minnesota's two-day orientation-registration is a period of testing, counseling, and registration of new students. This phase of the program is repeated at scheduled times during the summer months and is completed prior to the beginning of the new-student encampments. The new-student encampments are held at four sites prior to the beginning of welcome week. At these camps one faculty member is present for each seven student campers. Topics covered in discussion are university traditions, purposes of the university, responsibilities of the student and others related to adjustment and achievement in college living. In all, some 200 faculty members are reported to participate in the orientation of new students.

2. In its orientation center, the College of William and Mary offers a two-phase summer program for prospective college students. Phase I is a week-long program for high school juniors, seniors, and recent high school graduates. In this phase, students live on campus and participate in discussions of such topics as college and career, study habits, cur-

riculum requirements, and reading techniques. An analysis is made of each student's scholastic achievement, interests, and aptitudes. Individual conferences with counselors provide each student with a summary and interpretation of the total experience.

In phase II faculty members are widely involved. High school seniors and recent graduates who elect to do so remain at the college and attend appropriate classes during the summer session.

High School and Community Programs

Not all prospective new college freshmen find it necessary to journey to the site of the institution they hope to attend, in order to begin the necessary rites of induction. A small number of institutions have adopted procedures whereby the orientation process is begun in the student's own home community and in his high school. It is accepted practice for many colleges and universities to participate in traditional college-career-day programs by sending representatives to the high schools of the area they serve (see Chapter 11). This participation does seem to imply the inclusion of some of the functions of orientation to the extent of providing for prospective students information about the institution and its offerings and of developing some brief contacts of a counseling nature. At this level, however, recruitment and public relations are likely to overshadow any objectives of building toward students' adjustment to college and their appreciation of skills and understandings requisite to a successful college career.

Illustrative of programs which attempt to go beyond the "college-career-day"-level relationship with high school seniors and recent graduates are the preregistration meetings conducted by the University of Washington. These meetings, held in some twenty Washington communities, are planned so that newly accepted students, their parents or wives, and high school and junior college personnel are given an opportunity to meet in their own or nearby communities with representatives of the instructional and personnel staffs of the university to discuss registration, group living, costs, employment, and other topics related to beginning or continuing a college career. Faculty members, speaking from an all-university point of view, discuss the advisory system, curricula, study and academic adjustment, and university organization. It is intended that the meetings anticipate adjustment problems and help to build a feeling of security for students. The University Alumni Association sponsors preregistration meetings and provides hosts and hostesses for these occasions.

This type of activity also provides an opportunity to gain the active interest of parents and others by encouraging them to participate in an event involving college personnel, their own sons and daughters, and interested alumni.

The Extended Program

In many institutions the brief preclass program was not thought adequate for the orientation of new students, and a number of respondents, especially among institutions of moderate student population, indicated offering an extended orientation program in the form of a series of lectures, assemblies, or a required course. Such courses, lasting throughout the first semester or quarter, were usually said to carry college credit, although this was not always the case.

The faculty role may be seen as greatly expanded in this type of orientation program, which is accompanied by many of the concerns and problems that faculty persons are most accustomed to meeting day by day. An examination of manuals, syllabi, outlines, evaluations, and other printed materials would strongly indicate that in many respects the structuring of the orientation course is generally similar to that of other, more traditional freshman courses. They appear to be largely student-centered with wide concern for utilization of the most effective group processes and the creation of a classroom atmosphere that is conducive to good peer relationships and free interchange.

Some understanding of the content of orientation courses may be gleaned from a listing of some of the more common major topics or study units found in the printed materials mentioned above. Syllabi or manuals might typically include knowing the college (or university); understanding college standards, traditions, and regulations; adjusting to college life; seeking academic achievement through improved study habits, note taking, and reading skill; understanding of self-goals, attitudes, and interests; considering vocational choice; developing skills in human relations; understanding principles of human development; and building a philosophy of life.

These selected topics of study are perhaps even more meaningful if considered in the light of the stated purposes of orientation courses. Some specific statements of objective may be more helpful than a listing of such purposes. Some selected statements of objective are as follows:

SOUTHERN UNIVERSITY: This syllabus was written ... to help you to understand the body of traditions, regulations, activities, educational and vocational opportunities, here and abroad, and the counseling and other special services that make up Southern University's potentiality to you. This syllabus is further intended to help you grow in mental, physical and emotional maturity, and to help guide you toward adjustments that will make you self-directive toward your maximum and optimum development.

BAKERSFIELD COLLEGE: This course is to assist you in adjusting to college life. In it you are encouraged to set up and evaluate your college and life goals. You will be asked to analyze your personal resources in terms of your goals.

NORTHEAST MISSOURI STATE TEACHER'S COLLEGE: The purpose of this course is to assist freshman students toward making further adjustments in college life experiences and in human relations.

HOFSTRA COLLEGE: The purpose of orientation as we see it is to increase the student's receptivity to the total college experience.

Orientation through course work, apparently originating at Boston University about 1888, is not a new practice but has been rather slow in receiving widespread adoption. Currently, however, the trend seems to be in the direction of the inclusion of such courses in the college curriculum. Greene found in his survey of sixty-nine small colleges that thirty-six institutions were offering orientation courses and twelve of the remaining thirty-three planned to add them.[2]

In the more familiar course-work pattern of meeting the objectives of orientation of new students, the faculty member appears likely to contribute most effectively. There are many instances reported which indicate that faculty participation goes beyond usual expectations in attempting to help new students in achieving college goals. Some of these are outlined briefly below:

At Eastern Oklahoma Agricultural and Mechanical College, freshman students enroll in guidance courses taught by their faculty advisers. The class meets once each week but provides an opportunity for teachers to meet individual orientation needs of each student. This course is considered an extension of the advising program of the institution.

Faculty members of Brooklyn College present for the new student a conference featuring information regarding various careers and the types of curricula which relate to them.[3] Faculty members from different academic areas provide career information about those areas in a panel presentation. Curricular information is provided to students in small group settings by members of the broad academic areas involved.

The faculty of Morgan State College became aware of academic failure of freshmen which appeared to be attributable to inadequacies in such basic skills as reading, communications, and study habits.[4] From their deliberations on the causes of student failure, the faculty determined to reorganize the entire orientation program and to dedicate it to helping students to acquire essential academic skills. The new program covered

[2] George H. Greene, "Freshman Orientation Courses in Small Colleges," *Personnel and Guidance Journal*, 32:480–482, April, 1954.

[3] Joseph I. Shulin, "A Career-Curricular Conference," *Personnel and Guidance Journal*, 35:596–601, May, 1957.

[4] Otis D. Froe and Maurice A. Lee, "A New Emphasis in Freshman Orientation," *Personnel and Guidance Journal*, 34:360–365, February, 1956.

a period of two weeks, and the attendance of new students was required.

It was the decision of the faculty that each member would participate in the new program in order that there might be a small student-teacher ratio and in order that faculty might grow in sensitivity to student concerns.

A battery of achievement, aptitude, and interest tests provided initial data for faculty leaders who saw their groups of six or seven for instructional sessions or met their students individually for counseling. Each student had at least one individual conference with his adviser, and each received counseling regarding the significance of his test scores and the matter of exploring a major field. Test-retest evaluation indicated positive gains despite the seeming inadequacy of the two-week period.

At Appalachian State Teachers College, faculty members who teach orientation courses have initiated the use of the case-conference approach as a teaching device.[5] The instructor presents the "case" of a hypothetical student endowed with concerns and problems which appear most likely to be common ones of the students in the class. Class discussion centers about the problems and needs of this imaginary individual. These discussions often result in individual conferences as students are stimulated to explore further their own needs.

THE PERSONNEL AND THE PROGRAM

Neither planning nor execution of orientation programs appeared to be typically the exclusive function of any particular person, department, or group. Programs were said to draw leadership and direction from personnel officers, academic deans, faculty members or committees, and in some few instances from the students themselves. In the process of carrying out the planned activities of orientation, general participation appeared to be even more widespread, with alumni groups, civic and religious organizations, and others added to those already named.

As a result of reading the returned questionnaires and numerous bulletins, pamphlets, letters, and related printed materials regarding orientation programming, the author is impressed by the vast amount of planning and effort they represent. Certainly the induction of new students into college is a concern widely, almost universally, held in higher education. Indeed, one can believe with the late Dean Croft [6] that orientation is not a hodgepodge of activities but has become a program based on sound rationale and is now an integral part of higher education.

Impressive also were the similarities between the majority of programs

[5] Max R. Raines, "Helping College Freshmen Identify Problems Through a Case Conference," *Personnel and Guidance Journal*, 34:417–419, March, 1956.

[6] Lysle W. Croft, "Orientation Week Philosophy and Purposes," *Educational and Psychological Measurement*, 2:711–714, winter, 1951.

studied. It was especially true that among the "orientation-week" type of programs the general structuring of the programs, as well as their component activities, appeared quite similar. This is not to criticize but may be only a not-too-surprising result of the necessarily similar purposes of the orientation of new students, regardless of the type of institution or its geographical location.

The orientation-week program of the University of Maine in 1924, as outlined by H. J. Doerman,[7] lists the following features among its scheduled activities:

1. Lectures. Lecture topics included such things as use of the library, use of books, note taking, colleges of the university, social conduct, and college customs.

2. Tests and exercises. Among these activities were listed a psychological test, a mathematics test, and an exercise in written English.

3. Recreation. Featured among recreational activities were a general welcome, a dance (and games), a stunt-night program, and motion pictures.

4. Other events. Some other activities were a campus inspection, a physical examination, practice in the use of the library, and taking individual photographs.

With a few revisions, this pioneer orientation-week schedule would appear capable of serving as a framework for planning similar programs on many campuses today.

Might we conclude, then, that the differences in such programs lie not in the scheduled activities as they appear in printed pamphlets but rather in the philosophies of those who plan them, in the ingenuity and efficiency of their execution, and in the coordination of efforts which is achieved?

In short, the usefulness of orientation programs rests with people— the people who see them through from the first planning session to the final evaluation. It seems obvious, then, that the major factor is one of human relationships at a number of levels and in many combinations. First, there are the working relationships among and between those who coordinate the total effort and those who participate in carrying out its many and varied parts. Secondly, there are the relationships between those who work in the program and the new students in whose adjustment and welfare the program finds justification. A third type of relationship may be seen in one of orientation's common objectives, namely, the provision of an open, friendly atmosphere within the new-student group to facilitate the formation of class spirit and new friendship ties.

For many of those who work in the orientation endeavor, working

[7] H. J. Doerman, *The Orientation of College Freshmen*, The Williams & Wilkins Company, Baltimore, 1926.

relationships, especially as they touch directly the new student, may be brief ones. Whether programs are of the brief, preregistration variety or are extended through a quarter, semester, or more, their effectiveness is greatly curtailed unless means are found to provide direction and continuity to the success of adjustment. A brief period of a few days or a week can do little more than provide the relationship and the basis for its continuity. If such continuity is not forthcoming, the new student may find himself prematurely dropped or cut off from the assistance he had begun to find.

SUMMARY

Of all those who labor in behalf of the new student, the faculty member appears as a key figure in carrying forward the process begun in the early college days. His teaching role in the classroom, his advising role regarding course requirements and curriculum, his status role in the way students see him, and his many casual contacts with students comprise a medium for directing, extending, and refining the early relationship that is not readily available to the other members of the orientation team.

That many faculty members are willing to participate in orientation and other such endeavors is evidenced by the outcome of a recent experiment tried in the City College of New York.[8] Letters were sent to twenty-five faculty members, who had not previously reflected interest in extracurricular activities, inviting them to participate in the freshman orientation program. Of this group, twenty replied that they would be happy to participate, even though this meant relinquishing free week-end hours. Some of those accepting stated that they would have begun such participation earlier but they had never been asked and assumed that their help was not needed.

Faculty members, upperclass students, parents, and many other interested persons are capable of making valuable contributions to the orientation programs at almost any given college or university. Many institutions recognize this in the breadth of their planning, as may be seen by the variety of interests represented among the participants in orientation on some campuses. One respondent in the study previously mentioned stated realistically, "Everyone on campus helps."

The chapters which follow delineate some aspects of the roles that parents and upperclass students are capable of assuming in implementing the adjustment and development of the younger college student, provided that they too are "invited" to take part.

[8] Buell G. Gallagher, "A College President Looks at Student Personnel Work," *Personnel-O-Gram*, 10:58, June, 1956.

CHAPTER 13　*Parents in the Program of
Coordinated Counseling*

In a very real sense, the college student "leaves home" when he goes off to college. This is particularly true when the student leaves his hometown to enroll in a college or university at a distance from home. The leave-taking in some instances is matter-of-fact, with the son or daughter and the parents giving evidence that good preparation for the student's change of address has been made. In other instances, the leave-taking is more dramatic, with tensions evident on the part of the child or his parents. The role of the institution of higher education in this period of adjustment for the student is much in need of review.

Addressing themselves to the problem, representatives of a professional group point out: [1]

Attitudes of colleges toward the families of students reflect the institution's interest in the student's struggle toward adulthood. . . . College students are in every stage of dependence on their parents. Parental attitudes vary from dominating control over a nearly adult son or daughter to almost complete withdrawal of interest except for financial support, and even that may be lacking. No matter how rebellious the student feels toward his parents, he needs some assurance of their confidence and continuing concern for his welfare and achievement.

FOSTERING PARENT COOPERATION

In the poll of 218 institutions of higher education which has been cited throughout this book, respondents were asked to consider the question "What are the means used by your institution to foster cooperation with parents of students?" In their answers, respondents indicated that the chief means for coordinating the efforts of home and institutions of higher

[1] *Considerations on Personality Development in College Students,* Committee on the College Student of the Group for the Advancement of Psychiatry Report 32, May, 1955, p. 8.

education were (1) letters to parents, (2) campus visitation and tours arranged for parents, (3) individual conferences with parents, (4) booklets and other publications directed to parents, and (5) home visitations.

Generally speaking, the respondents felt that these means were "good" to "excellent" in their effectiveness. Some fewer respondents felt that the letters to parents and the conferences with them were only "fair" in effectiveness (see Tables for more detailed coverage).

The specific purposes for which each activity was employed among the 218 institutions surveyed were these:

1. Letters to report on the progress and general adjustment of the student; to give general information about the institution; to solicit the help or cooperation of the parent; to present details concerning special difficulties of the student—academic, disciplinary, personal, financial, etc.

2. Campus tours and visitation to provide orientation and information; to improve public relations; to serve recruitment ends

3. Conferences to share information concerning personal and academic problems of the student; to solicit the help and cooperation of parents in the guidance process; to promote better relations with parents; to allow for exchange of information between parent and institution

4. Booklets and other publications to present information concerning the institution and its offerings; to improve public relations; to serve recruitment ends

5. Home visitations to consider problems of deep or serious nature; to build good relations with the parents; to survey the student's background

Some of the specific practices among schools regarding these five categories of cooperative activity with parents are considered.

Letters to Parents

Institutions of higher education communicate with parents for a number of reasons. Some colleges and universities follow the practice of sending to parents a commendatory letter concerning the enrollment of son or daughter. Frequently this message is included with a brochure which covers some "minimum essentials" of information concerning the curriculum, institutional regulations, individual counseling, etc. At Bucknell University, the message to the parents is included in the bulletin prepared for use of entering students. (See App. O and Q for examples of letters sent by the General College of the University of North Carolina and by Hofstra College.)

Mimeographed letters covering general information about the institution and the orientation of the new student are sent to parents of students enrolling at East Texas State Teachers College (App. P), East Los Angeles Junior College, and Iowa State Teachers College.

In the category of information extended to parents by letter is the grade report, which is usually sent by the registrar. Differing opinion exists among professional personnel on the matter of "sending the grades home." Some feel that to follow this pattern is to prolong the practice of the elementary and secondary schools in issuing a report card. Some others, citing comments of parents or speaking as parents themselves, feel that the institution is obliged to give information concerning the progress of the student in view of the financial investment of the parent.

In one institution, the practice of sending to parents the report on mid-semester academic status of freshmen was questioned when personnel administrators expressed the feeling that the report was intended for counseling purposes *only*. The faculty adviser, residence counselor, and teacher working cooperatively with the student were viewed as able to effect greater gains than could parents who are removed from the scene. After deliberation, administrators recommended that parents be informed of the status of a student who receives an "unsatisfactory" notice in *more than three* subjects.

The impasse may hopefully be resolved after consideration of this statement: [2]

If the college views the parents as responsible for the student, it may send home report cards, call upon families to put pressure upon a son or daughter to do better work, and consistently involve the family in the student's career. Some students like and may need continued family involvement, but fostering this kind of relationship defers their maturation. The crucial question is how the college can strengthen the student's capacity for adult conduct and help him relinquish the remaining childhood patterns which get in the way of his growing up.

In addition to letters on academic status, there are communications which attempt to interpret the student—his motives, interests, and abilities—to the parent. The letters may inform a parent of a decision made by the student and his faculty adviser regarding a change of schedule or major in which the parent feels that he has considerable stake. An example of this type of communication is the following:

Dear Dr. P_____:

I have before me a copy of the schedule chosen for my son Robert by his faculty adviser. I would like to take this opportunity to voice my objection to such a program for several reasons. First, a load of twelve semester hours is hardly enough to keep him properly occupied, nor is it enough to enable him to graduate in eight semesters, according to your bulletin. The requirement seems to be an average of fifteen and one-half hours per semester, or am I mistaken?

Second, I had previously received from the head of the department a copy

[2] *Considerations on Personality Development in College Students, op. cit.,* p. 9.

of a four-year schedule of my son's chosen course in hotel management. The course now being given to him fails to include history, food and nutrition, physical science, and health education.

I am certain that you will agree with me that he should carry at least fifteen hours, as I feel that he is capable of so doing.

This matter is of great importance to me and I would appreciate your giving same your kind and prompt attention, as it is still early and nothing has been lost by the delay.

Kindly favor me with an immediate reply containing your opinions.

Sincerely yours,

Dear Mr. _____:

Thank you for your letter which arrived yesterday. Since receiving it, we have had the pleasure of talking with Robert. He came in at our request this morning, and we had a good talk concerning his course load.

At our institution we believe that students right out of high school have quite an adjustment to make to the college program. Our period of orientation to the university is rather short at mid-term. Robert arrived on Wednesday, for example, and this precluded his more leisurely orientation which had been set for new students—testing on Monday, January 31st, and counseling on Tuesday, February 1st. Hence, of necessity, he had to "make up for lost time" by being counseled and registered all in one day.

The chairman of the history sections for freshmen prefers that new students not enroll in History 101 until the fall semester. This prevents, in part, the "forgetting" on the part of the students over summer. Therefore, Robert can expect to take history beginning in the fall.

Robert tells me that mathematics and sciences were somewhat difficult for him in high school. His late arrival prevented his taking the mathematics placement test. This he can take in the fall when it is given again. Until that time, we feel it might be advisable for him to hold off until we have the test results which may point to the particular aspects of mathematics on which he should concentrate. The mathematics, in most instances, would be prerequisite to the chemistry and physical science.

Discussing the course work he is now carrying, Robert says the humanities class is requiring considerable reading—a chapter of the *Iliad* for tomorrow, for example. In addition, he feels the English 101 is exacting considerable time. My suggestion to him was to continue for another two days in order to get the "feel" of his course work. When he returns to see me on Thursday, we can get in touch with Mr. D_____, the faculty adviser, and make plans for adding a class or keeping the load as it is.

The typing (secretarial science) class Mr. D_____ felt would be good for Robert since he does not type well enough to do his own papers for the class requirements.

Last night Robert made up part of the initial testing missed Tuesday, February 1st, by taking two of the required examinations. I hope to have the results from these tests by Thursday when he returns. Robert, Mr. D_____, and I can then consider the addition of course work on the basis, in part, of his potential in the quantitative and qualitative areas of the examination. The students are told that the examination scores are used by counselors to adjudge their course load with respect to kind and type of subject.

I believe the foregoing covers, for now, the points I had in mind. Robert tells me he will continue to write you regularly. He realizes that—in being a long way from home—there is additional worry on your part about his welfare and his academic progress.

Be assured that we have Robert's best interests at heart. Today is a bright sunny day down here, and you can picture some several thousand students at our university starting out the new semester with considerable enthusiasm —Robert among them.

Sincerely,

_____

Director of Counseling

Campus Visitation and Tours

A number of institutions of higher education assume that the parents of new students will visit the campus at the time the son or daughter enrolls. In the bulletin for students entering Bucknell University, parents are informed that special meetings have been arranged for them at the time their son or daughter enters the university. These events include an opportunity for meeting the faculty and their wives in an informal greeting period; the opening assembly of entering students, at which time the president of the institution addresses the class; a parents' coffee hour which features members of the administration who speak on certain phases of university life; an informal reception at the president's home; and church attendance.

The president's reception at Temple University attempts to provide for entering students and their parents a brief orientation to aims and objectives of the institution. Smaller groups are formed during the evening, with discussions led by the deans of the college in which the student is enrolling.

The University of Missouri sponsors a parents' day early in the first semester. The program for this event includes an informal reception at which time the president, deans of various divisions, some faculty members, as well as members of the student government association and other groups, are on hand.

Parents' week end is held yearly at the State University of New York College for Teachers at Buffalo, the program including a convocation; tours and open-house events; fashion show; "meet the faculty" hour; buffet supper; dramatic production; tours of residence halls, campus school, and library; and president's reception.

Some institutions make a special effort to obtain the participation of parents in special events during the visitation—a request for their addressing small groups in the area of the father's or mother's occupational specialty; speaking at a luncheon or dinner meeting on a topic relating to the theme of the events; conferring with special administrative officers to give evaluative comments about the institution or advice about one phase or another of its operation. At Stephens College, for instance, fathers of some students have served on an advisory board for the business education department.

Conferences: Formal and Informal

At Princeton University the freshman parents' day includes conferences with the faculty advisers and heads of freshman courses of study. In most institutions, however, the opportunity for parents, faculty advisers, and deans to confer is not formalized. Some parents request a conference with a faculty adviser or professional counselor at the time the student enters.

In some instances, the parent may be passing through the city or near the institution on a business or vacation trip and may make an impromptu call. The author recalls the incident of a father who operated a small farm in central Georgia and who, when he received word from his daughter that she was taking "general-education" subjects, promptly got in his truck and set out for the university to find out just what these courses were. His expectation for her was that she take "business subjects" so that she could become a stenographer as soon as possible. A conference with the professional counseling staff and the faculty adviser served to convince him that his daughter "could use" some general education along with her business course work.

The more frequent conference is that initiated by the deans, director of counseling, or faculty adviser and covering some aspect of the student's adjustment. When the parent resides within fairly easy driving distance, or when living at greater distance he is willing to come to the college or university, there is likelihood that some basic planning can be effected in combination with several individuals.

This type of conference, which *does not* include the student in the initial stage, is held in many institutions. In one instance, a student with a speech impairment confided to his counselor that the goal of engineering had been set for him by his father. Performance in the basic courses in mathematics and drafting indicated that the student had little aptitude for the work. His preferences ran to art education and the teaching of industrial arts. In a conference with the dean of the College of Arts-Sciences, the director of counseling, the faculty adviser for engineering majors, and the speech clinician, the father admitted that he wished to promote the best interests of his son. Forthwith, he gave consent for the son to transfer from the engineering curriculum to the program in art education in which he eventually finished with a most creditable showing.

As can be expected, the conference of this type tends to reveal a great deal about the student's relations with his parents—the degree to which their expectations are forced on the student rather than suggested. When the parent is close enough, geographically or psychologically, to exert pressure on the student in a manner which deters his growth and maturity, the process of guiding the parent looms large. The case of Dean given at the conclusion of this chapter tends to illustrate this "parental interference," unwholesome in kind.

Sometimes an incident occurs that serves no real purpose other than the promotion of better relations with parents. A rather wealthy father, formerly from a large northern city but now retired, decided to visit the campus to "talk with everyone about his son." The father was a Scandinavian immigrant who had made a small fortune in this country through perseverance and toil, and he seemed very concerned that his boy work hard and make his own way, in order that it "make a man out of him." His son, enrolled on the campus as a freshman and working part time, had had no apparent academic, social, or financial problems. Nevertheless a conference was arranged by a professional counselor for the father together with the son's faculty adviser. At this time the father was able to relate his ambitions for the personal development of the boy. Eventually the conversation became more personal when the faculty adviser related that he too was of Scandinavian descent, and the father became relaxed and jovial. Even though the conference had not been necessary for solution of a particular problem, the faculty adviser obtained a better understanding of the background and parental expectations of his advisee, and the father returned home with a feeling of satisfaction that his son would not be lost in the sometimes impersonal atmosphere of a large university campus.

Booklets and Other Publications

The University of Rochester publishes a *Guidebook for Parents of Freshmen Women* which covers information on the work of the freshman adviser, the social adviser, the dormitory counselor, the work of religious counselors, health officers, vocational counselor, the opportunities for obtaining financial aid, class attendance, and travel regulations.

At Lafayette College, the dean of students prepares for distribution a leaflet titled *From My Side of the Desk*. Among the topics discussed are matters of college cost, fraternity membership, keeping a car on campus, parents' week end, religious development, and expectations of the college concerning the student. These leaflets are sent to parents together with each grade report.

At Kent State University, the president prepares a brochure which is titled *Footnotes* and which deals with the grading practices of the institution, its extracurricular activities, the health service, the food service, vocational choice, military deferment, etc. The office of dean of women in the same institution sends a booklet to parents of freshmen women which covers academic policies and procedures, time budgeting, social conduct, dormitory procedures, counseling, and education outside the classroom.

Any publications policy is based upon the idea that parents are interested in information about their son's or daughter's educational experiences and will, accordingly, take time to read it. The tie between campus and home is strengthened by the written word, appropriately illustrated and geared to the questions uppermost in the minds of parents.

Home Visitation

The visitation in the home of the college student appears to be the particular function of the preadmissions or admissions counselor in institutions where these officers are employed. The role of the admissions counselor may be described as follows: [3]

The admissions counselor confers with the student regarding plans, goals, interests, and achievements. In addition, he confers concurrently with parents to discuss the general-education program of a given college or university and the function of general education in meeting the needs, interests, and purposes of their son or daughter. After the student has entered college and the relationship has been established with his faculty counselor, the admissions counselor continues this interest in the student's progress by maintaining contact with the parents and the faculty counselor on campus.

In institutions not employing an admissions counselor, infrequent visitations of administrators and counseling and teaching staff may take place. The usual pattern is that in which the representative of the institution appears as a speaker or college-day participant in a given locality and is entertained or interviewed by parents of students residing in the area.

EXPECTATIONS FOR THE NEW STUDENT

A panel presented in a seminar for faculty advisers at Florida State University featured the subject "Expectations of the New Student." The

[3] Eugene L. Shepard, "The Role of the Faculty Counselor in General Education," in Melvene D. Hardee (ed.), *Counseling and Guidance in General Education*, World Book Company, Yonkers, N.Y., 1955, pp. 161–162.

point of view of each of the following was presented: the parent, the faculty member, the faculty adviser, the residence counselor, and the student himself. Two students, a freshman man and woman, reacted to the four presentations preceding theirs.

Dr. Mildred Morgan of the department of home and family life made the following points in discussing the expectations which parents have of their college-going son or daughter:

Really, I expect there are as many expectations on the part of parents as there are parents—and even *pairs* of parents. Many times the father and the mother do not expect the same thing. Differing expectations of parents are shown in the letters which parents write concerning their son or daughter. One letter which I scanned comments: "Our son has never been away from home for more than ten days at a time. He has had a very few of these trips —only to 4-H camp actually. He is our only child, and we were married thirteen years before we had him. We have always tried to keep him with us, hoping to prevent anything from happening."

These parents are going to expect a lot from the university and those persons in it who counsel. The son's personal-social guidance will be a big part of their expectation. His physical welfare is entrusted to you. His spiritual well-being is their concern transferred to you.

In another letter, I note that the mother comments: "Jane wants to teach, but I don't want her to become a teacher because I have taught for so many years." Here is a parent expectation which may be a little disconcerting to you. The request is for you to redirect the vocational goals of this student. And who at this moment knows whether the goal of teaching is *right* or *wrong* for this particular student? This is not a usual parent expectation, however.

A third letter comments: "Our boy needs special counseling. He is inclined to become depressed because of inability to grasp subject matter. He needs someone to give encouragement." Here is a plea for academic advisement together with such other specialized counseling as may be required. The faculty adviser must sense the need of the student at intervals for this special assistance —reading clinic, psychiatric aid, psychological counseling, or whatever appears to be the best referral.

Finally, I note this letter: "We feel she's searching for something which will be right for her. We know, however, that she must make her own choice to be happy in her life's work. Eventually, she will be a successful homemaker." This hope is a predominant one for parents of our women students. It goes without saying that parents would not send their daughters to a coeducational school if they did not hope that eventually they would find a mate there. So one parent expectation is for occasional wise and sympathetic guidance concerning the choice of a life partner.

All these expectations voiced by parents—for the academic, vocational, personal-social, health, spiritual welfare of their offspring—are important for a group such as you to consider. You see, I know the heartbeat in these letters, for my husband and I are parents of two college-age children ourselves, and for both Mary Ann and Tom we have at some time expressed hopes similar indeed to those on which I have commented today.

In reply to Dr. Morgan's remarks, Mr. John Blackburn cited his views:

We in the residence-hall counseling program are in a good position to view the dependency of the student upon his parent. Last night, for instance, there was a student who had to call his mother just the minute he got located in his room. This pattern oftentimes persists for several weeks. The same student seems not to be able to make any decision by himself; he must call home to see what "Mom" has to say about it. Of course, there is the other extreme, of the student who *should* get some assistance from home in making important decisions and who refuses to.

Yesterday we had a student who came to the residence hall with his father. As part of the procedure for entering, the boy was asked to fill out a cumulative record which asked for background information. The father stood beside him and directed his every move: "Son, put this here," or, "Now, I wouldn't put that there." The poor boy was embarrassed to tears. One of the assistant counselors started talking to the father about the World Series and maneuvered him away from the desk so that the boy could begin at that moment to think for himself. In the next hour, we gave the father a tour of the residence hall and explained some of the goals and expectations which we had for his son. The result was that the father saw a little more clearly that here was a place that "his boy" could, with assistance, become "a man."

At the conclusion of the panel, George Hill, a freshman, commented on his adjustment to the university, as follows:

When I entered college I found that the hardest thing for me to do was adjust to leaving home. To pull out of the small family group and to find my place among the thousands up here was no easy matter. I would like to add that it was just as hard for my parents to see me leave home as it was for me to leave! These telephone conversations that Mr. Blackburn has mentioned are as much for the adjustment of the parent as of the student. All of a sudden the parent finds that he hasn't anybody to give advice to or make suggestions for or shower his affection on, except maybe the family dog.

One of the biggest things I am learning is how to select my friends. At home we knew families and the idiosyncrasies of this person or that from long-standing acquaintance. Up here we are thrown together with all kinds of people, and out of the many contacts in classes, extraclass, residence hall we are expected to find the group in which we best fit. I am not sure that I am using the right scale for this selection process. I have these doubts probably because I am not sure just what kind of person I wish to become. If I were surer of my life goals, maybe I could select the activities *and the people* that would be *right* for my goal. It's at this point that I need some member of the faculty or of the counseling staff to talk with me about "Where do I go from here?" My folks would be mighty glad to know that I had such an opportunity to consider this with an adult.

THE INSTITUTIONAL POINT OF VIEW

From the foregoing it could be construed that all institutions of higher education cultivate the parent in the process of educating the student. That this is not universally true is attested by the following comment of a dean of students in a western state university:

> We do not ordinarily attempt to establish a working relationship with the families of our prospective students. In many instances, it would be absurd to do so, as the average age of our students is twenty-three years. Parents of students are always welcome to consult us, of course. Most of our students, however, consider themselves to be young adults, and they would be embarrassed to have us "cultivate" their families. Consultation with the families of students, unless they or the students request it, would in many cases cause resentment and loss of confidence on the part of students. Considerable tact is therefore required in this area in our institution.

The purpose and nature of the institution, the nature of the student group—these are a part of the over-all consideration with respect to enlisting the cooperation of the home in the program of coordinated counseling or guidance.

Increasingly, however, institutions are finding that the point of view of the parent—and his or her resulting actions—has much bearing on the performance of the student. An instance of counseling *in combination* with the home is herewith presented, with emphasis upon the fact that the student is a seventeen-year-old freshman.

The Case of Dean

The following information was taken from the application materials submitted to the registrar by Dean, his high school principal, and others.

Father: John R. Mills, businessman; grade school education
Mother: Emma B. Mills, housewife; grade school education
Son: Dean Mills, graduate of Denwood High School; fifty members in the class. Average grades B—; participated in band, baseball, and basketball; vocational interest, business administration with the idea of following in his father's business
High school tests:

	Percentile
Psychological	55th
English	42nd
Social studies	48th
Natural science	56th
Mathematics	61st

High school grades:

English	4 units	C
Civics	1 unit	C
History	2 units	BBBA
Algebra	2 units	BCCC
Geometry	1 unit	BC
Science	1 unit	B
Biology	1 unit	C
Chemistry	1 unit	B
Psychology	1 unit	B
Typing	½ unit	D
Band	2 units	BA

College tests taken during orientation week, freshman year, showed the following:

ACE Psychological Examination (national norms):

	Percentile
Quantitative	21st
Linguistic	33rd
Total	28th

Minnesota Personality scale (local norms):

	Percentile
Morale	75th
Social adjustment	70th
Family relations	30th
Emotionality	1st
Economic conservatism	95th

Voice, hearing, and articulation report: adequate; no defects

Mid-term reports on Dean for the fall semester were sent to the faculty adviser:

Unsatisfactory:

Development of modern society (history)
The humanities
Written communication (English)
Physical science

In early December, the director of counseling received a telephone call from the president of the college. The latter had received a letter from the student's mother, who had indicated the hope that Dean would be given help in his course work.

Dean, in interview, said that he felt that his basic problem was the result of poor preparation in English in high school. The director of counseling suggested that Dean discuss his work with the English teacher with the thought that a referral could be made to the English service (writing clinic) where Dean could have individual help over a longer period of time. Dean indicated his willingness to follow through on the suggestion.

In January, Dean's mother conferred with the faculty adviser, Mrs. Elmore, as follows:

At present, Dean is taking English 100 (a course in beginning English meeting five times per week with three-hours credit). He is seeing the instructor in the English service twice a week. I am wondering if he could arrange to take nothing but spelling next semester. Whenever Dean has to write in class within a time limit, he is unable to do so. On one occasion his teacher took him to his office and there Dean wrote a paper and made a C grade. Since he has such trouble in writing, he gets poor grades in everything. I think my son will gain back his confidence if he can make a few grades that are passing.

In addition, the mother spoke of the fact that Dean had trouble with his eyes and that in high school he wrote so poorly that his teachers were unable to read the work. To remedy his handwriting, the boy was helped on penmanship at night by a teacher. During this period his work seemed to improve. The mother concluded her visit with the comment:

We are not like some parents who put their children in college and then lose interest in them. We want to do all we can to help Dean. Our idea is not to interfere but to work with the instructors and other people who are trying to help him.

Dean's grades for first semester were:

Basic mathematics	C
Written communication	F
The humanities	C
Air science	B
Development of modern society	D
Physical science	C
14 semester hours	
10½ quality points earned	

In March, Dean's mother visited the campus and again conferred with Mrs. Elmore, faculty counselor. Several days later, Mrs. Elmore talked with Dean, summarizing the conference in a letter to his mother:

Dean called by the office today and had a talk with me. I trust we can find ways by which he can improve his quality of work. It is my plan to discuss Dean's work with each of his instructors this week in order that we see what progress he may be making as a result of his enrollment in the writing clinic.

A poll taken by Mrs. Elmore of the instructors in courses where there was real question of Dean's passing revealed the following:

DEVELOPMENT OF MODERN SOCIETY: Dean's grades in my class are low but he tries hard. He has difficulty in expressing himself in correct English. However, there is some improvement; he made F on the first test and a C on the second test. His over-all average is D. He seems very nervous, but he is interested in what he is doing and tries to participate in class. He will do better if he can overcome this nervousness.

THE HUMANITIES: His work in my class is below average. The main reason is that he has a very poor knowledge of English, both written and spoken. He cannot spell even the simplest words. I feel that he knows actually more than he is able to express or put down on paper. There is, occasionally, a lack of attention in class. I have seen him in a new car several times. Would he do better if he studied more and rode less? If you feel it would help, I would be glad to talk with the parents. In summary, I would like to help the student but cannot pass him unless he earns the grade.

WRITTEN COMMUNICATION: Dean is still not in the passing stage but he is slowly improving. It generally takes time for the "slower students" to catch on. Dean is conscientious and hard-working. From what I know, I would think the boy would do better if his parents would leave him alone. He is a fine boy but he seems always under pressure. If his parents would relax, the boy would be under less strain.

FRATERNITY ADVISER: I have talked with Dean's mother, and we agree that he has problems. I think they are accentuated by the anxiety of his mother— but I did not feel like telling her this. After all, he is her son and she will do pretty much as she wishes where he is concerned.

After a second interview with Dean, Mrs. Elmore, faculty counselor, made the following report:

Dean feels that his mother's ill health makes her overly anxious and inclined to worry unnecessarily. He hopes *she* won't bother us too much with her worries about him. I assured Dean that our job is to help parents and students and that he is always welcome in our office. Dean then volunteered this information: "My mother has always been extremely nervous. She reads the bad news —only murders and accidents in the newspapers—and then worries as if this news concerns her immediate family. She has been better until lately. Now the war scare in the headlines has put her back again. She is so afraid I will have to go to war that she is worse. My mother doesn't need to worry, financially, but this nervous trouble seems to run in the family.

A note from Miss Carleton, director of the English service, to Mrs. Elmore contained the following:

I'd count it a favor if you'd help me to get at Dean's problem. He hasn't a spark of spontaneity in his manner, never a hint of merriment in his face. Always he's prompt to keep appointments, dogged in his endeavor to do his assignments, courteous in acknowledging a favor. But he carries some terrible burden that will crush him—if it hasn't already crushed him. Will you call me sometime to make an appointment?

The mid-term report on Dean was as follows:

Unsatisfactory
    Written communication
    Development of modern society
    The humanities

In mid-May the instructor of the English class called the director of counseling to relate Dean's progress in her class, as follows:

I am really concerned about Dean at this time. It seems to me that we can only go so far with him on his writing problems and then we can go no further until other things are cleared. Up to now, I have had implicit faith in Dean— and I still do really—but I am wondering if he feels the *impossible* is being expected of him. I have a paper here which he purportedly wrote, but it is in such good form that I cannot accept it as his work. He tells me that the paper which he was asked to revise "blew out his car window" and hence he started all over and did this one which shows much too great a mastery of the language to be his. I am not reporting this incident to the student honor committee since they might not recognize the emotional involvements; instead I am calling you to see what you would suggest be done. In fact, I would appreciate your taking over from here.

Since the matter involved the student honor code and the disciplinary phases arising out of violations of the code, the matter was discussed with the dean of students. In the conference, it was decided that Dean should be referred to the health service where he would be free to discuss his problem with the staff psychiatrist.

An appointment was made with the psychiatrist. Dean was very willing to cooperate. In an oral report, the university psychiatrist indicated the following:

The student has evidenced real feelings of hostility toward his parents. He feels that they expect too much of him—hold him up to too high a standard of perfection. In my judgment, the boy might do better in a smaller school where there is less competition; however, that may not be too important a factor. The real problem is to get the father and mother to recognize the fact that they are producing extreme tension and anxiety in the boy by their overly high standards. He is physically and mentally quite all right, but his emotional state may lead to mental difficulties if the family persists in pressuring him.

The end-of-semester report from the faculty counselor read:

Dean is not achieving to the best of his ability; he is unable to meet emergencies of stress, and there are evidences of poor personality adjustment, and resulting health problems.

Within a few days and during the period of final examinations, Dean's mother unexpectedly visited campus, her wish being to learn about the honor-code violation. She confided:

I am really quite worried about Dean . . . you can see how my hands shake. Is there anything really wrong with him? I worry because of the nervous troubles I have had. I suppose he worries about himself, too, since he has seen me in a very nervous condition.

The director of counseling cited the wish on the part of the English instructor to believe Dean on the matter of the "lost" English paper and the "perfect" second try. Dean's mother recognized the fact that the English instructor was trying hard to accept Dean's statements as true.

The following information given by the English instructor was transmitted to Dean's mother:

Dean cannot pass the work in English until he has a tutor—someone who is sympathetic to his problems of spelling. In the last theme, for instance, there were sixty-three errors in spelling in the four pages. My opinion of Dean is still good, and I am convinced that he will make a good adjustment—even if he finds it necessary to take the work in the English course four or five times. Other students, on occasion, have had to do this.

In a telephone conversation with the psychiatrist, the director of counseling explored the matter of Dean's mother talking directly with him. This was effected. Following the conference, she returned to the counseling center.

In the second interview, Dean's mother spoke along these lines:

We are so very interested in what Dean does up here. He comes home every week end, or if he doesn't, we drive up here and spend Sunday with him and go to church with him. . . . One Sunday, I remember it was right after Easter, we came up and I found him sick. I told my husband it was probably a nervous upset, and I cautioned him not to mention the mid-term grade report. Instead, I told Dean he had done better than usual, and right then he seemed to brighten up and be like himself again. . . . I suppose Dean worries about me and what I am going to think about his grades. My sister, for instance, tells me that if I keep after Dean as I do he will end up a nervous wreck. My sister sometimes hides her son's books so he will not get so nervous and upset about his work. But we're the other way . . . we get down and help Dean or see to it that he gets his work. . . . I guess we have been too rigid about it all, now that I look back. If Dean takes on my worries, he's not going to be any good for his schoolwork, or *any kind of work*, I guess. Maybe if I am more happy-go-lucky about what he does, he will relax and not be so tense and anxious as his teachers say he is. . . . He *is* a good boy with a good personality, and all his teachers and fraternity brothers like him—so maybe that's the really important thing.

In this interview, Dean's mother gave some evidences of recognizing herself as one who created her son's tensions. On the matter of hiring a tutor for summer, Dean was to take the initiative. His mother expressed her great appreciation for the helpfulness of all the teachers, counselors, and administrators who had dealt with him. She was sure that Dean would want to return in the fall if his grades permitted.

A summary statement from Miss Carleton, writing clinic, to Mrs. Elmore reads as follows:

Dean needs more help than we have been able to give him this semester. Lately he has not been in attendance. I understand how students feel about attending the clinic when the credit work is demanding more and more of their time.

End-of-term grades for Dean were as follows:

Written communication	F
Sociology	C
Political science	C
Development of modern society	C
Physical education	B
The humanities	D
Air science	C

A follow-up letter sent to Dean's family contained the following:

By this time you will have received Dean's grades for second semester. The freshman year, we feel, is one in which students will explore their interests and abilities, develop their skills, and gain new understandings about themselves. In a very real sense, Dean has been able to do some of this exploration.

SUMMARY

As has been indicated in the earlier pages of the chapter, the success of a program of campus-wide counseling is based, in large measure, upon the kinds of working relationships engaged in by counselors, administrators, teaching faculty, and off-campus personnel. This relationship is shown through narration of what happens between offices, officers, and among student and faculty representatives in coordinating the various aspects of a student's problem.

In the case of Dean, a number of individuals within the institution pooled their ideas, but the picture did not assume completeness until the home and family aspects were taken into account. This would seem to indicate that the coordination of counseling services within a college or university is not limited merely to the campus but that, instead, the high school and the home, together with agencies in the local community, state, and region, are components. They are, indeed, part of the "central design" which good coordination seeks to keep intact.

One ingredient in counseling, long used in some institutions and of more recent use in others, is that of student assistance in counseling. The possibilities for use of students in responsible roles of guidance doubtless deserve systematic study. Most institutional planners will agree that students should be "involved" in institutional activities. The degree of involvement—its intensity and extent—is perhaps not clearly understood. In the chapter which follows, there are reviewed some of the ways in which students have been found to contribute, reciprocally, to the institution-wide program of advisement or counseling.

CHAPTER 14

The Student Who Assumes Counseling Responsibilities *

The preceding chapter has illustrated the role of the student in the home setting as that of a recipient of assistance. This has been the case to some degree also in the public school experience. Both parents and teachers have been accustomed to viewing the student in the familiar context of his home, school, and community and against a background of childhood artifacts, only recently outgrown. While this may in part be true also of the way in which college freshmen are viewed, developments within college counseling programs in the past two decades have brought about a considerable revision of the traditional stereotype of the student's role in the counseling process. For some time there has been a trend for the student to accept an increasingly greater role in his own counseling and guidance. At the present time this role, in many institutions, has been expanded to the end that he now serves as an active participant in the counseling of others, working in cooperation with student personnel administrators and faculty advisers.

On most campuses the freshmen and new students who arrive each fall within a brief space of time are so numerous that it is virtually impossible for each to receive immediate and individual attention from professional personnel workers and faculty members. Nor is there opportunity even to select those who most need attention. Experiencing needs for information, advice, friendship, and all manner of assurance and help in this period of adjustment, these students in residence halls, classrooms, soda shops, and on the campus turn for assistance to their more experienced peers. Not just in these early days of college life but throughout their college careers, students seek advice and information among their fellows. They, in turn, frequently render a similar service when they are asked—and perhaps often even if they are not asked— to do so.

* By Orrin B. Powell.

What quality of help in solving his problems of progress and adjustment does the student obtain from his friends and acquaintances? No doubt, he sometimes finds very good help, but oftentimes too much is left to fortuity; the process is too haphazard and the helper often too biased or ill-informed.

Many college planners and administrators have recognized in this situation both the need for this "first-echelon" type of counseling help and the resources within students themselves for providing it directly at the point of need. Such recognition has given rise to expanded personnel programs in which there are planned efforts to select students most capable of supplying this type of help, to train them, and to organize their efforts to the end of effective implementation of the counseling program.

SUMMARY OF SURVEY OF STUDENT–COUNSELING PRACTICES

In a survey of coordinated counseling practices conducted by the authors and described in part in preceding pages, some 181 respondents replied to questions regarding the participation of upperclass students in counseling roles within the counseling programs of their institutions. Of this number, 147 stated that students did carry on functions of this nature (see Table 8). The kind and the extent of "student-counseling-student" procedures appear worthy of further examination. In fifty-seven institutions, student counselors were said to be restricted to a single area in their counseling activities. In fifty-four instances, students who counsel were said to operate in two areas, in so far as such areas can be delimited, and thirty-six respondents indicated allowing their student counselors even greater latitude in the areas in which they work.

Areas of Counseling

The area in which students were most frequently said to counsel was that of personal-social concerns. Of those responding, 129 named this area as a major one. This is not surprising when one considers the setting in which such counseling takes place. By far the greater number of student counselors are to be found working within the framework of the orientation program for new students or in the residence halls where new students are housed. In both situations the general adjustment of the incoming college man or woman is a major concern of that particular time and place. That the upperclass student with his greater experience and sophistication in the rewards and exigencies of college life should be chosen to help in an area with which he is most familiar is logical. Academic problems, religious concerns, and vocational choices were areas also named in which students were counseling their more recently arrived college mates.

Responses received from thirty-four institutions indicated that students did not participate in the counseling of other students within the organized counseling program. A number of responses in this group indicated that, although there was no organized student-counselor program on a particular campus, the respondent was not unaware of possible benefits in such an undertaking, and a few even reflected having plans for a project of this kind in the near future. Only one respondent reported an administration unfavorable to this type of student responsibility.

Evaluation

There appeared to be some reluctance on the part of the respondents to rate the effectiveness of student counselors (see Table 9). Of the eighty-five attempts at such evaluation which were received, sixty were listed as good or excellent while twenty-five were given as fair or poor. Any attempt to summarize ratings of this sort may have little validity in view of the lack of standardized rating criteria and the differences in the kind and level of activities of a counseling nature in the various institutions.

Rationale

When questioned as to the importance of utilizing students in the counseling program, the majority of respondents indicated their belief that such procedure was of importance (see Table 10). The reasoning most frequently stated to support this belief was based on the peer group influence and relationship among students and the ensuing ease of communication and acceptance. Others saw in this type of situation good learning and leadership experience. Especially was this mentioned in responses from institutions where the major enterprise was that of teacher training. Other reasons were given in terms of (1) earlier detection of disturbed students whose problems were not being reported to, or discovered by, professional staff members; (2) helping to bring counseling services to more students than was possible for professional staff; (3) providing a good source of referrals; and (4) counteracting the influence of much of the informal, uninformed "counseling" carried on among students at all times.

Limitations of Student Counseling

Most of the respondents who reported procedures wherein students were utilized in implementing the counseling program were aware that limitations were needed (see Table 11). A majority stated that students did not counsel in major problem areas or at levels requiring the services of the professional. A number of responses indicated that counseling by students was confined to a specific time or need, as in the early orientation of new students or in residence-hall living. In a few cases, student counselors were required to submit a written report of each counseling interview as a means of control. Only a small number reported leaving limits of counseling activities to the judgment of the student counselor himself.

Selection

One might reasonably expect that students who are to be entrusted with responsibility for the counseling of other students would be selected with some care, and this expectation is supported by the respondents. Students, said to be counselors in the programs studied, were reported as upperclassmen selected for their personal qualifications and for their accomplishments as reflected by their records. Leadership appeared to play a weighty role in this selective process. Many of these young aides in counseling were said to be selected from student government bodies, from officers and leaders in YMCA, YWCA, service organizations, honoraries, religious organizations, and from recognized leaders in residence halls and other student groups.

An excellent example of the procedure for choosing student counselors is that described at Louisiana State University. Students are nominated by other students, deans, faculty, and staff members. Final choices are made by personnel deans after records have been carefully studied. The following characteristics are said to be sought in making final selections:

1. Well-balanced personalities
2. Creditable scholastic records
3. Active interests in campus affairs
4. Attitudes of appreciation for and cooperation with university standards and policies
5. A sense of responsibility
6. A wholesome capacity for fun
7. A sense of discretion regarding appropriate conduct, dress, and manner
8. A scale of values that lends purpose and meaning to life

In short, it would appear to be the hope of administrators that selectees might "counsel by example" of their own attitudes and behavior as well as by conference and discussion.

Training

Even the most careful selection, however, provides an inadequate guarantee that effective counseling will obtain. Some training appears necessary, and almost all programs utilizing student counselors were said to provide means of preparing selectees for this function.

Means by which training was provided for student counselors were reported to be workshops, conferences, lectures, group discussions, leadership training in organized government service, religious and other groups, and in a few instances through formal course work. This final means of preparation was named largely by teacher-training institutions. Personnel deans or other personnel officers were said to provide most of the leadership in the student-counselor training enterprise.

The content of training procedures varies considerably according to the function which students are expected to fulfill. From a scrutiny of manuals, memoranda, and other printed materials prepared to aid in this training, it seems that much of the training is intended to facilitate mechanical procedures. Student counselors are provided with schedules, lists of required activities, or similar materials and are instructed in the proper guiding of new students or checking on their early activity to see that schedules are adhered to and that requirements are met.

Other programs in which more thorough preparation is needed attempt to teach prospective student counselors something of the philosophy and objectives of the personnel program as a whole and the place of student counselors in the larger undertaking. Students are helped to understand their counseling responsibilities and the reasons why they were selected to counsel. These training programs also supply information regarding procedures and techniques which the young counselor might find useful in acquiring skills in conducting interviews and group discussions. Some training materials listed and described the more commonly encountered types of problems and explained ways of dealing with them. Found also were materials to aid the student counselors in making referrals easily and effectively. Resources for helping the students who were chosen as counselors to understand and recognize the limits of their own counseling functions were features of a number of programs of counselor preparation. For illustrative purposes, brief accounts of the major features of several training programs are reported.

BUFFALO (NEW YORK) STATE COLLEGE FOR TEACHERS: Selected junior counselors work closely with designated faculty advisers. Training is provided by seminars and interviews scheduled with the faculty adviser and with the dean of students. A handbook is furnished which provides a guide for study and a ready source of reference. Materials included deal with objectives of student counseling; the role and function of the junior counselor in specific periods, such as the summer recess or orientation; holding of group discussions; counseling procedures; and suggested references for study. Cautions to be observed are included in the materials concerned with counseling procedures.

KENT STATE UNIVERSITY: Upperclass "leaders" of new students are trained to assume responsibilities which are considerably beyond those attendant upon the role of the group "guide" as traditionally seen. Selected leaders are furnished with printed materials to aid in preparing them to carry out assignments which involve all early activities from the first greeting to the more serious business of first-quarter program planning with freshmen and registration. Preceding the arrival of new students, leaders participate in a work conference which provides opportunities for posing questions and eliciting discussion on any aspects that need clarification. (See App. L, item given new students.)

SOUTHERN ILLINOIS UNIVERSITY: Prior to the arrival of a new freshman class, student leaders attend a workshop for two and a half days. A printed manual, lectures, and committee meetings provide opportunities for leaders to learn of the responsibilities involved in aiding new students in their early adjustment. The manual for student leaders stresses the role of the leader as a friendly one and the need, on the part of the leader, to be alert to detect problems of special nature requiring referral to a professionally trained staff member.

SOME STUDENT–COUNSELOR PROGRAMS

In order further to illustrate these various factors of selection, training, function, and operation as they are met within the framework of individual programs of student participation in counseling, a number of brief accounts of specific programs are included. These examples will, it is hoped, also aid in gaining a clearer conception of the levels of such participation and the means for supervision and control of the student-counseling function.

OHIO WESLEYAN UNIVERSITY: An attempt is being made to bring advising and dormitory counseling together by using senior advisers to freshmen women as partial liaison between the counseling received from the faculty adviser or instructor.

TEACHERS COLLEGE, NEW BRITAIN, CONNECTICUT: Student counselors are selected from those students who by September will be in their third year. These counselors attend a series of in-service training meetings similar to those for the faculty advisers. Assignment of freshman advisees to student counselors is on the combined bases of their area of major academic interest, their commuter or resident status, and hometown area. During orientation week, the counselors attend with their counselees all of the meetings and events indicated. After the mid-point of each term, upperclass counselors report on the academic, personal, and social adjustment and the progress of advisees, the director of student personnel handling these reports. Anecdotes seeming to be of immediate concern are outlined in red. The counselor and the advisee are contacted by the director or dean where urgency is indicated. The dean of the college is notified when the problem relates to teaching or administrative policy. In addition, student-counselor reports are forwarded to the dean of women and men for their review. Sample:

Louise is debating as to whether or not she should withdraw from TCC. She feels that the teaching profession is not for her. Perhaps it is because she took the business course in high school and feels that secretarial work is what she wishes. I tried to tell her to wait until she took the course in principles of elementary education and perhaps that would give her a clearer idea of what the classroom situation really is.

UNIVERSITY OF PITTSBURGH: About fifty outstanding senior women are selected each year to work for the first ten weeks of the semester with freshmen in groups of five or six. For this work, seniors receive, under the direction of the dean of women, a week's intensive course in personnel work. These senior mentors make weekly individual reports to the dean of women's office on the progress of the girls as well as a final report which constitutes an estimate of her needs for the remainder of her student days. The discussion of the senior mentor with the new student is more on adjustment to life as young adults than on orientation to the special mores of Pitt.

CITY COLLEGE OF NEW YORK: Students do not officially counsel other students. . . . We do have a "big brother" program for the entering freshmen, and they often will aid the new freshmen in learning more about the college and what it has to offer the students. Students are valuable in the counseling area because they often are able to bridge a gap which might be overlooked by staff counselors. The student counselor is usually a referral agent unless it is a simple question of fact which may be gleaned from the college bulletin.

SOUTHERN METHODIST UNIVERSITY (COLLEGE OF ARTS-SCIENCES): Recently at the initiative of the student body, we revised the structure of our counseling program by admitting students as participants. Forty-one of the top-ranking students were selected to serve as assistants for the faculty counselors. One of our greatest difficulties is that of establishing an informal relationship between the counselors and their advisees. We feel that the principal service rendered by student counselors will be that of liaison between the faculty members and young students.

BROOKLYN COLLEGE: The department of personnel service is aided considerably in its freshman orientation program by the junior freshman committee. The members of this group are upperclassmen who are selected for this service on the basis of personality, participation in the extracurricular program, and scholarship. Each junior counselor is assigned eight to ten freshmen to whom he writes a personal letter about two weeks prior to registration. In his letter, the junior counselor extends his greetings to the entering student, makes an appointment to meet him during freshman week, and suggests that the freshman who has questions contact him before that time. At the meeting during freshman week, junior counselors explain registration procedures in great detail, conduct the students on tours of the buildings, and give information about the extracurricular program. In accordance with the department policy of encouraging self-responsibility among freshmen, junior counselors do not continue to make direct contact with new entrants. They do, however, stress their willingness to help the freshmen, and they invite the new students to telephone or write at any time the freshmen feel the need.

GETTYSBURG COLLEGE: Another phase of our counseling program is the employment of student counselors in the freshmen dormitories. These students are chosen on the basis of desire to counsel and on academic achievement as well as the usual character factors. It is their responsibility to achieve such a relationship with their freshmen, who number about fifteen, that they will be able to recognize some of the more typical problems of freshmen, such as their adjustment to campus living, moodiness, etc., and bring the problem before the dormitory committee, a group composed of student counselors and several faculty members meeting once a week to discuss and attempt to solve individual and group problems which arise.

MICHIGAN STATE UNIVERSITY: A student, serving alongside faculty members on the committee responsible for planning activities (in which student aides and faculty personnel work together) during orientation periods, comments as follows:

Naturally there are some things which administrators should not expect of student participants. Students may at first feel insecure. They may not understand all the problems to be faced. They have not benefited by learning which faculty members have acquired from experience over the years. On the other hand, the student *has* the student viewpoint and will reflect attitudes that might be expected from students who will be entering new. The student aide will be able to enlist the help of other students so that additional work can be done without diverting more faculty time to the project.

THE STUDENT COUNSELOR AS A TEACHER

Even though already participating in counseling, advisement, student-faculty liaison, and other related functions, the capable and informed upperclass student may have other contributions to make to the enterprise of education in his college or university. On a number of campuses, selected upperclass students were reported to be functioning in roles that contribute more directly to the instructional function as well. This type of relationship is organized in a number of ways. In some instances, scholarship clubs, honor societies, or other service groups offer help to first- and second-year students in subject-matter areas of the basic or general program of the institution.

One example of the student as a junior counselor-teacher may be seen in the roles of the student cadet officers of the Agricultural and Mechanical College of Texas. On this campus, where a strong military tradition exists, students are used extensively in the counseling of both the military and civilian components of the student body. For students in the corps of cadets, the military experience is a continuous one. Student officers, selected from juniors and seniors, serve not only in the traditional military function but in a guidance function as well. Each fall these students return to the campus several days in advance of their classmates in order to attend workshops which emphasize the guidance role. A number of student officers also serve as scholastic officers and assist students with academic matters. Scholastic officers work closely with the counseling, testing, and remedial personnel of the basic-division staff.

Another program incorporating students into the academic endeavor is that set up on an experimental basis at Brown University. This proposed program [1] is described as follows:

> Twenty senior engineering students will be assigned to counsel and assist in the teaching of the hundred freshmen entering the engineering division (in September). More than the necessary number of upperclassmen have volunteered for the work.
>
> Each student teacher will supervise the work of a group of five freshmen, giving one hour a week to a special class for discussion of the basic course, attending lectures with the new students, and giving each freshman a half-hour personal conference each week. They will also grade homework and go over the students' papers with them. They will be paid $600 for the year's work. The program is financed by a grant from the Ford Foundation for the Advancement of Education.

THE CASE FOR STUDENT COUNSELORS

The values to be derived from programs of student counseling, reported earlier in this chapter, appear to merit further consideration. Major factors in the importance of the inclusion of student counselors in personnel programs were reported by respondents largely in terms of utilizing the peer relationship for counseling purposes, of directing the inevitable and unstructured advising between students into constructive channels, of detecting unrecognized needs, of providing good learning experiences for those who counsel, and of bridging the gap between students and faculty.

These statements imply that there is value in the student-counselor program at several levels for persons involved in, or affected by, the student personnel program. There is implied value for the administration, faculty, and professional personnel worker; for the new students who are the focus of such counseling for periods varying from a few weeks to an entire school year; and for those upperclass students who are privileged to participate in counseling.

Assuming that the program in which the student counselor functions is carefully planned to include effective training and supervision and is

[1] "Students Will Be Hired To Help Teach Freshmen," *The New York Times,* Sunday, July 7, 1957, p. E7.

adequately coordinated with the total personnel program, there appear to be values inherent in all these areas.

From the viewpoint of the administration and staff of the institution, the student counselor may provide a service which Wrenn [2] sees as a combination "listening post and switchboard to the appropriate personnel staff." A function of this kind does, as a number of respondents pointed out, tend to bridge the gap between students and faculty and to provide a means of discovering more student problems requiring the services of the professional counselor.

The faculty member or personnel officer who finds himself closely associated with the student-counseling program is in a position of considerable advantage. Through his young co-workers he has an opportunity to widen his own influence in the teaching-guiding of students and is, at the same time, able to increase his own scope of understanding and appreciation of students, thus adding to his own professional competency and stature. The student counselor as an interpreter may then be seen carrying on a two-way role: first, interpreting student concerns to faculty and staff; and secondly, interpreting to new students the traditions and standards of the institution. Such an interpretive process, effectively done, appears potentially capable of contributing to the lessening of disciplinary problems and to enhancing the general smoothness and efficiency of daily functioning.

That the student-counselor program may be of real help to new students is perhaps the most easily recognized of its potential benefits. Many respondents indicated their awareness of the proximity factor in the student-to-student situation. That good peer relationships should obtain on any college campus is a common objective of administration and staff. That this normal relationship should be utilized for promoting the good adjustment of students seems only practical. Greater ease of communication, wider contacts with students, earlier detection of needs, and the useful structuring of an inevitable process all appear to be valid expectations in terms of assistance to the newer members of the student population.

The college campus as a community is a widely accepted concept. Whether or not the community is aided by well-planned social objectives and controls which might supply effective direction and meaning for its members, it remains the environment in which a significant portion of students' personal development takes place. Such development, whether considered in specific terms of social skills, attitudes, and value systems or in broad terms of personality development, might well be enhanced

[2] C. Gilbert Wrenn, *Student Personnel Work in College*, The Ronald Press Company, New York, 1951, p. 74.

by better leadership within the environment and on the individual's own level.

Many respondents indicated that they recognized that upperclass students who assisted in counseling their fellows also profited in the process. Such benefits were mentioned in terms of providing learning experiences, of supplying opportunities to develop and experience leadership, and of building morale through service. There is no denying that when individuals function in groups over a period of time there emerge leaders upon whose shoulders rests considerable responsibility for the total function. This process is repeated on the college campus, and those who accept leadership responsibilities often retain leadership roles of one kind or another throughout their lives. The training and guidance which the student counselor receives, together with his experience, should do much to help in raising the quality of his leadership above the superficial and the temporary to the end that attendant habits, skills, attitudes, and competency in dealing with human concerns may achieve better integration as factors of the maturing personality. The good counseling relationship with its characteristic attitudes rooted in acceptance of the worth of others may then become the basis for deeper and more meaningful human relationships for the individual in his everyday affairs.

Vital to the preservation of a democratic society is a sincere concern on the part of the individual for the welfare of the other members of his society. That such concerns seek expression is seen everywhere as individuals in all walks of life share their experiences with each other. The fortunate individual who receives effective training in this respect may well discover that his expressions of concern for human welfare become not only a helpful type of activity but a satisfying and creative one as well.

SAFEGUARDS IN STUDENT COUNSELING

At any level of counseling it is of importance that the counselor be capable of recognizing the point at which a situation threatens to exceed his own limitations for dealing with it. This implies, of course, the necessity for knowing what and approximately where these limitations are. The student counselor, with his brief training and experience, can hardly be expected to know his limitations at all times or to recognize them in a given situation. That there are dangers inherent in this situation probably needs little elaboration. Even in respondents' statements of recognized advantages of allowing students to counsel, there appear danger signals. For example, the assertion that students could counsel effectively because they are in a position to know and understand other students would also serve to imply that students understand themselves. Both of these assumptions are hardly safe.

In order to protect the counselor, the counseled, and the program as a whole, adequate safeguards must be devised and made operational in the process of student counseling.

Many respondents indicated that they were aware of the necessity for precautionary measures, but little information was volunteered as to the best installation of danger signals and safety devices.

The establishment of adequate safeguards is begun apparently in the process of careful selection of those students who are best suited to counsel. Well-planned, effective training programs; clearly established referral systems; and means for prompt reporting of interviews or group sessions add greatly to the safety factor. All these measures, however, leave too much to the judgment of the student counselor, and there is an additional need for clear and well-defined channels of communication between students who counsel and their professional counterparts if continuous supervision and coordination are to be maintained.

COORDINATION

To the college counseling program a new and potentially effective source of help for new students has been added wherever upperclassmen participate in the program as an organized adjunct to it. Attendant upon this company of new helpers, the program's coordinator finds new tasks and problems which confront him in his efforts to incorporate them into the counseling enterprise.

New channels of communication must be established with student groups and organizations which supply these counselor-aspirants. Adequate machinery for their careful selection and training must be established. The system of referrals must be expanded and perhaps better defined, and effective means of supervision devised and maintained. Personnel for professional leadership and guidance must be found among members of a staff which may be already carrying a full work load. Media for evaluation, experimentation, and improvement must also be supplied if the student counselor is to attain his best level of participation in the counseling of his fellows.

Finally, or perhaps first, the coordinator may often find that he must meet tactfully, but effectively, the opposition or apathy of a number of his colleagues. The traditional atmosphere often resists efforts to stretch it to shelter new and seemingly nonacademic procedures. The trend, however, seems to favor student counseling, and it would appear unlikely that a practice in which so much of potential benefit seems inherent should not be allowed an opportunity to prove its worth.

SUMMARY

College students turn naturally to their peers with their problems and concerns. From this normal relationship a great deal of "counseling" results. On a number of college campuses, those who administer the counseling programs are utilizing this peer-level relationship by the inclusion of selected upperclass students in the programs of their institutions.

Personnel administrators in many colleges and universities have indicated that the student as a junior counselor reaches many of his fellows whom the professional counselor seldom, if ever, sees, and he aids in detecting many needs and problems that might remain hidden from faculty and staff members. Other advantageous ways of utilizing students in the counseling program are reported to be in a liaison function— interpreting faculty and administration to students and vice versa— extending the influence of the personnel program, lending a measure of security to new students, implementing instruction, and providing a trained and informed source of leadership for the student population as a whole.

Despite potentialities in this type of counseling, certain limitations must be observed and safeguards established and maintained. Some major factors to be considered in the incorporation of students into the counseling program are as follows:

1. Careful selection of those who counsel
2. Provision of effective in-service training for would-be counselors
3. Continuous supervision of student counselors
4. Maintenance of good, clear channels for referral and general communication between students who counsel and professional staff members who supervise their efforts

Student counseling is effective only if it can be integrated into the existing program smoothly and with a minimum of conflict and misunderstanding. Thus, new and added problems must be solved by the individual charged with the coordination of the counseling service.

The theme of integration of instructional programs and student personnel services continuing, the attention of the reader is directed to two chapters to follow which show elements of coordination at work. Chapter 15 presents an example of a case conference, and Chapter 16, a case-study consideration.

It is to be recognized that no single case or two cases covering the problems narrated can be said to be entirely representative of the hundreds which are handled daily by counseling personnel in the 218 institutions polled. In Chapter 15, however, the case of a student from abroad was selected because of current interest, manifest on most campuses, in the adjustment of foreign students to "American campusways." The role of another specialist—the foreign-student adviser—is viewed.

In Chapter 16, the case of a student on rehabilitation scholarship is depicted. This choice was made in view of the current interest in and intensification of counseling with persons having physical impairment. Thus, while the content of Chapters 15 and 16 to follow may picture some patterns of case handling specific for one institution only, reflecting its educational philosophy and practice, there are elements in the narrations that are characteristic of many "cases" being handled by trained personnel in other colleges and universities.

CHAPTER 15 *Coordination Effected through the Case Conference*

In a work which discusses case studies and coordinative activities which are focused on the individual student, a team of writers introduces the case of Cradu, a foreign student enrolled at Brooklyn College, as follows: [1]

Although Cradu's previous academic record must have been well above average to secure his admission to college, the foreign-student counselor knows that, added to the difficulties which he will have in common with the graduates of local high schools, there will be special perplexities caused by different methods of instruction and by strange social customs. With most foreign students, the language of instruction is also unfamiliar. The counselor will help Cradu in his choice of courses and will keep in touch with him. The counselor will enlist the interest of his teachers . . . about his progress. If he lacks study skills necessary for success in college, the counselor will turn to a teacher who is giving remedial instruction in reading and study methods, and Cradu will be given the opportunity of joining this group. In short, all the resources of the college are drawn upon to guide Cradu and his fellow foreign students.

To show in somewhat more detail just how the resources of an institution are marshalled for the benefit of Cradu's "fellow foreign students," the particular case of Juan, narrated in this chapter, has been selected. There follows a transcribed version of an actual case conference held to review problems of a foreign student enrolled in a southern university. The conference was called by the director of counseling at the request of the student's faculty adviser, with the following persons participating:

Miss Calvin, supervisor of English service
Dr. Cato, therapist in the speech clinic
Dr. Leonard, general adviser for foreign students

[1] Ruth Strang, Mary C. Patton, Isabel J. Peard, Frank Piskor, and Catherine Reed (eds.), *Unity Within Guidance*, New York State Association of Deans and Guidance Personnel, Syracuse University Press, Syracuse, N.Y., 1953, pp. 84–86.

Mr. Kray, assistant dean of men
Mr. Wendell, residence counselor
Dr. Nash, teacher of the personal development course
Mr. Lorenzo, graduate student in psychology
Mr. Harriman, teacher of geography
Dr. Paul, teacher of English
Dr. Tillman, teacher of mathematics
Mr. Potter, faculty adviser for engineering students
Dr. Hale, director of counseling

CASE CONFERENCE: JUAN M.

DR. HALE: [States the problem.] Juan M., the subject of our conversation, entered school this fall. I saw him for the first time when Mr. Wendell, residence counselor, brought him in during orientation week. His problem then was a financial one, and we got him to the office of student aid for help. We knew at the time that Juan had a problem of communication, but we felt that time might take care of this. It did, but a little sadly for Juan. In October Juan was referred to speech clinic. That brings Dr. Cato into the picture. Then about two weeks ago, Juan was referred to the remedial English laboratory which Miss Calvin supervises. Now, perhaps, we can construct a picture of Juan as he appears from these clinical contacts. Dr. Cato, would you like to start?

DR. CATO: [Cites clinic record.] Well, I might say that I have looked over the records of Juan and find that his attendance at the clinics has been very irregular. Mr. Giles, who has been working with Juan, tells me that the last time he saw him was very close to a month ago. I told Mr. Giles last week to write Juan a note and ask him if he had something that conflicted with his schedule. Juan has availed himself of very little speech work this semester—perhaps four or five lessons.

DR. HALE: In those lessons you were working on rapid reading, isn't that right?

DR. CATO: [Cites technique used in clinic.] What we decided to do was to let the work on his articulation go for the time being. We thought that we would not try to check any specific errors of pronunciation, such as his tendency to use the vowel "e" in place of "i" in words like "sit," "bit," and would simply try to develop fluency in thinking in English terms. The only way we knew for getting this fluency was to read to him a little bit more rapidly than he thought he could understand and have him read just as rapidly as he could to us. The first lesson we tried to do some work with his speech, and occasionally we would remark about a pronunciation or articulation problem, but that is not the major purpose of our work. It is to develop rapid reading, at least intelligible, in an effort to give him a muscular pattern, you might say, of the language —to force him to think in the language and to make him read fast enough so that he can't think in Spanish.

HALE: And I think you said that you were using his textbooks for this.

CATO: That is right. We are using textbook material from his classes so that when we come across a word he doesn't understand we can explain it to him. We have been working on vocabulary as we go along. We always ask him what he has read, if he understands it, and what words he doesn't know. The reason we use the textbook rather than the simplified material we have for foreign students is that most foreign students when they come here have a basic vocabulary of household words. The words they need sorely are the words that they hear in their lectures. So, we have been concentrating on technical vocabulary.

HALE: Good; now, Miss Calvin, has Juan been regular in his attendance with you?

MISS CALVIN: [Cites clinic record.] He has missed two appointments, but I might say that one was not his fault. Our graduate assistant who teaches Juan was ill. The other absence Juan explained satisfactorily. We feel that he is making some progress. We have been dictating material from his textbook to help him in hearing the language. Then he reads that material back to us, but we make no point of anything more than his understanding the material. The speech work we are leaving to Dr. Cato. We do want to help Juan understand what he has himself written. When he writes something in class, he explains to us briefly what it is.

HALE: Now we can appreciate something of the two special remedial areas in which Juan is enrolled. Shall we swing our attention next to the classroom situation which five of you represent. Dr. Paul has Juan in English. What is he doing there?

DR. PAUL: [Cites responsibility to student.] Well, we might start off with a fundamental situation. It seems to me that, first of all, unless we do have a program specifically designed to teach English as a foreign language (which neither Miss Calvin nor Mr. Cato is actually doing) then I don't think we should admit a student who doesn't have the English language sufficiently mastered to use as a tool. However, I *do* think that, having admitted Juan, we very definitely have a responsibility for him. It would be rather an idiotic action on our part to flunk him for something he can't help. I am not sure whether we ought to establish something like the Army short courses in foreign languages here or simply not admit a student unless he were certified in English.

HALE: [Cites committee formulation.] Yes, you pose problems which a newly formed committee whose task is to plan for the foreign student recognizes. We have about sixty foreign students here now. Mr. Kray, Dr. Leonard, and I serve on this committee with some six others. You have stated some of the problems: (1) selective admissions based on language proficiency and (2) aid for the student who is admitted without such language proficiency.

DR. LEONARD: [Speaks to general problem of foreign students.] I think that we should work on the second point at this time because the registrar's office is not able to select these students on the basis of their letters of application. I received a student letter yesterday through the president's office which reflects a very good competence in written English, but I should hesitate very much to accept a student just from a sample of his written English. I would be more inclined to accept one who could carry on a conversation, because we can get him into some courses where he can develop some reading and writing knowledge. As for comprehension, I just don't know how we are going to test it. We have another case coming up of a Greek boy who definitely knows how to read and write, but the English which he has studied was the British model and it apparently didn't go very far into oral features. He has been accepted tentatively here and if he arrives in the second semester, I don't know what we are going to do with him except to do as we have done with Juan. If we could work out a program for "orientation in languages," oral languages particularly, which would be applicable to students from all parts of the world, I think that we would have use for it here.

PAUL: [Continues general discussion.] It seems to me that something else has worked well with some foreign students. For instance, some have come here for the first time during the summer sessions and have taken a very light load to become adjusted to the situation. Now, if we could direct their over-all activities a little more, rather than just putting them in a formal course, they could get English and other courses to put them on par with our other students. That would mean, though, that they might have to stay on our campus longer, but in the end I think they probably will anyway.

CATO: We discussed one time the possibility of giving credit to such a course in English because it would be a "foreign language" for the foreign student.

MR. KRAY: [Recalls centers for English study elsewhere.] Since we have less than a hundred foreign students, perhaps we could get these students to attend some of the language schools which they have on some campuses of the country. They go to that campus six or eight weeks to gain language proficiency. Getting back to what Dr. Leonard said awhile ago, I think that we can profit by the experience of some other universities. From my reading I find that many universities get the American consul or another officer from the American Embassy to administer a proficiency test before the student leaves. The results give the university some idea about the student's ability to speak the English language.

HALE: This semester we attempted to get all the new non-English-speaking foreign students in the same English 100 or English 101 classes. How about it?

LEONARD: We tried to get them together but it didn't work out very well. It was difficult to schedule them in spite of the help of the English department.

HALE: Now, swinging our discussion away from the English problems and over to a different kind of instruction, what would you say about Juan's ability in mathematics, Dr. Tillman?

DR. TILLMAN: [Cites performance of student in mathematics.] First of all, his attendance has been rather spotty. I can understand this since half the time he attended my class he did not know what went on. Undoubtedly he has not gotten anything at all out of the class period when he has been there. He has seen me individually three times outside of class. Juan has had the course in analytic geometry, which is the course he is taking now. He has a very fine notebook on the subject which contains about everything we would cover. He was absent one day during a test and the day after, but he came in to see me then last Wednesday. I made arrangements to give him a make-up examination. On Wednesday he came in, but he was late for that appointment. I gave him a make-up examination on which the score, I would estimate, was a D, but it showed only the knowledge that he had before he got here. Again, I don't blame him for not coming to class because I don't think he understands a word. He asks questions when he comes to see me. I can explain a matter two or three times to him. He will finally grasp it, but the language barrier is just too much for him.

HALE: The directions for doing a problem would confuse him?

TILLMAN: Yes, they are completely over his head. He sits there with his mind off somewhere else. He has ability in mathematics, however, despite all this.

HALE: Mr. Harriman, what is true in geography?

MR. HARRIMAN: [Cites student's performance in class.] Well, Juan's attendance in geography has been poor. Last month he didn't show any signs of comprehension in class. In fact, I tried to make two appointments with him, but we haven't been able to communicate with each other to make the appointment. I think that he is a peculiarly difficult case, and I doubt very much if a routine remedial course in English comprehension or reading would help him much. I think that he needs tutoring by someone almost night and day. In the past I have had a good many students who started about where Juan started, and nearly all of them within the first two months would show a very sharp rise in oral comprehension. I don't detect that at all with Juan. I don't think that he is particularly convinced of the importance of trying to adapt himself here. He has a very casual air and doesn't seem to be trying. From conversation with Juan, I am not certain as to his purpose in coming here. He seems to lack motivation.

MR. LORENZO: If he has a feeling of inadequacy about the language, this may be an emotional block in keeping him from becoming interested in what's taking place in these other courses.

CATO: Does he have competency in German, does anybody know?

HALE: What other languages does Juan know?

LEONARD: I don't recall. I always ask foreign students what other languages they speak, but I don't recall any other language which Juan mentioned.

MR. POTTER: He said that he has studied French. He didn't claim any great knowledge of it, though.

LEONARD: [Recalls item in culture of student.] About his absences, I might point out this one phase of his background. At the Naval Academy which he attended in his country, he was under strict discipline and he did attend classes regularly. But it is not customary in the Chilean University for any attendance record to be kept or for any daily grades to be given. Only the exam counts there, and frequently a man will take the course two or three times before he tries the exam. That's part of his background. Juan has not been to the university in Chile, but he knows how universities are geared.

HARRIMAN: How old is Juan?

HALE: The personal data summary [2] shows here that he was born in 1932. Dr. Nash, you see Juan in personal development class. What do you observe?

DR. NASH: [Gives general reactions and moves to specific observations.] Well, a personal reaction first. Because of present world situations, I am desirous that

[2] Supplied by office of personnel records. See Chapter 10 on the contribution of the records office to coordinated counseling.

our university work out a way that we may have as many foreign students as is practical here. As far as the requirements are concerned, it seems to me we must do two things: (1) determine the student's level of intelligence (I got the impression from hearing some of you talking that you think Juan is of fairly high intelligence level) [3] and (2) motivate these students to attend class. I just think of Juan in a different light from all the other students. I think of him as taking my course to try to learn to understand *me* as much as anything. Meanwhile, in our class we have two textbooks for the students to use who have reading abilities. Now, if students don't have reading or speaking ability or the ability to understand, then it's pretty hopeless. I'm hoping that Juan can develop enough reading skill to be able to pass the examination in personal development. Meanwhile, the rest of Juan's time in my class is spent in a very practical situation. He is trying to comprehend English, and I don't believe that all comprehension can be taught in a special foreign-language course. It comes through other contact.

Juan is starting to attend my class more regularly now. We are having a test Thursday. He came up today, and I listed the chapters he would be responsible for in the book. I had Chapters 3–7 on the board, but this hadn't much meaning for him. This use of a dash (3–7) mixed him up, and I had to explain it to him. He wouldn't be able to learn its meaning in a foreign-language book. I feel that he picks up a number of things like that from just actually being in a course. I would like to see us take students like Juan, pick their courses, keep them busy, but first be sure that they have the intelligence level to master the language. It seems to me that the first semester, even the first year at the university, should be chiefly spent not for credit but just for the student to become adjusted.

PAUL: May I ask how many courses Juan is taking?

HALE: Mr. Potter, as his faculty counselor, you have that.

MR. POTTER: [Cites course load.] Well, I think his courses are represented here by you people. It's twelve hours, plus the remedial work. That's not too heavy a program, if the boy is putting forth an effort and is able to carry the subject matter. Mathematics, for example, is primarily a language course for him. The English is certainly a language course. Dr. Nash just indicated that he considers his work in personal development primarily language training.

NASH: Juan claims that he is understanding a little more as he goes along, even with my southern accent. If he can learn to understand that along with these other accents of students from the rest of the South, he is doing well.

HALE: Are there other points which you want to bring up on the instructional phases or course load?

KRAY: I hope that you people will report these absences of Juan's to us; otherwise we have no knowledge.

POTTER: [Reviews progress of student in engineering-drawing class.] Well, I've known about his absences in Dr. Tillman's class but that's all I knew about. I would like to make one other comment on the work in engineering drawing. Juan is superior to those students who are further along than he is. I think that

---

[3] In the university in which Juan is enrolled, the non-English-speaking student is not required to take the ACE examination on entrance.

it stems from what Dr. Tillman indicated that Juan has known in the past. His technique of drawing is very good—that is, the detail of his drawing and the end product of his drawing. He is behind on his problems because of this same comprehension problem. Of course, I have the advantage over Dr. Tillman and some other instructors in that I can give him individual attention during the period he comes to my class, whereas they have to get with him outside class. He also comes in to me two days a week, not every week, but two days a week now and then for an extra hour which enables him to catch up. For one thing, Juan thinks in terms of the metric system and we think in the English system. I've had to convert him to that. This is a very definite problem, one that takes a certain amount of practice to master. In general, Juan exceeds the ability of many of the other students who are American students taking the course. This may be a clue to his intelligence.

NASH: [To Kray.] On that attendance report, I have noted his absences to you. Since you talked with Juan, he has improved in attendance.

HALE: Juan works in the college cafeteria, as you know.

POTTER: I asked him if the work conflicted with my class. It overlapped about a half hour and he has had the schedule of hours changed. Did you work that out with him [to Mr. Wendell, residence counselor]?

MR. WENDELL: No, he must have worked it out on his own.

KRAY: We have some information from the State Department in which the officials state that if any work outside class interferes with the student's class achievement, he will not be permitted to continue to work. Juan has only recently asked for permission to work.

HALE: [Reference to introductory statement.] Another facet to our problem in aiding foreign students is the financial aid. Juan didn't have any money for a long time. He got a loan from the university at the very beginning of school. It was a matter of his parents getting the money out of their country to him here.

KRAY: At first, there was a very unfavorable exchange rate between the countries but now it's remarkably good. He has been quite happy about that.

PAUL: [Brings focus of attention back to language proficiency.] Has anyone talked to him about his problem in Spanish? Could someone who knows Spanish very well get with him for two or three hours and find out what his peculiar problems are in class and exactly what we can do to make assignments more clear? As it is now, the barrier of personal communication is so great and he is so polite and agreeable that sometimes he pretends to understand when he doesn't.

NASH: [Suggests action to be taken by student.] I don't think we ought to be calling him in all the time, saying, "Now do you understand?" He must take the initiative. This is another example of where the different classroom situations will give him some learning experiences that he wouldn't get in a remedial class. Our writing as well as our speaking probably baffles him. We just scribble it up on the board and the students learn to understand our hieroglyphics after a while. He's probably having a great deal of difficulty reading my writing, and if he'll just come in and ask about it, I can help him. Juan has taken more initiative in my class in the last three weeks than he has in a long time.

HALE: How about a conversation with him in Spanish to probe his problems and attitudes? Dr. Leonard, would you have a thought on that?

LEONARD: Yes, I've thought about it, but I have not done it.

PAUL: I tried an experiment with the help of one of my students who speaks a little Spanish, and I was able to get through my ideas to Juan on that. But on the immediate problem of what we're going to do about grading him at the end of the semester—

HALE: Before we get to that, would you want to hear from the residence counselor on Juan's attitude. Is he well motivated?

WENDELL: [Gives impressions.] The notion I've gotten of Juan is that he is very cheerful, very cooperative, very conscientious, and—oh, for instance, we loaned him some bedding at the beginning of the semester. He didn't have any with him, and we had occasion about two weeks ago to ask for it back, because the residence halls needed it. I got across to him the idea that I had to have it back. He told me Monday that he was going down town to buy some. He remembers what I said although it's been two weeks since I talked to him about it. Then there's the situation I mentioned to you over the 'phone yesterday.

HALE: We might as well talk it out here, don't you think?

WENDELL: Well, I've had two or three complaints from the boys that Juan comes back to the dormitory at two or three o'clock on week ends and that he stands outside the building and tries out his vocal cords. He roars out his Spanish in song about three o'clock in the morning. It seems to please him, I guess, but it disrupts sleep throughout the building. I think it's a week-end affair—not many week ends in a row—but there have been complaints.

HARRIMAN: Maybe he needs to get into one of the courses in the school of music. [Laughs]

HALE: [Brings discussion again to immediate problem.] A moment ago Dr. Paul raised the question for which we really came together in this conference. What about a mid-term report on Juan? Will you send out a grade? It can't be much of a *grade*. Is there another alternative?

PAUL: Well, I was thinking more of what we were going to do at the end of the semester rather than right now.

CATO: We can't talk about that until we know whether this next period, after this present period, will be improved.

PAUL: Well, I mean I can pretty well tell now that Juan cannot possibly do satisfactory work in English composition this semester. But I might be wrong.

NASH: [Questions expectations of off-campus agency.] I'm willing to write off the first half of this semester as "no gain" and mark him on the basis of the second half and clearly explain to him what is being done. I see no reason why he might not eventually pass my course. What about the State Department in Washington? Is there any regulation on grades which he has to meet for their purposes?

KRAY; Yes, two boys came in this fall who are having a little bit of trouble now. The questions asked by the State Department are, "How many hours did you take last semester? What courses did you pass? What courses did you fail?"

LEONARD: It's twelve hours the State Department wants the student to take.

If there is any variance from that, it will take explanation. It doesn't necessarily mean twelve hours passed.

KRAY: They have to list the courses they fail. That's required.

NASH: What courses might Juan possibly squeeze through? I think he can get through mine, but he hasn't taken the test yet. It will count one-third. If he has reading comprehension, he can get through it and might even make a C.

CATO: Didn't someone suggest in our earlier conference the possibility of giving "incompletes"? In a very real sense that's what his work is.

HALE: These end-of-term incompletes will need to be made up by him within the period of time that the registrar indicates.

LEONARD: The usual limitation is one semester.

KRAY: [Cites case.] One of the students from Iceland received incomplete in English last time. He is now making it up because the English department didn't think his work last spring was of sufficient caliber to give him a passing grade. They didn't fail him; they gave him an incomplete.

TILLMAN: As far as his knowledge level is concerned, he has a passing grade in my course. If that meant that he would be encouraged to go ahead and take the next course, which is calculus, it would be unfair to him.

HALE: Then your recommendation would also be to give an incomplete, wouldn't it?

KRAY: It would have to be some sort of mark to make him repeat the course rather than go on to an advanced course.

TILLMAN: Repeating that course really wouldn't do him much good. He knows the basic subject matter, but until he can get to the point of understanding what is presented in this calculus course, which meets five days a week and is about as concentrated as any math course we have, he would really be confused.

POTTER: Juan should not take calculus unless he has that first course pretty well mastered. He should be able to complete my course in drawing in about a month, as it is just a matter of a lag between comprehension and the transferring of ideas from Spanish to English.

HALE: Then in March he would complete what other students finish in February?

POTTER: Yes, if he would be consistent in keeping up his work.

HALE: Mr. Potter, do you think you can work out a twelve-hour course load for second semester for Juan?

POTTER: [Sees conference results as aid to scheduling student.] I think so. I think that the important think now is forming the basis of next semester's scheduling for him. I think it is something that could have been done to his advantage prior to this semester, and we are just getting to it. Juan came up here all out of breath, literally, and wanted to register before we knew much about him. I think that may have been one of the difficulties. I do think that what we are discussing now would certainly be a basis for what we suggest that he take next semester.

KRAY: [Alternative idea.] Is Juan better off here or would he be better off down at the other state university, since he doesn't plan to stay here anyway? He's just here trying to learn English. Then he'll go to the other institution, assuming he acquires that knowledge, to take up engineering. Would he be better off down there where they have a hundred and some Latin American students?

POTTER: [Espouses idea.] I cleared him on that right at first. He said that there were too many students from Latin America down there, and that has been the reaction of some other foreign students. As I say, we are formulating the basis now for what we want Juan to do in his second semester to make the most efficient use of his time. Dr. Tillman says that he should not even think of going into advanced geometry or calculus. I say that he should not take the geometry for the same reason. The best procedure would be that he take regularly prescribed courses for preengineering students. He will only be here two years; he will then be admitted to junior standing at the other institution and will finish his work there. Maybe we need to change our program and say that what foreign students need here is *an extra year* of orientation. I think much of this will match up with what we want other foreign students to do.

KRAY: [Questions role of the university.] Yes, at the moment, but so far the two boys among our foreign students who have had the most trouble academically are two boys who are going to stay here only two years and then go to the other state school. Jose R. is having a lot of trouble. In fact, he may find himself out of school at the end of this semester if he isn't careful, and Juan is in the same situation. And Jose intends to transfer to the other state institution.

NASH: As I see it, that means that we are trying to turn our university into a type of orientation school for these people. I don't think that we have the time and facilities to do so.

KRAY: That's what I mean when I suggest that they go to the summer foreign-language institutes for a period of six or eight weeks.

NASH: Personally, I will do all I can if Juan is going to stay here for a four-year period and become an integral part of our society. That is one thing, but for him just to come here because he can't get oriented as fast at the university is another. Perhaps he had better go to a technical school.

LORENZO: Well, I still think that it is our duty to do something with him, rather than ignore his case.

NASH: Look at the man-hours consumed here today. I mean I'm glad to do it, but if it is on the basis of "personal attention in language" that we are going to draw students here, I would say that there must be other facilities in the nation already set up that could give that orientation more effectively.

CATO: [Suggests course with credit.] I think that brings up the necessity of some sort of organized program, in any case, at our school. You see, I am thoroughly in favor of the kind of courses that we talked about last time. It would be teaching English as a foreign language to these people and giving college credit. I don't think that we are going to solve anything by thinking of Jose or Juan as different kinds of cases, because the same problems are going to happen over and over with other students. We have these two people as our worst problems right now, but that's not going to hold forever.

I wonder if I could make another point about the math. Dr. Tillman said that he didn't think that it would be useful for Juan to take the course over, but the tool analogy has come up again and I wonder if maybe we can't push that a little bit further. Juan has a skill he's learned—let's say to saw a piece of wood straight across—and he learned with the *right hand*. Now, here he has to learn the same thing with the *left hand*, so to speak. He knows how, intellectually, to do this math thing, but he is having to do it *in a different way*. It seems to me that if he doesn't learn right off the bat to do with his left hand, then he has to keep trying. Now, when he learns to saw straight across a piece of wood with his left hand, he can go on to the next problem which is scroll sawing or something advanced, using his left hand.

HARRIMAN: [Predicts little progress.] I think you will observe at this point the by-factor—Juan's motivation or interest. I think that is one of his major troubles in the geometry situaton. He's seen most of this before, and there is no urgency about it at all. I think that, if Juan were to start over, it would be the same story. He'd be absent half the time; he would not get any more out of it by repeating.

TILLMAN: He doesn't respond to anything I've been able to say to him. I've gone over his notebook in Spanish with him. He's pointed out where something in it coincides with what we're doing. I don't think, however, that his attendance of my class is doing him any good because there is no response there.

NASH: Do we have a math course other than the one you're teaching which Juan could take?

TILLMAN: Yes, there are several.

NASH: Do you think that these might provide more motivation?

TILLMAN: But he is never going to make calculus, as near as I can tell, unless he has individual tutoring. I don't know anybody in the math department who has that much time to help him.

HALE: Harriman, I can see that you are ready to say something.

HARRIMAN: [Suggests screening process.] In line with my experience, I would like to state something to be considered. In instances where students obviously do not have oral comprehension in English, we ought to have them talk with a staff observer; even undergo some tests. Then the observer's impression could be transmitted to the counseling office. Secondly, we should try to find some student who speaks the same language to determine if there is a similar report on the student's problem. With those two reports, the counseling office could then brief the instructors on the student's problem in light of what has been learned. I think that would obviate most of the meetings of this type for foreign students.

HALE: Juan did come in late, but we had previously formulated a plan for each new student to screen through Dr. Leonard's office. Now we know, because of the decentralized arrangement here, that sometimes students don't always do that. Who saw Juan first in the early days of the semester?

LEONARD: I saw him, and I checked his English, oral English. He understood me quite satisfactorily, but during that check he also had the experience of not understanding one word which was spoken behind his back. To understand an individual directly in a one-to-one conversation and to understand a lecture in a group is an entirely different thing for Juan.

HALE: [Requests action from group.] Now, are we about to speak to the immediate problem? Shall we give Juan an incomplete for the end of the semester, or is that an individual assessment that we can't legislate on as a group?

NASH: I think that we agreed on giving either an incomplete or a grade—in other words, not flunking him.

HALE: Mr. Paul, I think you said he couldn't pass English.

PAUL: I don't see how he can. On the other hand, I'm not sure it's very intelligent to flunk him.

HALE: So, you might be constrained to give him a D or incomplete?

PAUL: I guess the incomplete is the best answer.

HALE: Would he register again for the English 100?

PAUL: That's the part I don't know. Should he reenroll in that course? Of course, an incomplete doesn't necessarily require that, does it?

HALE: Do *you* think he should reenroll?

POTTER: My best guess would be that he should.

KRAY: Should the person counseling Juan on his program tell him that he is probably going to be delayed for a year and that he needs to plan accordingly?

POTTER: He is taking twelve hours now whereas a normal load for the pre-engineering student is nineteen. That leaves seven hours short. I can tell him that.

HALE: Before you go, Miss Calvin, shall we assume that Juan will keep on working in the special clinic with you? [She agrees.]

NASH: In my class, I will give him either an incomplete or a grade, with the understanding that if he gets an incomplete he ought to take the course over.

HALE: [Cites contribution of group.] Now whether or not you realize it, you are setting some kind of precedent here. This is one of few instances where classroom teachers, clinicians, and counselors from the residence halls have sat down to frame what may become policy with respect to foreign students.

CATO: Do you have our recommendation on credit for English as a foreign language noted?

HALE: Yes—that this group recommends that remedial work, speech or writing, carry credit for foreign students.

CATO: I don't think that all remedial work should be given credit, because occasionally we are going to find people who lisp in Spanish as well as in English. Correction for this defect should not be given credit any more than should the same remedial work of the students who come to me as English-speaking students. I think that there should be a special course in English for foreign students for which foreign students should get training in reading, writing, listening, and speaking, for credit.

HALE: Then there would need to be a screening device set up in order that we know who needs to go into that course—English for foreign students.

PAUL: I've just realized something the last few minutes. We've been going at the problem as we see it ourselves, and we've come up with this problem of comprehension. Let's be sure that we get from Juan what he sees as his problem.

HALE: Could somebody, some Spanish-speaking somebody, talk with him about his problem? Could that be you, Dr. Leonard?

DR. LEONARD: I'll get at it.

NASH: It may be a cultural thing back in there that is blocking him.

CATO: There is another possibility. Dr. Leonard said that he doesn't understand English when you speak behind his back. Maybe he is hard of hearing, and so I will check his hearing the next time he comes to the speech clinic.

NASH: I have an idea. In addition to your talking to him, Dr. Leonard, could you get some Spanish-speaking student also to talk to Juan to see if anything comes out that doesn't show up in your conference?

LEONARD: I might be able to get some data through students I know.

HALE: How about another suggestion—that of investigating the offerings of foreign-language short courses on other campuses.

LEONARD: I think that we must beware of putting too much faith in some of these courses in other universities. Now the course in applied linguistics in one school, for example, is excellent for some purposes, but after talking with students who went up there last summer, I wonder if they really got what they wanted.

HALE: [Summary.] By way of summary, we have (1) entered into an agreement for assessing Juan's grades at end of term, (2) suggested that Dr. Leonard speak to Juan in Spanish about his problem, (3) suggested that Dr. Leonard talk with other foreign students to determine Juan's basic problems, and (4) agreed that Juan should continue his clinical work with Dr. Cato in speech and with Miss Calvin in speech and writing. By way of additional general planning for students from abroad, we have recommended that (1) credit be given for an orientation course in communication for foreign students, (2) study be made of offerings of foreign-language schools in short courses, (3) means be found for testing the communications abilities of foreign students before they arrive, and (4) we discuss with these students the advisability of spending a first semester in getting adjusted or oriented. This could conceivably prolong their period of study but be worth it in the long haul. Thank you so much for your attention and your good contributions here.

SUMMARY

Commenting on the effectiveness of the case conference, Warters [4] says that it is likely the best method for synthesizing, coordinating, and interpreting data gathered from various sources. In this instance, the process evolved when twelve conferees, representing the instructional program and student personnel services in a given institution, participated in the case review of Juan. It perhaps could be said that Juan had twelve sides and that when the twelve points of view were contributed then, and only then, was Juan completely visible.

If the reader is reluctant to accept this notion, he may agree with Wise [5] who comments:

[4] Jane Warters, *Techniques of Counseling*, McGraw-Hill Book Company, Inc., New York, 1954, p. 284.
[5] W. M. Wise, "The Implications of the Student Personnel Philosophy," *Educational and Psychological Measurement*, 2:684, winter, 1951.

No matter how many records we have obtained about the student, no matter how many test results we may have in front of us, no matter how many of our colleagues may sit and discuss the student, no matter how many conferences we may have with the individual himself, we still fall far short of having seen the whole student, for he is not really discernible even to himself. Indeed all that we can have are brief glimpses of the student. . . .

If the reader is hesitant to admit that the case conference has really produced a view of the "whole Juan," he may concede at least that the review has made Juan more of substance and less of shadow. Juan is not likely to be viewed as merely a student "number" in his classes or to appear as a blur in the surge of 500 men in the residence hall.

The case conference has served as a device for the in-service training of instructional personnel and student personnel workers. The conferees, in the course of the discussion lasting an hour and a half, have gained some appreciation of (1) the individualized teaching methods employed in basic course work, (2) the techniques adapted in the clinical setting, (3) the educative aspects of residence-hall life, (4) the cumulative concerns held in many quarters for the welfare of Juan, (5) the knotty problems that revolve around the admission of students from abroad, (6) the enmeshing regulations that bear down on Juan as he continues residence in the university, (7) the series of services that must be coordinated if their impact is to be truly beneficial for Juan, and (8) the sum total of these impressions which serve to create and reflect a philosophy of education particularized in the institution.

In addition, the case conference presented a review in some detail of specific areas in which the twelve conferees have participated or which they have observed. In this instance, discussion covered Juan's academic achievement, cultural background, social adjustment, achievement of communicational skills, economic and financial problems, and personal motivation. An appraisal of the resources of the institution in view of their possible assistance to Juan was made.

Finally, the deliberation, engaged in by twelve persons in various specialties, has contributed to the interdisciplinary view recommended in earlier chapters. The same benefits with respect to (1) in-service training of institutional personnel, (2) appraisal of the institution's resources for aiding a student, and (3) participation in interdisciplinary discussions could not have been achieved in a series of notes, telephone talks, or informal chats on campus.

CHAPTER 16 *The Coordination of Counseling: A Case Study*

Administrators, in an effort to describe working relationships, often point to organizational or structural charts, commenting, "This is how our program works." Likewise, officers in areas of student personnel and counseling enumerate their duties, as determined from a job analysis, explaining, "This is what I do in collaboration with such-and-such office."

Illustrating what can happen in "paper programs" of student personnel, Heaton [1] narrates the case of Dick Smith who, upon entering college, was given the usual psychological examination and other measures of achievement administered by the college for purposes of educational advisement. In the process of his induction, Dick filled in an entrance form or two in the office of the registrar. He was given a fairly searching health examination. The test scores, the personnel form, and the results of the health examination were *filed* each in the appropriate office. The boy, detached from these key data, went his unhappy way for two years, doing inferior work and troubling the instructors who felt that they dare not fail him because of his father's political power. Finally, an investigator with a "hunch" looked into the health file and noted a small entry to the effect that the boy had undergone eight years of treatment by a neurologist. Thereupon, a diagnosis was requested of the specialist, and the story of Dick's unhappy home relationships came out. As one phase of the treatment, the student had been advised by the specialist to increase his intake of carbohydrates and to proceed with medication intended to correct the metabolic condition.

Heaton concludes:

What difference would have resulted if the college physician, the student's adviser, the class instructors, the registrar, and the dietitian of the college

[1] Kenneth L. Heaton, "Kinds of Information Needed for the College Personnel Service," in John Dale Russell (ed.), *Student Personnel Services in Colleges and Universities*, University of Chicago Press, Chicago, 1941, pp. 115–116.

253

dining room . . . had come together in their concern for this student and decided what information was needed by all of them in order to adequately serve Dick's needs.

Organizational charts, line-and-staff diagrams, job analyses, and procedural summaries of an institution may tell only the surface story of case handling. Behind this façade proceed, in all probability, the series of day-to-day happenings which unfold, epic-like, telling the real story of working relationships between and among personnel. If coordination in counseling is directed toward (1) keeping intact a central design or pattern and (2) promoting an operating relationship by welding workers together through a recognition of a dominant idea, then the process of coordination is capable of illustration and dramatization.

This chapter attempts to show what can happen when persons sensitive to the needs of a student *do* come together to talk of ways in which they may more adequately perform. The intelligent, vigorous, persistent, and organized effort needed to promote coordination in counseling is observable in episodes, as selected, with the performers "speaking the speech" which reflects their concern. Their remarks, appropriately, are taken from actual "script," comments and observations contained in the student's cumulative record. The "thespians" in this instance include academic administrators, members of the teaching faculty, faculty advisers, residence and vocational counselors, the director of the counseling program, off-campus counseling personnel, graduate students—in short, most of those persons to whom this book is directed (see Preface).

The case chosen for portrayal is one of a student enrolled in a university on a vocational rehabilitation scholarship. In this day of increased interest in and preparation for the counseling of the handicapped, the case of Inez aims to do the following:

1. To show the practices employed within a particular institution for aiding the whole student

2. To show ways in which information is shared among personnel in an educational institution and a state-federal agency

3. To point up the process of decision making engaged in by a number of persons working cooperatively on a problem

4. To extend to the reader some responsibility for analyzing and evaluating specific action undertaken

The technique of presentation is one which permits each participant to reveal his point of view. The author's task has been to select dialogue and to supply stage directions which serve to "fill in" the narration. The result is both expository and narrative—and not a little didactic.

THE CASE OF INEZ

From the point of view of Mr. Ray, the district supervisor of
vocational rehabilitation

This client is eighteen years of age and is a graduate of Paramount High School. She has residuals of rheumatoid arthritis resulting in disabled hands and feet. It is believed that she can do college work and that she could become a teacher in the elementary grades. The purpose of the vocational rehabilitation plan is to assist her in earning a college degree. The client's wish is to do the four years' work in three years by attending summer sessions.

During her senior year in high school, the client felt that she wanted to become a religious-education worker, choosing to take training toward that objective. At the time, her rehabilitation counselor thought her objective satisfactory, basing his opinion on aptitude tests and on the idea that in religious work the client would find sympathetic employers. The counselor also felt that the client might consider library work. Early in the summer, with the client's aunt advising her and helping along the line of promoting assistance from relatives, the client decided that she should consider school teaching with a view to teaching in the elementary grades. The counselor and supervisor approved of this new objective, and the counselor drew a plan accordingly.

A summary of Inez's profile of interests and aptitudes as determined by the local rehabilitation counselor was available to the district supervisor:

Kuder Preference Record, Vocational, Form CH:

	Percentile *(national norms)*
Mechanical	96th
Computational	39th
Scientific	90th
Persuasive	25th
Artistic	32nd
Literary	75th
Musical	48th
Social service	31st
Clerical	5th

	Percentile
Army general classification tests: first civilian, edition— form AH	88th
Psychological corporation general clerical test	45th (high school girls)
Test of mechanical comprehension form AA (Bennett)	80th (college freshman)
Adjustment inventory student form (Bell)	Average

This information was transmitted to the counseling center before the arrival of Inez at the university. Copies of the memo were made at the counseling center and sent to (1) the records office and (2) the university hospital, where the department of physical education (correctives specialist) could have access to the information. A third copy of the memo was placed in the student's counseling folder for the use of Miss Perkins, the faculty counselor.

From the point of view of the admissions officer

The following information was taken from the application materials submitted by the student, her high school principal, and others.

Father: John David Doan, city policeman (retired); public school education
Mother: Myrtle Agnes Doan, deceased; public school education
Daughter: Inez Doan, graduate of Paramount High School; average grades, A—; member of National Honor Society and Baptist Young People's Union; vocational interest, elementary education; rehabilitation scholarship awarded
State high school tests:

Area	Percentile
Psychological	85th
English	98th
Social studies	58th
Natural science	76th
Mathematics	59th

High school grades:

English	4 units	ABAA
Spanish	2 units	AB
Civics	1 unit	A
History	2 units	B
Current events	½ unit	B
Social problems	½ unit	B
Algebra	2 units	AD
Biology	1 unit	B
Chemistry	1 unit	A
Speech	½ unit	A
Bible	1 unit	A
Home economics	1 unit	A
Office practice	1 unit	A
Physical education	½ unit	B

This information was transmitted by the admissions office to the records office, being recorded there as a part of the student's permanent record. A copy of this information, together with scores from the university entrance tests, was sent as a personal data summary to the counseling office. This information was placed in the students' counseling folder for the use of the faculty counselor.

From the point of view of the faculty counselor

The results made by Inez on the entrance tests were given to Miss Perkins, faculty counselor, as follows:

American Council on Education Psychological Examination (national norms):

	Percentile
Quantitative	23rd
Linguistic	46th
Total	34th

Minnesota personality scale:

	Percentile
Morale	75th
Social adjustment	35th
Family relations	10th
Emotionality	15th
Economic conservatism	50th

A telephone call made by Miss Perkins to the counseling office in November went as follows:

As you know, I am Inez Doan's faculty counselor. She has indicated an interest in elementary teaching. In my judgment, with the physical handicap which Inez has, she will find the work in elementary teaching very taxing. I have talked over with Inez the kind of preparation she will have to make and, beyond that, the rigors of playground supervision, the heavy class-teaching load, and the necessity for standing long hours on her feet. Right now I do not believe that Inez recognizes that she will have the difficulties in teaching that I have pointed out to her. I am wondering if you could arrange for someone to give her redirection toward her vocational goal.

As a result of this call, Mrs. Blake, vocational counselor, invited Inez to come in for conference.

From the point of view of the vocational counselor

Since it appears that counseling must continue for possibly a year, this statement deserves to be called a "progress report." Inez has been in for two interviews and plans to take the central aptitude test battery in January. She seems loath to give up her plans for work in elementary education but is making every effort to be open-minded and to investigate other fields. To this end, she is to see the assistant dean of the school of library concerning training on December 15.

A follow-up report by Mrs. Blake was made in January.

Results on General Aptitude Test Battery:

	Percentile
General learning ability	70th
Understanding of words	74th
Arithmetic ability	59th
Visualizing geometric forms	50th
Recognizing visual details	42nd
Clerical perception	35th
Eye-hand coordination	15th
Speed of hand movement	6th
Finger dexterity	27th
Manual dexterity	10th

This morning Inez came in to discuss the results of the GATB. Because of her physical disability, she did not do well on the apparatus part of the test and therefore no occupational patterns emerged; however, her performance on the parts of the test having to do with general learning ability and understanding of words show her to have good mental ability. I talked with her about the possibility of doing work that will not require much physical activity, such as proofreading in a publishing firm. We called the dean of the school of education to learn whether or not she would be granted a degree in education without serving an internship. He felt that the merits of the case would justify such action. Since Inez has her heart set on something in the field of elementary education, we thought that possibly she might deal with materials in elementary education or religious work. She said that the assistant dean in the library school agreed that she could take a minor in library science.

Inez seemed to accept the plan to continue in elementary education with the possibility that she might not be accepted for an internship and would need to prepare for work in a related field instead.

These reports were sent by Mrs. Blake to Miss Perkins, faculty counselor. Copies were likewise sent to the records office.

From the point of view of the residence counselor

Inez has a number of uncertain factors to deal with: health, finances, and vocation.

Between the time she was five to ten years old, she spent a great deal of time in the hospital with an onset of arthritis. Inez thinks that her mother's care of her brought her through to a point where she is not incapacitated completely. Two years before graduation from high school, Inez had another onset which she feels may have been caused by getting overtired. Again her mother took a good deal of responsibility for nursing care. She died soon after Inez was through this siege. Her father lives on a small retirement income on which he supports the home and a younger brother. Inez seems very fond of the young brother. Her father was a policeman who was retired early because of a back injury. He can give Inez no help in college. The rehabilitation office paid her fees and books this year. Three uncles have divided the other costs between them, supplying her with enough for food. Her spending money comes from indefinite sources, mostly friends who are interested in her, and she says that she has never lacked money but is always uncertain of any except her weekly food check. She has a good friend in New York who was a nurse in the hospital in which she received care. She frequently sends Inez money. She also was awarded an AAUW scholarship. She has been most uncertain of finances for next year because of changes in the uncles' situations. Recently, the rehabilitation service has said that they would pay all expenses next year, which has relieved her immeasurably.

She was interested in trying for a state teaching scholarship when there were openings for students now in college, but she was worried about the obligation to teach after graduation. She said that the doctors felt that there would likely be no recurrence of acute arthritis, but that this was still a possibility and should it happen, she might not be able to fulfill her responsibilities. At this time also, we learned from the counseling office that teaching has been questioned for her because of the slowness in her movements.

Inez was rather a forlorn child when she entered college. The students in her hall have welcomed her, giving her haircuts, helping her put hems in new skirts, typing her long "research" papers for her. She has "come out" a good deal and can hold her own in the group.

In early March, Miss Robb, the residence counselor, called the counseling office, saying:

Inez Doan, one of the girls in my hall, is, as you know, enrolled on the rehabilitation scholarship plan. I have had occasion to observe her as she prepares for her classes. It seems to take Inez a great deal of time to write her lessons in longhand for the reason that her disability has affected her hand and finger movement. The other day when Inez and I were talking, we thought of the possibility of a typewriter. Since she does not have too much strength in her hands and arms, the best device might be an electric typewriter. Do you know if the rehabilitation service would approve her having this kind of machine at their expense?

On the basis of this conversation, the director of counseling discussed the case in its evolvement with Mrs. Blake and with a graduate student, Miss Chance, who was doing a supervised internship in the office. Miss Chance requested Inez to come in to discuss her course work, Miss Robb having told Inez about the reason for the proposed conference.

From the point of view of the graduate-student intern

Inez states that her school work is not too difficult for her at this point, but because her hands are crippled it takes considerable time for her to prepare her written work. She thinks that an electric typewriter would enable her to decrease her actual writing time.

Inez stated that she had the feeling that no one thought she could succeed in any field because of her handicap. At one time she was sure that she could succeed in elementary education; however, she no longer is sure even of this field.

We discussed the possibilities of religious education in schools since at one time her interest was in religious work. Inez has tentative plans for attending summer school but again is undecided because of her physical condition. We talked of the number of hours she might carry in summer school, and Inez decided that she would work out the number of hours and then talk with the registrar about the amount of time required in class and the required outside work, before making her final decision.

Inez expressed the desire to come in and talk again with Mrs. Blake about her plans. Before the next interview she agreed to find out as much as possible about the opportunities in religious education, as well as the preparation required for the work so that she might explore this further.

At the end of the interview Inez added that, if she could obtain the electric typewriter to help her in her work, the girls on her floor in the dormitory would teach her the correct typing methods so that she might work at her own speed.

Miss Chance arranged an interview with Mr. Ray of the rehabilitation service to talk about the electric typewriter for Inez. It was found that, in the operation of an electric typewriter, just two *ounces* of pressure are required to shift the carriage as compared with fifteen pounds for shifting a regular typewriter carriage. The rehabilitation service subsequently bought Inez a used machine. Miss Chance obtained information on how to operate this typewriter and helped Inez to learn its operation. Inez's first year ended.

From the point of view of the orthopedic surgeon to whom Inez was referred by the rehabilitation service

The patient reported in for examination and was seen by me on August 26, with special reference to her hands and feet. She gave a history of onset of rheumatoid arthritis or Still's disease at the age of six years. This became quite severe and involved most of her joints including the knees, hips, shoulders and elbows, etc. The major joints, that is, the ankles, knees, hips, shoulders, and elbows, subsided satisfactorily and have a good range of motion at this time with little or no deformity. However, the hands and feet present a typical picture of burned out rheumatoid arthritis with obvious destruction of the interphalangeal and metacarpal phalangeal joints as well as the wrists. She has had no acute symptoms for more than five years. The second toe on the right foot is luxated dorsally and the metatarsal head beneath it is extremely prominent. She wears one type of shoe in which she can be comfortable, and, other than this, the feet do not give her any severe trouble. However, I think that eventually these feet will give her trouble and will probably need some corrective type of surgery. The changes in the left foot are less severe than those in the right.

The function of the hands is not bad considering the severity of the deformity. Her greatest difficulty is in writing, and she can even type a little bit. Examination of the back and hips is negative. The wrists show a flexion deformity on each side, more severe on the right, and it is only with the greatest difficulty that either wrist may be brought up to a neutral position. I think that it is remarkable that she is getting along as well as she is.

I see no reason for any active treatment at this time, such as whirlpool baths, paraffin baths, etc. I believe that the joint involvement is quiescent, and certainly no such treatment is going to decrease the deformity which she already has. Normal activity will maintain her function. I think that it would be to her advantage to see her again for a check examination in about three months.

Copies of this report were sent from the counseling office to the university hospital and the records office.

In February of the second year, the counseling center resumed work on the student's case in view of the fact that Inez would be approaching her teaching-internship experience. Mrs. Armont, graduate intern who succeeded Miss Chance, studied the case record, commenting that she believed that Inez was presently enrolled in the social work course which she was attending. Mrs. Armont asked Inez to come in for an interview.

From the point of view of the second graduate-student intern

Inez is enjoying her courses but is very anxious to find out *definitely* if she can intern as an elementary teacher and if she can be employed as a teacher. She felt that Mrs. Blake or I could get answers to these two questions.

I find that Inez has a good philosophy of life and a good attitude toward work. She is very optimistic and desires to earn her way, not to be employed out of sympathy only. She is interested in people and their problems. She likes her class in criminology very much and contributes valuable comments. Inez desires most of all a college education which will train her for some position in which she can earn the salary. I believe that Inez has changed her desire to be a teacher because she has learned what is required of a teacher.

From the point of view of the director of teacher internship

There must be some place in our society for a person with Inez's ambition and outlook. However, I must truthfully say that the elementary school *could* prove to be her undoing, with her limitations being what they are. In my judgment, she would have to be much more active and mobile in teaching younger children than she can possibly be with her handicap. It would not only be difficult for Inez to meet the situation, but it might also be hard for her pupils to accept her limitations. However, I do not wish to make this decision by myself. I would prefer to have the counseling office call a conference of those persons who know her well, including personnel from the district office of vocational rehabilitation. Let's see what the mutual deliberation of these individuals will reveal.

From the point of view of the case conferees

Twelve persons who had worked with Inez over the period of the two academic years were present at this meeting held in early April.

During the course of the hour and a half in which the group covered the problem, each person spoke of his or her acquaintanceship with Inez. The report from the instructor in correctives in physical education covered Inez's splendid cooperation and her high level of accomplishment in the modified physical education class. The report of the university physician mentioned loss of weight and possible nutritional or dietary deficiency. The vocational rehabilitation personnel felt that Inez's vocational objective could be changed without curtailment of her scholarship; in addition, they felt that the scholarship might be extended to cover training for the kind of work into which she would best fit, whatever that might be. The field of library work seemed to be a possibility except for the visual handicap, which was noted as "bilateral myopia" on the health report. Mrs. Armont recounted an interview with the dean of the School of Social Work, in which other possibilities for training Inez were considered. The group concurred in the feeling that, rather than have Inez apply for a teaching internship and then be denied, she be advised not to apply but to consider with Mrs. Blake and Mrs. Armont other types of preparation. The following action was outlined to conclude the meeting:

1. That Inez be examined by her physician and by an eye specialist during the approaching spring holidays, the examinations to be done at the expense of the rehabilitation service

2. That Mrs. Blake continue to work with Inez in exploration of a major, Mrs. Armont assisting

3. That Inez change from the School of Education to the College of Arts-Sciences if she felt that she needed more time to select her major, her classification in arts-sciences being "no preference as to major"

4. That Mrs. Armont poll members of the School of Social Work regarding opportunities for Inez in that area

5. That the director of counseling write Miss Darby, high school counselor, to enlist her help

The results of the case conference were summarized, with a copy filed in the records office.

From the point of view of Inez (in conference with the director of counseling)

A year ago I did not feel much like changing my mind about a field of work. But I know that you people have studied my problems and that you will help me to find the work I can do since teaching doesn't seem possible. I would like to know what I can do by the end of this school year. Do you think I can accomplish that?

You know, I don't intend to be a wheelchair case, and I certainly do not want charity. You can see that I do have more strength than many people who have had arthritis. I know that there is some kind of work I can do.

I talked to Mrs. Bazeman in the School of Social Work this week. She said that there *is* employment for handicapped people but that this type of employment would require at least two years of graduate study. As far as the study goes, I would like that all right if I knew pretty definitely that I could have a job when I was through. The people in the vocational rehabilitation office want me to let them know something definite by the middle of the summer. I don't know just what to tell them right now. But Miss Darby, my high school counselor, wrote me—after she heard from you—about possible employment this summer. Miss Darby has an idea that I might be able to work in the Children's Home for experience—not much money—and that this would give me a "look-in" on what service-type jobs other than teaching have to offer. As soon as I get home after school lets out here, I will apply in person at the Children's Home as Miss Darby suggests.

Narration and Conclusion

Over the summer, Inez worked in the Children's Home as she had planned. In a letter to Mrs. Blake she summarized her experience as "one more important to me than anything else which could have happened since it increased my self-confidence and skill in working with others." In addition, Inez took a trip East to visit her friend who was a nurse, observing in Baltimore and Philadelphia procedures in several social agencies.

Returning to the campus in the fall of her third year, Inez changed her major from education to social work and immediately began academic counseling with Dr. Peale, a faculty adviser in the School of Social Work. The office of vocational rehabilitation approved the change and reiterated its offer of aiding Inez in the new major. The district supervisor commented favorably upon Inez's achievement of forty-four quality points earned in carrying sixteen hours of work in the spring semester.

As Inez entered her senior year, she was asked to appear as a member of a panel in the seminar for counselors to discuss the manner in which her education-vocational aims had been clarified. Other members of the panel were Mr. Ray, Mrs. Blake, Miss Robb, Miss Perkins, Dr. Peale, and personnel from the counseling center. The "case of Inez" was narrated, in an abbreviated form, with use made of some of the material in this chapter. At the conclusion of the panel presentation, Inez was asked to make critical observations. She was asked specifically to answer this question posed by the director of counseling:

Inez, couldn't we have cut this process shorter and decided for you in your freshman year that a major in social work would be better for you than a teaching major?

Inez made the following reply:

No one else could have made the decision for me because no person could have known all that I needed at that time. I *do* feel, as I look back, that those who worked with me might have been more frank. Handicapped people must know the truth about themselves and their chances for placement sooner or later. As far as I am concerned, my feelings are not easily hurt, and I might have been given the truth straight out. On the other hand, though, each of you may have been trying to tell me the truth, in your way, and I may have been unwilling to listen to you then. It is a little hard for me to recall exactly how I felt those first two years, but I can say that this last year has been wonderful! I am looking forward to an internship in social work this spring and a job after graduation.

The expectation of Inez was fulfilled with her placement after graduation in the regional office of a welfare agency.

SUMMARY

In viewing the "educational epic," the author believes that the reader will discern varying degrees of intelligent, vigorous, persistent, and organized effort in the progression of the case. The reader is asked, as was Inez, to view the process critically and to adjudge wherein the objectives of good coordinative activity were met satisfactorily or wherein they fell short of expectations.

These things may be obvious:

1. Inez was viewed, as was Juan in the preceding chapter, from twelve or more "sides."

2. The assistance given to Inez was gauged, in so far as possible, to her need for help and to her own rate of maturation. She could not be hurried, mentally or physically, into an action.

3. The participants, faculty advisers and professional counselors, were patient, vigilant, and objective, though not impersonal. They appeared to be exploring *with Inez* the possibilities open to her. From this point of view, their participation in her case study was a type of in-service training.

4. Relations between "town and gown" were strengthened, particularly in the case conference, when three men from the rehabilitation office joined the campus group in the decision making. Interagency cooperation was explored in the process.

5. As is not always true, the student's "story" achieved institutional "closure" which produced for the participants somewhat the feeling of "play's ended" and resulted in something akin to a "curtain call." The case is frequently referred to in discussions of situations involving stu-

dents sponsored by the vocational rehabilitation service or council of the blind.

The succeeding chapter views another type of cooperative activity of administrators, professionally trained counselors, and faculty advisers— that of special study directed toward the needs and problems of contemporary students in higher education. The integration of effort of these practitioners is needed as new problems arise, as old problems persist, and as old and new combine to harass—and challenge—these educators.

CHAPTER 17 *Productive Inquiry:*
Solving the Unsolved

Turning back to the Preface, the reader will note the premises upon which this book was predicated. Cited were the following:

1. The faculty member is indispensable in the counseling process.

2. There are specific methods, philosophically sound and decidedly practical, which can be utilized in the in-service training of faculty members in their assignment to counseling.

3. The *diversity* of kinds of counseling to be found on college and university campuses is good as long as some *unity* can be effected for the benefit of both the student and the institution.

4. This unity of purpose and practice in counseling can be facilitated through the coordination of efforts of administrators, faculty members, and students, planning and working together.

5. The program of counseling in higher education builds upon the program of guidance in the secondary school.

6. The expectation of parents concerning the counseling of son or daughter is a factor to be reckoned with in present-day programs in higher education.

These premises may be said to have their roots in the statement made by a group of educators denoting one important future need: [1] to achieve a higher degree of integration between the student personnel services and instructional programs.

It is the purpose of this chapter to give some attention to special studies, with relation to the premises cited above, which (1) have been completed, (2) are in process of completion, or (3) deserve to be done.

A DEFINITION OF TERMS

A chapter of this nature is difficult to prepare in view of reader diversity. Cited in the Preface were the following persons visualized as

---

[1] *Future Needs in Student Personnel Work,* American Council on Education, Washington, 1950, p. 6.

readers: (1) general and academic administrators in colleges and universities, (2) administrators of programs of counseling, (3) teachers—both advisers and nonadvisers—in college and university, (4) graduate students preparing for posts as general or student personnel administrators or as teachers, and (5) personnel in the secondary schools—superintendents, principals, guidance directors, and counselors.

A detailed treatment of basic research in the area of student personnel services would likely be of limited interest to those in categories 1, 3, and 5 and to only a portion of the group in category 4. A more general treatment of feasible studies is given instead. In approaching the investigation of problems raised in preceding chapters of this book, the author differentiates between the terms *research* and *study*. Viewing the former term, Good notes: [2]

Research is the careful unbiased investigation of a problem based insofar as possible upon demonstrable facts and involving refined distinctions, interpretations, and usually some generalization.

That research, so defined and relating particularly to evaluation of counseling programs, is in need of being done is attested by Cottle: [3]

The review for the three-year period indicates the paucity and limited nature of published research on the evaluation of guidance services. There is great need for cooperative research among institutions and for research designs of better quality.

To meet this need, it is obvious that "careful, unbiased investigations ... based ... upon demonstrable facts and involving refined distinctions, interpretations ... and some generalization" must be made by persons qualified to do so. This task will be done, in large part, by persons who are specifically trained in student personnel work and counseling.

Commenting on the need for greater numbers of persons with less specialized training and with limited financial support to undertake investigations, Ginsburg writes: [4]

Unfortunately most people stand in awe of RESEARCH. The feeling that nothing can be done well that is not done with all the elaborate paraphernalia of large-scale research projects has been a serious deterrent. On the other hand there is growing evidence that, with a curious mind and a desire to learn more about what one is doing and the people with whom one is working, valid and useful studies can be carried out without either large foundation grants or the

[2] Carter V. Good, *Dictionary of Education*, McGraw-Hill Book Company, Inc., New York, 1945, p. 346.
[3] William C. Cottle, "The Evaluation of Guidance Services," *Review of Educational Research*, 27:234, April, 1957.
[4] Ethel L. Ginsburg, *The College and Student Health*, Based on the Fourth National Conference on Health in Colleges, National Tuberculosis Association, New York, May, 1954, p. 57.

268 *The Faculty in College Counseling*

other superstructures of formal research. Furthermore, it is being proved daily that students like to be asked to take part in research projects, and that they have much to learn from such participation. It has also been demonstrated that teaching and research go hand in hand—to teach effectively one must go on learning.

Reporting the ideas of a committee designated to outline principles to be observed in planning research in health, Farnsworth states: [5]

The committee noted that any one who makes observations, thinks about them, and relates them to theoretical concepts is in reality doing research. In such work, the curious mind, the keen eye, some knowledge of theory in the field, and an opportunity to exchange experiences with those in similar positions in other institutions are important. Research and service are closely related. If the health worker has an opportunity to do some teaching, he is thus encouraged to clarify thoughts derived from research. Thus, service, research, and teaching can be mutually facilitating if the college administration permits and encourages such well-balanced activity.

The "valid and useful studies" motivated by a "desire to learn more about what one is doing and the people with whom one is working" are those recommended by the author of this book. The "curious mind" and the "keen eye" are possessed by more than a few of the student personnel workers and the faculty members, in addition to health workers, who assist in advisement and counseling in every college and university. Thus, the emphasis in this chapter is laid upon special *studies* capable of being done by a number of persons rather than upon highly complex research to be done by the few. The objective of special study, like that of research, is to solve the hitherto unsolved problem. The difference between the two lies in the extent and depth of the activity, the refinement of process and interpretation. To draw a parallel, hopefully not too remote, the execution of a piano concerto would involve refined distinctions, interpretations, and generalization, the pianist demonstrating these with skill and brilliance. The ability of the artist so to perform would stem, in all likelihood, from a very considerable amount of practice in the execution of useful and valid studies—of finger exercises stressing fundamentals.

To a great extent, the studies discussed and recommended in this chapter are a type of "finger exercise" involving practice in fundamentals, basic to adequacy in counseling performance, but not in themselves "show pieces" of refined research. The motif or recurring theme for these exercises is the integration of student personnel services and instructional programs in all its aspects—of the facilitation of the "new creation" suggested in Chapter 1.

[5] Dana L. Farnsworth, *Mental Health in College and University,* Harvard University Press, Cambridge, Mass., 1957, pp. 180–181.

A PREVIEW OF STUDIES UNDERTAKEN

In the 1952–1953 poll of institutions (see App. A), Question 6 asked: "What studies have you done or are you now doing that relate to better administration and coordination of the student personnel services?" Of the eighty-nine institutions polled, some forty responded with these topics:

1. Study of the separate services in a decentralized program of counseling: precollege counseling, residence-hall counseling, advisement, vocational counseling, counseling for veterans, etc.
2. Study of the objectives of a counseling service
3. Study of problems encountered by first-semester freshmen
4. Study of methods for improving the coordination of counseling services
5. Evaluation of orientation procedures
6. Study of student withdrawals
7. Follow-up on students with low academic potential

Some fairly typical comments by respondents appeared as follows:

MIDWESTERN UNIVERSITY: We are experimenting with a new type of cumulative record which will be used by each of three key evaluation areas for the assistance of students.

EASTERN WOMEN'S COLLEGE: Every group of new students, at the end of three months, is given a mimeographed form to fill out, listing their reactions to the personnel services. This information aids us in making plans for the following semester.

SOUTHERN UNIVERSITY: We studied the coordination of student personnel services by means of a small grant.

WESTERN COLLEGE: An evaluation of our program of student counseling is being carried out by an advanced graduate student from nearby _____ University.

SOUTHWESTERN UNIVERSITY: At this time, we are completing a year-long departmental study of the objectives of our student services. Next year we will view the way in which the objectives are implemented.

MIDWESTERN TEACHERS COLLEGE: This year we are attempting to classify the problems for which students are referred to the counseling center.

In the 1956 poll of 218 institutions, respondents were asked in Question 15 (see App. B): "What changes in your program with reference to any of the foregoing do you foresee?" From the replies, it would appear that the greatest need was for providing a better program of training for faculty advisers (see Tables 16 and 7). Second in importance were changes in plan relating to the reorganization, improvement, and expansion of a single aspect of the program. A sizable number of the respondents saw a need for better coordination of the parts of the total program. Finally, respondents anticipated changes in the manner of selecting faculty advisers, of utilizing them in the program of counseling and in the improvement of working relations among personnel workers, administrators, faculty, and students.

The foregoing review of local studies seems to demonstrate the fact that much-needed investigations can be conducted although full-scale research, based on demonstrable facts and involving refined distinctions, is not feasible. At the risk of possible oversimplification, the author ventures to name some conditions basic to productive inquiry, in line with studies of the type emphasized in this chapter:

1. A conviction (more burning than simmering) that an idea or practice deserves to be studied

2. A sufficient amount of time (not all after-work hours or week ends) for investing in the study

3. Some know-how about ways of studying a problem and an ability to get the study "off the ground"

4. A persistence in following through, once the inquiry is begun, in the face of changing and sometimes adverse conditions

5. A sufficient amount of money for the "necessaries" in the study

6. A willingness to share the findings with others (persons on the local scene as well as those on other campuses)

In the pages which follow, consideration will be given to the several environments within which these studies, conducted singly, in a series, or as part of a constellation, may be made.

STUDIES CONDUCTED BY INSTITUTIONS IN SELF–SURVEY PLAN

As mentioned in Chapter 1, the growing number of institutional surveys denotes a recognition on the part of governing boards and administrators of the need to determine and define the underlying philosophical concepts of the institution and to review the activities which have evolved. In the process of self-survey, a searching study of the student personnel program is in order.

The institutional self-study tends to view "the whole student in the whole institution" in a fashion which the author adjudges as essential. The work of the student personnel administrator, the professionally trained counselor, and the faculty adviser is seen in relation to the total educational process—to the business and financial structure of the institution. The impact of curricular, extracurricular, and counseling activities upon students with differing abilities and motivations is viewed in some systematic arrangement.

Institutional self-studies proceed in a variety of ways, utilizing some or all of the following:

1. Visitation of consultants

2. Polling of faculty, staff, and students by questionnaire or in interview

3. Initiation of cost studies designed to compare *what is* with reference to *what should be*

4. Predictive studies which aim at the projection of planning into the immediate or long-range future of the institutions, etc.

At Tuskegee Institute, a two-year self-study proceeded under the direction of a steering committee, a faculty-member director, an off-campus adviser to the director, off-campus consultants for specialized areas, and numerous faculty committees. Among the recommendations designed to effect a greater degree of integration between the student personnel services and the instructional program was one specifying the organization of a one-year basic college, with the objective phrased as follows: [6]

... to bridge the gap, personally, between life in the home and life on campus; to allow for ample counseling and guidance by persons who are interested in helping freshmen understand and surmount their difficulties; to allow for personalized teaching designed to discover the learning problems of each student; to stimulate each student to deal with problems recognized by freshmen as significant.

From the report of a self-survey conducted by a large university is taken this excerpt relating to the orientation of new students:

The freshman orientation program should be altered to give more emphasis to academic matters. The student's first exposure should be academic orientation rather than an introduction to extracurricular activities. Student activities should be placed in proper perspective and described at a different time from that devoted to academic counseling.

In App. S will be found a fairly detailed check list devised by a team of student personnel workers and used in an institution's self-study for evaluating aspects of faculty advising on the freshman, upperclass, and graduate level. The instrument was constructed by the director of the guidance training unit, School of Education; the coordinator of counseling; and a graduate-student intern in guidance.

Answers to some of the questions posed in Chapter 1 will be found in institution-wide self-surveys: Is the student personnel service a kind of "Campus Colossus"? Is the growth in student personnel programs dwarfing development of the various academic areas? Within a given institution, is the presence of organized student personnel services in conflict with institutional philosophy? Are student personnel services out

---

[6] "Interim Report of the Steering Committee for Tuskegee Institute Self-study," Apr. 1, 1957, pp. 2–3.

of balance with respect to other program emphases? If so, how can balance be restored? If not, how can the impression of imbalance be corrected? These and other questions relating to the peaceful coexistence and the productive partnership of all areas of educational activity will merit attention.

STUDIES CONDUCTED BY DEPARTMENTS OR AGENCIES

With institutional self-surveys in progress or in prospect, or even without such possibility, certain studies should be made by departments or other units to produce evidence concerning the values deriving from programs of student personnel, bureaus of counseling, systems of faculty advising, and types of cooperative activity involving instructional and counseling personnel. Patrons of the institution, money-wise legislators, economy-minded governing boards—all are privileged to ask: What are the returns on the investment? The query extends to (1) the kind and type of services offered, (2) the competence and productivity of persons engaged in the venture, and (3) the adequacy of services.

To find concrete answers for the question as posed is not easy. There is usually no released time to enable staff members to carry on these studies. Frequently there is no money for any detailed scrutiny. But always there is urgency! The author recalls being stopped one evening after office hours by a legislative investigator and asked what proportion of the total staff time of the department was devoted to the personal counseling of students. Since counseling rarely divides itself neatly into categories—academic, vocational, personal, social, religious, etc.—an immediate and sharply definitive answer could not be given. It was necessary for the author to spend two hours that evening (since the information was needed the following morning) in constructing a carefully worded exposition designed to show that 100 per cent of staff time was devoted to "personal" counseling. The completed statement made use of a number of special studies (finger exercises in type) which had been carried on over a period of years by graduate students enrolled in the department as interns in counseling, by individual staff members themselves, and by the staff working in combination on aspects of a problem. In this particular instance, "time studies" depicting the manner in which the administrator or counselor spends his time were useful (see App. F-10). In addition, "face sheet" summaries of problems presented by students, together with the method of dealing with the problem, proved invaluable (see App. F-4). With impending action of a legislative group, a budget commission, or the business office resting upon statements of departmental performance, it behooves the chief administrator of the unit to be ready at a given moment with "the facts of life."

A few subjects for productive inquiry by a member of a department or a group of persons working together are these:

Mortality studies of incoming new classes
Reactions of students to academic advisement
Reactions of students to orientation procedures
Problems of incoming new transfer students
Follow-up on the progress of students on probation
Concerns of students from abroad
Referrals of residence counseling personnel to the faculty adviser
Referrals of the faculty adviser to the counseling center (App. K)
Evaluation of the service of upperclass students who are given counseling responsibility
Reaction of parents to the student's academic advisement
Characteristics of freshmen (or others) majoring in _____
                                                     (curriculum)
Choices of major as expressed by freshmen
Changes in choice of major from freshmen to senior year
Evaluation of _____ (printed form or record sheet)
Reaction of high school personnel to the college program of academic advising
Reaction of faculty advisers to the in-service training program
Recommendations made by faculty advisers for revisions in the counseling program
Uses made of personnel data on students by faculty advisers
Types of communication initiated between the faculty advisers and residence counselors
Study of training programs for students carrying counseling responsibilities
Etc.

In a number of the studies suggested, the faculty member who participates in the advisement program may be encouraged to contribute. Commenting on the ability of secondary-school guidance counselors to conduct prediction studies, Dyer states: [7]

Of course, a former Latin teacher recently turned guidance counselor will throw up her hands in horror at the thought of becoming enmeshed in the complexities of statistical research. She has always supposed this to be something strictly for the experts. Furthermore, she has never been able to understand higher mathematics. Even a made-over Latin teacher, however, can learn to put tallies in a scatter diagram and do the simple arithmetic that will convert it into a usable expectancy table. A practical prediction study needs to be little more than this, and any guidance worker is likely to be a better counselor for having gone through the procedure. The experts meanwhile might put their minds toward inventing some simplified methods for spelling out in nontechnical language the logical dangers to be avoided in the collection and interpretation of statistical information. It does not seem too wild a dream to

[7] Henry S. Dyer, "The Need for Do-it-yourself Prediction Research in High School Guidance," *Personnel and Guidance Journal*, 33:163, November, 1957.

expect that someday somebody will turn out a do-it-yourself manual on prediction research, which never once mentions a mean, a standard deviation, a correlation coefficient, or a regression weight.

The statement regarding the ability of the secondary-school teacher to conduct prediction studies is applicable to the ability of the college teacher to do not only prediction studies but also studies of the nature of those covered herein.

Among the valid and useful studies undertaken by selected departments or agencies are the following:

Feelings of Freshmen about College [8]

In the spring of 1953, 265 graduates of the class of 1952 of four high schools in Brooklyn and Long Island, attending 118 different colleges, were asked what they liked best and what they liked least about the institutions at which they were enrolled. No limitation was placed on the number of aspects of college life which could be mentioned with favorable or unfavorable comment. Responses were classified into three broad categories: human relations, courses and programs, and physical properties of the campus. In the tabulation, human relations showed 161 likes and 42 dislikes; courses and programs, 54 likes and 26 dislikes; and physical properties, 21 likes and 25 dislikes. On the basis of this one exploration there seem to be indications that data on human relations on various campuses should be added to material on educational opportunities at the colleges and on their physical properties, and that attempts to match students with colleges on the basis of personality adjustment and interest could be expanded and strengthened.

Evaluation of Freshman Counseling [9]

At Brooklyn College, as one measure of determining the successes and failures of the general counseling program after one year of operation, a check list and sentence-completion form were submitted to the entire spring 1956 freshman class of 452 students. Two hundred responses were adjudged as being an adequate sampling.

From the results, certain recommendations were framed: (1) 55 per cent of the respondents expressed a preference for drop-in, unscheduled appointments. An experiment was initiated using five counselors who are available without appointment on certain days and on other days, available with scheduled calendar; five counselors available at all times for unscheduled interviews only; five counselors available for regularly scheduled appointments only. (2) Students believe the main function of the counselor revolves around program planning. Yet 10 per cent feel the counselor does not know enough about the college, its resources, and curriculum for them to have faith in him. Sessions for counselors in these areas could, with profit, be held at intervals. (3) Six

[8] Norman Lowenstein and Vivian Yates, "How Freshmen Feel about College," *Personnel and Guidance Journal*, 33:379–380, March, 1955.

[9] Noman Kiell, "Freshman Evaluation of Faculty Counselors," *Personnel and Guidance Journal*, 35:361–364, 1957.

per cent of the students felt that too great dependence upon the counselor led to stultification or lack of incentive to think for oneself. Continued study was recommended. (4) Need was seen for an ongoing public-relations, information-giving program directed to students and citing the services offered by the general counseling program. The survey indicated a large number of 'incoming freshmen who are ignorant of and misinformed about counseling services.

Evaluation of the Counseling Process

Kamm [10] quotes a respondent who describes the study activities of his department as follows:

We know that the multiple R for the total English score, the science score, and the high school grade point average versus the first quarter grade point average for students who are counseled at the university is about 0.70. We know that by counseling and registration advising we can reduce this correlation to zero for students on the lower end of the scale. We also know that we lose half of our student population between the freshman year and graduation and we know that half of these students leave the university with grade point averages of 2 (C) or above. We are trying to reduce this dropout rate of 25 per cent for students who are succeeding.

Experiment in Selection of Student Counselors [11]

The resident staff in the women's residence halls met and pooled their information as to typical hall situations that a student counselor might have to meet (eighteen were cited). A selection committee was appointed consisting of five students, the resident from each hall, and the dean and assistant dean. This group was divided into smaller committees—these to meet with the applicants. The chairman explained to the assembled applicants that they would be asked to discuss various situations typical of the residence hall. They were given a dittoed copy of the situations. The selection committee took seats in the background and the applicants proceeded to discuss the situation together. Notes were taken by the committee and after all applicants had been interviewed, the selection committee met to discuss and select counselors. Advantages said to be forthcoming from this discussion method of selecting student counselors were cited: (1) time is saved; (2) applicants are less self-conscious; (3) method reflects actual way in which a student counselor would handle discussions with freshmen; (4) understanding is evident of relationships of student counselors to administrative personnel, etc.

Studies Relating to Cost of Services

In Chapter 6 reference was made to the fact that financing the program of counseling, specifically of faculty advisement, constitutes a

---

[10] Robert B. Kamm, "How Effective Are Our Student Personnel Programs?" *Personnel and Guidance Journal*, 33:321, February, 1955.

[11] Marna V. Brady, "Student Counselor Selection," *Personnel and Guidance Journal*, 33:289–292, January, 1955.

persisting problem. Commenting on studies productive of proof of worth of the counseling program, Chandler [12] states:

> Counseling can prove its value in dollars and cents. Fiscal people, both state and private, understand such views; therefore, those who believe in the value of counseling should be aware of the necessity of maintaining simple records to demonstrate this fact. An example of this proof is illustrated by one of the state colleges which developed and validated a good predictive test of achievement in its beginning chemistry course. This college can show that students making low scores on this test have a high record of failure. These low-scoring students can be counseled into either taking another chemistry course geared to their ability, or they can choose a different objective where mathematical and scientific skills are not so vital. Consequently, there are many less students taking and failing beginning chemistry, which is a relatively expensive course. It is also pointed out in the report that it is of little use to instruct students who are emotionally disturbed. It is a waste of their time and the instructor's effort to teach under these conditions. This is also expensive in money terms.

Unfortunately, however, all too little appears in the literature concerning the financial aspects of initiating and maintaining programs of student counseling and advisement. More—much more—needs to be explored and recorded concerning the cost factors in (1) releasing faculty members from one or more classes to do advisement of students, (2) reimbursement of faculty members who counsel, and (3) assimilating the costs of preparation of handbooks for faculty advisers, counseling folders of students, and special printed forms used in coordinating the counseling activities.

Evolution of Studies

Over-all, the foregoing are typical of those valid and useful studies undertaken by individuals within a departmental area who wish to learn more about what they are doing and about the people with whom they are working. Studies of this type done by several individuals within a department or agency evolve frequently in this fashion:

The idea

The involvement of persons in it

The formalization of a design

The search for support (variously defined)

The initiation of the study

The logical development of the plan

The frequent conference of participants on developing aspects

The emergence of data

[12] Everett M. Chandler, "Re-organization of the Student Personnel Progam in the California State Colleges," *Personnel and Guidance Journal*, 31:79, November, 1952.

The analysis of findings
The interpretation of results
The voicing of conclusions
The results shared
A new idea generated
A new study envisioned
The process initiated anew

This, in simple terms, could be the cycle of ongoing study, conceived to be a *part of* and *not apart from* day-to-day performance on the job.

The conditions basic to productive inquiry, as cited earlier in this chapter, hold:

1. The conviction that an idea deserves study
2. Time for such study
3. Some know-how concerning patterns of study
4. Persistence in following through on the study
5. Some money available for the absolute necessities of the study
6. A willingness to share the findings with others

Point 2, relating to time freed for study, should in no wise be minimized. The author would repeat: [13]

No articles were ever jointly authored by two deans writing at high noon in an administrative office or by counselors collaborating in a cubicle between student interviews. Conditions for writing have to be ordered and arranged for just as do committee meetings, report writing, and budget estimating.

INVESTIGATIONS MADE BY GRADUATE STUDENTS

It is sometimes possible for much-needed departmental studies to be made by qualified graduate students in partial fulfillment of requirements of the degree or as a special project separate from the degree requirements. The graduate student who is a full-fledged faculty member on leave from another campus may adopt for investigation a problem of importance for his home institution. Other graduate students, not on leave from their permanent posts, may be encouraged to undertake a project needing to be done on the campus where their advanced work is proceeding. In either case, the results, when "fed back" to the division or department seeking to resolve the problem, are likely to be enthusiastically received.

There follow here brief descriptions of pieces of investigative study from several campuses, all illustrating inquiries which would seem to have meaning for a number of institutions. Since the six studies cited here served in partial fulfillment of degree requirements, the term

[13] Melvene Draheim Hardee, "Stimulating Professional Publication," *Personnel and Guidance Journal*, 32:220, December, 1953.

"research" (careful, unbiased investigation based on demonstrable facts and involving refined distinctions, etc.) would apply to them.

A study by Gladys M. Engelbrecht, graduate student at the University of Connecticut, seeks to determine what actually happens, from an academic point of view, to the college student who effects a within-university change of school, college, or division. Respondents to the questionnaire are asked to provide objective evidence from which may be inferred (1) practical implications for administrative policy regarding changes and (2) the particular counseling of students who desire a change of school, college, or division during their undergraduate program.

A study by Harold W. Perkins of Pennsylvania State University makes inquiry into precollege counseling practices of larger institutions for the purpose of discovering a practical pattern of activities. Present and projected practices in testing, educational counseling, vocational counseling, convocations, counseling clinics, summer programs, personal interviews, etc., are reviewed.

The study of Harold W. Paulsen, graduate student, University of Michigan, seeks to establish criteria for evaluating guidance services in college departments of physical education. The investigator contends that at the present time the literature reveals no complete agreement among physical educators on guidance services that are essential or highly desirable for physical education departments.

A study by Carl O. Eycke, Ohio University, surveys the 367 state-supported colleges and universities of the United States to determine the degree to which these institutions make use of faculty members as counselors and the presence or absence of in-service training programs in these institutions. The study attempts to discern (1) the individual in charge of the in-service training program, (2) the criteria used in the selection of members of the faculty to do counseling, (3) the methods employed in in-service training as well as the content of the training programs for faculty who counsel, (4) the specific problems that colleges and universities have faced in program development, and (5) the changes that colleges and universities will initiate in their counseling programs.

A study by Mary Ann Tinsley,[14] Syracuse University, surveyed academic advising in the liberal arts colleges of nineteen universities. The liberal arts college was selected for study for the following reasons:

1. Liberal arts students have a greater variety of vocational interests than do students in more specialized colleges.

2. Many liberal arts students are dually enrolled and must meet the requirements of two colleges.

[14] May Ann Tinsley, "The Faculty Adviser in the Liberal Arts College," *Personnel and Guidance Journal*, 34:219–220, 1955.

3. Faculty advisers in the liberal arts college are less likely to be in the same field of concentration as their advisees because of the large number of separate departments.

A study by Lee Woolf, graduate student of the University of Florida, concerned itself with a comparison of the attitude of students and staff members at both the planning and the operational levels of the program of freshman orientation in three large universities. The investigator spent a period of time interviewing students, faculty advisers, and administrators at Florida State University, University of Miami, and the University of Florida.

Illustrating types of research productivity in the university, Pepinsky [15] comments that at Ohio State University an attempt is being made to learn about the theories of the university held by various groups within it. He cites the study by Hopwood of entering freshman women, results of which suggest that student expectations are highly stereotyped and platitudinous.[16] Research on college students' needs conducted by Jo Anne Johnson [17] of Denison University, completing work at Indiana University, covers kinds and frequency of problems which students voluntarily bring to a resident counselor. Structured interviews were held with members of the men's and women's staffs. The results showed that the most frequent areas encountered by the men in frequency order were requests for housing and dormitory information, intellectual discussions and questions, academic adjustment problems, vocational problems, and interpersonal adjustment. The least frequent were health and family relationships. For the women, the most frequent areas were housing information, interpersonal adjustment, academic adjustment, and intellectual discussions. The least frequent were financial problems and family relationships.

The investigations cited briefly in this section are unquestionably ones which are valid and useful for the local campus as well as for other institutions.

REGIONAL AND NATIONAL STUDY GROUPS

One real reward for graduate investigators cited in the foregoing section comes from sharing the wealth of their findings with cooperating institutions and others signifying an interest in the results. Regional or national clearing centers which distribute summaries of investigative method and findings appear to have considerable influence. The Western Personnel Institute, a voluntary, cooperative association maintained by

[15] Harold B. Pepinsky, "Productivity in the University," *Personnel-O-Gram,* 10:24, June, 1956.

[16] Kathryn Hopwood, "Expectations of University Freshman Women," *Personnel and Guidance Journal,* 32:464–469, April, 1954.

[17] From "Research Briefs," *Personnel-O-Gram,* 12:15–16, October, 1957.

and for western colleges and universities, serves as a clearing house for information useful to student personnel workers in member colleges.[18] It is, in reality, a center for cooperative study and experimentation.

The Regional Commission on Student Personnel Work, sponsored by the Southern College Personnel Association, aims at motivating cooperative study in the region and attempts to disseminate information relating to individual and group studies. The Southern Regional Education Board has assisted the SCPA in staging three workshops and in publishing reports emerging from them.[19] A current project of the commission concerns the use of a questionnaire on transition from school to college in the institutions of the region.[20]

A poll in 1957 of more than 400 presidents of southern colleges and universities produced a listing of studies thought important for their institutions. Some representative comments were these:

A WOMAN'S COLLEGE: Our institution would be interested in two aspects of study relating to faculty counseling—(1) the role of the faculty counselor in the student personnel program and (2) in-service education activities for faculty counselors.

A MEDICAL COLLEGE: We are interested in knowing more of the aims and accomplishments in counseling because we feel the necessity of having the right students channeled into medical education. As a professional school, our faculty exercises a limited amount of counseling in a restricted area. Should we be doing more?

A TECHNICAL INSTITUTE: We would be interested in the following: (1) the most effective means of training nonprofessional counselors, (2) the best devices or methods of evaluating the effectiveness of faculty counseling, and (3) the best system or means of counseling students above the freshmen level.

A LIBERAL ARTS COLLEGE: We are seeking answers to these questions: What is the ratio of counselors to counselees? The relationship of the faculty member to the professional counselor? What are chances for selected student participation in a program evaluating counseling?

From the foregoing, it is doubtless obvious to the reader that few local studies, whether they be departmental, divisional, or institutional in their original, will long remain "local." These studies rapidly become part of a larger whole. On occasion, results of departmental self-studies are used in an institutional survey. Institutional surveys are reflected, frequently, in state and regional surveys. These latter are discussed and aired in

---

[18] See publications of the Western Personnel Institute, Pasadena, Calif.

[19] *Reports of the Southern College Personnel Association Work Conferences*, August, 1952, and August, 1953. Dyckman W. Vermilye, *College Personnel Work in the South*, published for the Southern College Personnel Association by the Southern Regional Education Board, Atlanta, Ga., 1956.

[20] Permission granted by Harper & Brothers, New York, for use of the questionnaire devised by Educational Records Bureau and appearing in Agatha Townsend, *College Freshmen Speak Out*, 1956.

national groups. So it is, once there is word abroad concerning the existence of a study, whether it be in initial phases or completed, its local, provincial nature is diminished and its cosmopolitan aspects increased.

The national survey, vested in the President's Committee on Education Beyond the High School, has stimulated the regional review of problems in higher education. These questions have particular reference to student personnel work: [21]

1. For whom should education beyond the high school be provided?
2. What is the extent of local, state, and federal responsibility for full development of able youth?
3. Are expanded scholarship services a needed solution? How many? How financed? How large?
4. Are improved counseling and guidance services for our high school youth needed? How much? How financed? How organized?
5. Are additional studies of student motivation needed?
6. What other incentives are needed?

Question 4, bearing in considerable part on topics discussed in this book, will be answered largely on the basis of specific institutional practices. It is likely that the better answers will be forthcoming from departments and/or institutions which have encouraged and sponsored studies by an individual staff member or by staff members, within the institution or interinstitutionally, working *in combination*.

An example of a type of cooperative interinstitutional study appears in the report of the Sub-committee on Counseling of the State Colleges of California.[22] The study has concerned itself with (1) a survey of counseling practices in colleges and universities throughout the United States and (2) a detailed analysis of counseling activities in seven state colleges. The committee makes recommendations concerning numbers of counselors needed for regular, day, and graduate students; for clerical personnel to carry on an effective counseling program; and for space, equipment, and supplies which are required in this type of student service.

SUMMARY

Much of the motivation of the true educator comes from the challenge of finding answers to unsolved problems. Conditions replete with challenge are viewed by Williamson: [23]

[21] John K. Folger, "Discussion Guide," The Southern Regional Conference on Education Beyond the High School, Louisville, Ky., Apr. 23–25, 1957, p. 7.
[22] Report of the Sub-committee on Counseling in the California State Colleges, March, 1957. (Mimeographed.)
[23] E. G. Williamson, "Needed Research in Student Personnel Work," in J. B. Cul-

... there are no forbidden areas of investigation, no limitations on methods of inquiry, no restrictions on who does research, and no requirements that inquiry be confined to traditional problems and fields.

A consideration of some wide-open areas of investigation appears in this chapter, these relating to three study "environments." In this presentation, the author is aware of the fact that readers with differing views and abilities will conceive of the possibilities for study in a variety of ways:

1. The single investigator, who as a beginner may perform studies of "finger-exercise" nature, will consider the adoption of a fairly elementary design.

2. The single investigator, sophisticated in research processes, will visualize the more difficult project.

3. The team of investigators in a departmental, institutional, or inter-institutional setting may conceive of group activities ranging all the way from good two- or three-part simple "harmonies" to the most involved arrangement in research.

With respect to the pattern adopted for the most searching investigation, Wrenn [24] observes that the research design used must be that which is most appropriate to a comparison of the behavior with which the study is concerned with criterion behavior. He cites the special methods available, including measurement of interpersonal relations or case-study judgments treated quantitatively, emphasizing the fact that the most effective research design is that of longitudinal study involving a control group. Farnsworth,[25] reporting suggestions of a committee of college health workers, calls attention to the need for studies of the normal person and his relationships to the social structure, examination of problems of integration, and long-term longitudinal studies.

Suggestions for the evaluation of aspects of the program of student personnel and counseling are offered by Dressel,[26] Aiken,[27] and Tyler.[28] The recommendations include (1) the importance of starting with an all-institutional statement of philosophy and of objectives, both immediate and long-term, (2) the wisdom of laying out a master plan for evalua-

pepper and others (eds.), *Report of the Southern College Personnel Association Work Conference*, 1952, p. 30.

[24] C. Gilbert Wrenn, *Student Personnel Work in Colleges*, The Ronald Press Company, New York, 1951, p. 507.

[25] Farnsworth, *op. cit.*, p. 180.

[26] Paul Dressel, "Personnel Services in High School and College," *Occupations*, 29:335–337, February, 1951.

[27] Durward W. Aiken, "Counseling," in *Current Trends in Higher Education*, 1949, Department of Higher Education, Washington, D.C., pp. 24–25.

[28] Ralph W. Tyler, "Principles Involved in Evaluating Student Personnel Services," in John Dale Russell (ed.), *Student Personnel Services in Colleges and Universities*, University of Chicago Press, Chicago, 1941, pp. 291–300.

tion, (3) the need for establishing criteria for the evaluative study in terms of desirable changes in student behavior and attitudes, (4) the necessity for reviewing the variety of methods by which the evaluation may be conducted and for choosing those methods which are most appropriate to the study, and (5) the importance of involving as many personnel workers and faculty contributors as possible.

This chapter has given attention to studies—completed, in process, or deserving to be done—all with relation to the premises on which this book was based. Individual needs of institutional planners, as expressed through polls, were cited. Several kinds of productive inquiry were treated: (1) the institutional survey; (2) studies conducted by departments or agencies; (3) investigations made by graduate students; and (4) studies undertaken by regional and national groups. Some factors deserving attention in particular types of productive inquiry were reviewed. Over-all, the author urged that student personnel workers in greater number engage in useful and valid studies which would enlist, as often as possible, the interest and energies of students, faculty advisers, and other faculty members.

In the final chapter of this book, a summary through query is proposed, the author calling up for review a number of questions bearing upon the integration of effort of all those who work with the student. The queries relate to (1) the student who is the recipient of assistance; (2) the student who assumes counseling responsibilities; (3) the professionally trained worker; (4) the faculty adviser; (5) the coordination of counseling; (6) the articulation of secondary school and college; and (7) the working relationships between the college and the parents of students.

In viewing the concluding chapter of this book, the reader is asked to bear in mind certain aspects of higher education predicted for the future. Knowles,[29] in commenting upon these emerging features, lists thirteen possibilities. Selected examples of them are reproduced here:

There will be widespread growth of new two-year colleges with two years of college education becoming a commonplace experience for American youth.

Enrollment will exceed present predictions, possibly by as much as 50 per cent.

Commuting students will comprise the largest segment of the nation's undergraduate enrollment, with the dormitory type of college campus becoming relatively less significant.[30]

Existing colleges and universities will change in size and services to meet demands of a changing society.

[29] Asa S. Knowles, "Emerging Features of Tomorrow's Higher Education," *Educational Record*, 38:329–339, October, 1957.

[30] See also Margaret White Blair and Ruth O. McCarn, "Advising the Commuting Student," in Melvene D. Hardee (ed.), *Counseling and Guidance in General Education*, World Book Company, Yonkers, N.Y., 1955, pp. 266–283.

New patterns in high school and college relations will develop.

A new definition of educational functions will evolve from relations with foundations, industry, and government agencies.

College teaching will become one of the more attractive professions.

It is evident from even a casual review of these emerging features that the role of the faculty member as (1) counselor-confidant of the student and (2) as facilitator in the integration of student personnel services and instruction must be viewed in the framework of the future. The basic query is probably this: Can we obtain answers to questions fast enough and fully enough today to meet the demands imposed by the higher education of tomorrow?

CHAPTER 18 *Summary through Query*

In the opening pages of Chapter 1, a picture was drawn of the boom and bulge in student enrollment and the attendant expansion in buildings, staff, and services to students. Recounting his predictions to a group of educators, Darley[1] refutes the notion that the rising tide will be barbarian invasions of illiterates, vulgarians, and dubious intellectuals, overrunning the hallowed academic grounds. He predicts that the incoming groups will show ability ranges completely comparable with present generations but that educators will have to do a better job of educating than has been done in the past. To do this, they must learn to handle students more efficiently.

The reader will recall references in Chapter 1 to the several philosophies of education adopted or inherited by present-day institutions. Commenting on the effect that new social and technological concepts have upon educational philosophy, Tyler[2] observes that some current social changes are in direct conflict with our basic values. He affirms that the aim of education is not to teach students to adjust to these newer concepts but rather to overcome or surmount them. Hence, developments which deny the acknowledged dignity and worth of the individual and which exalt group conformity will not be taken by colleges as goals for their teaching but, instead, will suggest needed emphases in curriculum to counteract such trends.

The recognition of the basic dignity and worth of the individual will be emphasized not only in instructional programs but also in activities of the student personnel area. In student advisement and counseling

[1] John G. Darley, "What Modifications of the Present Structure Within Institutions of Higher Education Will Be Necessary or Desirable?" in *Current Trends in Higher Education,* Association for Higher Education, Washington, D.C., 1957, pp. 151–155.
[2] Ralph W. Tyler, "What Will Be the Emerging Curricular Implications for Colleges and Universities of the New Social and Technological Concepts," in *Current Trends in Higher Education,* Association for Higher Education, Washington, D.C., 1957, pp. 78–80.

there will be demonstrations of this belief which will serve to "educate" students as surely as classroom teaching aims to educate.

The present dual and difficult responsibility placed upon educators— administrators, teachers, counselors—is that they must (1) learn to handle the incoming wave of students more efficiently and (2) demonstrate to students—anew and continually—a belief in the basic dignity and worth of human beings. Thus, the focus of this book upon the integration of programs of instruction and student personnel services has immediate point. That students can be handled more efficiently when there is a merger of personnel effort in these groups has been illustrated. That an educational philosophy which affirms the basic dignity and worth of individuals is implemented by such integration is observed. Additional cooperative behavior to enable personnel to effect the efficient and humane handling of increasing numbers of new students is imperative.

In the initial chapter the Great Facilitator in the merger is indicated as the faculty member himself—he who serves as an aide in the program of student personnel, particularly in the program of faculty advisement. At present there is much speculation about the availability of faculty members for assuming responsibilities for student advisement. Great difficulty in recruiting personnel for teaching is evident. President Pusey [3] of Harvard points to the need for teachers who possess such qualities as devotion, knowledge, imagination, quick intelligence, patience, concern for others, awareness of beauty, grasp on principle, and attractive personality.

When teachers such as these are found, surely they deserve to be used in the program of advisement and counseling. But will they agree to serve? Many persons recruited to teach feel that their greatest productivity, in addition to teaching, lies in basic research and writing. Thus, a signal challenge exists for institutional planners and directors of programs of counseling—to attract well-qualified teachers to some types of service in the program of counseling. Once attracted, there is a twin challenge for administrators to effect a type of in-service education that is both swift and thorough. Following this orientation, there must be initiated a systematized study of how the faculty member dispatches the counseling obligation—how adequately, scientifically, creatively he performs in the helping role.

With this triggering of questions, others follow in swift succession. In days to come, *how* can the unsolved problems come closer to adequate solution? The succession of "hows" relate to problems of (1) the student who is a recipient of counseling-advisement; (2) the student who assumes counseling responsibilities; (3) the professionally trained worker;

[3] Nathan Pusey, "The Exploding World of Education," *The Fabulous Future, America in 1980*, E. P. Dutton & Co., Inc., New York, p. 70.

(4) the faculty adviser; (5) the coordination of counseling activities; (6) the articulation of secondary school and college; and (7) the working relations of the college and the parents of students.

Concerning the student

Williamson[4] comments that a most fruitful exploration for all higher education could be made of the developmental processes experienced by students as they move from the freshman to the senior year. Farnsworth opens up a series of questions calling for answers in the interest of efficient student handling:[5]

What are the most frequent background conditions of those students who are performing inadequately? What are the characteristics of undesirable parental-student relationships? What are the reasons for so many students leaving college within a few months or a year or two of entrance when they seemed well qualified at entrance? Can tests be devised which will indicate more accurately than heretofore those students who are likely to encounter emotional difficulties in college or in later life, in order that they may obtain help at the most effective time? Or is it more satisfactory to depend upon correlation of all existing data available when a student enters college, supplemented by an interview designed to evaluate his emotional stability? What are the attitudes that result in students' remaining dependent, resentful, or unwilling to extend themselves, and those which encourage independence, resourcefulness, and the capacity to undertake responsibility for their own intellectual development? What are the attitudes of members of the faculty toward psychiatry and emotional illness? Does it make any difference in the incidence or management of illness in students if these attitudes be stern and disapproving? What happens to students who "break down" in college, leave for a while, and then return? When they return do they do as well as other students? Do some groups do better than others? How long should a student remain away from college when he takes a medical leave of absence? How do those who have had adequate psychotherapy do in comparison to those who have none but merely change their type of activity for a while?

Questions raised in Chapter 2 of this book were these:

1. What is the nature of the contemporary student in higher education? What is he—intellectually, physically, psychologically, and spiritually? What are his hopes, dreams, and aspirations?

2. Whom (among adults in contemporary society) has the collegian chosen to imitate? For what reason?

3. What are the values of the college student? On what does his integrity waver? Remain unchanged?

[4] E. G. Williamson, "Needed Research in Student Personnel Work," in J. B. Culpepper and others (eds.), *Report of the Southern College Personnel Association Work Conference*, 1952, p. 35.

[5] Dana L. Farnsworth, *Mental Health in College and University*, Harvard University Press, Cambridge, Mass., 1957, pp. 181–184.

4. How does the college student make decisions? What are the intellectual processes of which he is capable? How have his emotions figured in his learnings? How will his emotions continue to educate him?

5. To what limits can the college-age adolescent stretch himself? How can he be helped to approach those limits?

Other important questions calling for review are these: How can the behavior of the college student be changed through counseling and advisement? What are the degrees of self-reliance which new students demonstrate? How is this self-sufficiency encouraged, utilized, and further developed? What type and quality of relationship can be established between the college student and the professionally trained counselor? Between the student and the faculty adviser? Between the new student and the upperclass student who is given counseling responsibilities?

Relating to the assumption of counseling responsibilities by students

McCracken [6] states that in areas such as religion, moral values, ethics, social responsibility, and aesthetic and intellectual appreciations, a younger student may be impressed more readily by a mature student than by a faculty member. He points out the obligation of the college for seeing that those students whose attitudes most closely parallel the goals of the college be given support and encouragement in their relationships with younger students. Some questions deserving attention are these:

1. What are the legitimate activities of the student who assumes responsibilities for counseling?

2. What types of special training do these activities require? How best can this training be provided?

3. How can the performance of students who carry counseling responsibilities be evaluated?

4. What quality of working relations may faculty advisers and student counselors effect? How can the partnership be facilitated?

Relating to the professionally trained personnel worker

Reminding his audience of their membership in one of the great "helping" occupations, Darley [7] presses toward the answering of three questions: Why are we trying to help people? How do we help people? How do we know that we have helped them?

Related to the second of these basic queries are others: What are the actual and assigned functions of each member of the student personnel

---

[6] Charles W. McCracken, "Teaching Beyond the Classroom," *Personnel and Guidance Journal*, 35:528, April, 1957.

[7] John G. Darley, "The Faculty Is Human, Too," an address to the Southern College Personnel Association, Atlanta, Ga., December, 1955.

and counseling staff? How is the objective "to help people" implemented by each staff member? What is the good adjustment toward which practitioners bend their efforts in the helping process? How do staff members, professionally trained, work effectively *in combination?* As reflected in part from Chapter 1, there are these questions:

1. Is there a particular counselor to whom a student must go when his problem is academic in nature? Personal? Vocational? Religious? Marital?

2. How are students informed of the counseling services?

3. May a student consult more than one person in the process of solving a problem? If so, how does he make the transition from one counselor to the other? From faculty adviser to professional counselor?

4. How shall a second counselor, working on the student's problem, be informed of the work of the first? How do professional counselor and faculty adviser work together?

5. Shall there be a report of the progress of the student as he works toward a solution of his problem? If so, to whom shall this report be available? At what intervals shall it be issued? With whom shall confidential information about the student reside?

6. Who shall receive results of the student's entrance tests and placement examinations? Who shall confer with the student on results of his aptitude, ability, and personality tests?

7. Shall there be a periodic check made to determine the progress which the student is making on his problem? How shall such a check be effected? What persons are involved? What is the role of the director of counseling?

8. If the progress of a student in his problem solving is slowed down, who shall recommend action to facilitate its solution? What is the role of the director of counseling?

9. What assistance shall be given to the student in summarizing and evaluating his counseling experiences? By whom?

Concerning the faculty adviser

Viewing the status of faculty advisement, MacLean [8] recalls that advising is a process which possesses a long and dignified history in college and university. It is, he recounts, an activity cordially hated by the majority of college teachers. However, as is frequently proven, through good advising many problems which might later become serious, exploding into the professional counselor's office, are circumvented.

It is undoubtedly obvious to the reader from a review of the preceding section that some questions stated there apply as much to the faculty

[8] Malcolm S. MacLean, "Counseling and the Tower of Babel," *Personnel and Guidance Journal,* 31:359, March, 1953.

adviser as to the professionally trained worker. The adviser, as pointed out, is likewise concerned with referral of advisees to other sources of help, with reports of student progress, with interpretation of selected test data, and with the student's evaluation of progress and summation of counseling experiences.

Reechoing from Chapter 5 are these questions: Is faculty advising largely "busy work"? Does it eventuate in relatively little service to students? Do faculty advisers make decisions for students? To what degree does faculty counseling disable the student in his attempts to walk alone? What is the minimum to which faculty counseling should be kept? What are the evidences of overzealous, inquisitive, incapacitating faculty counseling on local campuses?

Still to be solved are these perennials: How shall the program of faculty advising be organized? What is the optimum advising load for a faculty member? What is a system to be recommended for assigning students to the faculty adviser? How can the "clerk work" falling to the lot of the adviser be reduced? To what extent can group advisement of students be done effectively? How shall the load of faculty advisers be equated? What type of advisement do junior, senior, and graduate students need? How far should the faculty adviser go in counseling students on their personal problems? What are the elements in a systematic evaluation of faculty advising? Who shall initiate and contribute to this evaluation?

Concerning the coordination of counseling

Coordination, says Williamson, [9] is not a static form of administrative structure. Rather, it is a dynamic process constantly changing because of the personalities of workers, the demands made on the organization, the needs of clients, and the feeding of products of research into professional practice. Reiterated from Chapter 2 are the following:

1. Is there an over-all policy concerning the counseling of students? If so, is it understood by those who are charged with carrying out the program?

2. Are there definite procedures which have been established for carrying out the policy for counseling students? How did the procedures originate? Are the practices known to all officers participating in the counseling?

3. What are the responsibilities and duties of each officer who counsels students? Are these responsibilities and duties known and understood by the individual officers? By others who cooperate with him in the counseling program?

[9] E. G. Williamson, "Coordination by the Administrator," *Journal of Higher Education,* 19:301, 1948.

4. Does each person in the counseling program have authority commensurate with his assigned responsibilities? Are the limits of this authority clear?

5. Are the talents of the various experts in the program being used to good advantage? What are the tests applied to determine the best use of these abilities and skills? What are possibilities for better utilization of staff?

6. Is there an established channel of communication between the various officers who counsel? Is the channel used? Can it be used more effectively?

7. Is the program which is designed for the counseling of students effective? How well are the immediate and ultimate objectives of counseling being attained?

8. Is the policy for counseling students reviewed continuously in light of changes in the institutional philosophy and in society in general? Are the practices which implement the policy reviewed at intervals?

9. Is there opportunity for all staff members who counsel students to participate in revision of policy and procedures?

10. Is there a means by which the activities of staff members in the program of counseling can be integrated in counseling and instruction? What cooperative action can be initiated which will challenge the abilities and the efforts of total institutional personnel?

Problems concerning articulation with secondary school

The recommendations arising from the Report of the President's Committee [10] express hope that school systems will increase their emphasis on the development of sound guidance and counseling programs, that schools will increase their facilities for counseling parents of capable graduates of high school regarding education beyond the high school, and that colleges and universities will assist in stepping up programs for the recruitment and training of counseling personnel.

Institutions of higher education must begin to think about the implementation of the recommendation. How can secondary schools be assisted in initiating and developing their programs of guidance? What constitutes a "properly trained" counselor? What are the elements of successful parent interviews? How can values of education beyond the high school be dramatized to high school students and their parents? What means shall be employed for stepping up programs of recruitment and training for counseling personnel in graduate schools?

(An investigation relating to the training of high school counselors deserves to be cited. Through a grant made available by the Rosenberg

[10] The President's Committee on Education Beyond the High School, *Second Report to the President*, Washington, July, 1957, pp. 55–56.

Foundation, the counseling center of the University of California studied the in-service training of high school counselors and the techniques of training proving to be most effective. At the time the counseling center undertook the study, the university did not include in its regular offerings a full training program for professional personnel. The results emerging from the study are categorized in terms of recommendations regarding counselor preparation, in-service training, training methods, and administrative considerations.[11])

Concerning articulation with the student's home

Commenting knowingly on one phase of parent-college relationship, Ginsburg [12] states that every college has had its own painful experiences with overanxious mothers who expect the college to supervise son Johnny's daily bath and cut up his food in bite-size pieces. However, by far the majority of those who have established programs to benefit students find that parents respond favorably to what they judge is (1) a warm interest in the well-being of their children and (2) a program designed to foster the development of mature responsibility for health.

Some questions for discussion are conceivably these: What are desirable working relations to be effected in a given institution with parents of students? Are these two-way relationships, college administration and home, or are they three-way arrangements which include the student, his parents, and the institution? What support can the institution lend the student with reference to his growing independence? How can the faculty adviser assist parents in their view of the student's search for independence? What are the expectations of parents regarding the development of collegiate son or daughter? What are the expectations of parents regarding the contribution of the college to this "education"? What do parents expect of students in their development—"from here to maturity"?

THE STUDENT IS HERE

As enunciated earlier, the purpose of this final chapter has been to point out some seven areas wherein questions, in various stages of resolution or irresolution, lie. Two writers, Barry and Wolf,[13] exhort

[11] In-service Training of Secondary School Counselors, A Research Project of the Counseling Center, University of California, Berkeley, Calif.

[12] Ethel L. Ginsburg, *The College and Student Health*, Based on the Fourth National Conference on Health in Colleges, National Tuberculosis Association, New York, May, 1954, pp. 59–60.

[13] Ruth Barry and Beverly Wolf, *Modern Issues in Guidance-Personnel Work*, Bureau of Publications, Teachers College, Columbia University, New York, 1957, pp. 218–219.

their readers to shift their perspectives, to become experimentalists and synthesizers in difficult and challenging areas. They point to two tendencies which threaten to hinder progress: (1) an unwillingness of practitioners to proceed along different lines and (2) an inclination of educators to look at the past rather than to the future.

A scrutiny of the history of education reveals throughout a deep and enduring need to understand the student. Schoolmaster Matthew Arnold, for instance, affirmed a wish to see "the scholar" steadily and see him whole as a person. In this country, to see the student as a whole person is to see a unique being. Blakeley [14] explains:

> It has been calculated that with the coming together of two human beings there are genetical possibilities in the order of two to the 20,000 power; two multiplied by itself 20,000 times. This means literally that with all the billions of human beings that have existed since man became human, the mathematical possibilities of combination have only been scratched. Then when you realize that each individual has different experiences from every other individual; and then when you take the third factor, that each person is very likely to react differently to even the same experience from the way other individuals react, you see that we have literally in each human a unique creation. . . . We must learn how to liberate the powers of the individual . . . to use appropriate methods for unleashing human energy in individuals, appropriate to the fact that they are unique yet sharing common humanity.

In the face of this, present-day educators *must* think and act along different lines, assuming experimentalist roles—not in the distant future, but now. Knowledge about human learning, facts about students, about the constituency served, and about society's needs—these are currently available to institutions or can be readily collected.

By now, it must be obvious to the reader that the future is *present!* The crisis of impending greater enrollments is here. The matter of caring for numbers of students efficiently and with recognition of their basic worth is yet to be solved. The role of the faculty member in the total program of higher education—as the facilitator for integrating programs of student personnel and instruction, as an interdisciplinarian, gaining and giving new perspectives about the student—this is only now beginning to be understood.

Thus, in days to come, there will be much to do!

[14] Robert J. Blakeley, "Is Individuality Maladjustment?" in *Current Issues in Higher Education,* 1957, Association for Higher Education, Washington, D.C.

Tables

Table 1. Aspects of Counseling in Which Faculty Members Were Said to Participate

Kinds of counseling done by faculty members	By size of student population									
	To 750		750–2,000		2,000–5,000		Over 5,000		Total	
	n	%	n	%	n	%	n	%	n	%
Academic	59	100	76	100	48	100	35	100	218	100
Vocational	45	76	53	70	32	67	23	66	153	70
Personal-social	56	95	59	78	35	73	21	60	171	78
Religious	42	71	33	43	13	27	10	29	98	45
Health	33	56	31	41	11	23	9	26	84	38
Other	6	2	1	0	10	3	2	0	9	6

Table 2. Summary of All Respondents' Evaluations of Faculty Members' Participation in Counseling Services

	Excellent	Good	Fair	Poor
Academic	29	75	26	2
Vocational	14	34	37	5
Personal-social	17	45	28	6
Religious	11	28	14	1
Health	10	18	12	0
Other	5	3	0	0

Table 3. Means of Training Faculty Members for Participation in Counseling Services

Means of training	To 750	750–2,000	2,000–5,000	Over 5,000	Total
In-service (not explained)	13	17	8	6	44
Group meetings, various kinds	9	4	16	8	37
Conferences	6	16	8	4	34
Formal courses	10	11	...	4	25
Faculty workshops	6	3	...	...	9
Printed materials	5	8	6	4	23
Specialists and lectures	6	4	7	3	20
Experience	3	5	1	0	9
Little or none	4	7	4	5	20

Table 4. Evaluation of Training Provided for Faculty Members Who Participate in Counseling Services—by Area

Area	Excellent	Good	Fair	Poor
Academic	12	45	32	6
Vocational	3	24	22	4
Personal-social	5	29	21	4
Religious	3	16	7	1
Health	4	16	8	1
Other	1	6	0	0

Table 5. Summary of Respondents' Statements Concerning Importance of Utilization of Faculty Members in Counseling Services

	Total
1. The *faculty member* is in a *position to be of great help to students.* He is their first and nearest point of contact, and students know him better. He is most familiar with academic needs and with the content of his academic area.	66
2. *Counseling* is a *part* of the *educational program* or *function.* It is a natural result of the teaching-learning situation.	36
3. In terms of *student-faculty relationship,* it builds a better over-all relationship in the classroom and in the college community as a whole.	29
4. It *provides* the *means* for *faculty to know and understand students* better and adds stimulus for continued professional growth and development.	31
5. *In terms of administrative needs,* there are not enough professional counselors to meet the needs of all students or to carry the load alone. The success of the program depends upon the participation of everyone, and the faculty is the heart of the educational program.	28
6. It *aids* in *integration* of the various aspects of education; it relates counseling, teaching to student-life experience (idea of teaching whole persons).	26
7. It is a *service to students.* It gives them someone who is interested in them personally, makes counseling more accessible to them, and reaches more students.	20
8. It *adds* to the *effectiveness* of *teaching;* the teaching-learning process is improved.	18
9. Others.	6

Table 6. Summary of Responses Regarding Point of Need for Supplementation by Professional Counselors: Areas in Which Faculty Members Do Not Counsel

	Total
1. Cases of emotional or social nature or deviant behavior that are beyond the range of the reasonably normal and which require professional training in psychological (and related) skills	104
2. Counseling in areas specifically named (appears related to above in requiring special training and skill):	
a. Vocational	26
b. Personal-social	19
c. Religious	15
d. Health	29

> e. Financial   3
> f. Remedial (speech, hearing, etc.)   3
> g. Marital   1
3. Cases which the individual instructor feels need more than he has to offer in terms of time or background of training and experience (still a similar type of restriction)   22
4. Administrative and coordinative functions, such as policy, evaluation, planning, in-service training, approval of total program to graduate   24
5. Testing: interpretation and administration   38
6. Disciplinary functions   6
7. Any counseling beyond routine academic   11
8. Others   8

Table 7. Summary of Desired Revisions in Faculty Counselor Programs Named by Respondents

	Total
1. More and/or better in-service training for counselors	59
2. Adjustment of faculty counselor's load-time-pay in recognition of counseling duties	25
3. More and/or better coordination of the counseling program	13
4. Use of more faculty in the program, both in interest and participation; better faculty-student relations; in short, greater effort to promote the personnel point of view	31
5. More professionally trained counselors, or other personnel	24
6. Addition of services of a psychiatrist (on staff or available for referral)	4
7. More effective selection of faculty counselors who participate (not just assigned)	6
8. Change, expansion, improvement of whole program or on broad general basis	13
9. Addition or improvement of a specific service to students (as vocational counseling, testing, etc.)	12
10. Addition or improvement of a specific service for faculty counselors (as wider training, better materials, etc.)	10
11. More rigid requirements (of faculty)	2
12. Other	8
13. None	8

Table 8. Areas of Counseling Named in Which Students Participate

Kinds of counseling done by students	By size of student population									
	To 750		750–2,000		2,000–5,000		Over 5,000		Total	
	n	%	n	%	n	%	n	%	n	%
Academic	13	25	18	28	17	45	10	38	58	32
Vocational	10	19	7	11	6	16	7	27	30	17
Personal-social	35	63	51	78	27	71	18	69	129	71
Religious	16	31	19	28	8	21	8	31	51	28
Health	7	13	9	14	3	8	4	15	23	13
Other	7	13	4	6	4	10	4	15	19	10
None	10	19	13	20	7	18	5	19	35	19

Table 9. Total of Evaluations of Students' Participation in Meeting Counseling Needs

	Excellent	Good	Fair	Poor
Academic	5	16	16	2
Vocational	4	3	5	2
Personal-social	24	36	23	2
Religious	4	9	11	2
Health	2	7	4	1
Other	2	4	2	

Table 10. Summary of Responses Regarding the Importance of Utilizing Students in the Counseling Program

	Total
1. The peer group influence and relationship promote acceptance and ease of communication; share the student point of view; a peer-level contact.	88
2. It provides excellent learning experience for those who counsel; some in education need this experience.	24
3. It promotes a sense of responsibility and leadership and gives opportunity to exercise them.	14
4. It makes for a mutual effort in adjustment to college and group living.	7
5. It helps morale and spirit and aids the functions of student government.	6
6. It helps to reduce faculty load and bring counseling to a greater number of students.	11
7. It is effective in the orientation of new students.	3
8. It aids rapport between student leaders and faculty and interprets for them the student point of view.	4
9. It helps to reach the reluctant student and detect needs not otherwise apparent.	6
10. Students counsel each other regardless. Use of student counselors helps to channel these activities in useful directions and offset the influence of uninformed, incidental counseling.	5
11. Other.	18

Table 11. Summary of Responses Regarding Delimitation of Student Participation in Counseling Program; What Students Do Not Do

	Total
1. Any counseling in major problem areas which indicate need for services of trained professional worker	60
2. Definite services or functions prohibited:	
Academic	7
Vocational	7
Health	4
Discipline	6
3. Student counseling limited to a specific purpose (i.e., orientation, minor adjustment problems, dormitory affairs, referrals)	15
4. Relative: when student feels need for help, when counselee wants other help, depends on the case at hand	7
5. Matters which may conflict with the prerogatives or jurisdiction of faculty	5
6. Any activity involving administrative concerns or final acts and decisions	5
7. Other	10

Table 12. Means for Developing Cooperation and Articulation with Parents of Students Who Are Counseled

	Size by student population				
	To 750	750–2,000	2,000–5,000	*Over,* 5,000	*Total*
Letters	45	70	34	30	179
Conferences	38	63	33	31	165
Home visits	15	12	5	1	33
Brochures; printed materials	25	37	22	14	98
Campus tours; visits	24	47	21	12	104
Other	7	3	6	2	18

Table 13. Summary of Administrative Positions, Committees, and Methods Named as Instruments for Achieving Coordination of Efforts in the Counseling Program

Director:
1. Dean of students (or dean of guidance or of student life)   58
2. Dean of men and/or women   15
3. Director of counseling and guidance   25
4. Director of student personnel (or of student life or services)   26
5. President, vice president, dean of college, academic deans, and administrators   14
6. Other titles   14

Committee:
1. Counseling and/or guidance committee   29
2. Student personnel committee   27
3. Student life committee   4
4. Advisory committee   5
5. Committee on student affairs (or activities)   4
6. Other   27

Conferences:
1. Case conferences when needed or requested   15
2. Personnel administrator with counselors   13
3. Deans, department heads, administrators (top level)   6
4. Periodic meetings to plan and discuss   3
5. Faculty meetings   6
6. Others (grave disciplinary offenses, informal work with admissions and faculty advisers, communication between departments, student-faculty-administration)   9

Seminars and workshops:
1. With dean of students, director (or other officer) of personnel division   13
2. With president or other officer (administrative or academic)   7
3. Other: student affairs council; a discussion series; an administrative committee   3

Other means:
Working relationships and professional cooperation, written reports, printed materials, various policy committees, only by chance, formal course   10

Table 14. Summary of Responses Regarding Evidences of Quality of Working Relationships among Persons Participating in Counseling Programs

1. Counseling a joint effort; good personnel; academic work relationships	34
2. Greater interest and acceptance by faculty seen in wide referral, suggestions, and voluntary training	33
3. Statements by students—both oral and written	12
4. High morale, spirit, and cooperation result in good student activities	12
5. Observed behavior of students: better achievement, good integration, counseling sought	18
6. Administrative: recognition of efforts, reduction of mortality, acceptable policies	5
7. Growing program: constructive reorganization and improved services	10
8. Simplicity and informality of small college resulting in good work relationships	7
9. None	3
10. Other	6

Table 15. Summary of Responses Regarding Factors Serving to Militate against Effective Coordination in Counseling Programs

1. Attitude of (some) faculty; lack of understanding and sympathy	50
2. Lack of adequate time to counsel and develop program	36
3. Competition of departmental interests and demands	30
4. Budgetary shortcomings resulting in too little space, few counselors, facilities	31
5. Need for better training of those who counsel	21
6. Need for better communications—reports, correspondence, other	10
7. Need for administrative leadership (someone to head program)	10
8. Difficulty in reaching all students (evening or day students—divisions geographically separated)	6
9. Poor relationships between some faculty and some personnel workers	5
10. None	5
11. Others:	25

    a. Too little long-range planning, mostly expediency
    b. Problems from too-rapid growth of institution
    c. Hesitancy of students to ask for help
    d. Complexity of problems and diversity of services
    e. Program dependence entirely on one person
    f. Counseling in an individual college of the university
    g. Institution too large—turnover of students and faculty working against coordination

NOTE: Greater expression when discussing adverse factors (152 respondents give 229 responses) than in speaking of evidences of quality (107 respondents give 140 responses)

Table 16. Summary of Responses Regarding Proposed Revisions in Counseling Programs for the Near Future

1. Better program of training for those who counsel   29
2. Increase in the personnel staff   17
3. Better, expanded, or more efficient use of persons available   6
4. More careful selection of faculty on basis of potential for counseling   5
5. General revision, and possibly expansion, of the present program   6
6. Reorganization, improvement, expansion of a *part* of the program   21
7. Normal growth and development of present program rather than change   13
8. Better coordination of the "parts" of the program   27
9. Improvement in relationships of personnel workers: faculty, administration, students   9
10. None (stated by respondent; *not* implied by lack of answer)   32
11. New proposed innovations to aid and implement the program (see below)   7
    a. Evaluation of counseling services
    b. A strong student council organization
    c. Initiation of an orientation course to supplement counseling
    d. Use of dormitories as laboratories for group counseling
    e. Addition of training facilities for elementary school guidance
    f. Extension of freshman program to include sophomores
12. Recognition of counseling by adjustment of work load   5

Bibliography

Books

Aiken, Durward: "Counseling," in *Current Issues in Higher Education*, 1949, Department of Higher Education, Washington, pp. 19–25.

Andrews, Kenneth R.: *The Case Method of Teaching Human Relations and Administration*, Harvard University Press, Cambridge, Mass., 1953.

Arbuckle, Dugald S.: *Student Personnel Services in Higher Education*, McGraw-Hill Book Company, Inc., New York, 1953.

Barry, Ruth, and Beverly Wolf: *Modern Issues in Guidance-Personnel Work*, Bureau of Publications, Teachers College, Columbia University, New York, 1957.

Bennett, Margaret E.: "The Orientation of Students in Educational Institutions," in *Guidance in Educational Institutions*, Thirty-seventh Yearbook of the National Society for the Study of Education, Public School Publishing Company, Bloomington, Ill., 1938, part I, pp. 119–143.

Berdie, Ralph F.: "In-service Training in Counseling and Counselor Evaluation," in Ralph F. Berdie (ed.), *Counseling and the College Program*, Minnesota Studies in Student Personnel Work, no. 6, University of Minnesota Press, Minneapolis, pp. 11–18.

―――: "Some Relationship Problems in Counseling," in Ralph F. Berdie (ed.), *Roles and Relationships in Counseling*, Minnesota Studies in Student Personnel Work, no. 3, University of Minnesota Press, Minneapolis, pp. 20–30.

Bergstresser, John L.: "The Counseling of Students at the Level of General Education," in John Dale Russell (ed.), *Student Personnel Services in Colleges and Universities*, University of Chicago Press, Chicago, 1941, pp. 177–200.

―――: "Issues in Faculty Counseling," in E. G. Williamson (ed.), *Trends in Student Personnel Work*, University of Minnesota Press, Minneapolis, 1949, pp. 312–319.

Blaesser, W. W.: "Elements of a Well-rounded College Student Personnel Program," in J. B. Culpepper and others (eds.), *Report of the Southern College Personnel Association Work Conference*, 1952, pp. 8–18.

Blakeley, Robert J.: "Is Individuality Maladjustment?" in *Current Issues in Higher Education*, 1957, Association for Higher Education, Washington.

Bragdon, Helen D., and others: *Educational Counseling of College Students*, American Council on Education, Washington, 1939.

Brouwer, Paul J., and others: *Student Personnel Services in Higher Education*, American Council on Education, Washington, 1949.

Brown, Kenneth I.: *Not Minds Alone*, Harper & Brothers, New York, 1954.

Brumbaugh, A. J.: "Issues in the Administrative Organization for Student Personnel Services," in John Dale Russell (ed.), *Student Personnel Services* in College and Universities, University of Chicago Press, Chicago, 1941, pp. 96–106.

Brumbaugh, A. J. and Ralph F. Berdie: *Student Personnel Programs in Transition,* American Council on Education, Washington, October, 1952.

Callis, Robert: "The Relations of Counseling to Personnel Work in Residence Halls," in Ralph F. Berdie (ed.), *Counseling and the College Program,* Minnesota Studies in Student Personnel Work, no. 6, University of Minnesota Press, Minneapolis, pp. 38–43.

——, Paul C. Polmantier, and Edward Roeber: *A Casebook of Counseling,* Appleton-Century-Crofts, Inc., New York, 1955.

Considerations on Personality Development in College Students, Committee on the College Student of the Group for the Advancement of Psychiatry, Report 32, May, 1955.

Cowley, W. H., and others: *Occupational Orientation of College Students,* American Council on Education, Washington, 1939.

Darley, John G.: "How Does a College or University Build Effective Interdepartmental and Interschool Cooperation and Coordination?" in *Current Issues in Higher Education,* 1954, Association for Higher Education, Washington, pp. 159–163.

——: "What Modifications of the Present Structure Within Institutions of Higher Education Will Be Necessary or Desirable?" in *Current Issues in Higher Education,* 1957, Association for Higher Education, Washington, pp. 151–155.

——, and others: *The Use of Tests in College,* American Council on Education, Washington, December, 1947.

Davey, John R.: "Advising," in *The Idea and Practice of General Education,* University of Chicago Press, Chicago, 1950.

Deutsch, Monroe: *The College from Within,* University of California Press, Berkeley, Calif., 1952.

Doerman, H. J.: *The Orientation of College Freshmen,* The Williams & Wilkins Company, Baltimore, 1926.

Dressel, Paul L.: "Counseling as a Function of General Education," in Ralph Berdie (ed.), *Counseling and the College Program,* Minnesota Studies in Student Personnel Work, no. 6, University of Minnesota Press, Minneapolis, pp. 31–37.

——: "Evaluation in Counseling," in Ralph F. Berdie (ed.), *Concepts and Programs of Counseling,* Minnesota Studies in Student Personnel Work, no. 1, University of Minnesota Press, Minneapolis, 1951, pp. 70–81.

—— and Lewis B. Mayhew: *General Education: Explorations in Evaluation,* American Council on Education, Washington, 1954.

Farnsworth, Dana L.: *Mental Health in College and University,* Harvard University Press, Cambridge, Mass., 1957.

Feder, D. D.: "Selection and Training of Faculty Counselors," in E. G. Williamson (ed.), *Trends in Student Personnel Work,* University of Minnesota Press, Minneapolis, 1949, pp. 288–300.

Fletcher, Frank M., Jr.: "Problems Relating to Counseling Personnel," in Ralph F. Berdie (ed.), *Concepts and Programs of Counseling,* Minnesota Studies in Student Personnel Work, no. 1, University of Minnesota Press, Minneapolis, pp. 27–41.

Future Needs in Student Personnel Work, American Council on Education, Washington, 1950.

Gaus, John: "A First View: The University-wide Approach," in Joseph E.

McLean (ed.), *The Public Service and University Education*, Princeton University Press, Princeton, N.J., 1949, pp. 197–198.

Gibb, Jack R., and Lorraine Miller Gibb: *Applied Group Dynamics*, University Bookstore, University of Colorado, Boulder, Colo.

Giedion, S.: *Walter Gropius: Work and Teamwork*, Reinhold Publishing Corporation, New York.

Gilbert, William M.: "Training Faculty Counselors at the University of Illinois," in E. G. Williamson (ed.), *Trends in Student Personnel Work*, University of Minnesota Press, Minneapolis, 1949, pp. 301–309.

————: "Relationships Between Counseling Organizations and Other Divisions," in Ralph F. Berdie (ed.), *Concepts and Programs of Counseling*, Minnesota Studies in Student Personnel Work, no. 1, University of Minnesota Press, Minneapolis, 1951, pp, 42–55.

Gillin, John, and others: *For a Science of Social Man*, The Macmillan Company, New York, 1954.

Ginsburg, Ethel L.: *The College and Student Health*, Based on the Fourth National Conference on Health in Colleges, National Tuberculosis Association, New York, May, 1954.

Good, Carter V.: *Dictionary of Education*, McGraw-Hill Book Company, Inc., New York, 1945.

Gordon, Ira J.: *The Teacher as a Guidance Worker*, Harper & Brothers, New York, 1956.

"Guidance and Counseling," in Robert King Hall and J. A. Lauwerys (eds.), *The Yearbook of Education: 1955*, World Book Company, Yonkers, N.Y., 1955.

Gulick, Luther: "Notes on the Theory of Organization," in Luther Gulick and L. Urwick (eds.), *Papers on the Science of Administration*, Institute of Public Administration, Columbia University, New York, 1927, p. 3.

Gustad, John W.: "The Definition of Counseling," in Ralph F. Berdie (ed.), *Roles and Relationships in Counseling*, Minnesota Studies in Student Personnel Work, no. 3, University of Minnesota Press, Minneapolis, 1953, pp. 3–19.

Haggerty, William J., and A. J. Brumbaugh: *The Student in College and University*, North Central Association of Colleges and Secondary Schools, Commission on Institutions of Higher Education, Publication 13, 1939.

Hahn, Milton E., and Malcolm S. MacLean: *Counseling Psychology*, McGraw-Hill Book Company, Inc., New York, 1955.

Hammond, Kenneth R., and Jeremiah M. Allen: *Writing Clinical Reports*, Prentice-Hall, Inc., Englewood Cliffs, N.J., 1953.

Hardee, Melvene Draheim: "Counseling as an Integrating Factor in General Education," in Melvene D. Hardee (ed.), *Counseling and Guidance in General Education*, World Book Company, Yonkers, N.Y., 1955.

Havemann, Ernest, and Patricia Salter West: *They Went to College*, Harcourt, Brace and Company, Inc., New York, 1952.

Hawkes, Mrs. Herbert: "Importance of Student Personnel Services," in *Current Issues in Higher Education*, 1941, Department of Higher Education, Washington, pp. 117–118.

Heaton, Kenneth L.: "Kinds of Information Needed for the College Personnel Service," in John Dale Russell (ed.), *Student Personnel Services in Colleges and Universities*, University of Chicago Press, Chicago, 1941, pp. 107–126.

Higher Education in a Decade of Decision, The Educational Policies Commission of the National Education Association of the U.S. and the American Association of School Administrators, Washington, 1957.

Hilton, M. Eunice, and others: *Guidance in the Age of Automation,* Syracuse University Press, Syracuse, N.Y., 1957.

Hollingshead, Byron: *Who Should Go to College,* Commission on Financing Higher Education, Columbia University Press, New York, 1952.

Hopwood, Kathryn: "The Lion and the Lamb; Criteria for the Promotion of Faculty Serving Part or Full Time in Personnel Assignments," in *Proceedings of Student Personnel Workshop in Higher Education,* Florida State University, 1957.

Iffert, Robert E.: "Drop-outs: Nature and Causes; Effects on Student, Family and Society," in *Current Issues in Higher Education,* 1956, Association for Higher Education, Washington, pp. 94–102.

————: *Retention and Withdrawal of College Students,* Bulletin no. 1, Government Printing Office, 1948.

The Integration of Educational Experiences, Fifty-seventh Yearbook of the National Society for the Study of Education, University of Chicago Press, Chicago, 1957.

Johnson, B. Lamar: *General Education in Action,* American Council on Education, Washington, 1952.

Kelso, Paul C., and Melvene Draheim Hardee: "Cooperative Learning Experiences of the Faculty," in Melvene D. Hardee (ed.), *Counseling and Guidance in General Education,* World Book Company, Yonkers, N.Y., 1955.

Leonard, Eugenie Andruss: *Origins of Personnel Services in American Higher Education,* University of Minnesota Press, Minneapolis, 1956.

Lindbergh, Charles W.: *The Spirit of St. Louis,* Charles Scribner's Sons, New York, 1953.

Lloyd-Jones, Esther: "Changing Concepts of Student Personnel Work," in Esther Lloyd-Jones and Margaret Ruth Smith (eds.), *Student Personnel Work as Deeper Teaching,* Harper & Brothers, New York, 1954.

————, Ruth Barry, and Beverly Wolf: *Case Studies in College Student-Staff Relationships,* Bureau of Publications, Teachers College, Columbia University, New York, 1956.

Lovett, Robert A.: "A Business Executive Looks at Government," in Joseph E. McLean (ed.), *The Public Service and University Education,* Princeton University Press, Princeton, N.J., 1949, pp. 74–75.

MacIntosh, Archibald: *Behind the Academic Curtain,* Harper & Brothers, New York, 1948.

Marzolf, Stanley S.: *Psychological Diagnosis and Counseling in the Schools,* Henry Holt and Company, Inc., New York, 1956.

Mathewson, Robert H.: *Guidance Policy and Practice,* Harper & Brothers, New York, 1955.

Matteson, Ross W.: "Research in the Counseling Center," in Ralph F. Berdie (ed.), *Counseling and the College Program,* Minnesota Studies in Student Personnel Work, no. 6, University of Minnesota Press, Minneapolis, pp. 3–10.

Merriam, Thornton W., and others: *Religious Counseling of College Students,* American Council on Education, Washington, 1943.

Meyer, A. M., and Robert J. Hannelly: "The Student Personnel Program," in *The Public Junior College,* Fifty-fifth Yearbook of the National Society for the Study of Education, University of Chicago Press, Chicago, 1956, pp. 191–212.

Morse, Horace T.: "General Education and Individual Guidance," in Melvene D. Hardee (ed.), *Counseling and Guidance in General Education,* World Book Company, Yonkers, N.Y., 1955, pp. 3–25.

Mueller, Kate Hevner, and others: *Counseling for Mental Health,* American Council on Education, Washington, 1947.

Niles, Henry E.: "Principles or Factors in Organization," in Catheryn Seckler-Hudson (ed.), *Processes of Organization and Management,* Public Affairs Press, Washington, 1948.

Omer, Mary I., and Eugene L. Shepard: "How Records Contribute to Deeper Teaching," in Esther Lloyd-Jones and Margaret Ruth Smith (eds.), *Student Personnel Work as Deeper Teaching,* Harper & Brothers, New York, 1954, pp. 62–83.

Pace, C. Robert: *They Went to College,* University of Minnesota Press, Minneapolis, 1941.

Personnel Work in Education, Fifty-eighth Yearbook of the National Society for the Study of Education, University of Chicago Press, Chicago, 1959.

Prescott, Daniel A.: *Emotion and the Educative Process,* American Council on Education, Washington, 1938.

The President's Committee on Education Beyond the High School, *Second Report to the President,* Washington, July, 1957.

Pusey, Nathan: "The Exploding World of Education," in *The Fabulous Future, America in 1980,* E. P. Dutton & Co., Inc., New York, pp. 63–78.

Reed, Dudley B., and Charles B. Congdon: "The Health Service as an Agency for Understanding the Student," in John Dale Russell (ed.), *Student Personnel Services in Colleges and Universities,* University of Chicago Press, Chicago, 1941, pp. 143–157.

Report of the Southern College Personnel Association Work Conference, edited by J. B. Culpepper and Committee of the Southern College Personnel Association, 1952.

Report of the Southern College Personnel Association Work Conference, edited by L. L. Love and George Street of the Southern College Personnel Association, 1953.

Robinson, Francis P.: *Principles and Procedures in Student Counseling,* Harper & Brothers, New York, 1950.

Rogers, Carl R.: *Counseling and Psychotherapy,* Houghton Mifflin Company, Boston, 1942.

——— and F. J. Roethlisberger: in *Twelve Business Problems Analyzed,* Harvard Business Review, Boston, Mass., 1952, pp. 18–24.

Rothney, John W., and Bert A. Roens: *Counseling the Individual Student,* William Sloane Associates, New York, 1949.

Shank, Donald J.: "Some Questions about Faculty Counseling," in E. G. Williamson (ed.), *Trends in Student Personnel Work,* University of Minnesota Press, Minneapolis, 1949, pp. 312–319.

——— and others: *The Teacher as Counselor,* American Council on Education Studies, Washington, October, 1948.

Shepard, Eugene L.: "The Role of the Faculty Counselor in General Education," in Melvene D. Hardee (ed.), *Counseling and Guidance in General Education,* World Book Company, Yonkers, N.Y., 1955, pp. 161–178.

Shrewsbury, Thomas B.: "Legal Implications for Student Personnel Workers," in Esther Lloyd-Jones and Margaret Ruth Smith (eds.), *Student Personnel Work as Deeper Teaching,* Harper & Brothers, New York, 1954.

Sister Annette, "Psychological Principles," in Paul J. Brouwer (ed.), *Student Personnel Services in General Education,* American Council on Education, Washington, 1949, pp. 225–252.

Strang, Ruth: *Counseling Technics in College and Secondary Schools,* Harper & Brothers, New York, 1949.

———: "Personnel Services for Graduate Students in Education," in *Graduate Study in Education,* Fiftieth Yearbook of the National Society for the Study of Education, University of Chicago Press, Chicago, 1951, part I, pp. 83–113.

———: *The Role of the Teacher in Personnel Work,* 4th ed., Bureau of Publications, Teachers College, Columbia University, New York, 1953.

——— and others: *Unity Within Guidance,* New York State Association of Deans and Guidance Personnel, Syracuse University Press, Syracuse, N.Y., 1953.

Student Life in the United States, American Council on Education Studies, ser. 1, no. 57, Washington, October, 1953.

The Student Personnel Point of View, American Council on Education, Washington, 1949.

Sutherland, Robert L., and others: *Students and Staff in a Social Context,* American Council on Education, Washington, March, 1953.

Taylor, Harold: "The Philosophical Foundations of General Education," in *General Education,* Fifty-first Yearbook of the National Society for the Study of Education, University of Chicago Press, Chicago, 1952, part I, pp. 22–23.

Thorpe, Louis P.: "Mental-health Practices at the College Level," *Mental Health in Modern Education,* Fifty-fourth Yearbook of the National Society for the Study of Education, University of Chicago Press, Chicago, 1955, part II, pp. 236–270.

Townsend, Agatha, *College Freshmen Speak Out,* Harper & Brothers, New York, 1956.

Traxler, Arthur E.: *Techniques of Guidance,* Harper & Brothers, New York, 1957.

———: *How to Use Cumulative Records,* Science Research Associates, Inc., Chicago, 1947.

———: "What Methods Should Be Employed in Selecting College Students?" in *Current Issues in Higher Education,* 1955, Association for Higher Education, Washington, pp. 49–56.

——— and Agatha Townsend: *Improving Transition from School to College,* Harper & Brothers, New York, 1953.

Tyler, Leona E.: *The Work of the Counselor,* Appleton-Century-Crofts, Inc., New York, 1953.

Tyler, Ralph W.: "Principles Involved in Evaluating Student Personnel Services," in John Dale Russell (ed.), *Student Personnel Services in Colleges and Universities,* University of Chicago Press, Chicago, pp. 291–300.

———: "What Will Be the Emerging Curricular Implications for Colleges and Universities of the New Social and Technological Concepts," in *Current Issues in Higher Education,* 1957, Association for Higher Education, Washington, pp. 78–80.

The Undergraduate Student Counselor, National Association of Deans of Women, Washington, D.C.

Vermilye, Dyckman W.: *College Personnel Work in the South,* Southern Regional Education Board, Atlanta, Ga., 1956.

Warters, Jane: *Techniques of Counseling,* McGraw-Hill Book Company, Inc., New York, 1954.

White, Robert W.: *Lives in Progress,* The Dryden Press, Inc., New York, 1952.

Williams, Cornelia: *These We Teach,* University of Minnesota Press, Minneapolis, 1943.

Williamson, E. G.: *Counseling Adolescents,* McGraw-Hill Book Company, Inc., New York, 1950.

————: "Counseling from the Perspective of a Dean of Students," in Vivian H. Hewer (ed.), *New Perspectives in Counseling,* Minnesota Studies in Student Personnel Work, no. 7, University of Minnesota Press, Minneapolis, 1955, pp. 20–32.

————: *How to Counsel Students,* McGraw-Hill Book Company, Inc., New York, 1939.

————: "Needed Research in Student Personnel Work," in J. B. Culpepper and others (eds.), *Report of the Southern College Personnel Association Work Conference,* 1952, pp. 36–39.

————: "Student Personnel Work," in Walter S. Monroe (ed.), *Encyclopedia of Educational Research,* The Macmillan Company, New York, 1950, pp. 1290–1292.

———— and J. D. Foley: *Counseling and Discipline,* McGraw-Hill Book Company, Inc., New York, 1949.

Woolf, Maurice D., and Jeanne A. Woolf: *The Student Personnel Program,* McGraw-Hill Book Company, Inc., New York, 1953.

Wrenn, C. Gilbert: "Counseling with Students," in *Guidance in Educational Institutions,* Thirty-seventh Yearbook of the National Society for the Study of Education, Public School Publishing Company, Bloomington, Ill., 1938, part I, pp. 119–143.

————: "Some Emotional Factors in Counseling," in M. Eunice Hilton (ed.), *Guidance in the Age of Automation,* Syracuse University Press, Syracuse, N.Y., 1957, pp. 34–43.

————: *Student Personnel Work in College,* The Ronald Press Company, New York, 1951.

Wyatt, Dorothea E., "The Place of Student Personnel Services in Higher Education: Some Comments," in *Current Issues in Higher Education,* 1954, Association for Higher Education, Washington, pp. 165–168.

Periodicals

Aaronson, B. S.: "The Influence of Three Areas of Scholastic Maladjustment in Forcing Veterans to Leave School," *School Review,* 57:45–52, 1949.

Abrahamson, Arthur C.: "Counseling During a Three-Year Period," *Journal of Higher Education,* 25:384–388, 1954.

Adams, Clifford R.: "Marriage Counseling of College Students," *Educational and Psychological Measurement,* 9:594–601, 1949.

Adams, Harold A.: "One Phase of High School–College Relations," *Educational and Psychological Measurement,* part II, 9:457–469, 1949.

Aiken, D. W.: "Securing Faculty Cooperation in the Student Personnel Program," *Educational and Psychological Measurement,* 9:470–476, 1949.

The American Psychologist: 5:620–626, 1950; 6:57–64, 1951; 6:145–166, 1951; 6:428–452, 1951; 6:626–661, 1951; and 8:425–455, 1952.

Andrew, Dean C.: "Relationship Between Academic Load and Scholastic Success of Deficient Students," *Personnel and Guidance Journal*, 34:268–270, 1956.

Anthony, Vernon A., Colin Livesey, Peyton E. Richter, and Charles H. Russell: "The Team Approach to General Education," *Junior College Journal*, 26:319–327, 405–410, 1956.

Arbuckle, Dugald S.: "Our Semantic Wonderland in Counseling Theory," *Personnel and Guidance Journal*, 32:160–162, 1953.

Baller, W. R.: "Characteristics of College Students Who Demonstrate Interest in Counseling Services," *Journal of Educational Psychology*, 35:305–307, 1944.

Bennett, George K., Harold G. Seashore, and Alexander G. Wesman: "Aptitude Testing: Does It 'Prove Out' in Counseling Practice?" *Occupations*, 30: 584–593, 1952.

Berdie, Ralph F.: "Changes in Self-ratings as a Method of Evaluating Counseling," *Journal of Counseling Psychology*, 1:49–54, 1954.

————: "Improving Evaluation in Student Recruitment and Selection," *Personnel and Guidance Journal*, 34:481–486, 1956.

————: "Counseling—An Educational Technique," *Education and Psychological Measurement*, 9:89–94, 1949.

————: "Why Don't They Go to College?" *Personnel and Guidance Journal*, 31:352–356, 1953.

Bixler, R. H., and E. S. Bordin: "Test Selection: A Process of Counseling," *Educational and Psychological Measurement*, 11:361–373, 1946.

Blaesser, Willard W.: "The College Administrator Evaluates Student Personnel Work," *Educational and Psychological Measurement*, 9:412–428, 1949.

————: "Organization and Administration of Student-Personnel Programs in College," *Review of Educational Research*, 24:113–120, 1954.

Blum, L. P., A. C. Eichsteadt, Mary Ann Hunt, Florence Kleczka, and B. A. Sullivan: "Parent Reaction to College Counseling Reports," *Personnel and Guidance Journal*, 34:150–153, 1955.

Bordin, Edward S.: "Student Personnel Work and Personality Development," *Personnel and Guidance Journal*, 33:194–198, 1954.

Bowling, William G.: "Cantaloupes and College Catalogs and Minimum Essentials," *College and University*, 31:197–206, 1956.

Brady, Marna V.: "Student Counselor Selection," *Personnel and Guidance Journal*, 33:289–292, 1955.

Briggs, Ray: "Professor 1957 . . . A Profile," *Saturday Review*, Sept. 14, 1957, p. 19.

Brown, Louise B., and Alma Nemir: "Early Detection of Emotional Stress: Integration of Two Campus Resources," *Personnel and Guidance Journal*, 33:456–459, 1955.

Bryant, Arthur L.: "The Fraternity Adviser," *Personnel and Guidance Journal*, 36:203–206, 1957.

Budd, William C.: "Counselor Versus Student Prediction of Grade Point Average," in Research Notes, *Journal of Counseling Psychology*, 3:68–70, 1956.

Burns, Norman: "High School–College Articulation," *School Review*, 59:1–5, 1951.

Butler, John M.: "Measuring the Effectiveness of Counseling and Psychotherapy," *Personnel and Guidance Journal*, 32:88–92, 1953.

Calia, Vincent F.: "A Group Guidance Program in Action," *Junior College Journal*, 27:437–454, 1957.

Cameron, Marian L.: "An Evaluation of a Faculty Advisory Program, *Educational and Psychological Measurement*, 12:730–740, 1952.

Caravello, Santo J.: "Effectiveness of High School Guidance Services," *Personnel and Guidance Journal*, 36:323–325, 1958.

Carlson, Carol R., and John W. M. Rothney: "An Examination of a Method for Evaluating Counseling," *Personnel and Guidance Journal*, 35:584–586, 1957.

Carpenter, Marjorie, E. H. Hopkins, and M. Eunice Hilton: "College Guidance —Whose Job Is It?" *NEA Journal*, 42:272–274, 1953.

―――― and students: "High School–College Articulation," *NEA Journal*, 44:172–173, 1955.

Chandler, Everett M.: "Reorganization of the Student Personnel Program in the California State Colleges," *Personnel and Guidance Journal*, 31:76–82, 1952.

Chauncey, Henry: "From High School Into College," *Journal of the National Association of Deans of Women*, 13:124–133, 1950.

Clark, Selby G.: "Let's Make the Campus Disciplinary Program Effective," *Personnel and Guidance Journal*, 33:393–396, 1955.

Coleman, William: "Coordinating Specialized Student Personnel Services on the Campus," *Personnel and Guidance Journal*, 31:524–526, 1953.

―――――: "The Role of Evaluation in Improving Guidance and Counseling Services," *Personnel and Guidance Journal*, 35:441–444, 1957.

―――――: "Motivating Factors in In-service Training of Faculty Counselors," *Educational and Psychological Measurement*, 11:747–751, 1951.

Combs, Arthur W., Franklin J. Shaw, and Edward Joseph Shoben, Jr.: "Counseling as Learning: A Symposium," *Journal of Counseling Psychology*, 1:31–48, 1954.

Cooperman, Irene G., Clyde W. Gleason, C. Harold McCuly, and Bernard Peck: "Counseling and the Counseling Record," *Personnel and Guidance Journal*, 34:333–339, 1956.

Copeland, Theodore: "A Student-centered Program," *Journal of Higher Education*, 23:145–147 and 172, 1952.

Cottingham, Harold F.: "Roles, Functions, and Training Levels for College Personnel Workers," *Personnel and Guidance Journal*, 33:534–538, 1955.

Cottle, William C.: "Personal Characteristics of Counselors: I," *Personnel and Guidance Journal*, 31:445–450, 1953.

Cowley, W. H.: "Student Personnel Services in Retrospect and Prospect," *School and Society*, 85:19–22, 1957.

Croft, Lysle W.: "Orientation Week Philosophy and Purposes," *Educational and Psychological Measurement*, 2:711–714, 1951.

Curran, Charles A.: "Guidance and Counseling in Education," *Education*, 73:223–228, 1952.

Danskin, David G., and Collins W. Burnett: "Study Techniques of Those Superior Students," *Personnel and Guidance Journal*, 31:181–186, 1952.

Davis, Junius A.: "The College Teacher as Counselor," *Journal of Teacher Education*, 6:281–285, 1955.

Dement, Alice L.: "Good Students Want Counseling Too," *Journal of Counseling Psychology*, 4:113–118, 1957.

Dressel, Paul L.: "Counseling Caprices," *Personnel and Guidance Journal*, 33:4–7, 1954.

―――――: "Evaluation Procedures for General Education Objectives," *Educational Record*, 21:97–122, 1940.

Dressel, Paul L.: "Personnel Services in High School and College," *Occupations,* 29:331–340, 1951.

———: "Research in Counseling: A Symposium," *Personnel and Guidance Journal,* 31:284–287, 1953.

———: "Role of General Education in Articulation," *Junior College Journal,* 23:131–144, 1952.

———: "Working with Youth of Below Average Ability," *Personnel and Guidance Journal,* 34:348–350, 1956.

———, E. J. Shoben, Jr., and Harold B. Pepinsky: "Research in Counseling: A Symposium," *Personnel and Guidance Journal,* 31:284–294, 1953.

Dugan, Willis E.: "Counseling in Teacher Education," *Occupations,* 29:340–342, 1951.

Durnall, Edward J., Jr.: "Students Scrutinize a Guidance Program," *Personnel and Guidance Journal,* 31:187–188, 1952.

———, James F. Moynihan, S.J., and C. Gilbert Wrenn: "Symposium: The Counselor and His Religion," *Personnel and Guidance Journal,* 36:326–334, 1958.

Dyer, Henry S.: "The Need for Do-It-Yourself Prediction Research in High School Guidance," *Personnel and Guidance Journal,* 36:162–167, 1957.

Eckert, Ruth E.: "High School–College Cooperation," *NEA Journal,* 38:96–97, 1949.

Embree, Royal B.: "Developments in Counseling Bureaus and Clinics," *Educational and Psychological Measurement,* 10:465–475, 1950.

Evans, D. Luther: "The Professor and the Counselor," *Educational Research Bulletin,* Ohio State University, College of Education, 33:57–65, 1954.

Failor, Clarence W.: "Distinguishing Marks of Counseling," *Occupations,* 33:260–263, 1952.

Farnsworth, Dana L.: "College Health Services—Reality and Ideal," *Personnel-O-Gram,* 12:11–14, 1957.

———: "Psychiatry and Higher Education," *American Journal of Psychiatry,* 109:266–271, 1952.

Farson, Richard: "The Counselor Is a Woman," *Journal of Counseling Psychology,* 1:221–223, 1954.

Farwell, Gail F.: "A Coordinated Program of Admissions and Counseling," *Personnel and Guidance Journal,* 35:236–240, 1956.

Feder, D. D., William D. Kennon, Glenn R. Ross, Robert S. Wilson: "Noninstructional Services to Students," *Review of Educational Research,* 24:313–321, 1954.

Fick, Reuel L.: "The Problem Check List," *Occupations,* 30:410–412, 1952.

Fjelstad, Ralph S.: "The Carleton Faculty Study of Teacher Education," *School and Society,* 84:19–22, 1956.

Fontanella, M. A.: "The Military Instructor's Role in Guidance," *Journal of Higher Education,* 27:301–307 and 349, 1956.

Form, Arnold L.: "Measurement of Student Attitudes toward Counseling Services," *Personnel and Guidance Journal,* 32:84–87, 1953.

———: "Users and Non-users of Counseling Services," *Personnel and Guidance Journal,* 32:209–213, 1953.

Friedenberg, Edgar Z.: "The Measurement of Student Conceptions of the Role of a College Advisory System," *Educational and Psychological Measurement,* 10:545–568, 1950.

Froe, Otis D., and Maurice A. Lee: "A New Emphasis in Freshman Orientation," *Personnel and Guidance Journal,* 34:360–365, 1956.

Fuhr, Bernard, and Warren R. Baller: "Making Student Personnel Data Accessible," *Occupations*, 29:123–124, 1950.

Gallagher, Buell G.: "A College President Looks at Student Personnel Work," *Personnel-O-Gram*, 10:56–58, 1956.

Gerrity, Ellsworth M.: "Easing Transition from High School to College," *Bulletin of the National Association of Secondary School Principals*, 38:98–101, 1954.

Gibb, Jack R., Wilton Pruitt, James Pomeroy, and others: "Leadership Research and the College Student," *Personnel-O-Gram*, 11:32–33, 1957.

Gilbert, William M.: "How to Go About the Process of Evaluating Student Personnel Work," *Educational and Psychological Measurement*, 10:521–530, 1950.

Gillin, John: "The Role of the Interdisciplinary Faculty Member," *Personnel-O-Gram*, 10:27–35, 1956.

Ginzberg, Eli: "Toward a Theory of Occupational Choice," *Occupations*, 30:491–494, 1952.

Gluck, Samuel, and others: "A Proposed Code of Ethics for Counselors," *Occupations*, 30:484–490, 1952.

Goodhartz, Abraham S.: "Literacy on the Campus," *School and Society*, 83:147–149, 1956.

Goodrich, Thomas A.: "Gains in Self-understanding Through Pre-college Clinics," *Personnel and Guidance Journal*, 31:433–438, 1953.

Gordon, Ira J.: "The Creation of an Effective Faculty Adviser Training Program Through Group Procedures," *Educational and Psychological Measurement*, 10:505–512, 1950.

————: "Guidance Training for College Faculty," *Journal of the National Association of Deans of Women*, 16:69–76, 1953.

Gould, Samuel: "The Dimensions of a College," *School and Society*, 85:67–70, 1957.

Granick, Samuel, Walter J. Levy, and Murray Gunner: "Parental Attitudes and Vocational Guidance," *Occupations*, 30:21–23, 1951.

Grant, Claude W.: "How Students Perceive the Counselor's Role," *Personnel and Guidance Journal*, 32:386–388, 1954.

————: "The Counselor's Role," *Personnel and Guidance Journal*, 33:74–77, 1954.

Greene, George H.: "Freshman Orientation Courses in Small Colleges," *Personnel and Guidance Journal*, 32:480–482, 1954.

Greenschields, Myrel J., and Antonio Scarpelli: "A Pictorial Approach to Counseling," *Junior College Journal*, 27:327–332, 1957.

Guthrie, George M., and Harry W. O'Neill: "Effects of Dormitory Counseling on Academic Achievement," *Personnel and Guidance Journal*, 31:307–309, 1953.

Gwin, John P., Katherine Warren, and others: "Cost Studies Applicable to Student Personnel Functions," *Personnel-O-Gram*, 11:38–39, 1957.

Hackett, Herbert R.: "Evaluation of a Program of Counseling Students on Probation," *Personnel and Guidance Journal*, 33:513–516, 1955.

Hadley, Loren S., and panel: "Orientation—An Excellent Opportunity for Student Leadership," *Personnel-O-Gram*, 11:41–42, 1957.

Hahn, Milton E.: "Conceptual Trends in Counseling," *Personnel and Guidance Journal*, 31:231–235, 1953.

————: "Counseling Psychology," *The American Psychologist*, 10:279–282, 1955.

Hardee, Melvene Draheim: "A Program of In-service Training for Teacher-Counselors," *Junior College Journal*, 20:453–459, 1950.

———: "The Coordinator of Counseling," *Occupations*, 30:396–399, 1952.

———: "General Education and General Education Counseling," *School and Society*, 74:3–6, 1951.

———: "Stimulating Professional Publication," *Personnel and Guidance Journal*, 32:219–220, 1953.

———: "The Development of Character and Personality: A Shared Responsibility," *Journal of the National Association of Women Deans and Counselors*, 21:68–73, 1958.

———: "When Your Client Goes to College," *Journal of Rehabilitation*, 17:10–13 and 23, 1951.

——— and Margaret Bernauer: "A Method of Evaluating Group Discussion," *Occupations*, 27:90–94, 1948.

——— and Dorothy M. Pollock: "A Process of Investigation for Occupational Interests," *Junior College Journal*, 19:177–184, 1948.

Harvey, Martin L.: "The Selection and Training of Student Leaders in the Student Personnel Program," *Educational and Psychological Measurement*, 11:796–798, 1951.

Hayden, Velma D., and William D. Wilkins: "College Selection—Casual or Planned?" *Occupations*, 30:416–419, 1952.

Herrold, Kenneth F., Joel Davitz, David Fox, and Irving Lorge: "Difficulties Encountered in Group Decision Making," *Personnel and Guidance Journal*, 31:516–523, 1953.

Hopwood, Kathryn: "Expectations of University Freshman Women," *Personnel and Guidance Journal*, 32:464–469, 1954.

———: "Stability in Freshman Attitudes," *Journal of the National Association of Deans of Women*, 17:125–129, 1954.

Humphreys, J. Anthony: "Potential Contribution of Admissions and Registrars Offices to the Student Personnel Program, *Personnel-O-Gram*, 12:7–9, 1957.

Hunt, Herold C.: "Problems of Articulation Between High School and College," *Educational Forum*, 18:281–285, 1954.

Huntley, Charles W.: "Toward a More Effective Freshman Advisory System," *Journal of Higher Education*, 26:94–97, 1955.

Jamrich, John X.: "Organizational Practices in Student-Faculty Counseling Programs in Small Colleges," *Educational Administration and Supervision*, 41:94–97, 1955.

Jesness, Robert F.: "To Refer or Not to Refer," *Occupations*, 30:521–524, 1952.

Jex, Frank B., and A. Garth Sorenson: "G.A.T.B. Scores as Predictors of College Grades," *Personnel and Guidance Journal*, 31:295–297, 1953.

Johnson, B. Lamar: "Opportunity Ahead in Higher Education," *School and Society*, 84:115–118, 1956.

Jones, Edward S.: "Why Students Fail in College," *Association of American Colleges Bulletin*, 39:282–287, 1953.

———, and Gloria K. Ortner: "Articulation of High School and College," *Review of Educational Research*, 24:322–330, 1954.

Journal of the National Association of Deans of Women, 16:51–85, 1953. (Entire edition.)

Kamm, Robert B.: "An Inventory of Student Reaction to Student Personnel Services," *Educational and Psychological Measurement*, 10:537–544, 1950.

————: "Some Principles of Student Personnel Administration," *Personnel and Guidance Journal,* 34:13–17, 1955.

————: "How Effective Are Our Student Personnel Programs?" *Personnel and Guidance Journal,* 33:318–324, 1955.

————: "The Unity of the Educational Program, With Special Reference to Student Personnel Services," *Personnel-O-Gram,* 12:3–7, 1957.

Keniston, Hayward: "The Common Goals of Counseling," *Educational and Psychological Measurement,* 11:677–680, 1951.

Kerr, Clark: "The Student and His Total Environment," *Journal of the National Association of Women Deans and Counselors,* 20:158–163, 1957.

Kiell, Norman: "Freshman Evaluation of Faculty Counselors," *Personnel and Guidance Journal,* 35:261–264, 1957.

————: "Vocational Counseling of Fatherless Male College Students," *Personnel and Guidance Journal,* 34:369–370, 1956.

Kirk, Barbara A.: "Individualizing of Test Interpretation," *Occupations,* 30:500–505, 1952.

————: "Techniques of In-service Counselor Training," *Personnel and Guidance Journal,* 34:204–207, 1955.

Klingelhofer, Edwin L.: "The Relationship of Academic Advisement to the Scholastic Performance of Failing College Students," *Journal of Counseling Psychology,* 1:125–131, 1954.

Kneller, George F.: "Worldly View of Guidance and Counseling," *Journal of Higher Education,* 27:158–165, 1956.

Knowles, Asa S.: "Emerging Features of Tomorrow's Higher Education," *Educational Record,* 38:329–339, 1957.

Koile, Earl A.: "A Measure of Interest for Selecting Faculty Counselors," *Educational and Psychological Measurement,* 15:47–57, 1955.

————: "Characteristics of College Teachers Interested in Faculty Counseling Activities," *Journal of Counseling Psychology,* 2:32–34, 1955.

————: "Faculty Counseling Faculty Style," *Personnel and Guidance Journal,* 33:22–25, 1954.

————: "Faculty Counseling in Colleges and Universities," *Teachers College Record,* 55:384–389, 1954.

Kubie, Lawrence S.: "The Forgotten Man of Education," *Harvard Alumni Bulletin,* 56:349–353, 1954.

Lifton, Walter M.: "Counseling and the Religious View of Man," *Personnel and Guidance Journal,* 31:366–367, 1953.

Lindley, Clyde J.: "Are Your Records Sagging?," *Occupations,* 30:252–254, 1952.

Lott, George M.: "Clinical Problems Common Among College Students," *Mental Hygiene,* 34:641–645, 1950.

Love, L. L.: "The Faculty Advisory Program of the Ohio State University College of Education," *Educational and Psychological Measurement,* 9:477–481, 1949.

Lowenstein, Norman, and Robert Hoppock: "High School Occupations Course Helps Students Adjust to College," *Personnel and Guidance Journal,* 34:21–23, 1955.

———— and Vivian Yates: "How Freshmen Feel About College," *Personnel and Guidance Journal,* 33:379–380, 1955.

Ludeman, W. W.: "Trends in College Freshman Orientation," *Educational Forum,* 21:63–64, 1956.

MacKay, Kenneth C., and Kenneth W. Iversen: "An Experiment in Group Guidance for Freshmen," *Junior College Journal,* 19:195–199, 1948.

MacLachlan, Patricia S., and Collins W. Burnett: "Who Are the Superior Fresh-
men in College?" *Personnel and Guidance Journal*, 32:345–349, 1954.
MacLean, Malcolm S.: "Counseling and the Tower of Babel," *Personnel and
Guidance Journal*, 31:357–362, 1953.
Mahler, Clarence A.: "Evaluation of College Personnel Programs," *Personnel-O-
Gram*, 7:11–12, 1953.
Mathewson, Robert H.: "The General Guidance Counselor," *Personnel and
Guidance Journal*, 32:544–547, 1954.
Matteson, Ross: "Counseling Clinics for High School Grads," *Occupations*,
29:502–505, 1951.
———: "Individualized Admission Through Testing and Counseling," *College
and University*, 29:390–396, 1954.
———: "Self-estimates of College Freshmen," *Personnel and Guidance Jour-
nal*, 34:280–284, 1956.
McBride, Julia K.: "In-service Training of a Coordinator of Guidance," *Journal
of the National Association of Deans of Women*, 16:56–62, 1953.
McCracken, Charles W.: "Teaching Beyond the Classroom," *Personnel and
Guidance Journal*, 35:527–530, 1957.
———, William P. Wharton, and Gretchen Graff: "The Pre-college Clinic
Week," *Personnel and Guidance Journal*, 34:437–440, 1956.
McKeachie, Wilbert J.: "Anxiety in the College Classroom," *Journal of Educa-
tional Research*, 45:153–160, 1949.
Mehl, Walter J.: "Developing a College Orientation Program," *College and
University*, 31:53–61, 1955.
Messer, Nollie B.: "They Learn about Living," *Occupations*, 30:271–273;
1952.
Miller, Carroll L.: "Developments in Counseling by Faculty Advisers," *Educa-
tional and Psychological Measurement*, 10:451–454, 1950.
Mills, Thelma: "Job Analyses of Educational Personnel Workers," *Occupations*,
29:1–22, 1951.
Minkin, Vera F., and Nancy D. Stevens: "The Registrar," *Personnel and
Guidance Journal*, 32:221–222, 1953.
Murphy, Albert T.: "Counseling Students with Speech and Hearing Problems,"
Personnel and Guidance Journal, 33:260–264, 1955.
Myers, A. F.: "Articulation Between High School and College," *Journal of
Educational Sociology*, 29:193–232, 1956.
Neal, Ruth: "Counseling the Off-campus Woman Student," *Personnel and
Guidance Journal*, 36:342–343, 1958.
Nelson, A. Gordon: "The College Teacher as a Counselor," *Educational Forum*,
18:349–357, 1954.
Nelson, L. W.: "Secondary School–College Relations," *College and University*,
26:67–71, 1950.
Newton, David: "Dear Parents: Our College Cordially Invites You," *Personnel
and Guidance Journal*, 34:217–218, 1955.
O'Dea, J. David, and Franklin R. Zeran: "Evaluating Effects of Counseling,"
Personnel and Guidance Journal, 31:241–244, 1953.
Ohlsen, Merle M.: "Developments in Residence Hall Counseling," *Educational
and Psychological Measurement*, 10:455–464, 1950.
———: "An In-service Training Program for Dormitory Counselors," *Occupa-
tions*, 29:531–534, 1951.
———: "Evaluation of Dormitory Counselors' Services," *Educational and
Psychological Measurement*, 11:419–426, 1951.

Pepinsky, Harold B.: "Productivity in the University," *Personnel-O-Gram,* 10:21–27, 1956.

"Personal Guidance for the Prospective Teacher," American Association of Colleges of Teacher Education, Oneonta, N.Y., 1957. (Manuscript prepared by a committee of the Iowa State Teachers College staff.)

Phenix, Philip: "Barriers to Academic Communication," *Teachers College Record,* 59:76–88, 1957.

Pierson, George A.: "The Parable of the Teacher-Counselor," *Personnel and Guidance Journal,* 33:443, 1955.

————: "Utilizing Internship in Preparation of Counselors," *Occupations,* 29:92–94, 1950.

———— and Sydney W. Angleman: "From Adviser to Counselor," *Educational and Psychological Measurement,* 11:742–751, 1951.

Platt, James H.: "Speech Disorders and Counseling," *Occupations,* 30:102–105, 1951.

Ptacek, Paul H.: "A University's Attempt to Counsel Student Leaders," *Journal of Higher Education,* 28:137–142, 1957.

Rackham, Eric N.: "The Need for Adequate Criteria When Evaluating College Personnel Programs," *Educational and Psychological Measurement,* 11:691–699, 1954.

Raines, Max R.: "Helping College Freshmen Identify Problems Through a Case Conference," *Personnel and Guidance Journal,* 34:417–419, 1956.

"Research Briefs," *Personnel-O-Gram,* 12:15–16, 1957.

Rhulman, Jessie: "Securing Faculty Cooperation in the Student Personnel Program," *Educational and Psychological Measurement,* 9:482–487, 1949.

Richards, Laura E.: "The Integration of a Psychiatric Clinic with a Student Personnel Program," *Educational and Psychological Measurement,* 11:722–734, 1951.

Richardson, Lavange Hunt: "Guidance for College Students," *Educational Administration and Supervision,* 35:363–374, 1949.

Robertson, James H.: "Academic Advising in Colleges and Universities—Its Present State and Present Problems," *North Central Association Quarterly,* vol. 32, no. 3, January, 1958, pp. 228–239.

Rohrer, John H.: "An Evaluation of College Personnel Work in Terms of Current Research on Interpersonal Relationships," *Educational and Psychological Measurement,* 9:429–443, 1949.

Romney, Antone K.: "The Developments of a University Counseling Service," *School and Society,* 70:330–331, 1949.

Rothney, John W. M., and Robert L. Mooren: "Sampling Problems in Follow-up Research," *Occupations,* 30:573–578, 1952.

Ruja, Harry: "Vocational vs. Emotional?" *Personnel and Guidance Journal,* 31:99–100, 1952.

Saddlemire, Gerald L.: "A Current View of Men Personnel Administrators in Colleges and Universities," *Occupations,* 29:190–193, 1950.

Sageser, Henry W.: "Counseling in Their Colleges," *Occupations,* 29:348–349, 1951.

Samler, Joseph: "Professional Training—End Goal or Kick-off Point," *Personnel and Guidance Journal,* 31:15–19, 1952.

Sanford, Nevitt: "Personality Development during the College Years," *Personnel and Guidance Journal,* 35:74–80, 1956.

Seeley, John R.: "Guidance: A Plea for Abandonment," *Personnel and Guidance Journal,* 34:528–535, 1956.

Shaw, James G.: "An Evaluation of a Study Skills Course," *Personnel and Guidance Journal*, 33:465–468, 1955.

Shaw, Merville C., and Donald J. Brown: "Scholastic Underachievement of Bright College Students," *Personnel and Guidance Journal*, 36:195–199, 1957.

Shepard, Eugene L.: "A Three-level In-service Training Program for Advisers," *Personnel and Guidance Journal*, 36:48–50, 1957.

―――― and staff: "Meeting Student Needs through Counseling," *News Reporter*, Stephens College, 15, 1956.

Shoben, Edward Joseph, Jr.: "New Frontiers in Theory," *Personnel and Guidance Journal*, 32:80–83, 1953.

Shulim, Joseph I.: "A Career-Curricular Conference," *Personnel and Guidance Journal*, 35:599–601, 1957.

Smith, Elbridge M.: "Which Way to Junior College Guidance and Personnel Service Programs?" *Junior College Journal*, 28:186–189, 1957.

Smith, Robert E.: "Presenting the Psychological Dimensions of Classes to Instructors," *Journal of Educational Research*, 48:149–151, 1954.

Stewart, Lawrence H.: "Teachers and Counselors Look at Students: Some Implications for Guidance Practice," *Personnel and Guidance Journal*, 35:565–568, 1957.

Stoddard, George D.: "The Future of New York University: Interim Report of the Self-study," *School and Society*, 83:3–8, 1956.

Strang, Ruth: "Guidance of the Gifted," *Personnel and Guidance Journal*, 31:26–30, 1952.

―――――: "Major Limitations in Current Evaluation Studies," *Educational and Psychological Measurement*, 10:531–536, 1950.

Stroup, Herbert: "The College Teacher as Counselor," *School and Society*, 85:120–122, 1957.

―――――: "Letters to the Editor," *Journal of Counseling Psychology*, 4:248–250, 1957.

―――――: "Theoretical Constructs in Student Personnel Work," *Journal of Higher Education*, 28:319–326, 1957.

―――――: "Values and *Disvalues* of Faculty-Student Committees," *Personnel and Guidance Journal*, 35:289–292, 1957.

"Students Will Be Hired to Help Freshmen," *The New York Times*, Sunday, July 7, 1957, p. E7.

Stump, N. F.: "What Counseling Services Do College Freshmen Expect to Receive?" *School and Society*, 56:83–84, 1942.

Sturgis, Horace W.: "Trends and Problems in College Admissions," *College and University*, 28:5–16, 1952.

Super, Donald E.: "Testing and Using Test Results in Counseling," *Occupations*, 29:95–97, 1950.

Taylor, Harold: "Education: For What and for Whom?" *School and Society*, 83:39–43, 1956.

―――――: "Human Nature and Education," *Educational and Psychological Measurements*, 8:530–539, 1948.

―――――: "The Student as a Responsible Person," *Harvard Educational Review*, 19:67–79, 1949.

Tead, Ordway: "Integrating Personnel and Teaching Functions in College," *Educational Forum*, 17:401–411, 1953.

Thomason, R. Fred: "A Registrar Looks at Records," *College and University*, 30:186–193, 1955.

Thompson, Florence M.: "The Uses of Dormitories for Social Education," *Educational and Psychological Measurement,* 7:648–654, 1947.

Tinsley, Mary Ann: "The Faculty Adviser in the Liberal Arts College," *Personnel and Guidance Journal,* 34:219–220, 1955.

Travers, Robert M. W.: "A Critical Review of Techniques for Evaluating Guidance," *Educational and Psychological Measurement,* 9:21–25, 1949.

Traxler, Arthur E.: "Evaluation of Methods of Individual Appraisal in Counseling," *Occupations,* 26:85–91, 1947.

———: "Guidance Toward College Preparation," *School and Society,* 73:113–116, 1951.

Trout, David M.: "Why Define Counseling in Medical Terms?" *Personnel and Guidance Journal,* 32:518–523, 1954.

Tully, Glover E.: "Financial Aid to College Students," *Personnel and Guidance Journal,* 30:282–286, 1954.

Tyler, Leona: "The Initial Interview," *Personnel and Guidance Journal,* 34:466–473, 1956.

———: "Letters to the Editor," *Journal of Counseling Psychology,* 4:324, 1957.

Ulich, Robert: "Some Recent Tendencies in Educational Philosophy," *School and Society,* 83:26–30, 1956.

"Utilization of Faculty in Guidance Programs," Southern College Personnel Association *Newsletter,* 6:1, 1956.

Volpe, Edmond L.: "Schizophrenia on the Campus," *School and Society,* 82:165–167, 1955.

Von Berg, Dorothea: "Bridging the Gap Between High School and College," *Journal of the National Association of Deans of Women,* 17:35–42, 1953.

Vordenberg, Wesley: "The Impact of Personal Philosophies on Counseling," *Personnel and Guidance Journal,* 31:439–440, 1953.

Walker, Helen: "Methods of Research," *Review of Educational Research,* 36:323–343, 1956.

Warman, Roy E.: "A Study of Applicants for Readmission to College," *Personnel and Guidance Journal,* 34:553–558, 1956.

Weigand, George: "Adaptiveness and the Role of Parents in Academic Success," *Personnel and Guidance Journal,* 35:518–522, 1957.

Weitz, Henry: "Instruction and Guidance in Education," *Educational Forum,* 19:169–177, 1955.

———, Robert M. Colver, and J. Albert Southern: "Evaluating a Measurement Project," *Personnel and Guidance Journal,* 33:400–403, 1955.

Weitzman, Ellis: "The Meaning of a Comprehensive Student Personnel Program," *Educational and Psychological Measurement,* 9:671–677, 1949.

Wells, L. D.: "New Guidance Medium: Colorado Council on High School–College Relations," *Bulletin of the National Association of Secondary School Principals,* 41:45–47, 1957.

Williamson, E. G.: "A Concept of Counseling," *Occupations,* 29:182–189, 1950.

———: "Coordination by the Administrator," *Journal of Higher Education,* 19:306, 1948.

———: "Learning versus Fun in College," *Journal of Higher Education,* 28:425–432, 1957.

———: "Counseling in Developing Self Confidence," *Personnel and Guidance Journal,* 34:398–404, 1956.

Williamson, E. G.: "The Dean of Students as Educator," *Educational Record,* 38:230–240, 1957.

———: "Professional Preparation of Student Personnel Workers," *School and Society,* 86:3–5, 1958.

——— and E. S. Bordin: "The Evaluation of Vocational and Educational Counseling: A Critique of the Methodology of Experiments," *Educational and Psychological Measurement,* 1:5–24, 1941.

——— and W. Max Wise: "Symposium: Residence Halls in Higher Education," *Personnel and Guidance Journal,* 36:392–401, 1958.

Williamson, B. Lois, and Daniel D. Feder: "Scholarship Winners," *Personnel and Guidance Journal,* 31:236–240, 1953.

Wilson, Frances M.: "What Makes an Effective In-service Training Program?" *Journal of the National Association of Deans of Women,* 16:51–56, 1953.

Wilson, H. K., and W. Scott Gehman: "The Division of Intermediate Registration," *School and Society,* 72:68–71, 1950.

Wilson, Margaret: "Dynamics of a Residence Hall Program," *Occupations,* 29:116–122, 1950.

Wise, W. M.: "The Implications of the Student Personnel Philosophy," *Educational and Psychological Measurement,* 11:681–690, 1951.

Woolf, Maurice D.: "Securing Cooperation of the Faculty in the Personnel Program," *Educational and Psychological Measurement,* 9:488–495, 1949.

Wrenn, C. Gilbert: "Counseling Methods," *Annual Review of Psychology,* 5:337–357, 1954.

———: "The Administration of Counseling and Other Student Personnel Services," *Harvard Educational Review,* 19:110–120, 1949.

———: "The Ethics of Counseling," *Educational and Psychological Measurement,* 12:161–177, 1952.

———: "The Evaluation of Student Personnel Work: A Critique of the Guidance Movement," *School and Society,* 52:409–414, 1940.

———: "The Role of Faculty Advisers in a Personnel Program," *Occupations,* 19:506–508, 1941.

———: "The Selection and Education of Student Personnel Workers," *Personnel and Guidance Journal,* 31:9–14, 1952.

———: "Trends and Predictions in Vocational Guidance," *Occupations,* 25:503–515, 1947.

——— and Robert B. Kamm: "A Procedure for Evaluating a Student Personnel Program," *School and Society,* 67:266–269, 1948.

Young, F. Chandler: "College Freshmen Judge Their Own Scholastic Promise," *Personnel and Guidance Journal,* 32:399–403, 1954.

———: "Evaluation óf a College Counseling Program," *Personnel and Guidance Journal,* 33:282–286, 1955.

Speeches

Atherton, Audrey: "Articulation in Counseling," in a panel presentation, American College Personnel Association, Buffalo, N.Y., 1954.

Birdwhistell, Ray: "Contemporary Youth in Higher Education," an address to the Third Annual Work Conference, Southern College Personnel Association, Mars Hill, N.C., August, 1954.

Darley, John G.: "Diversification in American Higher Education," an address to the National Association of Student Personnel Administrators, University of California, June, 1956.

————: "The Faculty Is Human, Too," an address to the Southern College Personnel Association, Atlanta, Ga., December, 1955.

Hardee, Melvene Draheim: "Studies in Behavior in Human Relations Education," from a panel discussion, American College Personnel Association, Chicago, March, 1955.

————: "Counseling in General Education," in a panel presentation for Division 17, American Psychological Association, New York City, September, 1954.

Hobbs, Nicholas: "The Social Scientist in the Field of Guidance," an address to the Southern College Personnel Association, Nashville, Tenn., November, 1953.

McConnell, T. R.: "A University President Looks at Student Personnel Work," an address to the American College Personnel Association, Buffalo, N.Y., 1954.

Murphy, Gardner: "The Cultural Context of Guidance," an address to the American College Personnel Association, Chicago, 1955.

Dissertations and Theses

Atherton, Audrey: "A Study of the Undergraduate Educational Counseling Services in the School of Education," dissertation submitted in partial fulfillment of the requirements for the Ed.D. degree, Florida State University, 1953.

Brunson, May A.: "Integrating Student Personnel Work with the Educational Program of the Campus," thesis submitted in partial fulfillment of the requirements for the Ed.D. degree, Teachers College, Columbia University, 1957.

Clark, T. C.: "A Plan for Improving the Student Personnel Program of the Department of Educational Administration, Teachers College, Columbia University," thesis submitted in partial fulfillment of the requirements for a doctor's degree, Teachers College, Columbia University, 1953.

Copeland, Theodore H., Jr.: "Freshman Orientation Programs: A Study of Their Development and Present Status with Special Reference to Middle Atlantic Colleges," in partial fulfillment of requirements for the Ed.D. degree, Teachers College, Temple University, 1953.

Eycke, Carl O.: "A Survey of In-service Training Programs for Faculty Counselors in State Supported Colleges and Universities in the United States," thesis presented in partial fulfillment of the requirements for the M.A. degree, Ohio University, June, 1956.

Farwell, Gail F.: "An Analysis of Factors and Criteria Related to the Admission of Borderline Cases at Michigan State College, Fall Quarter, 1952," unpublished doctoral dissertation, Michigan State College, East Lansing, Mich., 1954.

Glanz, Edward C.: "Case Studies of Faculty Counseling Programs," dissertation on file, Teachers College Library, Columbia University, New York.

Rackham, Eric N.: "The Determination of Criteria for the Evaluation of Student Personnel Services in Institutions of Higher Learning," unpublished doctoral dissertation, University of Michigan, 1950.

Vogel, Fred J.: "Study of the Concepts and Practices Relating to the Allocation of Certain Student Personnel Responsibilities in Selected Institutions of Higher Learning in the United States," dissertation submitted in partial fulfillment of the requirements for the Ed.D. degree, Florida State University, 1958.

Mimeographed

Basic Facts, Office of High School Cooperation, Michigan State University, East Lansing, Mich.

Directory of University Student Personnel Agencies and Staffs, University of Minnesota, September, 1957.

Folger, John: *Discussion Guide,* The Southern Regional Conference on Education Beyond the High School, Louisville, Ky., Apr. 23–25, 1957.

Functions of a Mentor, Carnegie Institute of Technology.

Glanz, Edward C.: *A Guidance Program in Action.*

In-service Training at Stephens College, report of the Committee on In-service Training to the Board of Curators, 1947.

In-service Training of Secondary School Counselors, research project of the counseling center, University of California, Berkeley, Calif.

Interim Report of the Steering Committee for Tuskegee Institute Self Study, Apr. 1, 1957.

Jones, Lonzo: *Bulletin for Lower Division Counselors,* Indiana State Teachers College.

Raushenbush, Esther: *Education and Guidance,* Sarah Lawrence College.

Report of the Committee on Instruction, Local Chapter, A.A.U.P., University of Kansas, Lawrence, Kans., Feb. 26, 1957.

Report of the Sub-committee on Counseling in the California State Colleges, March, 1957.

Statement of the Development of the Counseling Service in the New York State College of Home Economics at Cornell University, Ithaca, N.Y., April, 1955.

Appendixes

Return to Mel Hardee, Coordinator of Counseling
Florida State University

REVIEW OF PROCEDURES IN COORDINATION OF COUNSELING SERVICES — 1952

1. What types of student personnel services are available in your institution?
   Qualify any of these.

   ___ Educational counseling
   ___   Freshmen only
   ___   All classes

   ___ Residence counseling

   ___ Psychological services

   ___ Psychiatric services

   ___ Vocational counseling

   ___ Placement

   ___ Religious counseling

   ___ Remedial reading

   ___ Speech and hearing

   ___ Marriage and family
        adjustment counseling

   ___ Veteran's problems

   ___ Health counseling

   Others:_____
          _____
          _____

2. (a) What is the title of the officer who is responsible for the <u>administration</u> of
       <u>student personnel services</u>?

   (b) What are some special means by which his/her administrative duties are
       performed? (Example: Periodic meetings of the officers in the area?
       bulletin? individual conferences?)

3. (a) Is this same officer (see 2a) responsible for the coordination of services <u>for
       students</u>? Explain briefly.

   (b) How do students become informed of the offerings in student personnel?

   (c) What evaluation of the use of those services <u>by students</u> has your institution
       made?

4. (a) What working relationship is there between (1) the officers who are responsible
       for administration or coordination of the various student personnel services
       and (2) the academic deans and department heads?

   (b) What working relationship is there between (1) the officers who are responsible
       for administration or coordination of the various student personnel services
       and (2) the general teaching faculty?

5. (a) What are the <u>benefits</u> resulting from your particular kind of student personnel
       administration? coordination?

   (b) What are the <u>shortcomings</u>, in your opinion?

6. What studies have you done or are you now doing that relate to <u>better administration</u>
   or <u>better coordination</u> of the student personnel services?

Signed:_____

Institution:_____
                        MDH

Appendix B

Return by July 1 to Dr. Melvene Hardee
Florida State University

THE COORDINATION OF COUNSELING SERVICES: A SURVEY 1956

1. Counseling in our institution is considered to be

    ____ Part of the instructional program   Other: _____

    ____ A series of separate services.   _____

    ____ A centralized service   _____

Teaching Faculty

2. Members of the teaching faculty participate in the counseling of students as follows: they are trained for this responsibility as indicated; in both instances the success of their counseling and training is adjudged:

(a) Types of counseling in which faculty serve	(b) How successful	(c) Means by which they receive training	(d) How successful
____ Academic			
____ Vocational			
____ Personal-social			
____ Religious			
____ Health			
Other:			

3. If written materials concerning 2 (a) to 2 (c) above are available, how may they be obtained?

4. State why the use of teaching faculty in these areas is considered important.

5. With reference to 2 (a) above, at what point are the services of the professionally trained counselor needed? In other words, what specifically does the teaching faculty not do in your program?

6. What improvements or changes would you make in any of the above?

The Students

7.

(a) Types of counseling in which students serve	(b) How successful	(c) Means by which they receive training	(d) How successful
____ Academic			
____ Vocational			
____ Personal-social			
____ Religious			
____ Health			
Other:			

8. If written materials are available on 7 (a) to 7 (c) above, how may they be obtained?

9. State why the use of students in these areas of counseling is important.

10. At what point are the services of professionally trained counselors needed to supplement the work of students? In other words, what does the student-counselor not do?

The Parents

11. What are the kinds of cooperation which your institution fosters with respect to the parents of students who are being counseled or guided?

    (a) Activity   (b) For what   (c) How
                                     purpose   successful

_____ Letters_____
_____ Conferences_____
_____ Home visitation _____
_____ Booklets-brochures_____
_____ Campus tours _____
Other:_____

Coordination

12. How is the work of the professional counselors, administration, teaching faculty, and the students drawn together (coordinated)?

    (a) Method of   (b) Designation   (c) How
            coordination   successful

_____ Director of counseling_____ Title:_____
       or coordinator or
       similarly named individual
_____ Committee (formal) appointment_____ Its name:_____
_____ Conferences (informal) _____ Explain: _____
_____ Seminars, workshops, etc._____ Under direction of: _____
Other:_____

13. What evidences do you have of the quality of the working relationships? Give examples of this working partnership.

14. What factors prevent the best type of coordination in your counseling program?

15. What changes in your program with reference to any of the foregoing do you foresee in the near future?

16. How do students learn of the counseling services available? How do faculty and staff learn of the services?

                                      _____
                                      Officer reporting

                                      _____
                                      Institution   Location

Appendix C
ORIENTATION PROGRAMS AND PRACTICES: A SURVEY

Please supply any of the information requested here that is not to be found in the printed material you are sending. If more space is needed, use the reverse side of these pages or additional sheets as you may wish. Your further comments on any of these, or other, items will be very welcome. Return to O. Bert Powell, Florida State University, Tallahassee, Florida.

Institution_____by_____

1. (a) When is your orientation program held with respect to registration and the beginning of classes?

   (b) What form does your orientation take? (i.e., testing and introductory activities, an extended lecture series, a course)

2. (a) When was your orientation program first begun?

   (b) What has been the general trend in terms of time and activities: to expand? to decrease?

   (c) What plans are seen for the future?

3. (a) What faculty or staff persons contribute to planning the orientation program?

   (b) Who is in charge of the program?

   (c) What persons help to carry out the program in its operation?

4. (a) For what students is the program planned?

   (b) What students aid in planning or carrying out the orientation program?

5. (a) What tests are given to new students as a part of the orientation process?

(b) What is the total testing time?

(c) How soon after testing are test results available?

(d) What use is made of test data, and by whom is it used?

(e) What referrals of students result from these tests?

6. (a) What social and recreational activities are provided in the orientation program?

7. (a) What preregistration counseling is available to new students?

(b) What, if any, preregistration counseling is required for new students?

(c) How is registration carried on? (i.e., by mail, on campus, over a period of time, everyone at same time, other)

8. (a) What evaluation of orientation program has been done by students, faculty, or others?

9. (a) On your campus what is generally accepted as the purpose of the orientation program?

10. (a) Have any unique or especially helpful practices developed? Please explain.

11. (a) What persons (students, parents, high school personnel for purpose of better college-high school articulation, etc.) receive the printed orientation bulletin?

(b) How is the bulletin delivered? (by mail, called for, only on request, etc.)

(c) When is the bulletin delivered? If it is delivered before arrival on campus, how long before?

RELATIONSHIP BETWEEN RESPONSIBILITIES ALLOCATED TO STUDENT PERSONNEL AREAS IN INSTITUTIONS OF HIGHER LEARNING IN THE UNITED STATES AND STUDENT PERSONNEL ADMINISTRATOR'S OPINION RATINGS OF THESE ALLOCATIONS

Function or Service	Responsibility Rating										vs.	Opinion Rating								
	A 1	2	3	4	5	B 1	2	3	4	5		C 1	2	3	4	5	D 1	2	3	4	5
Administration																					
The orientation of students	30	24	2				23	22	9				3	5	36	13	1				
The orientation of new faculty and staff	6	12	2			1	8	20	10				3	3	14	4			3	2	2
Procedures involved in the registration of students	9	5	1			2	17	31	8		1	1	4	8	12	5	1				
Policies concerning admission to the institution						1	20	27	8			4	10	54	13					1	
Policies concerning curricula offerings of the institution	46	24	2	1			4	12	5		1	1		2						1	
Regulations dealing with out of class student conduct							13	12			1		3	3	2		1				
Policies concerning probation and dismissal of students	16	12	1				31	32	2		2	1	24	58				1			
Policies dealing with faculty conduct						2	1	6					2	1	1						2
Disciplining of students	32	27	1			2	16	17	1		4	3	6	18	5			1	1		
Functions of undergraduate recruitment	4	6	3	1			20	31	3		4		6	18	3						
Policies dealing with student community relationships	16	23	1			2	18	33	5		1	3	8	3					1		
Assigning personnel functions to instructional staff	8	6				4	29	36	4		3		4	4						1	1
Employment of additional professional personnel staff	44	14				3	18	15	1		2		4	4						1	1
Defining job functions of professional personnel workers	58	12	1			3	15	10	1		1	1								1	1
Vocational guidance and placement																					
Vocational guidance and counseling of students	19	29	1				32	16	2		1	1	2	2	1			1	1		
Assisting students secure part time employment	40	21	4			2	24	2			3	2	9	4							1
Helping students obtain permanent employment upon graduation	13	14	2			1	19	14	3		1	13	8	7	3					1	1
Awarding of institutionally controlled undergraduate scholarships	16	7	1			1	33	23	2		1	3	3	7	3					1	1
The loaning of money to students	35	13	1	1	1	1	23	17	1		7	3	1	3			2	1		1	1
Collection of delinquent student loan payments	13	6	1				19	17	6		7	2	16	11			1			1	1
Health and remedial services																					
Providing health services for students	54	11					10	8			9	1	4	3		11	12	4	5	1	
Providing psychiatric services for students	32	7				1	10	7			3		5	1		15	14	5	5	2	
Providing dental services for students	9	1					5				1	3	2	5		14	5	6	24		
Providing remedial study skills services for students	15	10	1	1		1	25	20	3		5	1	5	5		5	2	2	3		
Providing remedial reading services for students	14	9	3	1		2	24	18	3		6	6	6	7		2	1	2	1		
Providing remedial speech and hearing services for students	7	1	1			1	24	21	3		11	9	10			1	3	3	4	1	
Providing health and accident insurance for students	25	10				1	13	9			3	1	3	6		7	7	4	7	4	

Source: Fred J. Vogel, "Study of Concepts and Practices Relating to the Allocation of Certain Student Personnel Responsibilities in Selected Institutions of Higher Learning in the United States" (104 institutions surveyed).

Function	A	B	C	D	(opinion rating counts)
Housing					
Assignment of students to dormitory rooms	70	3			3 7 · 2 2 · 2 1 · 4 4 · 1 1 · 1 1 · 2
Rules and regulations regarding on campus housing	58	11			5 14 · 2 5 · 1 1 · 1 2 · 1 1 · 3 3
Rules and regulations regarding off campus housing	61	11	1		1 14 · 3 2 · 2 1 · 2 3 · 1 1 · 3 3
Fixing and collecting rent of on campus housing	9	1	1		21 18 18 · 2 4 2 · 1 1 1 · 1 1
Functions relating to food services in dormitories	17	2	1		18 10 5 · 5 12 6 · 1 2 4
Functions relating to food services on campus	13	2	1		10 9 4 · 8 10 18 12 · 1 1
Counseling					
Over-all policies concerning the counseling of students	46	21	2		19 13 · 3 3 · 4 4 · 4 7 · 1 1
Academic advisement of students	7	18	3		13 35 9 · 7 1 · 5 2 · 2 18 · 1 6 · 1
Coordination of academic advisement of undergraduates	18	7	1		12 25 18 · 5 6 · 5 4 · 1 1 · 1 1
Collecting and maintaining personnel files on all undergraduates	54	20	1	1	2 12 7 · 1 1 1 · 1
Guidance and counseling of students with minor problems	34	19	2		1 17 29 · 2 2 · 2 2 · 1 26 · 2 3 · 1 1
Guidance and counseling of students with major problems	45	8	2		1 15 14 · 2 2 · 2 2 · 2 20 26 · 2 1 3 · 3 2
Guidance and counseling of faculty and staff with problems	2				1 10 20 3 · 2 20 · 2 26 · 2 1
Spiritual guidance and counseling of students	14	7	1		2 23 39 1 · 2 2 · 2 1 · 3 · 1 1
Activities					
Functions relating to fraternity activities on or off campus	52	17	1	1	1 9 2 · 6 10 35 25 · 7 1 1 1
Functions relating to sorority activities on or off campus	51	17	1	1	1 8 2 · 4 11 28 16 · 8 1 1
Student social activities	52	22	1	2	2 16 9 · 1
Intercollegiate sports	3	6	1		4 7
Intramural sports	5	4	1	1	14 13 5
Functions relating to student union activities	37	13	1	3	3 14 9 · 2 5 3 · 2 4 · 2 1 1
The assignment of space for out of class campus activities	30	7	1		21 17 · 5 3 · 3 1 · 6 1 · 2 2 · 1 1
Coordinating the campus activity and academic calendars	34	14	5	2	20 19 · 7 · 3 1 · 6 33 · 1 · 1 1
Functions relating to alumni activities	3	4	1		7 7 4 · 14 33 20
Encouraging off campus student participation in campus activities	29	20	3		3 24 15 · 2 6 14 · 1 1 · 1 · 2 1 · 1 1
Foreign student activities	25	18	6		1 27 10 1 · 2 1 · 1 · 2 · 2 · 6 1
Determining policies governing student publications	15	4			23 20 5 · 5 11 10 6 · 1 · 2 1 · 1
Student recreational (physical, hobbies, crafts, etc.) activities	7	8	3		37 23 3 · 1 6 11 2 · 1 · 2

Key for Interpretation of Table

The following letters indicate allocation of responsibility:
A – Sole responsibility of the student personnel area
B – Shared responsibility of the student personnel area
C – Not the responsibility of the student personnel area
D – This service is not provided at this institution currently

The following numbers indicate individual opinion rating of responsibilities:
1 – I believe this is the sole responsibility of the student personnel area.
2 – I believe this is primarily the responsibility of the student personnel area, but it may be shared with another division(s) of this institution.
3 – I believe this responsibility should be shared with another division(s).
4 – I believe that even though this is not essentially a student personnel responsibility, the student personnel area could share in it.
5 – I believe the student area has no responsibility for this function.

University of Rhode Island
Office of Advisement and Counseling
Marvin Rife, Coordinator

1 South Hall
January 27, 1956

SUMMARY OF SEMINAR FOUR
January 9 and 12, 1956

What is the place of faculty advising in higher education?

A. The first part of each session was devoted to presentation of significant trends in coordinated programs of advisement and counseling in higher education throughout the United States. Developments include:

1. Improvement in selection of faculty members best suited for advisement responsibilities

2. Orientation and in-service training for faculty advisers

3. Providing advisers with adequate background information about their advisees (personal and objective data)

4. Follow-up counseling with students referred by faculty advisers and others

5. Evaluation of the effectiveness of advisement programs

6. Involvement of faculty in active discussion of and deliberation upon problems in guidance of students

7. Obtaining student interest and participation in suggestions for improvement of faculty advising

8. Providing handbooks and other helpful information to faculty as guides for more effective advisement services

9. Stressing the student-centered approach to faculty advising, for the purpose of helping the student recognize and face his own problems, make his own decisions, and act responsibly upon such decisions

10. Making available to students information on sources of help from the university on problems related to improved academic performance (example: Problems? Here's Help! U. of Texas)

11. Developing improved means of effective communication with parents regarding the academic progress of students

12. Stimulation of greater concern for and understanding of the important supplementary services for student morale and academic efficiency:

    a. Counseling in student living quarters
    b. Creative and high quality student activities
    c. Preventive and remedial health services
    d. Concern for community influences
    e. Rapport with the commuting student
    f. Religious counseling

13. Bringing the results of research and other studies on academic advising to the attention of faculty, administration, and students

14. Long-range planning for development of adequate future facilities and services related to the improvement of academic performance of students

B. Discussion in the two seminar sessions emphasized the following issues:

1. What are the bases for mutual confidence and respect between faculty adviser and student? Loss of personal respect for faculty is often more serious than loss of academic respect. Students tend to respect firmness from a teacher so long as it has with it fairness and impartiality.

2. Do student activities play too large a role in campus life, to the detriment of academic achievement? Greater emphasis should be placed upon the quality of creative and cultural activities consistent with the high standards of the university. A larger proportion of the student body should be involved in active planning and participation in significant extracurricular activities.

3. Should all faculty members be faculty advisers? Many administrators operate on the assumption that competence to be a college faculty person implies competence to be an adviser. Actually, not all faculty have the interest and ability to perform this important function at a high level. It is the task of the in-service advisement program to work with the administration and faculty to improve the quality of advisement generally.

4. What kinds of knowledge, background, and skill are essential for competent advising? Most advisers operate along five basic channels in helping the student to help himself:

   a. Understanding the background of experience, aptitude, achievement and interests of each student. It is helpful that the faculty person was once a student himself and that he was once the same age as the student, since this may help to sharpen the adviser's perceptiveness of the advisee's goals and aspirations.

   b. Establishing rapport and a sound two-way communication relationship with the student. Initial interviews help pave the way for future contacts; some understanding of the dynamics of individual and group behavior is essential.

   c. Listening to the student and his expressions of interest and concern for the business at hand. Faculty adviser should be adept at restraining his own impulses to do a lot of talking.

   d. Interacting with the student in the cooperative exploration of his problems. Faculty adviser should know enough about the curriculum to give helpful information, but should recognize his limitations and be willing to call upon other university resources when he doesn't have the "answer."

   e. Not giving advice, but placing responsibility upon the student to weigh the evidence and make decisions within the framework of university policy. (This calls for review of the basic responsibility of the faculty adviser for the student's program. Should the student not be held responsible for meeting all the requirements of the university for graduation and for knowing what those requirements are?)

Florida State University
Office of Coordinator of
Counseling and Guidance

NOTICE OF APPOINTMENT TO FACULTY ADVISERS

The dean of your school has indicated that you have agreed to serve in the program of faculty advisement for the coming year. We are indeed happy to learn of your acceptance of this important University service.

At this time we are making preparation for the Fall Orientation Week Program. It is our plan to devote the morning of Wednesday, September 12, to the Seminar for Faculty Advisers, with time to be spent in group study of the new General Education requirements and related matters. A program of the Seminar will be sent you via campus mail in late July.

The Bulletin for New Students listing the details of Orientation Week will also reach you later. However, you may wish to hold the following items in mind as you view your departmental and area obligations for this period.

The Group Meeting with your students will be held Friday, September 14, from 11:00 a.m. to 1:30 p.m. In addition, you will be participating in the individual conferences with students on Monday (all day), Tuesday (half day), and Wednesday (all day), September 17, 18, and 19. Details of these meetings will be covered with you fully in the Seminar.

The staff of our office extends you best wishes for a good summer. Needless to say, we are looking forward to your participation in the program of University counseling and advisement this Fall.

Sincerely,

Melvene Draheim Hardee
Coordinator of Counseling

MDH: mm

September 9 and 10, 1955
Opperman Music Hall

FALL CONFERENCE OF THE
FLORIDA STATE UNIVERSITY FACULTY

Friday, September 9

9:00 - 9:30 a.m.   Welcome and Introduction of New Faculty Members: President Doak S. Campbell, presiding

The Student Honor Court: Barbara Graham, Chief Justice of the Honor Court

9:30 - 9:40 a.m.   General Session continued: Dr. Melvene Hardee, Coordinator of Counseling and Guidance, presiding. Introduction of platform guests from high schools of Florida and the State Department of Education.

9:40 - 10:15 a.m.   Symposium: "These are the Students, Teachers and Curricula of the High Schools of Florida"

Moderator: Dr. Harris Dean, Chairman, Florida Committee of the Southern Association of Colleges and Secondary Schools

"The Students in the High Schools of Florida": Dr. Joe Hall, Assistant Superintendent, Dade County Public Schools

"The Teachers and What They Teach in High Schools of Florida": Dr. J. T. Kelley, Director of the Division of Teacher Education and Certification, State Department of Education

10:15 - 10:30 a.m.   Recess

10:30 - 11:15 a.m.   Panel: "These Are the Students We Teach at Florida State University"

Moderator: Dr. R. R. Oglesby, Dean, Division of Student Welfare

"What the Students at Florida State University Think They Are": Dr. Ralph Witherspoon, Professor of Psychology and Director of Child Development Program

"What the Tests Say the Students Are": Dr. M. H. DeGraff, Director, Test Service Bureau

"What Happened to the Class Entering in 1950": Dr. W. Hugh Stickler, Director, Educational Research and Service

11:15 - 12:15 p.m.   Introduction of Speaker: President Doak S. Campbell

Address: "The Future of Higher Education in America": Dr. Benjamin Fine, Education Editor, New York Times

12:15 - 2:00 p.m.   Luncheon. Suwannee Room
Faculty members will be guests of the University

1952 SEMINAR FOR FACULTY ADVISERS AT FLORIDA STATE UNIVERSITY
CHAIRMAN: MEL HARDEE, COORDINATOR OF COUNSELING

8:30 - 8:40   Introductory Remarks: Dr. J. B. Culpepper, Dean, Division of Student Welfare

8:40 - 9:00   The Students Look at the Counseling Program: Students selected from freshman, sophomore, and upper level groups in panel discussion

9:00 - 9:20   An Evaluation of the Educational Counseling Program for Entering Students, 1951-52

9:20 - 10:00   Decision Making in Educational Counseling: A panel including the following faculty advisers:
       Miss Audrey Atherton, School of Education
       Miss Inez Frink, School of Business
       Dr. Vincent Thursby, College of Arts-Sciences
       Mr. Dean Johnson, School of Social Work

10:00 - 10:15   General Announcements

10:15 - 10:30   Recess

10:30 - 10:40   Distribution of Packets of Counseling Materials Assembled by Office of Coordinator of Counseling

10:40 - 11:00   Explanation of:
       The Decentralized, Coordinated Program of Counseling
       Use of the Directory of Guidance Services

               The Student and the Military Service: Arranged by Sam Baptista, Graduate Assistant, Office of Coordinator of Counseling

11:00 - 11:45   Timely Information about the Draft: Mr. John Flournoy, Director of Personnel Records

               Army Ordnance Program: Colonel Cornell D. Booth, Professor of Military Science and Tactics

               Air R.O.T.C.: Colonel Bernice S. Barr, Professor of Air Science and Tactics

12:00 - 1:30   Lunch

1:30 - 2:30   General Education: the Present Program at Florida State University: Dr. W. H. Stickler, Coordinator in Charge of General Education.

2:30 - 2:45   The Student Wishing a Short-term Educational Experience: Comments from representatives of particular schools.

2:45 - 3:15   The Plan for Orientation Week: Mel Hardee

3:15 - 3:30   Recess

3:30 - 4:45   Group meetings of counselors by special designation:
       Group I   Freshman counselors new to the program
       Group II   Freshman counselors with a year or more of experience in the program
       Group III Counselors for transfer students in the various schools

WORKSHEET FOR STUDENT CASES: OFFICE OF COORDINATOR OF COUNSELING

Name of student_____ Referred by:_____
Date:_____
In:_____
Case handled by:_____ To:_____

Problem as seen by referrer:

Request of referrer:

Collection of information: (use reverse also)
 1. Personnel record shows:

 2. Faculty adviser:

 3. Residence or day counselor:

 4. Teachers:

 5. Check with others (specify):

 6. Conference with the student:

Action taken to assist the student (brief outline by steps):

Reports: Personnel Records Office_____ Referrer_____ Additional reports (oral
 or written) to_____

Case continuing_____ closed_____ or_____ Date_____

SUMMARY OF PERSONAL DATA
(for educational counselors)

Counselor	
Office address	Phone

SECTION I
(Data obtained from Office of Personnel Records)

Name_____ Sex_____ Date of birth_____

Home address_____

High school_____ Location _____

Other colleges_____ Dates_____

Residence Counselor_____

Distribution of High School Credits

Academic Units	Units	Grades		Units	Grades	Nonacademic Units Subj.	Units	Grades
Languages___			Mathematics___			Agriculture___		
English___			Algebra___			Home econ.___		
French___			Pl. geometry___			Bookkeeping___		
Latin___			Trigonometry			Typing___		
Spanish___			Science___			Band___		
Social studies___			Biology___			Glee club___		
Civics___			Chemistry___					
History___			Physics___					

Data from Standardized Tests

High School Tests:

%

Psychological (19___H.S. Ed.)_ _ _ _____
English _ _ _ _ _ _ _ _ _ _ _ _ _ _ _ _ _____
Social sciences _ _ _ _ _ _ _ _ _ _ _ _ _____
Natural sciences _ _ _ _ _ _ _ _ _ _ _____
Mathematics_ _ _ _ _ _ _ _ _ _ _ _ _____

Orientation Week Tests:

Psychological:
   Q score _ _ _ _ _ _ _ _ _ _ _ _ _ _ _____
   L score _ _ _ _ _ _ _ _ _ _ _ _ _ _ _____
   Total score _ _ _ _ _ _ _ _ _ _ _ _ _____

Result of placement tests
   English_ _ _ _ _ _ _ _ _ _ _ _ _ _ _ _____
   Mathematics_ _ _ _ _ _ _ _ _ _ _ _ _ _____
   Music _ _ _ _ _ _ _ _ _ _ _ _ _ _ _ _____
   Foreign language _ _ _ _ _ _ _ _ _____

Vocational plans of students expressed on application_____

High school activities:_____

Name of student_____

Campus address_____

SECTION II

(Data to be obtained from student by Educational Counselor)

Educational Data

1. What was the size of high school senior class with which you graduated?_____
   _____ Your rank in class?_____
2. What school subjects did you like best?_____
3. What school subjects did you like least?_____
4. In what subjects were your highest grades?_____
5. In what subjects were your lowest grades?_____
6. What other colleges have you attended?_____
7. If you have transferred from another college, for what reason did you make the change?_____
8. What were your outside activities in sports, school paper, clubs, and organizations? (High School and College)?_____
   _____
   _____

Work History and Experience

If no record of work, check here_____

Job _____ Year_____
Duties_____ Wages_____
How long did you keep this job?_____
Employer_____ Address_____

Job _____ Year_____
Duties_____ Wages_____
How long did you keep this job?_____
Employer_____ Address_____

What are your plans for financial support in college?_____

Do you type?_____ Speed?_____Take dictation?_____ Speed?_____

Additional Information

1. Student's reason for coming to college_____

2. What personal benefit does the student expect from college?_____

   _____

_____
Educational Counselor

Please return to Mel Hardee
by October 17th if possible

TOPICS FOR DISCUSSION

To Heads of Clinical and Counseling Services:

A. In view of the meeting of director-heads of clinical and counseling services on October 9th, would you be interested in other meetings of this group in the 1956-57 school year? Please elaborate a bit on your answer:_____Yes_____No If you checked "yes" above, would you consider the following?

Frequency of meeting_____Nov._____Jan._____March_____April_____May (check) Suggested day of week and time:

Do you think refreshments are essential or not?

B. What type of meeting would you consider to be of interest to you or the group you represent?
_____1. Speaker and discussion
_____2. Discussion
_____3. Other:

C. What topics among these (or others) would you like to have covered?

_____1. An observer of the counseling program at FSU has commented, "I am alarmed at all the 'counseling' going on here." Is there a real basis for this alarm? What are the levels of (a) advisement, (b) counseling, (c) therapy, etc. that you see?

_____2. Limitations in counseling: If there are budgetary and staff limitations existing at FSU, can limits be set for (a) numbers of students accepted for "counseling" or remedial work and (b) length of time offered them for this specialized help?

_____3. "Preferential assistance": If only a certain number of students can be taken for remedial or therapeutic assistance, how shall they be selected?

_____4. Voluntaryism in counseling: To what extent can we rely on the student's voluntarily seeking counseling help? In what instances shall the referral for help be a requirement?

_____5. Cooperation with the home: In what instances shall the counselor enlist the support of or give information to parents? When shall the student be "protected from" the parent? Are there legal aspects as well as professional-ethical ones?

_____6. Motivation and tension: What degree of tension in the student is desirable with reference to his goal achievement?

_____7. Self-reliance or reliance on counselor: To what extent can the counselor rely on the resources within the student? To what extent is the manipulation of the environment of the student by the counselor advisable?

_____8. Adjustment for the college age: What are the evidences of optimum or adequate adjustment in the college student? Are these the same as for the non-college-going young adult population?

(Use other side for your suggestions about additional topics or a rephrasing of the ones above.)

ANALYSIS OF MIDSEMESTER UNSATISFACTORY STATUS

1. Student's evaluation of the probable causes of unsatisfactory status: (narrative statement)

Additional factors which, in the judgment of the student, pertain to specific subjects. Please indicate subject: (English, history, etc.). Check appropriate item.

	Subject	Subject	Subject
Do not study			
Have reading problem			
Do not hand work in on time			
Am excessively absent			
Am frequently late to class			
Do not spend enough time on lessons			
Have health or other personal problem			
Do not seek help from teacher			
Have poor background for subject			
Am not interested in subject			
Am working too much outside school			
Have too many outside activities			
Cause unknown			
Other			

_____
Signature of student

2. My evaluation of the foregoing with respect to the student's understanding of his problem is this:

3. In conference, the student and I effected the following action relating to the above:

_____   _____
Signature of adviser   Date

Note: This sheet is to be completed in conference with the student. If the student does not appear for conference, please turn in this form with notation.

This report is to be sent to the Office of Coordinator of Counseling on date specified.

END-OF-YEAR REPORT ON FRESHMAN ACADEMIC ADVISEMENT
For the Permanent Record in the Office of Personnel Records

_____ has been my advisee during the period of time between _____
_____ and _____. The summary below covers this period.

_____
Adviser's signature

1. With respect to academic performance, my advisee seems to have achieved (check in the appropriate space):

   _____ To the maximum of his/her ability
   _____ Almost up to his potential
   _____ Beyond what was expected of him
   _____ Below the level of his abilities
   _____ Inconsistently

2. Factors militating against his fullest achievement may have been (please estimate in your own words):

3. Factors aiding or stimulating achievement may have been (please estimate in your own words):

4. In the advisement of this student, the following actions were taken:

   (a) Referrals to:
   _____ Office of Coordinator of Counseling
   _____ Academic dean or department head
   _____ Instructors
   _____ Reading service
   _____ Speech clinic
   _____ English service
   _____ Help sessions
   _____ Residence counselor
   _____ University hospital
   _____ Other administrative offices or community agencies
   (list)_____

   (b) Other types of action:

5. Further attention should probably be given to these special needs:

6. Regarding my estimate of the student's progress, I should say (you may wish to consider such factors as maturity, use of time, study habits, initiative, cooperation, friendliness, concept of self and goals, social attributes, general progress and personal development, etc.):

Florida State University
November 19, 1956

MIDSEMESTER PROGRESS REPORT

We regret that this report to you is not an individualized one. With the time before the Christmas holidays being short, we find it necessary to use a general notification of this type.

Attached you will find a copy of the midsemester report sent to the student named. We are sure that you, the parent, will be interested in reviewing the report which indicates that the student is doing unsatisfactory work in three or more subjects. We call your attention to these things:

1. The report is issued for the purposes of counseling the student who is doing unsatisfactory work at midsemester. Unsatisfactory is here defined as "D" or "F."

2. It is our observation that students are often able to take action of a kind which will result in the improvement of the academic status by the end of the semester.

In this connection, we would suggest that the student (1) consult his faculty adviser or Dr. Melvene Hardee, Office of Coordinator of Counseling, 301 Westcott Building, who supervises the work of faculty advisers; (2) confer with the teachers of the courses in question; or (3) talk with other members of the administrative or counseling staff with whom he or she is acquainted.

The matter of the academic adjustment of first-year students at Florida State University is an important one. In this regard, we appreciate the cooperation of the parents and the home.

Charles H. Walker
Registrar

lh

Office of Coordinator of Counseling
301 Westcott

TABULATION OF DAILY CONTACTS

Date _____

	Personal	Telephone	Mail—outgoing
Office of President			
Offices of Academic Deans			
Department Heads			
Office of Registrar			
Dean of Student Welfare			
Office of Dean of Men			
Office of Dean of Women			
Office of Personnel Records			
Office of Student Aids			
Test Service Bureau			
University Hospital			
Educational Counselor			
Teaching Faculty			
Parent or Relative			
Clinician			
Speech _____			
Reading _____			
Psychological _____			
Psychiatric _____			
Other _____			
Residence Counselor _____			
Vocational Rehabilitation Office _____			
Veteran's Administration _____			
Students _____			

Special events:

A. and M. College of Texas

GUIDANCE SERVICES

Introduction

The following attempts to answer in part, at least, such commonly asked questions as, "What guidance services are available on this campus?", "What are the primary responsibilities of various offices and counseling personnel?", and "How can we avoid unnecessary overlapping and duplication of services?"

Many people on the campus contribute to the guidance effort: teachers, student leaders, military personnel, specially trained counselors, activity advisers, and medical personnel, to name but some. Special emphasis should be placed on the guidance role of the teaching staff member. Along with academic advisement and such individual counseling as time permits, is the unique opportunity afforded the teacher to observe students regularly. It is urged that all teaching personnel note out-of-the-ordinary behavior and make referral, wherever such seems wise, to the appropriate office, as indicated below.

It is suggested that this sheet be located for ready reference, either on your desk or on a nearby bulletin board. Your suggestions and active participation in the guidance effort of this campus are cordially welcomed and appreciated.

At-a-glance Guide to Guidance Offices and Services

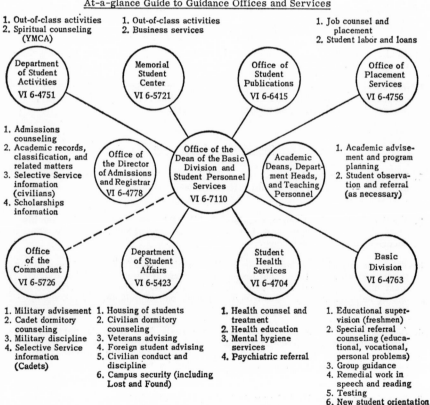

1. Out-of-class activities
2. Spiritual counseling (YMCA)

1. Out-of-class activities
2. Business services

1. Job counsel and placement
2. Student labor and loans

Department of Student Activities VI 6-4751

Memorial Student Center VI 6-5721

Office of Student Publications VI 6-6415

Office of Placement Services VI 6-4756

1. Admissions counseling
2. Academic records, classification, and related matters
3. Selective Service information (civilians)
4. Scholarships information

Office of the Director of Admissions and Registrar VI 6-4778

Office of the Dean of the Basic Division and Student Personnel Services VI 6-7110

Academic Deans, Department Heads, and Teaching Personnel

1. Academic advisement and program planning
2. Student observation and referral (as necessary)

Office of the Commandant VI 6-5726

Department of Student Affairs VI 6-5423

Student Health Services VI 6-4704

Basic Division VI 6-4763

1. Military advisement
2. Cadet dormitory counseling
3. Military discipline
4. Selective Service information (Cadets)

1. Housing of students
2. Civilian dormitory counseling
3. Veterans advising
4. Foreign student advising
5. Civilian conduct and discipline
6. Campus security (including Lost and Found)

1. Health counsel and treatment
2. Health education
3. Mental hygiene services
4. Psychiatric referral

1. Educational supervision (freshmen)
2. Special referral counseling (educational, vocational, personal problems)
3. Group guidance
4. Remedial work in speech and reading
5. Testing
6. New student orientation

Guidance Personnel: Their Duties and Limitations

Student advisers (Cadet officers, civilian housemasters, and aides): Guidance duties limited primarily to information giving, setting of good examples of college citizenship, and observation of own groups of students for "danger signals," with subsequent referral of problems noted. In addition, cadet officers provide guidance in military matters.

Tactical officers: Military guidance; cadet dormitory life and military discipline; guidance and supervision of cadet officers; and observation of individual students for problems, with subsequent referral, as warranted.

Civilian counselors: Primarily concerned with civilian group living conditions, including living unit government, activities, and student conduct. Also, guidance and supervision of housemasters, and observation of individual students for problems, with subsequent referral, as warranted.

Academic advisers (Teaching personnel, department heads, and academic deans): Primarily concerned with academic advisement and program planning of students enrolled in their respective colleges, with some attention to general student problems. Also, observation of students for problems, with referral to appropriate agencies, as warranted.

Counselors, basic division: Academic advisement of basic division students. Also, vocational planning, emotional counseling, and remedial assistance in reading, study skills, and speech, for all Texas A. and M. students.

Medical counselors: Physical and mental health treatment and counsel, and psychiatric referral.

Miscellaneous guidance personnel: Veterans adviser; foreign-student adviser; general secretary, YMCA (for religious counsel and referral): and manager, student labor and loans (for financial assistance).

The Making of Referrals

1. When any professional person sees that a problem is beyond his competency or area of responsibility, he should refer the student to more appropriate or specialized services.

2. A referral, in its best sense, consists of aiding the person concerned to see his problem, to want to work on it, to know where he can get help, and to take steps to secure appropriate assistance.

3. The basic attitude in referrals, as in all counseling, is a fundamental respect for the individual, and a belief that (except in extreme deviate cases) the individual must ultimately resolve his problem in his own way. The counselor's job is one of helping, but not "spoon-feeding"; it is one of guiding, but not manipulating.

4. Generally, staff personnel should make referrals directly to the person designated to handle the particular problem. Student advisers should, on the other hand (except in emergency situations), report problem cases to their Tactical Officer or Civilian Counselor, who will make the referral, if such seems wise.

5. Do not expect miracles to be worked on cases referred. Usually, basic attitudes are involved in behavior, and such are changed slowly.

HANDBOOKS AND GUIDES FOR FACULTY COUNSELORS
(Collected and examined by Hardee)

1. Alabama Agricultural and
   Mechanical College
   Normal, Alabama
   Guidance Handbook for Advisers

2. Alfred University
   Alfred, New York
   Handbook for Freshman and
   Sophomore Faculty Advisers

3. Arizona State College
   Tempe, Arizona
   A Manual for Faculty Advisers

4. Carleton College
   Northfield, Minnesota
   Manual for Counselors

5. Central Missouri State College
   Warrensburg, Missouri
   Adviser's Manual

6. Chico State College
   Chico, California
   Faculty Adviser's Manual

7. College of Wooster
   Wooster, Ohio
   Counseling Manual

8. Drake University
   Des Moines, Iowa
   Source Book for Counselors

9. Hofstra College
   Hempstead, New York
   Orientation at Hofstra: A Manual
   for Faculty

10. Kentucky State College
    Frankfort, Kentucky
    A Manual for Faculty Advisers

11. Kent State University
    Kent, Ohio
    A Guide for Faculty Advisers

12. Knox College
    Galesburg, Illinois
    Manual for Academic Counselors

13. Lindenwood College
    St. Charles, Missouri
    Notes to Counselors

14. Morgan State College
    Baltimore, Maryland
    A Manual for Faculty Counselors

15. New Jersey State Teachers College
    Newark, New Jersey
    Student Personnel Services

16. New Haven State Teachers College
    New Haven, Connecticut
    Student Personnel Services Handbook

17. North Dakota Agricultural College
    Fargo, North Dakota
    A Manual for Arts and Sciences
    Registration Advisers

18. Ohio University
    Athens, Ohio
    University College Counselor's
    Handbook

19. Ohio State University
    Columbus, Ohio
    Adviser's Manual for Education
    Survey 407

20. Sacramento State College
    Sacramento, California
    Manual of General Faculty Advising

21. San Francisco State College
    San Francisco, California
    Adviser's Handbook

22. Southeastern Louisiana College
    Hammond, Louisiana
    Handbook for Faculty Advisers

23. Stephens College
    Columbia, Missouri
    Manual for Advisers

24. Southwestern State College
    Weatherford, Oklahoma
    Junior College Advisory Handbook

25. University of Alabama
    Tuscaloosa, Alabama
    Faculty Advisers Manual

26. University of Bridgeport
    Bridgeport, Connecticut
    Handbook for Faculty Counselors

27. University of Connecticut
Storrs, Connecticut
Manual for Academic Counselors

28. University of Kansas City
Kansas City, Missouri
To You, the Faculty Adviser

29. University of New York
Buffalo, New York
Faculty Adviser Handbook

30. University of New Hampshire
Durham, New Hampshire
Handbook for Advisers

31. University of Wisconsin, College
of Letters and Science
Madison, Wisconsin
Advising Handbook

32. University of Wyoming
Laramie, Wyoming
Information for Faculty Advisers

33. Vassar College
Poughkeepsie, New York
Handbook for Academic Advisers

34. Wheaton College
Wheaton, Illinois
Counselor's Manual

35. Willamette University
Salem, Oregon
Manual for Faculty Advisers

Southern Illinois University

ACADEMIC ADVISEMENT CENTER

To New Students:

Welcome to Southern Illinois University! Your academic advisor is anxious to meet you and to talk with you about your plans for the coming year.

This university provides an opportunity for students to complete their registration for the Fall Quarter during the summer as well as during New Student Week. May I remind you that you may complete this advanced registration between July 11 and August 6 and August 15 and August 27? If you register during this latter period, you should come prepared to pay your fees. You should plan to arrive on campus to care for your entire registration prior to 3:00 p.m.

I hope you will take advantage of this advanced registration period. By doing so, you will find that the advisement and registration process is rather pleasant. You will also have a wider choice of courses than if you wait to register during New Student Week. Registration in advance does not excuse you from New Student Week, however, since many other activities are outlined for this week in addition to registration.

If you do find it convenient to register early, you may follow the steps outlined below:

1. Check your certificate of admission to determine to what college or school you have been admitted. (If you feel an error has been made or if you have changed your mind, contact the Office of Student Affairs.)

2. Check this folder to learn the name of your adviser and his appointment schedule.

3. Mail the enclosed appointment schedule card to the Academic Advisement Center.

4. Report to your academic adviser at the appointed time and bring with you your certificate of admission.

Sincerely yours,

Willis E. Malone, Secretary
Council of Chief Academic Advisers

Procedures for Determining Name and Office Hours of Your Adviser

1. Students should check their certificate of admission to determine the college or school to which they have been admitted.

2. Determine the name of your adviser from the information below.

3. All advisers for the colleges and schools on the main campus are located in the Office of Student Affairs Building on Harwood Avenue. The advisers for the Vocational Technical Institute are on the Southern Acres Campus in Building T2.

4. During this period of registration, July 11 to August 6, the office hours for the advisers will be as listed below.

5. During the registration period of August 15 to August 27 all of the advisers will be on duty from 8 a.m. to 12 a.m. and 1 p.m. to 3 p.m.

College of Education

Students admitted to the College of Education are assigned to advisers according to their major interest as outlined below:

		Mon. through Fri.
Mr. Willis Malone, Chief Academic Adviser		10:00 – 12:00
Business		1:00 – 3:00
Speech correction		
Undecided		
Miss Florence Denny		8:00 – 10:00
Art	Journalism	2:00 – 3:00
Foreign languages	Phys. ed. for women	
Home economics	Nursing education	
Mr. Neal Phelps		8:00 – 10:00
Elementary education		1:00 – 2:00
English		
Music		
Mr. Ernest Brod		8:00 – 10:00
Elementary education		1:00 – 2:00
Kindergarten-primary		
Special education		
Mr. Claude Dykhouse		Tues., Thurs., Fri.
Undecided	Industrial ed.	8:00 – 11:00
Geography	Social studies	Mon. and Wed.
Government	Sociology	2:00 – 5:00
History		
Mr. Cecil Franklin		10:00 – 12:00
Mathematics	Health ed.	1:00 – 2:00
Phys. ed. for men	Physics	
Botany	Zoology	
Chemistry		

College of Liberal Arts and Sciences

Students admitted to the college of Liberal Arts and Sciences may select one of the following advisers.

	Mon. through Fri.
Mr. Claude Coleman, Chief Academic Adviser	8:00 - 12:00
Mr. Amos Black	1:00 - 5:00

School of Business and Industry

Students admitted to the School of Business and Industry are assigned advisers according to their major interest as outlined below:

	Mon. through Fri.
Mr. Paul Hoffman, Chief Academic Adviser	9:00 - 10:00
Business administration	1:00 - 3:30
Economics	
Mr. Gallington	10:30 - 12:00
Industrial education	2:00 - 3:30
Pre-engineering	

Home Economics

July 11 - August 6   August 15 - August 27
Dr. Eileen Quigley   Mrs. Mary L. Barnes

School of Communications

Students admitted to this school are assigned to:

	Mon., Tues., Thurs., Fri.
Mr. Paul Hunsinger, Chief Academic Adviser	10:30 - 11:30
	1:00 - 2:00

School of Fine Arts

Students admitted to this school are assigned to:

	Mon., Tues., Wed., Fri.
Mr. David McIntosh, Chief Academic Adviser	9:00 - 10:00
	Tues. 2:00 - 4:00

School of Rural Studies

Students admitted to this school are assigned to:

Mr. John Hosner, Chief Academic Adviser	Thurs.	1:00 - 5:00
	Mon.	8:00 - 12:00
Mr. Herbert Portz	Tues., Fri.	2:00 - 5:00
	Wed.	10:00 - 12:00

Vocational Technical Institute

Students admitted to the Vocational Technical Institute are assigned to Mr. Harry B. Bauernfiend. His office is located on the Southern Acres Campus in Building T2.

SUGGESTIONS FOR REFERRAL

Area	What to Look For	Things to Do	Places to Refer Students for Help
Extracurricular	Overload Inactive but wants to get into things Low marks, question of too much to do In activities, but no chance for leadership Use of campus buildings for social affairs	Analyze time schedule to determine use of time Take to group meetings Report student's talents to group leaders	Dean of Men or Women Dean of University College Group officers Registrar
Social life	Not making friends Too popular for own group Shy and withdrawing	Introduce to others Take to social events	Dormitory Directors Dean of Men or Women Organization heads
Scholastic	Low marks Dissatisfaction with courses Inability to manage time properly Change or drop a course Admission or transfer of credits	Urge conference with instructors Help make time budget Study together or help contact others in class Tutor	Instructors Dean of College Dean of Men or Women Office of Admission
Health	Frequent colds Tired all the time Nervousness, irritability, constant worry Headaches and other evidences of eye strain or infection	Get student to health office Check on room lights Check on eating and sleeping habits	Health Office Dean of Men or Women Resident Counselor
Financial	Worries about money Talks about not being able to go more than a year Borrows money Spending a lot	Check with Personnel Deans on financial aid application Discuss money with counselee (individual or with group)	Dean of Men or Women Treasurer
Vocational	Worried because not vocationally decided Seems ignorant of job requirements Worries for fear no job will be open upon graduation	Refer to Personnel Dean Show career material in library and testing bureau Urge to take interest tests and get test interpretation	Dean of Men or Women Testing Bureau Library Dean of University College Placement Bureau

Area	What to Look For	Things to Do	Places to Refer Students for Help
Housing	Dislikes roommate Finds dorm noisy Room not satisfactory	Refer to house director Talk with roommate	Dean of Men or Women House director
Employment	Needs money Long work hours Dislikes work Sticks to one routine job that is of little training value	Refer to employment service or to Dean of Men or Women if a good student is in need of board or room	Dean of Men or Women Employment Bureau
Home	Gets a letter from home every day Rarely gets a letter from home Delays all decisions until parents have ruled Completely ignores parents in making decisions	Talk over home relations in early counselee meeting Encourage to write home once a week Encourage students to make decisions as they need to be made	Dean of Men or Women Dean of University College Resident or Dorm Counselor
Emotional	Extreme nervousness Extreme indecision Crying and outbursts Moodiness Threats of suicide Unpopularity	Encourage "talking out" problems Refer to appropriate people Be patient Don't judge	Dean of Men or Women Dean of University College Health Center
Religious	Loses faith Ignores religious activities Scoffs at religion Excessively "pious"	Encourage discussion Refer Recommend student to go to church with another student	Dean of Men or Women Minister, Rabbi, or Priest Dean of University College
Tests	Thinks he is dumb Worried about success Too confident of success Very undecided as to courses or vocation	Refer to Dean of University College or to Testing Bureau for tests, thorough test interpretation, and perhaps further tests	

Kent State University

YOUR GUIDE TO PERSONNEL SERVICES

This material will acquaint you with both the general and special personnel services which the University provides for all students. In addition to the regular faculty, there are other University offices and officers who are ready to assist you in achieving maximum success in your educational experience. The careful use of this material will aid you in availing yourself of these services, and also can help you avoid unnecessary mistakes.

These services are described only briefly here.

Most of your advising or counseling will be done with four persons or offices. These four, who are the core of the University regular guidance organizations, include:

Your Faculty Adviser

Is the first one to see on program planning
Can give answers to many problems
Is able to refer you to special services when you need intensive counseling
Must sign your registration cards, withdrawal slips and most forms connected with program

Your Personnel Dean
(Dean of Women - Dean of Men)

Is the one to consult on most general nonacademic problems, including problems of interpersonal relationships
Has general supervision of all extracurricular activities, including social activities and living arrangements
Will help you find the answers to any questions you may have about the University and its services
Is the one to see when you wish special consideration in any matter

The Director of Student Advising

Can assign you to a faculty adviser or discuss need for a change
Approves overloads
Advises on change of colleges or of curriculum objectives
Handles advisory problems beyond the scope of your faculty adviser

The Academic Dean's Office

Can clear up curriculum and course of study questions
Determines graduation status, probation and dismissal
Authorizes major and minor sequences, eligibility for certain programs within the college and all special academic permissions

Special Services for Student Problems

In addition, the University maintains some special services to help with your problems. These services are all:
Free
Confidential
Eager and ready to help
Easily approached
Your faculty adviser or any member of the university staff may suggest your using these and help you make an appointment.

The Guidance Testing Office

When do you use its services?
To help plan a vocational goal
To help plan a college program to meet that goal

What do its services include?
Gives aptitude and other tests
Counsels through interviews
Maintains a complete library of information about occupations
Helps you think through your problems of vocations

The emphasis is on helping you make your own decision.

How do you use it?
Go to 303 Kent Hall at any time to make an appointment.

Psychological Clinic

When do you use its services?
To help with personal problems arising from academic work
Social relationships
Self-adjustment
Future plans
Or when you have that "all mixed up" feeling

What do its services include?
Administers psychological tests
Gives personal counseling with a psychologist or a psychiatrist

Services are on an individual basis and are confidential

How do you use it?
Go to 219 Kent Hall any day that the university is in session to make an apointment.

The Reading Center
When do you use its services?
To improve your reading ability
To get any needed help on how to study effectively
To enrich your reading experiences

What do its services include?
Administers tests to evaluate your reading rate
Gives a series of lessons to improve your reading rate and skill
Gives help in how to study

How do you use it?
Go to 117 Kent Hall for information about enrolling in Speech 150.

Speech and Hearing Clinic
When do you use its services?
To correct any kind of speech or hearing problem such as
Poor articulation
Stuttering
A hearing loss
To improve your voice quality

What do its services include?
Diagnoses speech and hearing problems
Administers tests
Provides therapy for university students with speech or hearing handicaps

How do you use it?
Go to the clinic at 204 Kent Hall to make an appointment.

The Health Center

When do you use its services?
When you are ill, feeling below par, or notice any deviation from your normal well-being
Have questions concerning the healthful environment of the university or desire any health information

What do its services include?
The entire lower floor and a part of the third floor, staffed with physicians, nurses, health educators, and clinicians with X-ray, basal metabolism, electrocardiograms, and laboratory tests for your use each day school is in session
Regular hospital service (major surgical cases are not taken care of on the campus)

How do you use it?
Present yourself at the receiving room from 8:00 a.m. to 5:00 p.m. any school day (Saturday 8:00 a.m. to 12:00 noon); a hostess will direct you to the proper room
For any sudden illness outside these hours which is an emergency go to the health center, ring the emergency call bell and the nurse will come down to take charge of you; the nurse will put you to bed and contact the physician on call
There is an emergency call bell at each entrance

How do you get to the Health Center?
At any time, day or night, that you are unable to get to the Health Center through your own arrangements, you should do one of the following:
1. Call the campus police to take you
2. Call any of the city ambulances
These services are free to you.

The only foolish question is the one you don't ask!

Central Michigan College

TEACHER'S REPORT TO THE STUDENT PERSONNEL DIVISION

(Concerning students doing unsatisfactory work)

Concerning_____ Course_____ No. _____

Date_____ , 19____   Teacher_____

Do you wish the information on this report kept from the student?_____

If the interview with the Personnel Counselor brings out significant information

    affecting this student's progress in your course would you like a reply?_____

Which of the following difficulties are you reporting?

    Scholarship—present mark

    Personality problems—describe_____

    Other—describe_____

Other relevant facts:

What explanation has the student given you regarding the difficulty?

What suggestions have you given the student which might aid the Personnel Counselor

    in dealing with the problem?

Form SP 38

Central Michigan College
Student Personnel Division
Counseling Office

RESPONSE TO TEACHER'S REPORT

Dear_____   re:_____

Regarding your: Date:_____
____ SP-38 Form   ____ Note
____ Telephone call   ____ Absence report
____ Personal contact   _____ (other)

The following information is presently available:

Absences

_____ 1. Has withdrawn from college
_____ 2. Is withdrawing from college
_____ 3. Has been ill
_____ 4. Was called home
_____ 5. No adequate reason given for absences
_____ 6. Is withdrawing from your course
_____ 7. Has agreed to see you regarding his absences
_____ 8. Away on college-sponsored trips
_____ 9. Other_____

Grades

_____ 1. Student has not applied proper effort; will try to correct difficulties
_____ 2. Is doing poorly in several other courses
_____ 3. Poor reading skills
_____ 4. Inadequate background for course
_____ 5. Poor study habits
_____ 6. Student desires a conference with you
_____ 7. Has personal problems preventing study (I will contact you later.)
_____ 8. Has not learned to listen and take notes
_____ 9. Part-time job occupies too much time
_____10. Student appreciates your report and interest in his achievement
_____11. Appointment to see me has been made; will notify you of results
_____12. Student considers his case somewhat hopeless
_____13. Needs to reconsider choice of curriculum
_____14. No relevant causes for poor work discovered
_____15. Too occupied in social activities

Personal, Social, Emotional, Other Problems

_____ 1. Working with the student; will inform you of progress being made
_____ 2. Student does not desire help at this time
_____ 3. Referred student to _____

_____ Have been unable to contact student as of this date

Comments:

                                            Sincerely yours,
                                            _____
                                            Personnel Counselor

INTERVIEW REPORT FORM

1. Check the services listed below with reference to the frequency of your departmental use of them. In addition, in column 5 indicate the value of the service to your department by encircling the appropriate letter (E-excellent, M-medium, P-poor):

	Frequent	Occasional	Rare	Never	Value
Office of Dean of Student Personnel	____	____	____	____	E M P
Office of the Coordinator of Counseling	____	____	____	____	E M P
Office of the Dean of Men	____	____	____	____	E M P
Office of the Dean of Women	____	____	____	____	E M P
Office of the Director of Vocational Guidance and Placement	____	____	____	____	E M P
Office of the Director of Personnel Records	____	____	____	____	E M P
Office of the Registrar	____	____	____	____	E M P
University Health Services	____	____	____	____	
Test Service Bureau	____	____	____	____	E M P
Psychological Services (Dept. of Psychology)	____	____	____	____	E M P
Psychiatric Services	____	____	____	____	E M P
Speech and Hearing Clinic	____	____	____	____	E M P
Marriage and Family Counseling (School of Social Welfare)	____	____	____	____	E M P
Family Living Counseling (School of Home Economics)	____	____	____	____	E M P
Foreign Student Adviser	____	____	____	____	E M P
Residence Counselors (Men)	____	____	____	____	E M P
Residence Counselors (Women)	____	____	____	____	E M P
English Service (Writing Laboratory)	____	____	____	____	E M P
University Chaplain	____	____	____	____	E M P

What are your over-all comments with regard to the functioning of University personnel services for students? Be specific and constructive._____
_____
_____

2. Check the ways by which faculty departmental advisers obtain information about the availability of University-wide personnel services:
   ( ) University Bulletin (catalogue)
   ( ) Directory of Guidance Services (publication of Office of Coordinator of Counseling)
   ( ) Counseling and Guidance at FSU (publication of Division of Student Welfare)
   ( ) Word-of-mouth information from staff members
   ( ) Student's comments about the availability of the service
   ( ) Conference with the director of the service
   ( ) Visitation to the office or agency
   ( ) Others (describe):_____

3. Rank the following factors which serve as the basis of contact with the University student personnel services:
   ( ) Knowledge of the function of the office
   ( ) Personal acquaintance with head of service or staff
   ( ) Demonstrated efficiency of the service
   ( ) Others (describe): _____

4. In the following, indicate by encircling the letter A the statements which you feel illustrate the purposes and objectives of student personnel at FSU which are in agreement with the point of view of your department. Indicate by encircling the letter D the statements which you feel illustrate the purposes and objectives of student personnel at FSU which are in disagreement with the point of view of your department.

Appendix O

The University of North Carolina

Chapel Hill
August 10, 1957

The General College

308 South Building

OFFICIAL INFORMATION

To the Members of the Class of 1961:

In order that you may get to the University and be registered with the least possible confusion, I am calling your attention to the following schedule of what you should do:

I. BEFORE LEAVING FOR CHAPEL HILL:

1. You should have completed your arrangements for a room.

2. Be sure to tell your family and all who may be writing to you to use your room address on your mail. Mail without room address will have to be called for at the General Delivery window, and may be delayed many days in reaching you.

II. ON LEAVING FOR AND ARRIVING IN CHAPEL HILL:

1. If you have not had the North Carolina Entrance Tests you should leave in time to be in 106 Carroll Hall on Thursday morning, September 12, at 8:30. (Results of these tests are prerequisites for your registration). If you have had these tests, your first appointment will be in Memorial Hall at 7:00 Thursday evening as indicated below in paragraph IV.

2. Students come to Chapel Hill by bus, train, automobile, or plane. If you come by train you should buy your ticket to Durham, N. C. You should leave the train in Durham and take a bus from there to Chapel Hill. Planes arrive at the Raleigh-Durham airport.

3. Your trunk can reach here by express, train, or bus. If you come on the train and check the trunk to Durham, you may have the trunk delivered to your room by the express company.

4. The first thing to do is to locate your room. If you are renting a dormitory room, the key may be secured by the deposit of fifty cents at Room 2, New East Annex. Dormitories will be open for occupancy on the morning of Wednesday, September 11, 1957.

5. Students in dormitory rooms provide their own linen and personal supplies. The minimum consists of 4 single sheets, 1 pillow, 2 pillow cases, 2 blankets (in time for cold weather), and sufficient towels.

6. You may secure information that you need from the dormitory manager, the information desk on the first floor of South Building or from this office, South Building 308, third floor.

III. PAYMENT OF FEES:

All students should be prepared to pay their tuition and fees in full at the time of registration. The University operates under strict regulation fixed by State Law and the Trustees. The University accepts personal checks in payment of accounts, but to provide money for his own use each student should bring certified or travelers' checks. Only a small amount of cash should be brought because of the risk of loss.

IV. REGISTRATION:

The registration program proper begins with a meeting of the entire class of 1961 in Memorial Hall promptly at 7:00 P.M., Thursday, September 12. Bring a pen or pencil. The registration program includes physical and mental examinations, meetings with Advisers and Counselors, final registration for classes, talks by upperclassmen on campus life, and dormitory get-together meetings. This program begins at 7:00 P.M. Thursday and continues through the following Wednesday. It is **essential** that you be in attendance **right from the beginning.**

If I can be of any service to you between now and the time of your arrival, please write to me.

Cordially yours,
CECIL JOHNSON
Dean of the General College.

Note — IMPORTANT:

Your General College Adviser's name is ....whose office is South ....

You will be a member of Orientation Team Number ....

Bring this slip with you to the meeting on Thursday, September 12 at 7:00 P.M. You will have to know your Adviser's name and Orientation Team Number to find your proper place at the meeting.

SCHEDULE OF EVENTS DURING FRESHMAN WEEK, 1957

Every freshman is urgently requested to be present at Memorial Hall promptly at 7:00 o'clock on Thursday evening, the twelfth of September.

THURSDAY, 12th

8:30 a.m.   Meeting of all freshmen who have **not** had North Carolina Entrance Tests in 106 Carroll for instructions.

9:00 a.m.   and 1:30 p.m. English, Mathematics and aptitude tests for those who have **not** had North Carolina Entrance Tests. A freshman must take the North Carolina Tests even if he has had the College Entrance Boards or other comparable tests.

7:00 p.m.   Meeting of Freshman Class:
      Men in Memorial Hall, Jerry Oppenheimer, presiding.
      Women in 106 Carroll Hall, Sue Mayhew, presiding.

8:00 p.m.   Meetings with Advisers and Counselors. A detailed schedule of Orientation will be supplied each student at these meetings.

FRIDAY, 13th

8:30 a.m.   and following: Physical examinations as scheduled and NROTC and AFROTC interviews for those interested.

9:00 a.m.   to 1:00 p.m. Library Tours for those not scheduled for physicals.

1:00 p.m.   to 3:00 p.m. Honor System Lectures for Freshmen.

3:00 p.m.   Greek and Latin Placement interviews for all freshmen who have had two or more years of Latin or Greek in high school whether they plan to continue the language or not.

8:00 p.m.   General Assembly in Memorial Hall.

SATURDAY, 14th

8:00 a.m.   NROTC and AFROTC interviews.

8:30 a.m.   Physicals as scheduled.

8:30-10:00 a.m.   Library Tours.

1:30 p.m.   Language Placements for all freshmen who have had two or more years of French, Spanish or German in high school **whether they plan to continue the language or not.** These Placements not only aid in putting a student in the work for which he is best qualified but offer opportunities for advanced standing.

3:00 p.m.   Honor System lectures.

8:00 p.m.   Party on Tennis Courts with WCUNC freshmen as guests.

SUNDAY, 15th

Morning: Services in Chapel Hill Churches.

2:30-5:30 p.m.   Chancellor's Reception.

5:30 p.m.   Supper in the Churches.

8:30 p.m.   Student Government Meeting in Memorial Hall.

MONDAY, 16th

8:00 a.m.   Registration, as scheduled, at Woollen Gym.

1:30-4:30 p.m.   Physicals as scheduled.

8:00 p.m.   Faculty Panel, Memorial Hall.

TUESDAY, 17th

8:00 a.m.   to 5 p.m. Registration as scheduled.

8:30 a.m.   to 4:30 p.m. Physicals as scheduled.

WEDNESDAY, 18th

8:00 a.m.   to 5:00 p.m. Registration as scheduled.

9:30 a.m.   Tests for **ALL** freshmen.

2:00 p.m.   Tests for **ALL** freshmen.

THURSDAY, 19th

8:00 a.m.   Classes begin.

WELCOME TO THE UNIVERSITY

Chancellor Aycock, the Faculty Advisers, the Student Counselors, and I hope that each contact which the University has with you will express our pleasure in welcoming you into the company of Carolina students. We shall greet the incoming class at the reception on Sunday afternoon of Freshman Week.

AN EXPLANATION OF FRESHMAN WEEK

This is the thirty-third year that we have had a Freshman Week at registration time. It grew primarily from the necessity of helping freshmen like you to become adjusted. There is not a single item in this schedule that we can leave out, and we ask you to go through the whole of it. A student who has had the Entrance Tests will find his orientation somewhat simplified but he will need to be here for the whole period.

INTRODUCTION TO THE LIBRARY

In order to acquaint new students with the University Library, the Reference Department has arranged a series of lectures. These lectures will familiarize the student with the general reference books, card catalog, periodical indexes, and the general location of materials which he will need throughout his college career.

A test will be arranged on September 16 through 18 for all students whose previous experience will enable them to make use of the University Library with no further instructions. New students who pass this test will be excused from the lectures and problems. Students who feel qualified to take this test should apply at the reference desk on the second floor of the Library.

Because of their importance, the lectures are required. To receive any grades for the fall semester, freshmen, unless excused, must attend the library lectures and complete the problems accompanying them. These problems are brief exercises intended to give the student practice in the basic procedures necessary to effective use of the Library.

PHYSICAL EXAMINATION

The physical examination is the University Physician's and your means of learning about your physical condition. You must have completed the physical examination before registering.

ATHLETIC ACTIVITIES

All freshmen are encouraged to take part in some physical activity during Freshman Week and to acquaint themselves with facilities available. On completion of the physical examination by the University Physician, all facilities of the Department of Athletics and Physical Education will be available, including: (1) swimming pool, (2) handball and squash racquet courts, (3) badminton and volleyball courts, (4) softball, touch and tag football fields, (5) tennis courts.

AUTOMOBILES

By trustee regulation freshmen are forbidden to keep automobiles in Chapel Hill. The Office of Student Affairs may make exception in the case of a veteran, a commuter, or a handicapped student. Beginning in the fall of 1957 cars are forbidden to sophomores who have less than a C average.

MEETING WITH ADVISER AND COUNSELOR

Your General College Adviser and Student Counselors will meet with you and the others of your group immediately after the first assembly of the class on Thursday, September 12. They will explain more fully the program of the week and begin an active personal relationship which will continue throughout the year. Please remember this so as to do your part in registration without confusion or delay. (Your Adviser and Team number are indicated on page 1.)

OPPORTUNITIES DURING FRESHMAN WEEK

The way to approach the events of Freshman Week is to enter into all of them whole-heartedly and make your first week representative of what you hope will be a most successful four years. Meet your appointments faithfully and promptly. Get acquainted with the campus, your General College Adviser, your Student Counselor, and the members of your class. Make of your room an attractive place in which to live and work. Most important of all, get better acquainted with yourself by asking again what you really want to be and seeing clearly just how your college career can help you toward that end.

As you enter the University you become a part of a great tradition. We hope that you will have a better and fuller life because you have been here and that the University will be better and finer because you have been a part of it.

East Texas State Teachers College   February 20, 1957

LETTER TO PARENTS

Welcoming your sons and daughters to East Texas State Teachers College each spring is a pleasure to those of us on the staff. These first days are packed full of activities for both students and staff members. We would like to tell you something about the program of orientation during the first few days and counseling activities that follow.

We attempt to present activities designed to acquaint the student with the campus, the community, the college staff, and his classmates. Naturally, planned activities during three or four days do not begin to answer the puzzling problems of college life. For college becomes an individualized experience for each student by having a program of individual guidance. In this program a faculty counselor is assigned to each student. Thus each student has one particular faculty member to whom he can go for information about courses of study, different occupations, and for information on various other questions about college life. The main purpose of this program is to help each student succeed as a person and to get the most out of college life.

"Good" grades may not necessarily be the most important goal for students, but we feel that it is important to chart each student's academic progress. At mid-semester we check with instructors for information on the progress each student is making in his classes. Students having difficulties are invited to see their faculty counselors and other instructors who attempt to help them overcome the difficulties.

I am serving as your son's faculty counselor. We have already had a chance to do some talking about his course of study and plans, and I hope that he will feel free to return at any time. In this program we have set aside several periods during the semester for conferences.

If, in the future, you would like to discuss your son's progress, please feel that a letter or personal conference will be most welcome.

                                        Sincerely,

                                        Faculty Counselor

Hofstra College

LETTER TO PARENTS

To the Parents of Hofstra College Freshmen:

Approximately thirty faculty members have been chosen to act as advisors to the members of the freshman class at Hofstra College. During the first semester these counselors see the students individually for half-hour sessions about once every two weeks and meet them in groups of fifteen or twenty for an hour session twice a week.

This program of individual and group counseling is called Freshman Orientation and is designed to help your son or daughter make the necessary academic, social, and personal adjustment to college.

_____ has been named as_____
Orientation Counselor for the present academic year. This counselor will have a close personal relationship with each of the fifteen freshmen in his charge and will know each one of them better, probably, than anyone else in the College.

We have found that the counseling assistance given through Orientation can play a large part in the academic success and the personal happiness of beginning students at Hofstra. I hope that all parents will encourage their sons and daughters at Hofstra to take advantage of the services available to them through the Orientation Program.

You, as a parent, are free to get in touch with the counselor named above, either by phone, by letter, or by a personal visit to the College. If you prefer to get in touch with me and let me help you make contact with the counselor, I shall be very happy to hear from you.

Sincerely yours,

Randall W. Hoffmann
Associate Dean of Students

P. S. A description of the Orientation Program of Hofstra College appears inside

Freshman Orientation at Hofstra

When young men and women start their college careers at Hofstra, they are usually at a stage of life characterized by (1) a desire to be independent of parental control, (2) a somewhat unrealistic notion of their ability to cope with life's problems, great or small, and (3) a tendency to feel reluctant to seek out help when they need it.

Here at Hofstra we realize that such attitudes can make life somewhat difficult, and we have tried to set up a safeguard against them. We know that many young men and women of eighteen are not yet completely ready for independence, and that they are not able alone to cope with all of life's problems. We also know that when a counseling service becomes an automatic part of their freshman program they do not feel hesitant to take advantage of it.

Hofstra College has set up just such a counseling service—called Orientation—in which all freshmen are required to enroll for the first semester and for which they receive college credit toward the requirements for graduation. Each student becomes a member of a small group which meets with the counselor for three hours each week, at which time the student has the opportunity of learning such skills as study habits and techniques, notetaking, report writing, and time budgeting. If his psychological tests show that he is having difficulty with reading, he is assigned to Orientation 1, which combines all the features described herein with intensive training in reading. This training will stand the student in good stead all through his college career.

At the group meetings he also can learn the place of extracurricular activities in the college picture, can bring up, and have discussed, his problems of vocational choice, can add to his knowledge of social usage and to his skill in human relations. In addition to all this he can, in the group or in individual conferences with his counselor, give voice to whatever personal problems he may have and with the guidance of the counselor approach a solution for some of these problems.

These counselors are selected for their warm interest in students as persons, for their knowledge of the academic and extracurricular organization of the College, and for the wisdom they can bring to bear on the problems of young people. They give generously of their time and energy. Their purpose, however, is not to force unwilling students to work, neither is it to guarantee that inferior students will succeed, nor is it to do for the student what the student should do for himself. Rather their purpose is to usher the student toward an acceptance of his responsibility to himself and society, to help him learn how to handle the freedom and independence he is trying to achieve, and finally to help him learn how to make the most out of college and how to let college make the most out of him.

These aims cannot be realized without the help of the parents. You can supplement and reinforce the work of the Orientation Counselor in several ways:

1. By encouraging your son or daughter to make and keep a close, friendly relationship with the Orientation Counselor.
2. By encouraging regular hours of study. (It should be remembered that college is a full-time job and that a student taking a normal program would find it necessary to spend about four hours per day, seven days a week, in study and preparation.)
3. By a quiet but insistent emphasis on the fact that achievement in the other important aspects of college life is meaningless without success in the academic subjects.

The Dean of Students Office

When an Orientation Counselor is presented with problems that require specialized attention, he has available the counseling services of the Dean of Students Office. Students are referred to this office who are having more than the usual difficulties in personal and social adjustment, in finding their vocational objectives, in acquiring the skills necessary for scholastic achievement, and the like.

The Dean of Students Office is staffed by competent counselors, is equipped to get at the root of most difficulties encountered by college students, and is ready to help any student in working out his personal problems. Parents should feel free to telephone, write, or visit the Dean of Students Office for information about the College or for help in understanding the problems confronting their son or daughter at Hofstra.

Hofstra College   Hempstead, New York   Ivanhoe 9-7000

Stephens College

ADVISER'S ANNUAL REPORT

Name of advisee	Name of advisor	Date

Please check in appropriate column at right:

	Superior	Above average	Average	Below average	Poor	No basis for judgment
Adaptability.						
Alertness						
Appearance						
Common sense.						
Consideration for others . . .						
Cooperation						
Industry						
Initiative						
Judgment						
Leadership ability						
Manners (etiquette).						
Punctuality						
Responsibility						
Trustworthiness						
Vitality						

Please check appropriate phrase or phrases below:

1. Attitude toward college regulations

_____ Actively cooperative
_____ Cooperative
_____ Constructively critical
_____ Passively accepts them
_____ Conformative but not constructive
_____ Destructively critical
_____ Other:_____

2. Relations with others

_____ Exceptionally well liked
_____ Well liked and accepted
_____ Accepted by small group
_____ Unnoticed by others
_____ Avoided by others
_____ Member of nonconformative group
_____ Other:_____

3. Emotional stability

_____ Exceptional balance
_____ Well balanced
_____ Usually well balanced
_____ Easily moved to anger or de-
            pression
_____ Unresponsive and apathetic
_____ Constantly upset
_____ Other:_____

4. Family and social background

_____ Conducive of wholesome develop-
            ment
_____ Conventionally good (average)
_____ Certain difficulties
_____ Seriously interferes with develop-
            ment
_____ Suitable development in spite of
            background
_____ Other:_____

5. Self-confidence

_____ Wholesomely self-confident
_____ Reasonably assured
_____ Uncertain of self in new situations
_____ Completely lacking in assurance
_____ Unsure of self and aggressive
_____ Unsure of self and withdrawn
_____ Other:_____

6. Oral expression

_____ Exceptional facility
_____ Converses easily and naturally
_____ Conventionally correct (average)
_____ Sometimes awkward and slipshod
_____ Persistent difficulties
_____ Other:_____

Please answer to the best of your ability:

Has she had financial assistance?

Will she need financial assistance for further training?

If not graduating or returning, why?

What is her class attendance record?   Health?

What are her special abilities and talents?

What handicaps or limitations does she have?

Do you recommend her for further schooling? with reservations?
    without reservations?   (explain if "with reservations")

Do you recommend her for employment? with reservations?
    without reservations?   (explain if "with reservations")

Extraclass record: Please list those activities in which she participated while at Stephens and comment on the degree of her participation, i.e., membership only, actively interested, held office, acceptance of responsibility in this area, etc. Please list any special honors or achievements.

Summary essay: (Refer to Manual for Advisers, page 2-10 for sample.)

Appendix R-2

ANNUAL REPORT FORM – 1956-57
SPECIAL COUNSELING AND PERSONNEL SERVICES

Name of counselor reporting_____

1. Quantitative data summary

____Number of students counseled this year

____Estimated number seen on short-term basis (once or twice)

____Estimated number counseled over an extended period (more than twice)

2. Referral sources:

____Estimated number of students referred by advisers

____Estimated number of students referred by residence counselors

____Estimated number of students who were self-referred

____Estimated number from other sources such as teachers, admissions coun-
selors, etc.

3. Appraisal of results of counseling (make a statement in space below concerning
following points):

   (a)   Attitude of the students toward the counseling given them.

   (b)   Type of problems encountered this year. (Differences and similarities in
quality, quantity, acceptance of responsibility for working on their problems,
etc.)

   (c)   Observations and judgments as to percentage of counselees showing:

   ____ Apparent improvement (in behavior, attitudes, or received the information
needed)

   ____ No apparent change

   ____ Insufficient evidence for judgment

   (d)   Needs and/or other comments:

Return to: Eugene L. Shepard on or before May 20.

Stephens College

EVALUATION OF COUNSELING

The Counseling Service staff is interested in evaluating the effectiveness of its counseling. One means of doing this is to secure the observations and opinions of those who have referred students for counseling. Our records indicate that _____ _____came to the Counseling Service at your suggestion. Will you please check these questions in regard to this student.

1. Why was the student referred? Please check one or more of the appropriate responses.

   Personal problem   _____

   Educational and/or vocational planning   _____

   Achievement-ability discrepancy   _____

   Other (specify)   _____

   _____

2. Do you feel that the student benefited from the counseling?

   Yes   _____

   Apparently, but it is too early to tell   _____

   No   _____

   No basis for judgment   _____

3. If your answer to no. 2 is <u>favorable</u>, please check one or more of the following. As a result of the counseling the student appears

   To have achieved some self-understanding   _____

   To have acquired needed factual information   _____

   To be more self-directed   _____

   To evaluate herself more realistically   _____

   Other (specify)   _____

   _____

4. If your answer to no. 2 is <u>no</u>, please check one or more of these responses. The student

   Learned nothing about herself she didn't
   already know   _____

   Appeared to view herself in much the same
   way as she did prior to counseling   _____

   Was disappointed in the counseling   _____

   Other (specify)   _____

   _____

5. Other comments which you feel might be helpful to us in terms of improving our services:

Stephens College

STUDENT OPINION SURVEY

The Counseling Service staff is eager to secure your opinions regarding the effectiveness of the counseling being done this year. One means of doing this is to get the judgments and the reactions of those who have been to the Counseling Service. Will you please answer the following questions and return the sheet to us in the envelope provided.

1. For what reasons did you come to the Counseling Service? Check one or more if appropriate.

   A personal problem   _____

   An emotional problem   _____

   Educational or vocational planning   _____

   Other (specify)   _____

   _____

2. Do you feel that you benefited from the counseling?

   Yes   _____

   Apparently, but it is too early
        to tell   _____

   No   _____

3. If your answer to no. 2 is <u>favorable</u>, please check as many of the following as apply. As a result of the counseling I feel that

   I have achieved greater self-
        understanding   _____

   I have acquired needed factual
        information   _____

   I am more self-directing and
        less dependent   _____

   I received needed reassurance   _____

   I am able to evaluate myself
        (strengths and weaknesses)
        more realistically   _____

   Other benefits (specify)   _____

   _____

4. If your answer to no. 2 is <u>no</u>, please check one of the following. I feel that

   I learned nothing about myself that
        I didn't already know   _____

   I was disappointed in the counseling   _____

   Other (specify)   _____

   _____

5. Other comments which you feel might be helpful in terms of improving our service. Please be frank.

Florida State University
Subcommittee on Counseling
University Study Committee

EVALUATION OF STUDENT ADVISEMENT

Introductory Remarks

In evaluating student educational advisement services provided by faculty advisers, any study must recognize that at FSU separate provision is made for (1) advisement of freshmen students, (2) advisement of upperclass students and (3) advisement of graduate students. The former program is carried out by what are now called "educational counselors" under the supervision of the Coordinator of Counseling, while the latter two services are provided through departmental activities, under the general direction of the school or college concerned. The accompanying questionnaire is concerned only with advisement services provided for upperclass and graduate students.

In the following material, a distinction is made between (1) advisement functions provided primarily within the department and (2) advisement functions involving other university student personnel services. (Note: this same distinction will apply to the program of freshmen advising when it is reviewed by questionnaire at a later date.)

As department members consider the following questions, they are urged to seek a group agreement on the best answer, i.e., a departmental opinion is desired. Where complete agreement is not possible, and there may be several such instances, opportunity is provided at the conclusion of the questionnaire for a "minority report". In cases where some faculty members dissent from the departmental stated opinion, they are urged to utilize this part of the questionnaire in explaining their position.

Glossary of Terms

Educational advisement: A term used to denote services provided by faculty members to students wherein attention is given to individual and group assistance in furtherance of educational planning and adjustment.

In-service training: A general expression used to include a variety of professional procedures seeking to upgrade, through on-the-job training, those persons working directly with students (example: case conference, lectures by professional people in guidance and personnel, orientation sessions, seminars, course work, planned departmental discussions, supervision by trained personnel workers, etc.).

Student personnel services: Refers to the administrative organization and facilities for meeting various adjustment needs of students in colleges or universities. Does not include the curriculum, but may include such services as counseling services (which include educational, vocational, personal-social, and health), admissions, personnel records, clinical services, and personnel research units.

Group methods: Similar in meaning to "group guidance," i.e., group approaches to meeting the adjustment needs of students. Includes such activities as certain classes (occupational investigation and self analysis), orientation meetings, selected club programs, seminars, discussions, and lectures which deal with specific phases of student problems.

Guidance: A term generally applied to elementary and secondary schools and counseling centers where individual adjustment services are available; has broader application relating to education; refers also to the developmental experiences that an individual undergoes in resolving his difficulties; is not limited to vocational or educational problems.

Coordination: The process of integrating and cooperatively organizing a series of varied yet related personnel services toward a more effective over-all program.

Counselor: A term reserved for persons with some degree of professional training who work with individuals in resolving personal, vocational, educational, or other problems; the professional training varies with the institution and the individual, but should include work in psychology and education, as well as personnel techniques (principles of guidance, methods of testing and approach, counseling functions, informational services, organization of student personnel service, and techniques of placement and follow-up.)

Part I. Academic Advisement of Upperclass Students

This section of the questionnaire pertains to the educational advisement of upperclass students (sophomore, junior, and senior) and is not intended to include a consideration of the University-wide program of freshman advisement (which is a separate function of the Office of Coordinator of Counseling), or of the advisement program of graduate students.

1. Check the person responsible for the coordination and supervision of departmental upperclass advisement activities:

   ( ) none   ( ) Department
   ( ) Dean   ( ) Specially designated person
   ( ) Assistant Dean   (title):_____
   ( ) Department head   _____

2. Check the bases upon which the individual doing the coordinating and supervising of departmental upperclass advisement is selected:

   ( ) Aptitude   ( ) Point of view
   ( ) Interest   ( ) Free time
   ( ) Leadership ability   ( ) Other (describe):_____
   ( ) Maturity   _____

3. To what extent does this individual in charge of departmental educational advisement encourage faculty participation in planning the advising functions:
   ( ) Regularly seeks faculty suggestions for planning
   ( ) Occasionally seeks faculty suggestions
   ( ) Never asks for faculty suggestions

4. Check the person(s) responsible for the educational advisement of upperclass students who are majors in your department:

   ( ) Dean   ( ) Department teacher
   ( ) Assistant Dean   ( ) Specially designated person
   ( ) Department head   (title):_____

5. Rank in numerical order the relative importance your department places upon the bases on which these persons are selected for advising duties:

   ( ) Aptitude   ( ) Maturity
   ( ) Interest in advising   ( ) Point of view
   ( ) Personality traits   ( ) Free time
   ( ) Training   ( ) Other (describe):_____
                                _____

Appendix S   371

6. Rank in order of desirability the following areas of professional preparation for educational advisers:

(   ) Subject-matter competency
(   ) Knowledge of counseling techniques
(   ) Knowledge of tests and measurements
(   ) Knowledge of principles of vocational guidance
(   ) Psychology of individual differences
(   ) Others (list):_____

7. Rank in order of usage those of the following in-service training procedures employed in your department:

(   ) Group discussions
(   ) Special courses
(   ) Reading of printed materials
(   ) Department head lectures
(   ) Outside nondepartment speakers
(   ) Others (describe):_____

8. In terms of the following scale, insert the number of advisees assigned to the typical upperclass adviser:

(   ) Minimum
(   ) Average
(   ) Maximum

9. In making adjustments to the teaching load of faculty members who are assigned upperclass advising functions, which of the following are considered as equivalent to advising duties (use average load in #6 above as a basis for answering this question)?

(   ) No adjustment made
(   ) One 3-hour class
(   ) A field or extension duty
(   ) A year-long committee duty
(   ) A year-long research project
(   ) Other (describe):_____

10. Check the statement which best describes your intradepartmental coordinative activities in relation to upperclass student advisement activities:

(   ) Regular and consistent attempts made to plan and provide for advisement functions.
(   ) Occasional and sporadic attempts made to plan and provide for advisement functions.
(   ) No attempt made to plan and provide for advisement functions.

11. Check the phrase which best describes interdepartmental coordinative activities concerning student advisement services:

(   ) Hold regular meetings with other departments within the school or division.
(   ) Meet with other departments on occasions for purposes of discussion.
(   ) Work in isolation; never meet with other departments within the school.

12. Check the appropriate column best describing services available for special groups of students:

	Transfer	Foreign	Failing
Special provision for advisement	_____	_____	_____
Limited provision for advisement	_____	_____	_____
No special provision made for advisement	_____	_____	_____

13. Which of the following statements best describes the viewpoint of your department with regard to the basic responsibility for decision-making in the advisement of upperclass students?

( ) We recognize and subscribe to the philosophy that the student's independent judgment is of basic importance.

( ) We are aware that the student's independent judgment is important but may be influenced by the maturity and experience of the counselor.

( ) The maturity and experience of the adviser justifies ignoring the student's judgment.

14. To what extent do upperclass faculty advisers in your department discuss as a group the importance of considering the personal integrity of the student in contrast to the possible bias of judgmental thinking of the faculty-adviser?

( ) Frequent discussions
( ) Occasional discussions
( ) No discussions

15. To what extent is there lack of agreement among departmental advisers about serving the best interests of the student and serving the best interests of the department? (Examples: student recruitment versus individual needs of students; employment trends and societal needs versus individual needs of students; etc.)

( ) Considerable lack of agreement
( ) Moderate amount of agreement
( ) Considerable agreement

16. Indicate in order of importance the most commonly used methods of acquainting students with vocational opportunities:

( ) Included as part of introductory required course
( ) Suggest exploratory courses
( ) Recommend interview with expert in the field
( ) Point out pertinent readings in current publications
( ) Suggest visitation to offices, businesses, institutions, etc.
( ) Others (describe):_____

17. Rank in order of importance the sources used within the department for obtaining information about the student:

( ) Standardized achievement tests
( ) End-of-course examinations
( ) Case conference or faculty group discussion
( ) Anecdotal records, rating scales, check-lists, etc., noted by department faculty
( ) Personal conferences
( ) Other (describe):_____

18. Check the appropriate column in relation to data which would help your department in gaining a better understanding of your students:

Data Source	Pertinent	Would Be Desirable	Available and Used	Available and Not Used
ACE test	_____	_____	_____	_____
Minnesota personality test	_____	_____	_____	_____
General culture test	_____	_____	_____	_____
Family background	_____	_____	_____	_____
Grades from high school	_____	_____	_____	_____
Scores from high school tests	_____	_____	_____	_____
Grades made in college	_____	_____	_____	_____
Extracurricular activities engaged in high school and college	_____	_____	_____	_____
Work experience	_____	_____	_____	_____
Other (describe):	_____	_____	_____	_____

19. Does your department sponsor printed materials to facilitate the educational advisement of your students? Yes____No____.
Describe:_____

_____

20. Check the appropriate statement regarding the procedures by which departmental advisers function as resource people for the teaching faculty on common problems of students:

( ) Organized and systematic exchange of student information
( ) Casual and informal exchange of student information
( ) Advisers not used as resource people

21. As a department, do you feel that classroom instruction has been influenced by advisement responsibilities? Yes____No____If yes, list specific ways in which teaching practices have been affected:_____

_____

22. In advising students, how extensively does your department relate group methods with individual advisement procedures?

( ) Regular efforts to integrate group advisement and individual student advisement
( ) Sporadic efforts to integrate group advisement and individual student advisement
( ) Relatively little effort to integrate group advisement and individual student advisement

23. List the most effective methods employed by your department in coordinating group work (e.g., seminars, exploratory courses such as Ed. 105, etc,) with individual advisement:_____

_____

24. How adequate for advisement are your departmental physical facilities (sufficient space, type of room, equipment, privacy, etc.)?

( ) Adequate
( ) Acceptable but limited
( ) Inadequate

25. Indicate by checking for each level the type of administrative support given advisement activities in your department:

Support	By Departmental Administration	By School or College Administration
Strong	_____	_____
Limited	_____	_____
Weak	_____	_____

26. List specific improvements relative to administrative support of the advisement program that would be desirable from:

Departmental Administration	College or School Administration
_____	_____
_____	_____
_____	_____

27. State any specific administrative procedures that would provide a more effective basis for voluntary student adviser contacts, i.e., avoiding required conferences, yet encouraging greater utilization of departmental advisers:_____
_____
_____

28. Indicate the approximate average annual turnover of educational advisers in your department.

( ) 0% -24%   ( ) 25% -49%   ( ) 50% -74%   ( ) 75% -100%

29. What suggestions can you offer to reduce undesirable turnover among departmental educational advisers?_____
_____
_____

30. Does the same adviser normally stay with the upperclass student throughout his college course? Yes____No_____

31. List any suggestions for the improvement of departmental upperclass advisement services:_____
_____

32. Departmental minority reports in regard to the answers supplied for Part I of this questionnaire are requested on separate sheets (to be attached at this point in the report).

Part II. Relationships with Student Personnel Services

The following questions are directed toward determining the relationship between upperclass educational advisement (that which is above freshman level) and the other University student personnel services.

Grinnell College
Faculty Counseling

INTERVIEW REPORT FORM

Do not write here   Student_____

Read by   Date_____
Dean _____
                                           Counselor_____
Director of Counseling_____

Use ratings where applicable by circling appropriate words. Rate only those characteristics observed in this interview. Write a summary on the back to amplify ratings, or give additional information if needed.

1. Personality and social adjustment

Adjustment to roommate	Unusually happy	Normal	Unhappy
Emotional control	Overcontrolled, inhibited	Poised, relaxed	Emotional excess
Home adjustment	Indifferent	Normal relations	Worry
Adjustment to college living	Dissatisfied, fearful	Fits in well	Enthusiastic
Social participation is source of	Satisfaction	Normal concern	Real worry
Health is source of	No undue concern	Necessary concern	Undue worry
Relations with instructors seem	Very good	Average	Strained

2. Academic and vocational adjustment

Grades are	Weak	Average	Strong	Improving, becoming poorer
Grades cause	No concern	Usual interest		Real worry
Study habits are	Poor	Good	Superior	Improving, becoming poorer
Study habits cause	No concern	Normal concern		Real worry
Were college requirements discussed in this interview?			Yes	No
Vocational goals are	Undefined	Tentative	Well defined	Realistic, unrealistic
Thinking about vocation is	Indifferent		Constructive	Anxious
Are financial problems uppermost in the student's thinking?			Yes	No

3. Additional information (including examples and comment):

A D The consideration of the total educational experience of the student is of more importance than is the single consideration of vocational competence.

A D The student's choice of a major should be based upon his interest and abilities rather than the need of departments to build enrollment.

A D The high school background and achievement of the student are points to be considered in predicting the student's performance in college.

A D The out-of-class experiences of the student will effect performance within the classroom.

A D The aims and objectives of parents need to be considered in viewing the performance of college students.

5. The following are considered to be basic policies underlying sound student personnel administration. Please encircle the appropriate letter which indicates your reaction to each of the following statements (A–agree, I–in doubt, D–disagree). Fundamental needs in student personnel administration are:

(a) To achieve a better degree of integration between the student personnel programs in secondary schools and institutions for higher learning A I D

(b) To achieve a higher degree of integration between the Student Personnel Service and instructional programs A I D

(c) To assist college administrators in translating the student-centered concept of education in specific institutional objectives against which the effectiveness of the institution can be measured A I D

(d) To bring about wider recognition of the fact that if adequate personnel services are desired they must have a substantial and secure place in the institutional budget A I D

(e) To develop over-all administrative plans and procedures which will enable the specialized personnel staff to integrate their work with other phases of the institutional administration A I D

(f) To improve both quality and quantity of research on the instruments, processes, and programs of student personnel work A I D

(g) To provide for the active participation of students in shaping policies and procedures of the student personnel program A I D

(h) To make better use of advisory committee in improving integration between various student personnel services; for example, establishing an advisory committee of students, faculty, and administrators to work with the Office of Coordinator of Counseling A I D

(i) To develop student personnel services primarily in view of a systematic study of needs of students A I D

6. Check the items below which would indicate the manner in which University student personnel services can be better coordinated with departmental educational advisement:

( ) A study of needs of the department with reference to educational advisement (study made by whom?):_____

( ) Provide greater release of time for members of the department for purposes of visitation and conference with special University officers (name such officers):_____

( ) Others (describe):_____

7. Departmental minority reports in regard to the answers supplied for Part II of this questionnaire are requested on separate sheets.

Florida State University

STUDENT QUESTIONNAIRE*

The School of Education is making an intensive effort to improve the effectiveness of the undergraduate educational counseling services. We feel that you, as a student in the School of Education, can be of great help to us in this investigation. We shall appreciate your cooperation in responding to this questionnaire. Thank you.

School or college	Classification	Teaching area

A. In the following problem areas, indicate by marking in the appropriate column the extent to which you feel counseling services in the School of Education are functioning—in other words, to what extent service is being given. Instead of the usual check mark, please use the following symbols, according to the basis for your judgment:

P -Personal experience with the counseling service
F -the experience which your friends have had
PF-Personal experience plus that of your friends

No Basis for Judgment | None | Little | Some | Great

_____ 1. Selecting a desirable teaching area
_____ 2. Learning about teaching opportunities
_____ 3. Interpreting test results (Minnesota personality test, psychological exam)
_____ 4. Selecting combination of teaching areas
_____ 5. Planning four-year program of course work
_____ 6. Working out schedule of classes for each semester
_____ 7. Making available information about student remedial services (speech clinic, English clinic)
_____ 8. Arranging for correspondence study
_____ 9. Suggesting methods of improving unsatisfactory grades
_____ 10. Helping with recommendations for study habits
_____ 11. Assisting in informing about loans, scholarships, and student work
_____ 12. Informing about procedures for internship
_____ 13. Evaluating professional education courses for transfer students
_____ 14. Arranging for dropping and adding courses
_____ 15. Informing about draft and military status
_____ 16. Assisting in explaining course work in terms of certification requirements

*From study of Audrey Atherton, "The Undergraduate Educational Counseling Services in the School of Education, Florida State University" (an adaptation of this form was also sent to graduates of the School of Education).

No Basis for:
   Judgment   None Little Some Great

_____ 17. Helping to choose electives   ____ ____ ____ ____

_____ 18. Helping to explain certification
requirements in states other
than Florida   ____ ____ ____ ____

_____ 19. Assisting in interpreting the
college catalog   ____ ____ ____ ____

_____ 20. Helping to clear necessary procedures for graduation   ____ ____ ____ ____

_____ 21. Choosing course work which will
be applicable for transfer to
another college   ____ ____ ____ ____

_____ 22. Choosing appropriate or desirable
internship location   ____ ____ ____ ____

B. Do you know who your counselor is in the School of Education? If answer is "yes",
please check the remaining items. If your answer is "no", please omit this section
and go on to Section C.

      Yes_____No_____

Check in the column to the right your reaction to the following aspects of your
counseling experiences in the School of Education. If you mark the column, "improvement needed", please write your suggestions or comments in the space provided below the items.   Adequate   Improvement Needed

1. Accessibility of your counselor   _____   _____

2. Enough time with your counselor   _____   _____

3. Competency of your counselor   _____   _____

4. Privacy of the counseling situation   _____   _____

5. Interest of your counselor in you   _____   _____

6. Your understanding of the function of
your counselor   _____   _____

7. Confidence in your counselor   _____   _____

8. Attitude of your counselor toward you   _____   _____

9. Please write in any other suggestions or comments you would like to make regarding the relationship between you and your counselor.

_____

_____

C. Place a check mark in the appropriate column to the right if you feel there is a need for expansion in the amount of help and/or change in the method of giving help through the School of Education in the following problem areas. If you feel a change is desirable, please write in your suggestions below the items.

                                                    Expansion   Method

1. Services which help you learn about teaching as
   a career   _____   _____

   Suggestions for expansion:_____

   Suggestions for method:_____

   _____

   _____

2. Services which help you plan your course work   _____   _____

   Suggestions for expansion:_____

   Suggestions for method:_____

   _____

   _____

3. Services which help you with your personal and
   social problems   _____   _____

   Suggestions for expansion:_____

   Suggestions for method:_____

   _____

   _____

4. Services which help you learn about certification requirements   _____   _____

   Suggestions for expansion:_____

   Suggestions for method:_____

   _____

   _____

5. Services which help you with your health
   problems   _____   _____

   Suggestions for expansion:_____

   Suggestions for method:_____

   _____

   _____

6. Services which help you with general univers-
   ity regulations   _____   _____

   Suggestions for expansion:_____

   Suggestions for method:_____

   _____

   _____

Index